The Learning Guide to Computers

The Learning Guide to Computers

Gini Courter
Annette Marquis

SYBEX®

San Francisco • Paris • Düsseldorf • Soest

Associate Publisher: Amy Romanoff
Acquisitions Manager: Kristine Plachy
Acquisitions & Developmental Editor: Sherry Schmitt
Editor: Bonnie Bills
Technical Editor: Stephen Bigelow
Book Designer: Lorrie Fink at Seventeenth Street Studios
Graphic Illustrator and Photoshop Specialist: Inbar Berman
Electronic Publishing Specialist: Kate Kaminski
Production Coordinator: Anton Reut
Indexer: Nancy Guenther
Cover Designer: Ziegler Designs
Cover Photographer: Gary Buss

Cover photo appears courtesy of FPG International.

Screen reproductions produced with Collage Complete.

Collage Plus Complete is a trademark of Inner Media Inc.

SYBEX is a registered trademark of SYBEX Inc.

TRADEMARKS: SYBEX has attempted throughout this book to distinguish proprietary trademarks from descriptive terms by following the capitalization style used by the manufacturer.

Netscape Communications, the Netscape Communications logo, Netscape, and Netscape Navigator are trademarks of Netscape Communications Corporation.

For an alphabetical list of manufacturers and trademarked products that are referenced in this book, see the Appendix.

The author and publisher have made their best efforts to prepare this book, and the content is based upon final release software whenever possible. Portions of the manuscript may be based upon pre-release versions supplied by software manufacturer(s). The author and the publisher make no representation or warranties of any kind with regard to the completeness or accuracy of the contents herein and accept no liability of any kind including but not limited to performance, merchantability, fitness for any particular purpose, or any losses or damages of any kind caused or alleged to be caused directly or indirectly from this book.

Photographs and illustrations used in this book have been downloaded from publicly accessible file archives and are used in this book for news reportage purposes only to demonstrate the variety of graphics resources available via electronic access. Text and images available over the Internet may be subject to copyright and other rights owned by third parties. Online availability of text and images does not imply that they may be reused without the permission of rights holders, although the Copyright Act does permit certain unauthorized reuse as fair use under 17 U.S.C. Section 107.

Copyright ©1997 SYBEX Inc., 1151 Marina Village Parkway, Alameda, CA 94501. World rights reserved. No part of this publication may be stored in a retrieval system, transmitted, or reproduced in any way, including but not limited to photocopy, photograph, magnetic or other record, without the prior agreement and written permission of the publisher.

Library of Congress Card Number: 96-70744

ISBN: 0-7821-1968-9

Manufactured in the United States of America

10 9 8 7 6 5 4 3 2 1

To our parents, Helen and Norman Marquis and Erma and Guy Courter, for always encouraging us to look to the future.

Acknowledgments

Making this book happen took a real team effort. Tracking down photos, contacting the sources, following up with those who needed it, and then figuring out what was actually received took much more effort than any of us expected. We can't begin to thank Sherry Schmitt, our Acquisitions & Developmental Editor, for her enthusiasm for the book and her appreciation for the challenges this project presented.

Our Editor, Bonnie Bills, was phenomenal in making order out of what seemed like total chaos at times. Thanks, Bonnie, for being patient, making us laugh, and keeping us sane. Heather O'Connor was an incredible help, making contacts to obtain photos for the book. We also want to thank Karla Browning who, even though she picked up the project in midstream with very little background information, used a lot of initiative and friendly persuasion to beg photos out of people. When she couldn't get them, she went out and took them herself. The book wouldn't be in print without her help. Thanks to all of you for your persistence.

Electronic Publishing Specialist Kate Kaminski and Photoshop Specialists Inbar Berman and Franz Baumhackl did a fabulous job in laying out the book and making the photos and graphics look their best. Production Coordinator Anton Reut kept the project moving forward, despite some unexpected delays. Thanks to you all for all your work.

Dennis Dougherty, our academic reviewer, provided us with valuable feedback to make sure the book was understandable to new users and useful in introductory computer courses. Thanks, Dennis, for your helpful comments.

It's always a challenge to write a computer book and make sure that the information being presented is not only interesting but technically correct. Our technical editor, Stephen Bigelow, was fabulous in praising the worthy and educating us when we needed it. Thanks, Steve, for making up for all the physics courses we never took.

Finally, we want to thank the companies and individuals who gave us interviews, researched photos, and provided background information. We especially want to thank Amy Courter and Lynn Newbound-Stump from Valassis Communications, Inc., Dr. Richard Ward from Henry Ford Health System, Jim Flury from IntegrationWare, Ed Haswell of EDesign (for the Assembly language code in Session 6), and Jim Willing from Jim's Computer Garage on the World Wide Web. These people helped us make sure that this book is well grounded in the real world of business. Thanks to each of you for your contributions.

Contents at a Glance

Introduction	xv
Part I: In the Beginning	**2**
Session 1: Exploring Computers	3
Session 2: From Chisels to Computers	25
Session 3: The Age of Titans	49
Part II: PCs Take Center Stage	**74**
Session 4: The Personal Computer Revolution	75
Session 5: The Ins and Outs of Personal Computer Hardware	99
Session 6: Personal Computer Software	125
Part III: Up Close and Personal	**150**
Session 7: Family Computers: Knowledge and Entertainment	151
Session 8: Productivity at Home	175
Session 9: Doorway to the World: Online Services and the Internet	201
Part IV: Computers in Business	**226**
Session 10: Business Systems and Software	227
Session 11: Connectivity: From LANs to the Internet	255
Session 12: Computers in Production	281
Session 13: Computers in Distribution	301
Session 14: Computers in Service Industries	325
Session 15: New Technologies, New Challenges	347
Appendix: Manufacturers and Products	363
Glossary	369
Index	386

Table of Contents

■ Introduction — xv

PART I: IN THE BEGINNING — 2

Session 1 ■ **Exploring Computers** — 3

    Section 1.1: What Is a Computer? — 4
        A Computerless Society — 4
    Section 1.2: An Increasing Dependence — 8
    Section 1.3: Benefits of Computers — 10
    Section 1.4: Costs of Computerization — 11
    Section 1.5: Exploring Computers — 13
        Careers in Computers — 14
        Workplace Computer Skills — 15
        Personal Computer Skills — 16
        Personal Enhancement — 16
    Section 1.6: The Types of Computers — 17
        Supercomputers — 18
        Mainframe Computers — 19
        Minicomputers — 19
        Microcomputers — 19

Session 2 ■ **From Chisels to Computers** — 25

    Section 2.1: In the Beginning — 26
    Section 2.2: Bones and Machines — 28
    Section 2.3: Computers in the Nineteenth Century — 30
    Section 2.4: Making the Census Count — 35
    Section 2.5: Computing in the Twentieth Century — 38
    Section 2.6: The Computer Goes to War — 39

Session 3 ■ **The Age of Titans** — 49

    Section 3.1: Generations of Computers — 49
        First Generation: Vacuum Tubes (1942-56) — 50

	Second Generation: Transistors (1956-63)	52
	Third Generation: Integrated Circuits (1964-71)	54
	Fourth Generation: Microminiaturized Circuits (1971-?)	58
	The Fifth (and Future) Generation	60
	Section 3.2: Parts of a Computer System	61
	Input	61
	Memory	61
	Processors	66
	Storage	67
	Output	71

PART II: PCs TAKE CENTER STAGE — 74

Session 4 — **The Personal Computer Revolution** — 75

Section 4.1: The Dream of Personal Computing	76
Companies Take Up the Challenge	77
Bringing Down the Cost and the Size	78
An Act of Desperation	79
And the Revolution Begins	80
Section 4.2: The Dream Takes Shape	82
Storage for the Rest of Us	82
Apple Takes the Lead	84
The Computer Wars Heat Up	85
Section 4.3: The Dream Becomes Reality	87
Section 4.4: Pieces of the Dream	90
Microprocessors	90
The PC System Board	91
Storage Devices	93

Session 5 — **The Ins and Outs of Personal Computer Hardware** — 99

Section 5.1: An Overview of Input and Output	100
Section 5.2: Input Devices	100
Text-Entry Devices	101
Pointing Devices	102
Audio, Video, and Graphics Input	107
Source Data Automation Input Devices	108

	Section 5.3: Output Devices	110
	Monitors	110
	Printers	113
	Sound Output Devices	118
	Section 5.4: Input/Output Devices	118
	Sound and Motion	118
	Fax Machines and Modems	120

Session 6 Personal Computer Software 125

Section 6.1: Introduction to PC Software	126
Section 6.2: System Software	126
Operating Systems	127
Device Drivers	133
Utilities	133
Programming Languages	134
Section 6.3: Applications Software	140
Section 6.4: Software Development	144
Development Teams	144
Systems Analysis and Design	144
Information Engineering	145

PART III: UP CLOSE AND PERSONAL 150

Session 7 Family Computers: Knowledge and Entertainment 151

Section 7.1: Not a Couch Potato Anymore?	152
Capturing an Audience	152
Section 7.2: Educational Software	153
Reference Tools	154
Interactive Learning	159
Educational Simulations	162
Section 7.3: Entertainment Software	166
Arcade-Style Games	168
Traditional Games	168
Puzzle Games	168
Adventure Games	170
Military and Strategy Games	170
Sports Games	171

Session 8		**Productivity at Home**	**175**
		Section 8.1: The Big Three	176
		Word Processors	176
		Spreadsheets	177
		Databases	178
		An Office Suite at Home	179
		Section 8.2: Financial and Legal	180
		Financial Management	180
		Tax Preparation Software	183
		Electronic Legal Help	184
		Section 8.3: Hobbies and Recreation	184
		Planning a Vacation	184
		Genealogy and Family History	187
		Design Tools	189
		Section 8.4: Printing and Publishing	190
		Desktop Publishing	190
		Why Not Use a Word Processor?	192
		Clip Art and Photo Collections	192
Session 9		**Doorway to the World: Online Services and the Internet**	**201**
		Section 9.1: The Birth of Online Communication	202
		Standardized Protocols	202
		Electronic Bulletin Boards	203
		Commercial Online Services	204
		The World Wide Web Takes Control	206
		Section 9.2: The Internet Today	208
		Services of the World Wide Web	208
		Other Common Internet Services	209
		Accessing the Internet	213
		Internet Addresses	214
		Section 9.3: Tools to Explore the Web	216
		Browsers	216
		Search Engines	217
		Audio and Video	220
		Section 9.4: Becoming a Contributor to the Web	220
		Creating a Web Page	221
		Making a Web Page Come Alive	222

PART IV: COMPUTERS IN BUSINESS — 226

Session 10 — **Business Systems and Software** — 227

    Section 10.1: Information Systems — 228
        Types of Information Systems — 228
    Section 10.2: Transaction Processing Systems — 228
    Section 10.3: Management Information Systems — 232
        Data Warehousing — 235
        Data Mining — 236
        The Changing Role of Data Management — 236
    Section 10.4: Expert Systems — 238
    Section 10.5: Office Automation Systems — 240
        Integrated Office Suites — 240

Session 11 — **Connectivity: From LANs to the Internet** — 255

    Section 11.1: Connectivity Basics — 256
    Section 11.2: Communications Systems — 257
        Communications Modes — 258
        Communication Verification — 258
        Communications Media — 260
    Section 11.3: Computer Networks — 262
        Network Hardware Basics — 263
        Network Software Tasks — 263
    Section 11.4: Local Area Networks — 264
        Peer-to-Peer Networks — 265
        Client-Server Networks — 265
        Networking Software — 266
        Wide Area Networks — 268
    Section 11.5: Using a Network — 268
        Network Security — 270
    Section 11.6: Network Applications — 270
        Electronic Mail — 270
        Scheduling — 272
    Section 11.7: Distributed Systems — 272
        Client-Server Applications — 273

	Workgroup Software	274
	The Internet and Intranets	274
Session 12	**Computers in Production**	**281**
	Section 12.1: Creating a Product	282
	Section 12.2: Designing a Product	283
	Using Computers to Design Advertising Inserts	284
	Designing Hardware and Software	286
	Computerized Prototype Testing	288
	Virtual Manufacturing	289
	Section 12.3: Using Technology in Manufacturing	289
	CAM and CIM	289
	Computers and Just in Time	290
	Section 12.4: Managing Product Quality	292
	Quality Methods	292
	Measuring Quality	293
	Section 12.5: Managing Production with Computers	295
Session 13	**Computers in Distribution**	**301**
	Section 13.1: Distributing Goods and Services	302
	Section 13.2: Warehousing and Inventory	302
	Item Identification	302
	Distribution Centers	304
	Inventory Control Systems	305
	Inventory Tracking	306
	Section 13.3: Computers in Transportation	308
	Transportation Scheduling Systems	309
	Transportation Tracking Systems	310
	Transportation for the Service Sector	313
	Section 13.4: Computers in Marketing and Sales	314
	Marketing	314
	Sales	315
	Sales and Marketing on the Internet	318
Session 14	**Computers in Service Industries**	**325**
	Section 14.1: Defining Service Industries	326
	We'll Leave the Computer On for You	326

XIV TABLE OF CONTENTS

Virtual Real Estate Shopping	327
Managing Your Money Electronically	328
Digital Entertainment	329
Section 14.2: Improving Your Health	332
The Evolution of Health Care Information Systems	332
Section 14.3: Computers in the War on Crime	337
Section 14.4: Libraries	339
Digital Libraries	341

Session 15 ■ **New Technologies, New Challenges** **347**

Section 15.1: Putting the Personal into Personal Computers	348
Making Friends with Your Software	349
Section 15.2: Connecting the World	351
Making the Internet Safe and Available	351
Simplifying Internet Access	352
Section 15.3: New Ways to Interact with Computers	353
"Open the Pod Bay Doors, HAL"	353
Look, Ma, No Hands!	354
Section 15.4: Phenomenal Storage and Memory Advances	355
Faster than a Speeding Bullet	355
Section 15.5: Moving Computers Beyond the Desktop	356
Receding into the Shadows	357
One Thing's For Sure	359

■ **Appendix: Manufacturers and Products** **363**

■ **Glossary** **369**

■ **Index** **386**

Introduction

We assume that if you are reading this book you could be relatively new to the world of computers. Or you may already be using a computer, but conversations with friends and colleagues let you know that there is information you are missing. Or you may not have openly embraced this new technology, but have decided that the world will leave you behind if you don't get ready to catch the wave. We began by assuming that you know nothing at all about computers and built from there. We'd be surprised, however, if all of the information in this book is completely new to anyone. Computers have infiltrated our society much too deeply for many people to be immune, and it's next to impossible not to have heard at least a few of the basics.

Whatever your previous relationship with computers, this book was meant to fill in the gaps, to provide you with a solid foundation about where computers came from, their myriad parts and pieces, and how they are used today. We endeavored to make this exploration interesting, a little humorous at times, and always historically and technically accurate. We sincerely hope that you will find topics that fascinate you and that when you finish the book, you'll be interested enough to work more with computers. At the very least, you'll be proud of the fact that you are up to speed in this constantly changing and challenging field.

ABOUT THIS BOOK

This book is divided into four major sections. Part I, "In the Beginning," provides you with a look at how we got to where we are today: how computers developed over time and how mainframe computers influenced our image of computing. Part II, "PCs Take Center Stage," provides you with an overview of personal computers. You'll learn how and why they were designed, and how PC hardware and software gives us incredible flexibility and power not available in mainframe systems. In Part III, "Up Close and Personal," you'll learn about PCs for home use and how the Internet has changed the face of computing in this decade. Part IV, "Computers in Business," gives you an in-depth look at how computers, especially PCs, are used in different business settings. You'll go inside several companies and see firsthand how they apply computer technology to various aspects of their businesses. There is no better way to evaluate career options and what skills might be expected of you when you go to work for today's companies.

At the beginning of each session, you will find a vocabulary list that identifies words in the session that may be unfamiliar to you. When these terms are defined in the text, they will be printed in **bold** to give you an easy reference point for review. Following the vocabulary list at the beginning of the session is a list of objectives that identify what you will learn in the session.

At the end of each session, you will find a summary followed by a series of focus questions about concepts covered in the session. You will also find exercises to reinforce what you have learned in the session. Your answers to many of the questions can be a source for papers or used to generate discussion in a classroom or small group.

We also know that many people using this book are or will be in the job market soon. You may have already decided what career you want to pursue, but may not know how much you will need to know about computers. We hope the last four sessions will help to prepare you for whatever career you choose. For those of you who have not yet decided or may be changing careers, we have included Career Capsules, like the one shown below, throughout the book. These show you the education required, the expected salary range, and a brief description of the career. We hope they will help to give you a feel for some of the jobs that require computer skills.

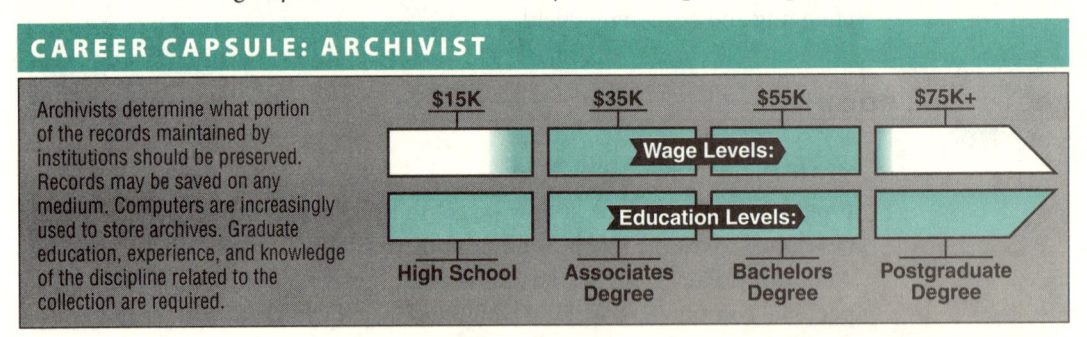

CAREER CAPSULE: ARCHIVIST

Archivists determine what portion of the records maintained by institutions should be preserved. Records may be saved on any medium. Computers are increasingly used to store archives. Graduate education, experience, and knowledge of the discipline related to the collection are required.

Wage Levels: $15K – $75K+
Education Levels: High School, Associates Degree, Bachelors Degree, Postgraduate Degree

Although this book is designed to be used in a lecture course, it's helpful if you can access the World Wide Web and actually visit the Web sites listed in the "Further Exploration" sections at the end of each chapter. These will give you a great overview of the types of sites on the Web and the amazing amount of information that is available for the asking. We've also listed books and other reference materials that will help you develop a solid understanding of the topics covered in the session.

If you enjoy what you learn here, don't stop at the end of this book. Enroll in hands-on applications courses and start finding out directly how computers can make your life easier. You'll be glad you did.

We hope you enjoy using *The Learning Guide to Computers*. We would love to hear your comments on this book. You can contact us at the following address:

Gini Courter and Annette Marquis
c/o Sybex Inc.
1151 Marina Village Parkway
Alameda, CA 94501
e-mail: *triad@kode.net*

PART 1

In the Beginning

Vocabulary

- computer
- computer-literate
- computer system
- desktop computer
- input
- hardware
- mainframe
- microcomputer
- minicomputer (mini)
- multimedia
- multiuser
- output
- personal computer
- program
- software
- supercomputer
- tower computer
- workstation

SESSION ONE

Exploring Computers

AS THE NEW MILLENNIUM APPROACHES, people training for careers in just about every field are finding that knowledge of computers is essential. Once used only by those with technical know-how, today computers play an important role in the work routines of most professionals—from bankers to farmers, health professionals to athletes. To begin thinking technologically, you must first understand what computers are and the role they play in our lives today. At the end of this session, you will be able to

- Chronicle some of the ways society relies on computers
- List benefits of using computers
- Relate some of the costs of computerization
- List reasons people study computers
- Classify computers by size

3

SECTION 1.1: WHAT IS A COMPUTER?

An automobile is just a vehicle that allows passengers to travel to a destination, a simple invention in many ways. But drivers and passengers of early automobiles could not have predicted the societal changes cars, trucks, and motorcycles would lead to. An extensive billion-dollar interstate highway system, suburban sprawl and the resulting decline of urban centers, environmental pollution, and the importance of OPEC countries half a world away are directly related to the development of the automobile. The automobile also sparked increased job opportunities for rural and small-town dwellers, fast food drive-up windows, and the ability to easily visit friends and family who live more than 20 miles away.

Like the automobile, the computer is rapidly transforming society. A **computer** is a simple electronic device that takes data, processes the data according to a series of instructions called a **program**, and produces information. Data you enter into the computer is called **input**; the information that is produced by the computer is called **output**. A **computer system** is composed of a number of individual electronic components called **hardware.** In order to qualify as hardware, a component has to be a *physical* part of the system. Because programs are not physical components, a program or a collection of programs is referred to as **software**.

Until the 1980s, computers were so expensive only big business and government organizations could afford to take advantage of their benefits. Today, we feel the presence of computers in nearly every part of life. Technological change is hard to measure while it's happening, but you can begin to understand how much computers have changed our lives by thinking about life without them.

A Computerless Society

Imagine you woke up this morning and there were no more computers. Or—if you like a good conspiracy theory—imagine that for years, computer manufacturers around the world have been placing devices in computers that would allow them to be remotely disabled. And today is the day they chose to shut them down. (The manufacturers are, of course, demanding a large ransom in exchange for enabling the computers again.) You may prefer to construct your own imaginative scenario to explain this situation, but the question remains: how would your life and the lives of others be changed if there were no computers?

Do you wake up to an electric alarm clock? Power companies use computers to regulate the flow of electricity, from the point of generation through cables and substations to your home. The alarm would never go off if the power wasn't flowing in your home's circuits.

Eventually, you'd wake up, with or without an alarm. But the world you would wake up to would be more silent than usual. Radio and television stations are completely computerized, so forget *The Today Show* or waking up with National Public Radio. And if you want to know about the weather, look out the window. (Is that an electric coffee maker in the kitchen? That's unfortunate.)

Have a nice breakfast—but don't count on hot food. While your refrigerator may have few if any computerized parts, the electric stove and microwave both include computerized features. (Of course, without electricity, everything in the freezer is defrosting, the food in the refrigerator will be warm by tomorrow, and the electric stove won't work anyway.)

It would be nice to call someone to find out what's going on, but telephone calls are switched by computer. You can't call your employer, so you might as well go to work.

That late model car in your garage won't start: it has a computerized ignition system. You can take a bus, but avoid the trains: computerized systems keep them from running into each other. If you have an older car, this is your lucky day. But be careful driving in major metropolitan areas where traffic signals are switched by computer. Even in rural areas, many of the traffic lights use computerized timers to switch from red to green. Railroad crossing lights and barriers are computerized, too.

> *The most powerful technologies are those that disappear. They weave themselves into the fabric of everyday life until they are indistinguishable from it.*
> —*Mark Weiser,* Scientific American, *1995*

You can stop for a fast food breakfast, but it won't be fast. Without computerized registers, the cashiers have to look at the menu board to determine the price of each item (they can't, after all, just press a button that says "Breakfast Burger") and total all the orders in their heads. Orders then have to be passed to the kitchen on paper or by shouting. And there's bedlam in the kitchen: without computerized timers for fryers and grills, the cooks are guessing when the hashbrowns and burgers are done. The beverage machine, computerized to dispense the right amount of carbonation and flavoring at the push of a button, isn't dispensing anything at all. When you get your food, savor every bite—like all other businesses, fast food companies will need a bit of time to efficiently deliver product without computers.

While you've been waiting for your slow fast food, there has been a rush on the grocery stores. People are buying all the nonperishable goods they can, and standing in long lines to pay for purchases that are being totaled by hand. Stores are only taking cash—the systems that verify checks and credit cards are computerized. Computers, such as the one shown in Figure 1.1, help retail stores to do everything from processing receipts to managing inventory.

Figure 1.1
Computers in retail stores have made processing receipts and tracking inventory more manageable tasks.

Courtesy of Twilight Technologies

But even getting cash (see Figure 1.2) isn't easy with the failure of all the automated teller machines.

You can go into the bank, but without computers, they won't be able to check account balances, because the Federal Reserve System clears checks and balances the accounts for the banks by computer. When the supply of cash held by local banks runs out, they will be hard-pressed to get more cash from the highly computerized Federal Reserve system. Wall Street and the financial markets, chaotic enough *with* computers, are in trouble, too. Without computerization, buy and sell orders will take weeks to be executed.

Figure 1.2 Millions of people have grown dependent on the easy availability of money from automatic teller machines.

Getting information from one place to another will be a major challenge. Every method of transmitting information is computerized: the postal system, package delivery systems, electronic mail, telephone, telegraph, cellular systems, broadcast television, and radio will all be crippled until antiquated, more manual forms of switching, tracking, and engineering are in place. Ham radio operators with older equipment will help fill the communications gap until we relearn how to keep in touch without the aid of computers. This might be a good time to visit parents and grandparents who like to relive the old days.

Entire international systems rely on computers. For example, think about air travel: airline reservations are all maintained on computers; the security machines at airport terminals are computerized; and commercial airliners are wonders of computerization. Importantly, the air traffic control system is extensively monitored with the use of computers. (There are frequent pleas to update the system, adding even more computer power to assist air traffic controllers, as you'll learn about in Session 12.) Without computers, we'd all be grounded.

> **NOTE**
>
> For a relatively thoughtful and action-packed look at air traffic's dependence on technology, see the 1990 Bruce Willis movie *Die Hard II*.

There are, of course, many other things that will be difficult to do in this new, noncomputerized world. Industry, transportation, service, and nonprofit companies rely on computers to maintain shipping and accounting records, employee and production schedules, and client and customer information. It isn't even noon in our imaginary world without computing power, yet it is already clear that it will take a long time to rethink and retool the way business—and, in fact, life itself—is conducted.

SECTION 1.2: AN INCREASING DEPENDENCE

Heavy dependence on computers is a recent phenomenon. This trend began in the late 1950s, when computers began to augment manual systems. Insurance records, for example, were computerized; however, all paper records were also stored in large filing cabinets, so if the computer failed, employees could still pull records by hand to answer questions and handle claims. Today, insurance records are kept electronically, and often there is no paper backup. Rates for insurance policies are also calculated by computer. Similarly, many hospitals and clinics that once kept paper medical records stored in cabinets or vaults, today can't even schedule a patient appointment when the computer is turned off. Hospital admitting offices, such as the one shown in Figure 1.3, are able to record patient information, verify the patient's insurance, and assign a patient to a room.

In the first half of the century, manufacturing involved people using tools and machines to create products. This began to change in 1958, when the first industrial robot was put into service. By the 1970s, many robots were installed in manufacturing facilities, replacing the workers with computerized machines. Even after the robotics invasion, however, skilled draftspersons, engineers, and mechanics were responsible for prototyping—that is, creating a single

Figure 1.3
Admitting a patient to a hospital involves entering a significant amount of data into a patient database system, usually using a mainframe terminal.

Courtesy of Kingswood Hospital

engine, door panel, seat belt, or airplane wing—and new aircraft and automobile body prototypes still had to be tested in wind tunnels to ensure the finished product would be aerodynamic. By the early 1980s, as design enhancements required new prototypes and more extensive wind tunnel tests, this too began to change. Manufacturers began creating computer models of parts, and prototyping became a thing of the past. Designers found that testing could be done with more precision using computers. Today, many products are created and tested using only computers.

Computerized airline reservations weren't a reality coast to coast until 1964, with the advent of SABRE, a computerized telecommunications network from IBM and American Airlines. Airline reservation agents, such as the one in Figure 1.4, rely entirely on computerized systems. And it wasn't until 1976 that SABRE was installed in its first travel agency. Today, you don't even need a travel agent; you can make your reservations yourself on SABRE or a number of other online reservation systems, using a personal computer in your own home.

Commercial airline flights operated a bit differently 25 years ago, too. Commercial flights were monitored with radar and radio until the early 1970s, when the U.S. computerized air traffic control system was installed in major U.S. flight zones. In today's aircraft, computers provide a constant flow of navigational information, monitor instrument readings, automatically pilot the aircraft, regulate cabin pressure, respond to radio signals, turn on emergency systems, and record cockpit conversations and instrument readings. The famous "black box," which provides investigators with important data about an aircraft's condition prior to a crash, actually contains a computer chip that stores thousands of readings about an aircraft's functioning.

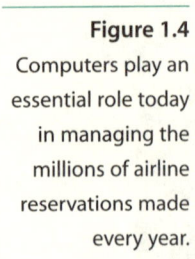

Figure 1.4
Computers play an essential role today in managing the millions of airline reservations made every year.

©1996 Paul Loven

In every field, every type of business, and every aspect of our lives, computers are becoming indispensable. Increasingly, it is the manual human system that is becoming redundant.

SECTION 1.3: BENEFITS OF COMPUTERS

Computers have gained popularity for a number of reasons. Most importantly, there are tasks that computers do very well—better, even, than human beings. These include

- Storing or "memorizing" large amounts of information
- Quickly recalling a single piece of information
- Rapidly performing a series of sequential tasks
- Carrying out a specific action based on sensor readings or other quantifiable information

Computers also have other attributes that businesses find useful. They

- Are never late or absent and won't ask for a raise
- Turn out work of a fairly consistent quality

- Have limited social requirements, so they don't need a company picnic
- Don't require an hourly wage
- Can work under conditions that are ill-advised for human employees, including 24-hour workdays with no breaks and toxic environments

And yet, all these advantages wouldn't explain the recent influx of computers without one additional factor: a reasonable price. In the last 20 years, the combination of technological developments and mass production of computer components has caused the price of computers to drop dramatically. Computers are now affordable for even the smallest businesses, so it isn't surprising that many businesses have embraced computers with open arms. And business use of computers is only one aspect of the computer revolution. Individuals have also been quick to put computers to use in the home as personal and family tools.

SECTION 1.4: COSTS OF COMPUTERIZATION

Despite the drop in computer hardware prices, our increased dependence on computers has a price tag. Prior to computerization, individuals who could calculate rapidly were often referred to as "human computers." Memorization and retrieval skills, difficult for many people to develop, were valued and compensated. Insurance company employees who could quickly find and retrieve customer files from hundreds of filing cabinets advanced to the top of the clerical pool. Young attorneys who could look through volumes of cases and determine which might be applicable to a current case secured jobs as research assistants in law offices. Good research skills became a prerequisite for advancement in a firm. Manufacturing engineers who had a depth of experience to diagnose potential machinery failures were vital in an industrial setting. And managers who could assess potential consequences of changes in price, sales, employee compensation, or equipment purchases were recognized as experts in cost analysis.

Although human beings are still necessary to evaluate the quality and implications of the information received, computers can outperform human beings in many of the specific tasks required to be a research assistant, insurance clerk, supervising engineer, or numerical analyzer. Human "computers" can be replaced by anyone with enough skill to use a pocket calculator. The United States Postal Service provides a good example of one of the costs of increased computerization. Ten years ago, each piece of mail delivered by the

United States Postal Service was sorted manually at least three times. After mail was collected from mailboxes and brought to the Post Office, a postal system employee working at a sorter read the address and zip code then pressed a series of three code keys to sort the letter into a bin. All letters in the bin shared a common destination: the same country, state, city, or postal code. The contents of the bin were then placed in bags and transported to the destination. Later, an employee at the destination postal center would again sort the letter to the correct carrier route. Finally, before delivery, the postal carrier would hand sort each letter for their route into a manual sorting rack that separated mail for each address.

Sorters are among the highest paid postal employees, because each sorter has to memorize an entire set of national zip codes or local street addresses and their corresponding three digit codes, and process one letter per second with 99 percent accuracy. Today, the human sorters have largely been replaced with machine sorters. Stacks of letters with addresses facing the same direction are placed into a computerized machine that reads the address and zip code, then sprays a bar code on the letter, as shown in Figure 1.5. The letters are then fed into a bar code sorter that reads the code and sorts the letter into the proper bin. When the letter arrives at its destination, another bar code sorter is used to sort the letter to the carrier route.

Figure 1.5
Adding a bar code to an envelope speeds processing by the Post Office.

The result of computerization in the Postal Service is that fifteen to twenty sorters are replaced by each set of computerized bar code equipment, and jobs are created for only one or two technicians who maintain the equipment. This is a pattern that is being repeated in financial institutions, manufacturers, animation studios, printing plants, and other businesses all over the world, resulting in a short-term loss of highly paid jobs in some industries. This is nothing new. Major changes in technology always lead to a change in the list of skills required for secure employment. When automobiles replaced horses and trains as the primary means of travel, blacksmiths and railroad engineers found themselves without jobs. When automobile manufacturers replaced metal car bodies with plastic car bodies, many welders were out of work and had to retrain in different fields. And now, computers have again changed the employment landscape.

One price of increased computer use is a shift in the employment markets, resulting in a shortage of computer technicians and a pool of unemployed or underemployed people who often lack computer skills. Another consequence of increased dependence is the cost associated with implementing new computerized technologies. While computers continue to drop in price, the number of computers required to remain competitive in today's business environment continues to increase. The cost of the computer itself is less than half the cost of computerization. Computer programs and training more than double the cost of implementing new computer technology. If a computer system is working (even if it isn't working well), it can be hard for managers or directors to channel resources to update it. The costs of purchasing new technologies and retraining employees to use them create technology gaps, with some parts of a system using advanced technology, and other parts using computers and programs that are decades old.

Workplace stress is another cost of technological dependence. Computers are able to respond quickly to requests for data, creating an environment where quick response times are expected. Recent studies of business dynamics indicate that today's office has become a highly stressed, rapidly paced workplace, with twice as many requests for quick information and decisions as the office of the early 1980s. As demands and the resulting stress increase, job satisfaction decreases. Some researchers believe that increased workplace stress reflects a gap between people's expectations of technology and its actual performance. Hopefully, as society becomes more familiar with technology, we will be able to develop more realistic expectations of the technology—and of the people who are being asked to use it.

SECTION 1.5: EXPLORING COMPUTERS

Perhaps you're not certain why you chose to take a computer course. You may know that you need computer skills for a potential job; or maybe you were feeling adventurous, or just plain curious. While each of us has specific motivations, the general reasons for exploring the world of computers tend to fall into four broad categories:

- To find a career in computers
- To develop workplace computer skills
- To acquire personal computer skills
- For personal enhancement

Careers in Computers

As computers become more capable, new careers in computers are created. If you enjoy working with math, logic, machines, or people, you might consider a career in the computing field. According to the U.S. Bureau of Labor Statistics, two of the five fastest-growing jobs in the next 10 years are in the computer field, and as shown in Table 1.1, the computer jobs pay significantly more than the other three fastest-growing jobs.

Table 1.1
Fastest-Growing Jobs

Job Title	Growth 1994–2005	1994 Median Weekly Earnings
Personal and home health care aides	119%	$258
Home health aides	102%	$278
Systems analysts	92%	$845
Computer engineers	90%	$845
Physical and corrective therapy assistants and aides	83%	$296

Source: Bureau of Labor Statistics; *USA Today* research by Nicole Carroll 6/26/96

Computing careers are not limited to systems analysts and engineers. Other possible careers include programming/software design, computer education and training, computer operations, multimedia and desktop publishing, computer repairs and electronics (shown in Figure 1.6), and hardware and software sales. You'll find information about these jobs and others like them in Career Capsules in later sessions.

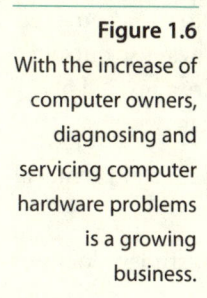

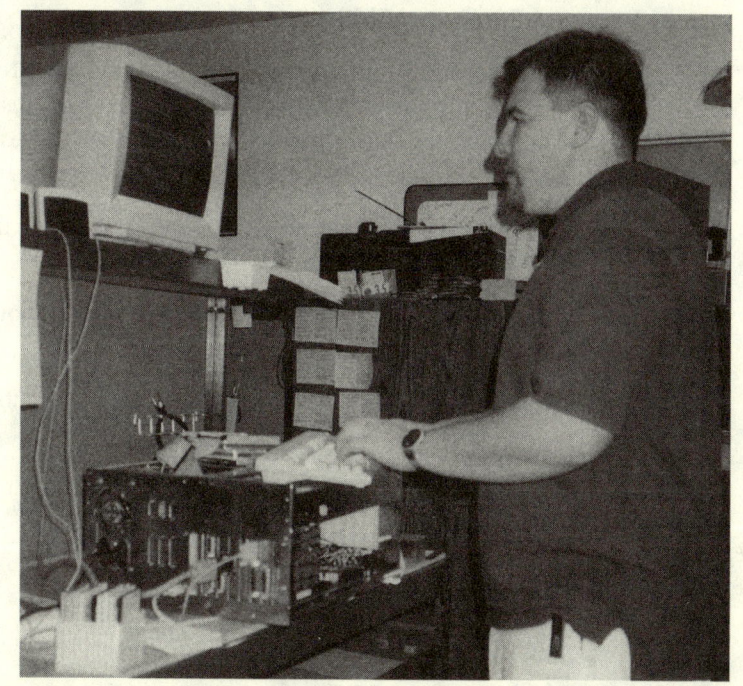

Figure 1.6
With the increase of computer owners, diagnosing and servicing computer hardware problems is a growing business.

Courtesy of Twilight Technologies

■ Workplace Computer Skills

As the computer revolution continues, it is becoming increasingly difficult to find a job that doesn't require some knowledge of computers. The manager of the 1990s uses computers to create reports, analyze budgets, send electronic mail, and schedule resources for a new project. The tens of thousands who worked in secretarial pools, typing and taking shorthand, are now administrative assistants with sophisticated computer skills. Draftspeople and graphic artists have traded pencils, pens, and brushes for desktop computers and graphic design software. Restaurant employees place food and beverage orders on a computer screen, and retail employees ring up sales with a scanner.

Today's workplace is a computerized workplace, so whether you are working in the computer field or not, most jobs today require computer skills. Even executives are finding themselves spending more time in front of a computer screen. The more extensive your computer knowledge is, the more job opportunities will be available to you.

■ Personal Computer Skills

You don't need to have career aspirations to have a desire to use a computer. In 1995, computers designed for home and small business use outsold televisions, becoming the home appliance of choice. There are a myriad of ways to make use of the power of a computer at home. You can

- Quickly access information on thousands of topics, from stain removal to CPR to home schooling
- Analyze data to aid in personal decision making about student loans or mortgages
- Create professional-looking correspondence and published materials
- Learn new languages and skills
- Keep track of information about investments, assets, collections, and family genealogy
- Maintain a budget
- Communicate with colleagues and friends worldwide
- Telecommute—work from your home rather than driving to an office
- Play single and multiplayer games

When you become a competent computer user, you can perform many tasks more easily and produce a higher quality product. A creative individual with a computer can construct reports, presentations, and newsletters that rival those created by professional typesetting firms. Connect your computer to the Internet, and you can conduct research at remote libraries in Washington, D.C., Indiana, Japan, Germany, and Israel. Even if you don't do much more than play games, using a computer at home opens new horizons and introduces you to new ways of seeing the world.

■ Personal Enhancement

People study and learn to use computers for the same reason others climb mountains: because it can be personally rewarding. It's a field of knowledge that is changing rapidly and growing at an exponential rate, and keeping up with the changes—or trying to—is a great way to stay on the cutting edge of technology.

In spite of the benefits of computers, some people are afraid of the impact of computers on their personal right to privacy. In the novel *1984*, George Orwell paints a vivid picture of a future where Big Brother maintains surveillance and records of the most intimate details of individuals' lives. Orwell's vision of big government exerting control with large computers didn't come to pass in 1984, and isn't likely to in the near future. But even though Big Brother has not materialized the way Orwell described it, don't assume that your private life is private. Your personal information is housed in dozens or even hundreds of computers owned by credit bureaus, banks, federal and local government agencies, utilities, and retail stores. Increasingly, this information is sold or shared with other businesses and agencies.

It is sometimes unclear how computerized information relates to the issue of personal freedom. New Jersey is introducing a new driver's license in 1997 that includes a small computer chip containing your driver's license information and emergency medical information. The identification card could easily include other information that could be accessed by law enforcement agencies—past driving violations, criminal record, a history of substance abuse, or credit information—and such inclusions are being considered. Some find this idea comforting; others find it terrifying. As a result of issues like these, some people study computers for the sake of self-protection.

Finally, people might want to learn about computers because all of their friends and family have an understanding of computers and how to use them. In other words, their friends are **computer-literate**. Tired of not being able to understand conversations about their grandchildren's homework projects or their spouse's job, or casual conversation in the workplace or gym, they decide that its time to take a look at the information superhighway.

SECTION 1.6: THE TYPES OF COMPUTERS

In the next three sessions, you'll see how the dreams and visions of a multitude of engineers, mathematicians, philosophers, and scientists have combined to form the computers of today. Throughout the text, you'll learn about different types of computers, from handheld units to giant computer installations. When reading about computers, it's helpful to have a system that allows you to compare one computer to another based on different characteristics. One way to categorize computers is by size. As computers were refined, four different sizes of computers developed. Although size is becoming less relevant than it once was in designating the power of a computer, it is still the easiest way to divide the broad spectrum of computers.

Supercomputers

The largest computers are called **supercomputers**. Like the Cray T-90 shown in Figure 1.7, each supercomputer is custom constructed for a specific purchaser with extremely large data processing needs. The supercomputers in the Cray T-90 series are capable of processing up to 60 billion calculations per second. Most supercomputers are owned by governmental agencies, research institutions, and Fortune 100 companies. However, according to Cray, more industrial companies are turning to supercomputers to manage their production computing work. There are fewer than 10 companies in the world who manufacture supercomputers.

Supercomputers are used for scientific research in astronomy, physics, mathematics, and genetics. For example, the National Center for Atmospheric Research uses a supercomputer to visually model changes in the earth's climate based on changes in other variables, such as changes in the Sahara desert and the earth's ozone layer. Boeing, Apple, and Chrysler are among the companies that use supercomputers to help design products and determine the cause of problems found in existing products. A supercomputer supports NASA's Ames Virtual Windtunnel, a virtual reality environment where space shuttle design aerodynamics are tested.

Figure 1.7
Cray Supercomputers, built for extremely large data processing needs, can process up to 60 billion calculations per second.

Courtesy of Cray Research

■ Mainframe Computers

The next size of computers—and the size that has been around the longest—is the **mainframe** computer. Until the 1970s, mainframes were the bread and butter of the computer industry. Because mainframes can be used by many people at the same time, they support the **multiuser** computing environment that is required in large businesses.

■ Minicomputers

Like mainframes, **minicomputers** (or, simply, **minis**) are multiuser computers, but they are smaller than mainframes. As minicomputers have become more powerful, the lines between the different sizes of computer have become less clear. It isn't unusual for employees in a company to believe the computer they use is a mainframe computer, when they are actually using a computer the manufacturer describes as a "super-mini" or minicomputer.

In 1977, Digital introduced the VAX family of computers, including the VAX 11/750 (shown in Figure 1.8), which utilized 32-bit processors. VAX computers can be configured together in clusters and are used in settings where a large number of users need to access a computer concurrently.

Other companies that build minicomputers and mainframes include Digital Equipment Corporation (DEC), Unisys, and IBM. The minicomputer pictured in Figure 1.9 is an IBM minicomputer.

■ Microcomputers

Microcomputers (also called **personal computers**) come in all shapes and sizes—from powerful desktop models to handheld models with limited functionality. Over the past 25 years, microcomputers have become smaller, faster, and more powerful. As users have demanded flexibility, ease-of-use, and mobility, manufacturers have worked to meet their expectations, producing personal computers for just about every purpose. No longer content to look at a black screen and type in commands, users want full-color video and audio with stunning graphics and sound capabilities called **multimedia**. We want computers we can take on the road, use in airports and construction sites, and even mount on tractors and harvesters.

Figure 1.8
The interior view of a Digital VAX 11/750

Courtesy of Jim Willing.

While many large corporations make microcomputers, individual computer components can be purchased separately. There are hundreds of thousands of computer manufacturers worldwide, including small mom-and-pop computer shops in storefronts, basements, and garages. The abundance of manufacturers helps keep microcomputer prices low, but also makes knowledgeable personal computer purchasing riskier and more difficult.

Figure 1.9
IBM minicomputers are multiuser computers that are smaller than mainframes but with generally more computing power than personal computers.

Courtesy of International Business Machines Corporation. Unauthorized use not permitted.

A **desktop computer** is designed to lay flat on a desktop. It is composed of a box-like case that holds most of the electronic components that make up the computer. When this case is surrounded by all of its external components, such as a keyboard, monitor and printer, it is often referred to as a **workstation**. A **tower computer** (see Figure 1.10) is similar to a desktop except the case stands upright. Tower computers have more room to add expansion devices like additional disk drives and backup storage devices. A desktop or tower computer typically has one or two input devices (a keyboard and a mouse), an output device (the monitor), a second output device (a printer), a storage device or two (the floppy disk drives), and, finally, the case which holds the microprocessor, among other things. All of these individual parts, in addition to a growing number of add-on components such as CD-ROM drives and speakers, make up the entity we call a personal computer.

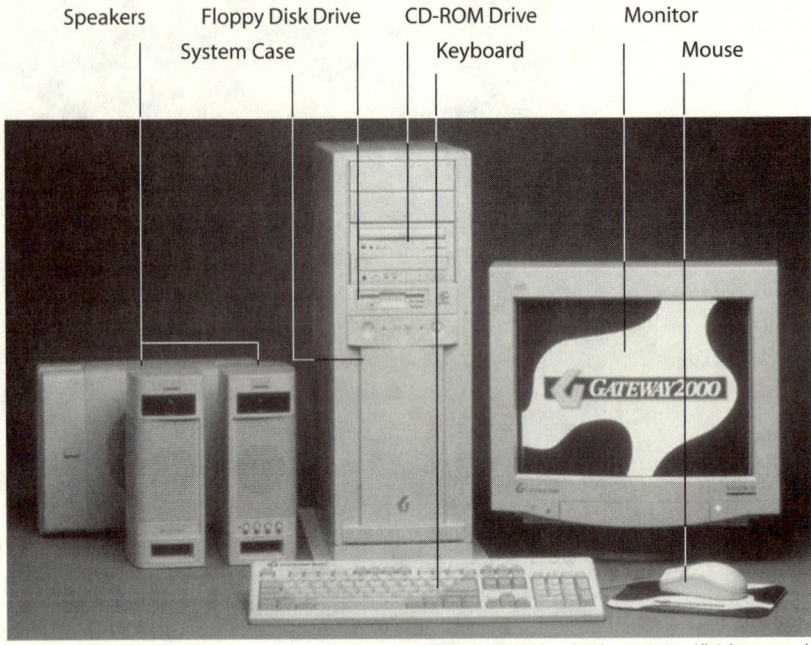

Figure 1.10
A Gateway personal computer

Speakers · Floppy Disk Drive · CD-ROM Drive · Monitor
System Case · Keyboard · Mouse

©1996, Gateway 2000, Inc. Reproduced with permission. All rights reserved.

As the age of the personal computer advances, the variety of shapes, sizes, and capabilities of personal computers continues to expand. In fact, the power of the personal computer continues to double every 18 to 24 months. As microcomputers become more powerful, manufacturers of mini and mainframe computers work to enhance their products. Innovation fuels a desire for further innovation, as you will see in Session 2.

What You Have Learned

Computers have become a significant factor in almost every aspect of modern life. Whether a person plans to work in the computer industry or not, becoming computer literate is an important part of preparation for any type of job. Computers provide a number of benefits that many feel outweigh the costs. Computers can store large amounts of data, sort through it and recall a single piece of information quickly, provide valuable communication tools, and work longer and in more dangerous conditions than humans. Because computers can effectively replace humans in certain tasks, people are forced to adjust by retraining for different jobs that incorporate the use of computers. The range of

FOCUS AND EXPLORATION

computers available—from supercomputers to mainframes, minis, and personal computers—means that there are computers for a growing number of applications and industries. As technology moves forward, people are finding ways for computers to enhance life both personally and professionally.

Focus Questions

1. What is a computer?
2. What types of tasks can computers do more easily than people?
3. Why do individuals choose to learn about computers?
4. Explain some of the costs of our increased dependence on computers.
5. What are the four sizes of computers, from smallest to largest?
6. Name three hardware components of a personal computer.

Knowledge Reinforcement

A. You are the owner of a small business, and are considering purchasing one or more computers for your clerical staff to use. What types of costs will you need to consider as part of your decision? Of these costs, which will be the hardest to quantify? Which will be the easiest?

B. Why are you studying computers? What kinds of knowledge do you want to acquire?

C. In your experience, how have computers changed the way you bank? Purchase gasoline? Travel from one place to another? File income tax returns?

Vocabulary

- abacus
- Howard Aiken
- Analytical Engine
- John Atanasoff
- Atanasoff-Berry Computer (ABC)
- Charles Babbage
- George Boole
- Vannevar Bush
- Colossus
- cuneiform
- Difference Engine
- Differential Analyzer
- John Presper Eckert
- EDVAC
- ENIAC
- EDSAC
- Herman Hollerith
- Hollerith card
- Jacquard's loom
- Augusta Ada King, Countess of Lovelace
- John Mauchly
- Napier's bones
- Blaise Pascal
- Pascaline
- Wilhelm Schickard
- stored program
- Alan Turing
- UNIVAC
- John von Neumann

SESSION TWO

From Chisels to Computers

COMPUTERS ARE NOT AN INVENTION OF the twentieth century. The idea of computing has been with us for centuries but it took the convergence of knowledge from a number of fields to make computers what they are today. Understanding how computers developed helps to determine where they will be going as we approach a new millennium. At the end of this session, you will be able to

- Outline the importance of mathematics to the development of computers
- Chronicle the development of the first electronic computer
- Reproduce von Neumann's conceptual computer
- Describe the contributions of key people to the evolution of computers
- Identify the role computers played in World War II

25

SECTION 2.1: IN THE BEGINNING

Before breathalyzers, traffic offenders suspected of being inebriated were often asked to look at a police officer's hand and state how many fingers the officer was holding up. The ability to count from one to ten is a skill that children learn before they enter school. Most of us could easily count to a million but would probably get bored and quit somewhere along the way.

But counting is not a human universal. Our distant ancestors, living off the land, had little need for counting. Even in this century, anthropologists have encountered groups of hunter-gatherers that use only three numbers, which we would interpret as having the values *none*, *one*, and *many*. You either don't have any yams, you have the one yam you need for lunch, or you have more yams than you need: many yams (two yams and five hundred yams both are many). Counting only becomes important when you need to compare or plan—to make sure that the number of cows that come back in the evening is the same as the number that left in the morning, or to know whether you have set aside enough seed for the next season's planting. When people began to settle in agricultural communities, they had a need to count so they could create a strategy for the coming seasons.

Anthropologists assume that people began counting by using their fingers, holding up one finger to represent one item being counted. (Why not? Fingers were handy.) Tallying systems used to keep score in games still reflect the shape of the human hand:

Counting on your fingers doesn't seem like a large mental leap, but it is. Imagine the first person counting sheep on their fingers and trying to explain it to the neighbors: "I have this many sheep…" "Those aren't sheep—those are your fingers. Sheep are woolly animals with four legs." Even after the abstract idea of using fingers to represent sheep or bushels of grain was accepted, there was still a problem: if you need to keep track of sheep and grain, you either need another set of hands, or a way to record the number of sheep before you begin counting the grain bushels. People eventually developed a system of abstract symbols that could be scratched into rocks or drawn on other surfaces to represent the sheep *and* the grain. The earliest evidence of writing is from Mesopotamia (in what is now Iraq) around 3500 B.C.E.

The writing, called **cuneiform** (from the Greek words meaning "wedge shaped") used different symbols for 1, 5, 10, and other numbers. Its invention divided human time into two eras: prehistory and history. History began when people first recorded information in writing. Interestingly enough, much of the early writing that has been found are records of tax assessment rolls.

> **NOTE**
>
> Cuneiform also used written symbols to represent individual words, similar to the writing used in China during the same period. Two thousand years later, another abstract concept revolutionized language and writing—the invention of the alphabet, in which written symbols stood for sounds rather than entire words. Since there are fewer sounds than words, the alphabet that was spread throughout the Middle East by the Phoenicians was easier to learn, allowing more people to learn how to write. By 640 B.C.E., the first library had been created to store written records.

Once the tax collector had counted and recorded ten farmers' sheep herds, all the herds needed to be totaled. The **abacus**, shown in Figure 2.1, allowed users to make computations by sliding stones on a board or beads on a series of wire racks. There are records of abacus use in Egypt as early as 500 B.C.E., in the time of the Pharaohs. Invented somewhere in the Middle East or India, the abacus is considered to be the first computing device.

> **NOTE**
>
> The abacus was in use in Europe at the time of the American Revolution in the late 1700s. Although it wasn't introduced in China until the 1200s and even later to Korea and Japan, the abacus is still used in parts of Asia today.

Figure 2.1
The abacus allowed users to make computations by sliding stones on a board or beads on a series of wire racks.

Courtesy of Linden High School

Over the next nine hundred years, the time of the Roman Empire, great strides were made in mathematics. Algebra books were written, geometry was conceived, and Roman numerals were developed. The fall of the empire in 410 C.E. marked the beginning of the period of European history known as the Dark Ages. For the next ten centuries, anything new or innovative in the former Roman Empire was suspect. In Europe, simple skills like adding and counting were lost. The spirit of invention remained suppressed until the Renaissance began in the 1400s. It was nearly two thousand years after the invention of the abacus before anyone would improve upon it.

NOTE

During the Dark Ages of Europe, mathematics was kept alive by Arabs like Muhammed ibn Al-Khwarizmi, who conceived the positional numbering system we use today, with a "ones place," "tens place," and so on.

SECTION 2.2: BONES AND MACHINES

John Napier was born in Edinburgh, Scotland, in 1550. He was a mathematician, and is best known as the inventor of logarithms. Napier spent a great deal of time trying to find shortcuts for mathematical operations. One of Napier's shortcuts was a device he named the Rabdologia, but which others called **Napier's bones.** The bones were strips of wood, bone, or ivory with numbers painted or etched on them that could be arranged to multiply two large numbers. Napier's bones could also be used to assist with division. Napier wrote a description of the bones that was published in 1617, the year he died. Use of Napier's bones spread rapidly throughout Europe. Improvements in the bones led to the development of the slide rule, which was used extensively into the early 1970s.

> **NOTE**
>
> Moveable type print was in use in China in the 1400s. In 1454, German Johannes Gutenberg invented the moveable type printing press. The ability to create hundreds of copies of books and articles (such as the description of Napier's bones) meant that scientific ideas could quickly spread to a wider audience, which resulted in a permanent acceleration in the rate of innovation. It also made it harder for governmental and religious authorities to completely suppress new ideas.

Napier's contemporary **Wilhelm Schickard** was a German professor of languages, mathematics, and astronomy. He was also a friend of the astronomer Johannes Kepler and a tinkerer who could build intricate devices. In 1623, Schickard built the first mechanical adding machine, a version of Napier's bones on cylinders. He sent a description and drawings of the machine to Kepler, but neither Kepler or Schickard tried to market the device. In fact, the machine and all knowledge of it was lost until one of Schickard's drawings was found in some of Kepler's papers in the 1960s. As a result, Schickard wasn't given credit for his invention. Instead, credit for inventing the first adding machine is often given to the French philosopher and mathematician, **Blaise Pascal.**

Pascal was born the year Schickard constructed his adding machine. An impressive thinker, Pascal wrote a geometry book when he was 16 years old. When he was 19, he designed a machine that could add and subtract, the **Pascaline** (shown in Figure 2.2), to help his father with his work as a tax collector. Pascal was unsuccessful in trying to have his machine built by others. He spent the next few years learning to build his own machines, improving on the Pascaline in the process, and eventually patenting it in 1649. Although the Pascaline worked, it was a commercial failure. An abacus was cheap, and fingers were free; in comparison, the Pascaline was quite expensive. Pascal might have persevered and found a way to construct a less expensive machine, but in 1652 he was almost killed in an accident. This near-death experience changed his interests from mathematics to philosophy, which he continued to study until his death at age 39.

In 1669, two mathematicians working independently developed the theories that underlie the field of calculus. One of the mathematicians, Sir Isaac Newton, is also known for his work in physics, including the well-known Laws of Gravity. The other, Gottfried Wilhelm Liebniz, continued Pascal's work on mechanical calculators. (Liebniz's other contribution to the field of

Figure 2.2
The Pascaline, a machine that could add and subtract, was designed by Blaise Pascal to help his father in his work as a tax collector.

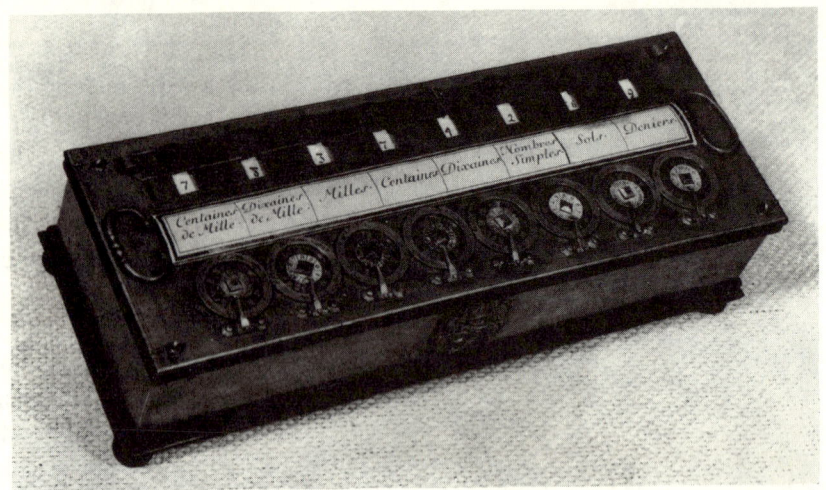

computers was his initial explorations into the binary numbering system used in modern computers.) In 1671, Liebniz designed a machine that could multiply numbers. A French clockmaker finished building the Liebniz multiplier in 1674. Although both Liebniz's and Pascal's calculating machines worked, the mechanical technology of their time did not support the finely detailed machines that they designed, so their machines were error prone and required frequent maintenance. The industrial production base needed to execute their designs didn't develop until the next century.

SECTION 2.3: COMPUTERS IN THE NINETEENTH CENTURY

The nineteenth century began with two inventions that made important contributions to modern computers. In 1800, the Italian physicist Alssandro Guiseppe Volta invented the first electric battery, using plates of zinc and copper combined with salt-soaked cardboard disks. Volta's large, wet battery was the predecessor of batteries used to power portable computers today.

The second important invention, called **Jacquard's loom,** was a pattern-weaving machine invented by Joseph-Marie Jacquard. The loom was controlled by a series of punched cards with holes that represented the pattern of the cloth being woven. Levers on the loom were lined up with the cards and triggered by the holes. Jacquard's loom is the first machine controlled by information—the weaving pattern stored on cards—rather than by a human operator. It was also the first machine to use a **stored program** like a modern computer program.

With James Watt's invention of the steam engine in 1765, and the earlier work of Pascal and Liebniz, all the pieces were now in place for an automated calculating machine. All that was required was someone to put the pieces together.

Charles Babbage, the son of a London banker, educated himself in mathematics by reading the works of well-known mathematicians like Liebniz. When he entered college at the age of 20, he found that he was more knowledgeable than many of his teachers. He helped found the Analytical Society to promote mathematics in England. When he was in his late twenties, Babbage (shown in Figure 2.3) was working with error-ridden sets of tables that were used in astronomy. Creating tables of numbers seemed to be a perfect job for a machine.

Babbage quickly realized that a machine was needed that could calculate the tables and then store the results to be used in other calculations—to create, for example, subtotals that could then be used in a grand total. Numerical problems could be entered from a punched card system similar to that used by Jacquard. Since errors in numeric tables were often introduced when results were handwritten or typeset, Babbage also wanted his machine, called the **Difference Engine,** to be able to print numbers directly rather than having a human operator read and then write numbers on paper.

Babbage completed his first diagram of a steam-powered Difference Engine in 1822. He then obtained British government support to build a complete model that would calculate and print tables. The terms of the grant were vague: Babbage thought that he would be given enough money to complete the engine; the government, however, felt no such obligation, and quit supporting Babbage's project. Work on the nearly completed Difference Engine was terminated in 1833. Figure 2.4 shows the ill-fated Difference Engine. While Babbage might have been able to fund the completion of the work, he was already thinking of his next project, the **Analytical Engine**, a general purpose computing machine that would be able to multiply and divide large numbers with great accuracy. Numbers would be read from punched cards, and results placed on another set of cards for reuse in later calculations.

Figure 2.3
Charles Babbage

Charles Babbage Institute, University of Minnesota, Minneapolis

One evening I was sitting...with a table of logarithms lying open before me. Another [Analytical Society] member coming into the room and seeing me half asleep called out "Well, Babbage, what are you dreaming about?" to which I replied "I am thinking that all these tables might be calculated by machinery."

—Charles Babbage, 1821

In 1840, Babbage traveled to Italy and gave a series of lectures on the Analytical Engine. An Italian summary of the series was produced, and Babbage asked **Augusta Ada King, Countess of Lovelace** and daughter of Lord Byron, to translate the summary into English. Lady Lovelace, shown in Figure 2.5, worked closely with Babbage, adding so many notes that they more than doubled the length of the summary. Based in part on descriptions in her notes, Lady Lovelace is recognized as the first computer programmer,

Figure 2.4 Even though it was never completed, Babbage's Difference Engine was the first machine to use a punch card system to calculate numbers.

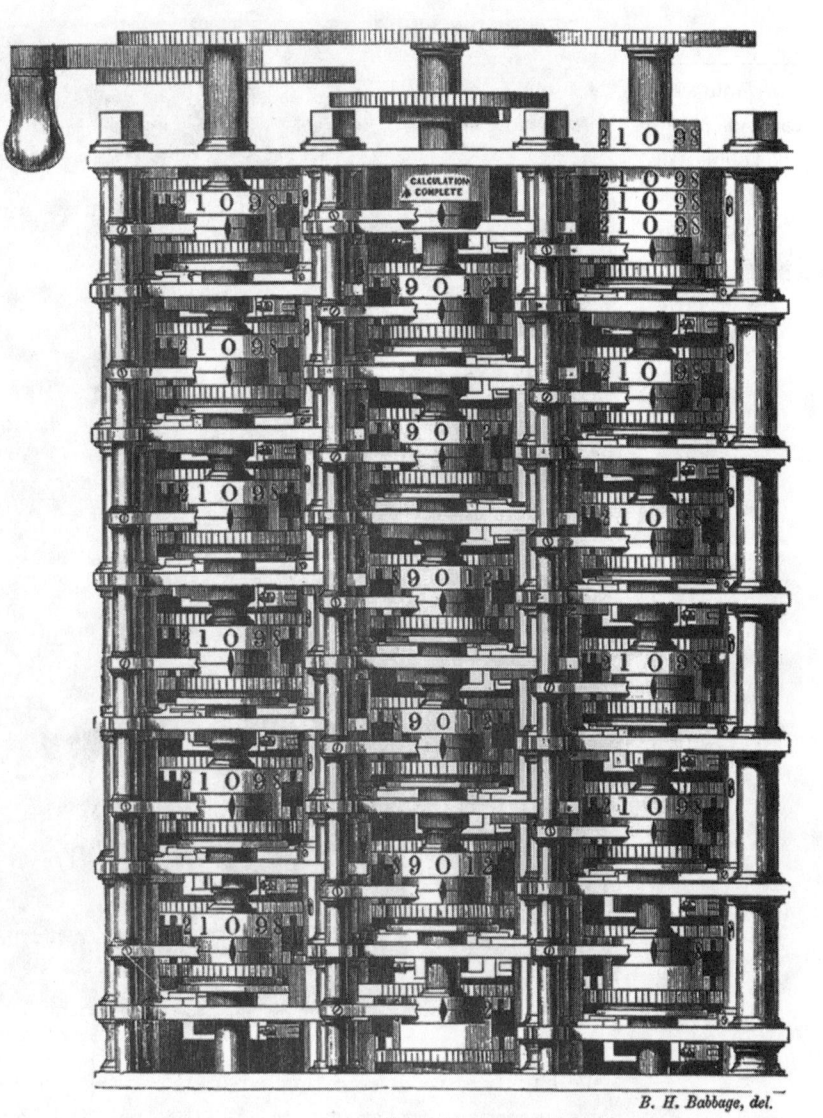

B. H. Babbage, del.
Charles Babbage Institute, University of Minnesota, Minneapolis

although there are scholars who feel this credit is not deserved. There is disagreement about Lady Lovelace's involvement with the Analytical Engine. Some feel she was intimately involved in revisions of the machine and programs, and helped Babbage obtain his original government funding. Others feel her role was only that of a translator. Despite the conflicting opinions, the programming language of the United States Department of Defense was named Ada in her honor.

Figure 2.5
Lady Ada Byron, the Countess of Lovelace, is considered by some to be the first computer programmer.

Crown Copyright

Perhaps because of his earlier experience with government funding, Babbage made no real attempt to build the Analytical Engine. Instead, he roughed out the overall design and completely designed and modeled some of the individual components of the machine, like the improved printer. New improvements were continuously added to the design (which ultimately contained over fifty thousand parts), and Babbage was still working on his machines on and off up until his death at age 80. While the Analytical Engine was never completed, Babbage had designed the forerunner of the modern computer.

> **NOTE**
>
> After Babbage had spent most of the money from his father's estate on his machines, Babbage and Lady Lovelace tried to construct a mathematical scheme to predict the outcomes of horse races. It didn't work.

There were other inventions of the mid-1800s that make our computing life easier today. The electric generator was invented by Michael Faraday in 1831. The first telegraph line between two major metropolitan areas was completed by Samuel Morse in 1844, linking Baltimore, Maryland, and Washington, DC. For the first time in history, news could travel between cities faster than a horse or train could travel. In 1858, the first transatlantic telegraph cable was completed, linking the United States and Europe and providing a sense of human community larger than one's nation or continent. The telegraph was the first strand of the World Wide Web, a step toward the modern vision of an interconnected global village.

Mathematician **George Boole** published his first papers on symbolic logic (also called Boolean algebra) in 1847. Boole expanded on the work of Liebniz almost two hundred years before and described a way to use binary values (variables that can have one of two values like true/false, yes/no, and on/off) to make comparisons and logical decisions. Modern computers use binary logic made possible by Boole's work.

In 1867, Christopher Sholes invented the typewriter, direct ancestor of the computer keyboard. Alexander Graham Bell's telephone (1876) amplified the effect of the telegraph and created a focus on sound technologies. The next year, Thomas Edison's phonograph demonstrated not only that sound could be transmitted and received, but that it could be stored. Edison followed this invention with the invention of an affordable electric light and motion pictures.

SECTION 2.4: MAKING THE CENSUS COUNT

The United States Constitution requires a decennial census of the population, so every decade employees of the Census Bureau count all the residents of the United States. The census of 1880 took over seven years to complete. The need for detailed information was growing with each census. With the dramatic increase in immigration, the bureau feared that the 1890 census could not be completed within ten years.

Herman Hollerith, an employee of the Census Bureau, thought there should be a way to mechanize the census process. In 1882, Hollerith left the bureau and started work on a machine to tabulate census information. Hollerith used the punched card ideas that Jacquard and Babbage had employed, but in a different way. Rather than using punched cards for instructions, Hollerith used the cards, shown in Figure 2.6, to record specific pieces of census data.

Figure 2.6
The Hollerith Card was the first method used to store machine-generated data.

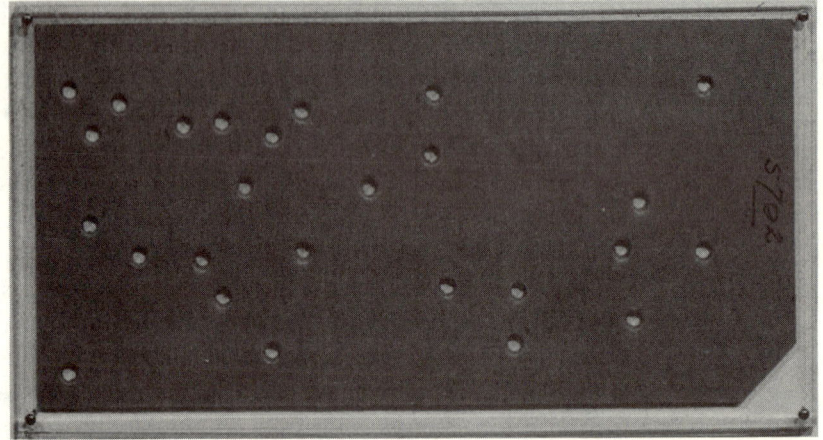

Smithsonian Institution Photo No. 77034

The **Hollerith card** was divided into sections for each piece of census information: gender, age, occupation, race, marital status, and so on. Information was recorded on the card by punching a hole through "M" for male or "F" for female; and "M" for married, "Dv" for divorced, or "Un" for unmarried. (Unlike the 1990 census, the census of 1890 didn't ask about domestic partners.) Once data had been entered on a card, the card was placed on a machine mounted in a desk. Mercury-filled wells lay under each of the possible holes in a card; the wells were connected with wire to counters. A press with metal pins was lowered onto the card. Where there was a hole in the card, a pin passed through to the mercury well, completing an electrical circuit and turning the hand on the counter one notch.

Hollerith filed a patent for his system in 1887, and did some trial runs using census-like data—Army medical statistics. In 1889, a competition was held to select a system for the 1890 census. Hollerith's system, one of three entrants, was the clear winner. The punched card system had a definite advantage: data only had to be entered once. And the cards served as a storage system, so the data could be reused in other tabulations. The census of 1890 was completed with over one hundred Hollerith machines, and was a tremendous success. The first count of the census was completed in weeks, and all the tabulations were completed late in 1892. Whereas Babbage had dreamed of working with steam engines to create a mechanical computer, Hollerith was able to work with electricity to create the first *electro*mechanical computer (see Figure 2.7).

Figure 2.7
Hollerith Tabulating Machine, the first electromechanical computer

Courtesy of International Business Machines Corporation. Unauthorized use not permitted.

The success with the census made Hollerith a very popular man. He traveled and advised extensively in Europe, and then, in 1896, he turned his business into the Tabulating Machine Company. Because Hollerith's big business was still census work—generally done every ten years—the Tabulating Machine Company needed something to keep it busy for the eight years between censuses. Hollerith began marketing tabulating machines to railroads, insurance companies, and manufacturers. With an increased customer base, the Tabulating Machine Company took off. In 1911, Hollerith sold the company to Charles Flint, who merged it with two other companies to form a corporation named CTR (Computing-Tabulating-Recording Company). In

1914, Thomas J. Watson became president of CTR, and was president in 1924 when the company changed its name for the last time to International Business Machines—IBM.

SECTION 2.5: COMPUTING IN THE TWENTIETH CENTURY

While Hollerith was successfully building and selling computers, other inventors were making contributions to the computer age. In 1901, an engineer named Guglielmo Marconi sent a radio broadcast from England that was received in Newfoundland. Radio received a great deal of attention in the popular press, and research about broadcast frequency modulation later contributed to the invention of the transistor.

John Ambrose Fleming's 1904 invention of the electronic rectifier vacuum tube received a quieter reception, but was required for later advances in computing and communications. The electronic rectifier only let electricity pass through in one direction; its invention was the starting point for the electronics used today in all computers, telephones, televisions, and audio equipment.

By 1908, Henry Ford was using assembly lines in Michigan for mass production of automobiles. Mass production would one day contribute to the low costs of computer components and fuel the computer revolution.

During World War I, research dollars were focused on the tools of war—and computers were not on the list. As a result, the next significant computer innovation didn't occur until 1930. An American electrical engineer, **Vannevar Bush**, produced the first machine that could actually solve differential equations, hard-to-solve equations that were used extensively in engineering and science. With differential equations, the rate of change in a function is based on changes in the variables underlying the function. Bush's machine used a feedback loop to put results from the function calculations back into the variables. Part electronic but largely mechanical, **Differential Analyzers** were the first automatic, general-purpose computing devices.

In 1936, British mathematician **Alan Turing** wrote a paper about mechanical logic and mathematical processes. Turing wasn't interested in building a computer, but he was interested in thinking about the kinds of problems that could be solved by machines. According to the conceptual paper Turing wrote, the Universal Turing Machine would receive a set of numbers preceded by instructions about what should be done with the numbers. Turing called his device *universal* because the inclusion of the instructions (program) as well as the data meant the machine could be instructed to do any task which could be broken into a series of mathematical problems. Conceptually, the Universal Turing Machine could play chess as well as compute differential equations. Turing's paper came at a critical time in computer development, and broadened the vision of the capabilities of the new computing machines.

I think there's a world market for about five computers.
—*Thomas J. Watson Sr., 1943*

Iowa State College (currently Iowa State University) professor **John Atanasoff** developed the idea for an entirely electronic computer in 1940 and convinced the university to let him hire a graduate student, Clifford Berry, to help build the computer. The ABC (**Atanasoff-Berry Computer**), completed in 1942 and shown in Figure 2.8, was based on Boolean algebra because of the Hollerith-style punched cards Atanasoff used—there either is or isn't a hole at any specific point in the card., The ABC used Fleming's vacuum tubes rather than mechanical gears, and was the first electronic computer.

Figure 2.8 Atanasoff-Berry Computer, the first entirely electronic computer

Iowa State University Library/University Archives

SECTION 2.6: THE COMPUTER GOES TO WAR

World War II was the first war in which computers played a major role. Both the Axis and Allied powers spent incredible amounts of money on technology, including computer research. Computers were used in Germany to design missiles and aircraft. But the war was won by Allied computers.

Axis troops and agents sent messages that were encoded and decoded using a simple device called Enigma. Enigma fit into a suitcase, and had been sold in Europe and the United States in the 1930s. Although the Germans modified their Enigma coders, shown in Figure 2.9, enough was understood about the basic design to allow the Allies to freely decode Axis radio messages during the last two years of the war, using a code-breaking machine named Bombe.

Figure 2.9
Messages from German Enigma coders, like this one, were broken by the Allies using the Bombe Code Breaking Machine.

Smithsonian Institution Photo No. 90-3649

But highly classified messages weren't sent over radio; they were sent by teletype and coded with a machine built in Germany. The British (including Alan Turing) developed a secret computer named **Colossus**, designed specifically for cryptanalysis: analyzing and decoding messages. Colossus was the world's first large electronic valve programmable logic calculator. Before the end of the war, up to 10 different Colossus computers were built, but the existence of Colossus remained a secret until 1976. Detailed information is only today becoming known about Colossus, since all of the original drawings were destroyed in a fire in 1960. It is known, however, that information obtained from decoding German transmissions was vital to the success of the Allied invasion of Europe on D day. Because the secret of Colossus was so well-protected, the computer had little effect on the computer innovations that followed.

The war stimulated other, less secret computer developments. **Howard Aiken**, a Harvard engineer, created the Harvard-IBM Automatic Sequence Controlled Calculator, also called the Mark I, in 1944. The Mark I was an electronic calculator used to create gunnery tables for the Navy.

In 1943, **John Mauchly**, an instructor at the Moore School of Engineering of the University of Pennsylvania, and **John Presper Eckert**, a graduate student at the school, submitted a proposal to the U.S. Army to create a general-purpose computer. Mauchly had studied the Moore School's Differential Analyzer, which was being used full time to calculate gunnery firing tables for the military. Mauchly discovered that the Differential Analyzer couldn't keep up with the demand. It was clear to Mauchly that the Army needed another computer. The Army agreed, and funded Mauchly's and Eckert's proposal for $400,000. Project PX was begun. In 1946, months after the end of World War II and three years after the computer was conceived, Mauchly and Eckert unveiled the Electronic Numerical Integrator and Computer (**ENIAC**). ENIAC, shown in Figure 2.10, included over 18,000 vacuum tubes, weighed 30 tons, and was over one thousand times faster than the Mark I. ENIAC's manual, written by Adele Goldstine, contained all the computer's technical descriptions, including the specific vacuum tubes used.

Figure 2.10
ENIAC, the first general purpose computer, included over 18,000 vacuum tubes and weighed 30 tons.

Smithsonian Institution Photo No. 53192

Even while Mauchly and Eckert were developing the ENIAC, they knew there was a problem with it. Although the computer could complete a task at speeds never before achieved, its programming was *hard wired*—electrical wiring was run to create new connections—by programmers like mathematician Kay McNulty Mauchly. It would take days to run the wiring to set up a program that only took minutes to run. Mauchly and Eckert reasoned that if the program could be stored in memory (like the data) and fed to the computer, new programs could be started quickly without rewiring.

Late in 1944, John von Neumann, shown in Figure 2.11, a member of the Manhattan Project team that developed the atomic bomb and a consultant to many scientific endeavors during the war, visited the ENIAC project. After discussions with Eckert and Mauchley, von Neumann conceptualized a stored program technique and wrote a paper, "First Draft of a Report on the EDVAC," in which he described a digital computer design.

Figure 2.11
John von Neumann conceptualized the first digital computer, a computer that could use stored programs.

Courtesy of Richard Goldstein, RAND Corporation.

The computer von Neumann conceived, shown in Figure 2.12, had five basic parts:

- An input unit like a keyboard for entering information into the computer
- A memory area to hold programs and data
- An arithmetic unit to perform calculations
- A control unit that would move program instructions and data between memory and the arithmetic unit
- An output device such as a printer

Figure 2.12 Von Neumann's conceptual computer

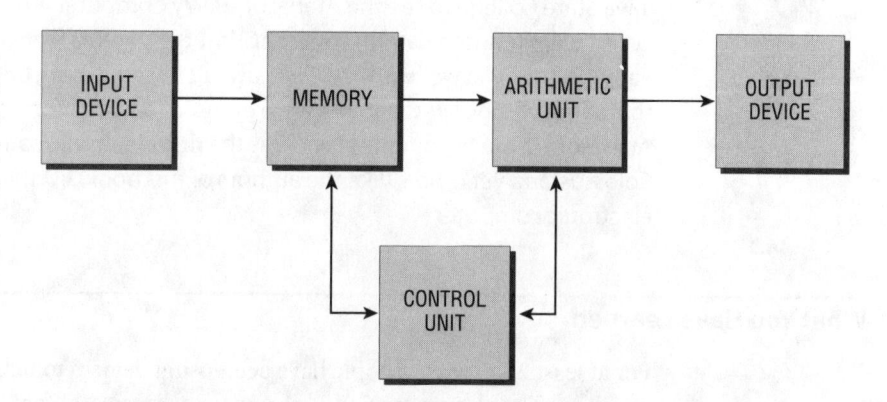

Von Neumann's paper was widely published, and it significantly changed the way computers were designed. (Almost all computers built since ENIAC have been von Neumann computers.) Based on von Neumann's technique, the ENIAC team applied for and received additional funds to build an Electronic Discrete Variable Computer (**EDVAC**), a computer that that would use stored programs. But before they could build it, the Moore School had another visitor, Cambridge University's Maurice Wilkes. Wilkes visited in 1946, and based on what he had learned from Mauchly and Eckert, began work on a von Neumann computer when he returned to England. Wilkes completed work on the Cambridge **EDSAC** (Electronic Delay Storage Automatic Calculator) in 1949. EDSAC, the first stored-program computer, was used by Cambridge faculty and students until 1958.

Mauchly and Eckert left the Moore School in 1946 to form the world's first electronic computer company, the Electronic Control Company. They applied for and received patents on ENIAC, and tried to find investors and purchasers for electronic computers. The U.S. Census Bureau, which was looking for a replacement for Hollerith's machine, was their only customer. Out of funding, and unable to entice investors in their company, Mauchly and Eckert sold the Electronic Control Company to Remington Rand in 1950. Terms of the sale included employment for Mauchly and Eckert at Remington Rand, and in 1951, their **UNIVAC** computer was completed and delivered (late and severely over-budget) to the Census Bureau. UNIVAC marks the beginning of the next step in computers: the age of commercial computing.

NOTE

ENIAC designer John Mauchly corresponded with John Atanasoff and visited Iowa State College to see the Atanasoff-Berry Computer in 1941. Mauchly and Eckert were granted patents for ENIAC, but the patents were revoked in the early 1970s *Honeywell v. Sperry Rand* lawsuit based, in part, on the judge's ruling that some of the ENIAC patents were granted for work done earlier by Atanasoff. Some histories list ENIAC as the first electronic computer, others Colossus, and yet others (like the authors of this book) list the ABC as the first electronic computer.

What You Have Learned

For at least 2500 years, people have been using devices to help them calculate numbers. The abacus reigned supreme for centuries, before being gradually replaced by mechanical and then electrical devices. This transition didn't occur, however, until the development of a system to record data. Punched cards were first used to store instructions for a mechanical device. Herman Hollerith was the first to use punched cards to record specific pieces of data that could then be used in other calculations.

With the discovery of electricity, computing machines moved into a new era. Computers such as Colossus were instrumental in decoding secret German transmissions and ultimately contributed to the Allied victory in World War II. ENIAC, the first general purpose computer, used over 18,000 vacuum tubes and weighed 30 tons. John von Neumann's stored program technique and conceptual computer changed the way computers were designed and ushered in the age of commercial computing.

■ FOCUS AND EXPLORATION

Focus Questions

1. What was Napier's bones and what computing device did it largely replace?

2. What was the significance of the development of Jacquard's loom?

3. List three developments in the nineteenth century and indicate how they contributed to the modern computer.

4. How did Hollerith use punch cards differently than Jacquard and Babbage?

5. What is the significance of the ABC?

6. How did computers contribute to the winning of World War II?

7. What are the five parts of a von Neumann computer, and what is the function of each part?

Knowledge Reinforcement

A. Our decimal numbering system is based on 10. What other numbering systems do you know about and how do they work?

B. Do you think Charles Babbage was viewed as a success or a failure by his contemporaries? If you had lived in Babbage's time, would you have been interested in his work?

C. What kinds of tasks are completed by modern computers that fit within Babbage's vision of a computer as a calculating machine? What types of tasks fit within Turing's scheme of a Universal Machine?

D. Why might the Allies' governments have kept Colossus a secret for thirty years?

Further Exploration

Asimov's Biographical Encyclopedia of Science and Technology (2d rev. ed.). Isaac Asimov. Doubleday & Company, 1982, 0-385-17771-2. Brief biographies of significant scientists and inventors, including Babbage, Napier, and others.

Asimov's Chronology of Science and Discovery. Isaac Asimov. Harper & Row, Publishers, 1989, 0-06-015612-0. History of discoveries and inventions in science.

The Colossus Rebuild Project:
http://www.cranfield.ac.uk/CCC/BPark/colossus

Computing Before Computers. William Aspray et al. Iowa State University Press, 1990, 0-8138-0047-1. History of computing devices from the abacus to electronic calculators.

The Difference Engine. William Gibson and Bruce Sterling. Bantam Books, 1991, 0-5532-9461-X. An alternate histories novel set in an England where Babbage's Analytical Engine was actually constructed.

Enigma. Robert Harris. Ballentine Books, 1995, 0-8041-1548-6. A novel about Enigma codebreakers.

The First Electronic Computer: The Atanasoff Story. Alice R. and Arthur W. Burks. University of Michigan Press, 1989, 0-472-08104-7. A detailed description of the invention of the ABC and the ENIAC patent trials.

History of Computing Information—ENIAC's 50th anniversary:
http://ftp.arl.mil/~mike/comphist/

Past Notable Women of Computing (Kay Mauchly, Adele Goldstine, and many others):
http://www.cs.yale.edu/homes/tap/past-women.html

They All Laughed. Ira Flatow. HarperCollins Publishers, 1992, 0-06-092415-2. Information on the role of Colossus in World War II.

A World Lit Only by Fire. William Manchester. Little Brown and Company, 1992, 0-316-54531-7. The Dark Ages and the Renaissance.

SESSION THREE

The Age of Titans

Vocabulary

- access time
- arithmetic logic unit
- artificial intelligence
- ASCII
- binary digit (bit)
- byte
- cache
- capacity
- central processing unit (CPU)
- COBOL
- compiler
- conceptual computer
- control unit
- coprocessor
- direct (random) access
- DRAM
- gigabyte (GB)
- Grace Hopper
- input
- integrated circuit
- Intel
- kilobyte (KB)
- machine language
- magnetic storage media
- megabyte (MB)
- megahertz (MHz)
- memory
- microminiaturized circuit
- microprocessor
- millisecond
- nanosecond
- operating system
- optical storage
- output
- RAM
- ROM
- register
- semiconductor
- sequential access
- storage
- swap file
- transistor
- virtual memory

WHILE COMPUTERS HAVE A RICH history, many of the discoveries and improvements that culminated in the PC on your desktop have been made in your lifetime. This session looks at more recent developments in computers and the culture of technology. At the end of this session, you will be able to

- Discuss the different generations of computer hardware
- Use the conceptual computer to explain parts of a computer system
- Explain how computer capacity and speed are measured
- Compare types of storage devices

49

SECTION 3.1: GENERATIONS OF COMPUTERS

On election day in 1952, Remington Rand's UNIVAC was introduced on national television. Dwight D. Eisenhower and Adlai Stevenson were running for United States President, and as election returns came in from the east coast, Remington Rand employees entered the results into UNIVAC, which was programmed to predict the election winner based on the early returns. The CBS television network was supposed to announce UNIVAC's winner at nine o'clock, but at the scheduled time, CBS commentators announced that UNIVAC had no prediction. In truth, UNIVAC did have a prediction: its calculations indicated that Eisenhower would win by a large margin. The commentators had refused to announce the prediction, because they (along with everyone else in the country) thought the election would be close. Later in the evening, when it was apparent that UNIVAC had predicted the results correctly, CBS announced the earlier result, and UNIVAC's credibility was immediately established in the eyes of the American public.

UNIVAC's televised abilities allowed the large majority of Americans who weren't involved with computer science to see computers in a new way, and helped set the commercial computer age in motion. Beginning with UNIVAC and other similar computers, there have been four distinct stages of commercial computer development, called the generations of computers. Today, we are poised on the edge of the fifth generation.

First Generation: Vacuum Tubes (1942-56)

Electronic, first-generation computers like UNIVAC processed data using the vacuum tube technologies pioneered in the ABC, ENIAC, and EDVAC computers. These first-generation computers were called *mainframe* computers, a reference to the metal frames used to hold the racks of vacuum tubes. Vacuum tubes are like large light bulbs that require time to warm up and throw off tremendous amounts of heat. The thousands of vacuum tubes in computers like ENIAC meant there were thousands of tubes to warm up, and, when the computer quit working, thousands of tubes to check to see which one had burned out. Vacuum tubes are so large that if computers were still constructed using them, modern mainframes would need to be as big as skyscrapers.

First-generation computers contained magnetic drums for storing data. Stored programs were written in binary **machine language**, a series of 0s and 1s that directly reflected the computer's debt to George Boole. Each manufacturer created its own machine language.

Grace Hopper, who had worked with Howard Aiken on the Mark I calculator in the 1940s, went to work for Mauchly and Eckert after they left the Moore School. Hopper, shown in Figure 3.1, developed the first **compiler**—a program that turns programming language into machine language—in 1952. The compiler changed the face of programming, allowing programmers to enter numbers and letters rather than simply the 0s and 1s of machine language. This breakthrough also created a definite increase in the number of people who were willing to learn how to program computers.

Figure 3.1
Admiral Grace Hopper, a mathematician and physicist, developed the first computer compiler.

Navy Photo by James S. Davis

■ Second Generation: Transistors (1956-63)

In 1948, three Bell Labs physicists—William Shockley, Walter Brattian, and John Bardeen—discovered a new type of crystal called *germanium*. Germanium didn't conduct electricity as well as copper or steel, but it did conduct electrical current better than glass or rubber. This type of material was dubbed a **semiconductor**.

Other semiconducting materials were discovered, including silicon, that were made from easily available raw materials—rocks or sand. The physicists found that by adding other materials to the semiconductor (a process called *doping*), they could create a material that would act as an electrical rectifier or amplifier—in other words, a material that could take the place of a vacuum tube (shown in Figure 3.2). The new devices created from semiconducting materials were called **transistors**.

Figure 3.2 Computers like ENIAC used thousands of vacuum tubes.

Smithsonian Institution Photo No. 64934

Transistors (see Figure 3.3) were much smaller (one-fiftieth the size of a vacuum tube), more energy efficient, and sturdier than the fragile glass vacuum tubes. In 1953, the first transistorized device for public purchase was released: a hearing aid that fit into the ear opening. By the end of the decade, transistors were replacing tubes in computers, televisions, and "transistor radios"—the first radios small enough to carry in your shirt pocket. Appliances that used transistors were dubbed "solid-state" because the transistors were solid.

Figure 3.3
Transistors, made of semiconducting materials, quickly replaced vacuum tubes in electronic devices.

Courtesy of International Business Machines Corporation. Unauthorized use not permitted.

The new solid-state technology was used to build the first supercomputers (see Session 1), which were giant computers developed to handle large amounts of data and rapid calculations. During the 1960s, second generation mainframe computers were manufactured by companies like IBM, Honeywell, and Sperry-Rand (now part of Unisys), and were widely used in large businesses.

In 1957, Grace Hopper developed a business programming language called Flow-Matic. In 1960, Hopper was one of the co-inventors of **COBOL**, the Common Business-Oriented Language. Based on Flow-Matic, COBOL was the first high-level computer language that wasn't specific to a particular machine. (High-level computer languages resemble English, unlike the 0s and 1s of machine language.) Programs written in COBOL were then translated into machine language with a COBOL compiler. Most business programs were written in COBOL until the 1980s; scientific programs were written in FORTRAN (Formula Translator).

High-level programming languages like COBOL and FORTRAN combined with von Neumann's stored program concept in the second generation to create truly flexible, general-purpose computing machines. A program could be quickly loaded into a computer's memory (made of transistors rather than tubes), run, and then replaced with yet another program. With better programming languages and more computers, new occupations were created: computer programmers and systems analysts.

In 1957, IBM released the first disk drive that could both read information from a disk and write information on a disk. In 1959, Digital Equipment Corporation (DEC) created the PDP-1 minicomputer, shown in Figure 3.4. Smaller than mainframe computers, minicomputers were marketed as powerful compact computers. Most importantly, minicomputers were inexpensive. The PDP-8 minicomputer cost less than $10,000.

The end of the 1950s saw another first: checks cleared by computer, rather than by hand. The Bank of America, the world's largest bank, was concerned with how long it took to post checks to accounts. So in 1959, General Electric installed the new Electronic Recording Method of Accounting (ERMA) at Bank of America. ERMA used computers to record checks that had been numbered with magnetic ink, and could sort and post twice as many checks in a minute as a human bookkeeper could post in an hour.

NOTE

By the early 1960s, Bank of America wasn't hiring any more bookkeepers, and Americans began to suspect that computers could replace people. A Katharine Hepburn and Spencer Tracy movie of the period, *Desk Set* (1957), featured a computer named EMERAC that was replacing human reference workers (just before the holidays, of course), and accurately reflected the fears of the time. *Desk Set* is available on video.

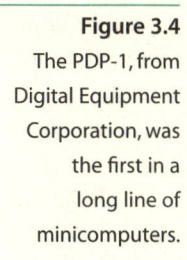

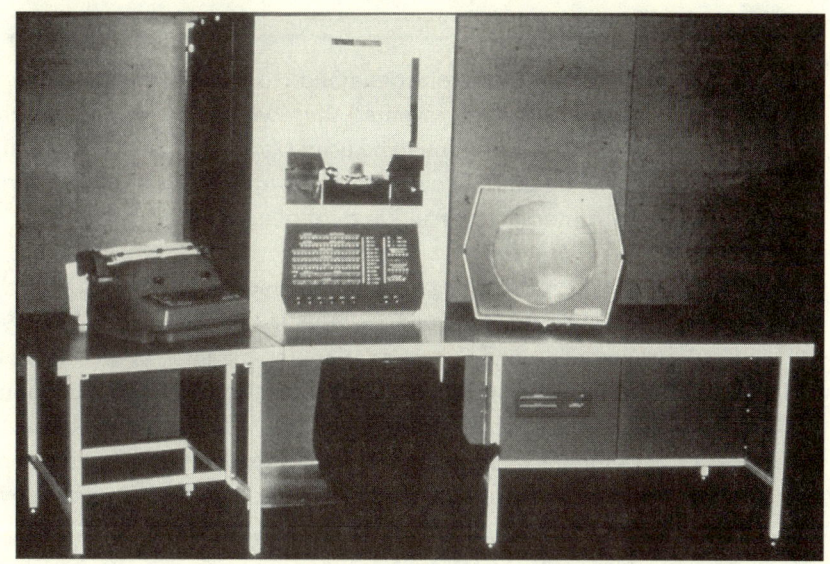

Figure 3.4
The PDP-1, from Digital Equipment Corporation, was the first in a long line of minicomputers.

Courtesy of Digital Equipment Corporation, Corporate Photo Library

The second generation also included the first patent on a robotic device, granted to George Devol Jr., and Joseph Engelberger in 1954. In 1958, Devol and Engelberger installed the first industrial robot, UNIMATE, in a General Motors assembly plant. In the same year, Chester A. Carolson created the first photocopying machine: the Xerox.

Third Generation: Integrated Circuits (1964-71)

By the beginning of the third generation, transistors had been around for a dozen years, getting more compact and more reliable as manufacturing processes were continually improved. By the end of the 1950s, transistors had gotten so small that it stood to reason to manufacture multiple transistors as a single unit. Jack Kilby, an engineer, developed the quartz integrated circuit in 1958. The first integrated circuit had three components in a single module made of quartz silicon.

A group of engineers at Fairchild Semiconductor (the first company in Silicon Valley, California) was also working on the idea of putting transistors and circuits on one chip. Engineer Jack Hoerni figured out how to make flat transistors, which then allowed for flat integrated circuit modules—computer chips. Increasing improvements led to the inclusion of more components on each chip. Computers were shrinking in size, but the cost of chips was still higher than the cost of individual transistor components.

> **NOTE**
>
> The change from one generation to the next doesn't happen overnight. When the transistor was invented, there were still plenty of vacuum tubes sitting in warehouses, waiting to be used. Many early second-generation computers included both vacuum tubes and transistors, and transistors were used along with integrated circuits in third-generation computers.

The race to get a man on the moon helped drive down the price of chips. The Soviet Union launched the first satellite, Sputnik, in 1957. In 1961, U.S. President John F. Kennedy, looking for a way to increase national confidence, committed the United States to sending a man to the moon by the end of the decade. The cost of such a venture wasn't an issue—but size was. In order to computerize spacecraft, more compact integrated circuits needed to be built by companies like Fairchild. And, in turn, the increased government support for research and production of integrated circuits helped create more complex chips at a lower cost.

Another major improvement of the third generation was the development of operating systems. **Operating systems** are programs that control the basic functions of a computer, including moving instructions and data in and out of memory, printing, and reading information from a disk (see Section 3.2 for information on memory and disks). Before operating systems, for example, each program had to include many lines of code that specified exactly how to open a file. With an operating system, a program only has to have enough code to send the open request to the operating system, which issued a system call. The system call handles the actual task of opening the file. Standardized operating systems allowed other programs to be written more quickly and with fewer lines of program code.

Despite these advances in computer technology, the personal computer of today was still a long way off. Instead, *time-sharing* was the buzzword of the 1960s. With time-sharing, users no longer had to line up to use a computer; instead, the computer rotated between simultaneous users, giving each a small slice of time. Since computers work more rapidly than people, it was possible for users to work at a constant pace and never notice that the computer had been "out working with someone else" for the last one-tenth of a second. The predominant vision of computing's future was that several incredibly large computers would each accommodate thousands of time-sharing users, all of whom would enter information on punched cards and get output from a printer.

3.1 ■ GENERATIONS OF COMPUTERS   57

Engineer Douglas Engelbart (pictured in Figure 3.5) of the Stanford Research Institute had another vision: individual computers that produced output on television-like cathode ray tubes (rather than printouts) and let users manipulate pictures as well as type in text. In the fall of 1968, Engelbart presented his vision at a computer conference, demonstrating a new word processor with a computer that included both a keyboard and a new pointing device he called a mouse.

Figure 3.5
Douglas Engelbart envisioned and designed the first models of the easy-to-use, mouse-driven, graphically oriented, networked computers of today.

Provided by Douglas C. Engelbart and the Bootstrap Institute

By 1970, Engelbart was demonstrating multiple-window user interfaces, the predecessors of Windows, and had implemented a large mainframe-based electronic-mail system. Engelbart hoped his vision of personal computing would radically change the direction of computing at companies like IBM, Sperry, and DEC—but the large companies still didn't believe there was a market for easy-to-use, graphically oriented computers.

■ Fourth Generation: Microminiaturized Circuits (1971-?)

In the early 1970s, integrated circuits continued to get smaller. Using large-scale integration (LSI), manufacturers could fit hundreds of separate components on a single chip. LSI was replaced with VLSI (very large-scale integration) with hundreds of thousands of components per chip. Ultra-large-scale integration (ULSI) pushed the number of components per chip into the millions.

In 1971, a small company named **Intel** (currently the world's foremost chip manufacturer), put all the critical components of a computer onto one chip: the microprocessor. **Microprocessors**, like the one shown in Figure 3.6, were stand-alone products—a microprocessor could be put into any computer, or any appliance. Computers broke out of their metal cases and found their way into cars, microwaves, and stereo systems. And microprocessors were cheap when compared to the processors used in mainframes and minicomputers.

Figure 3.6
A microprocessor from Intel sitting on an aspirin.

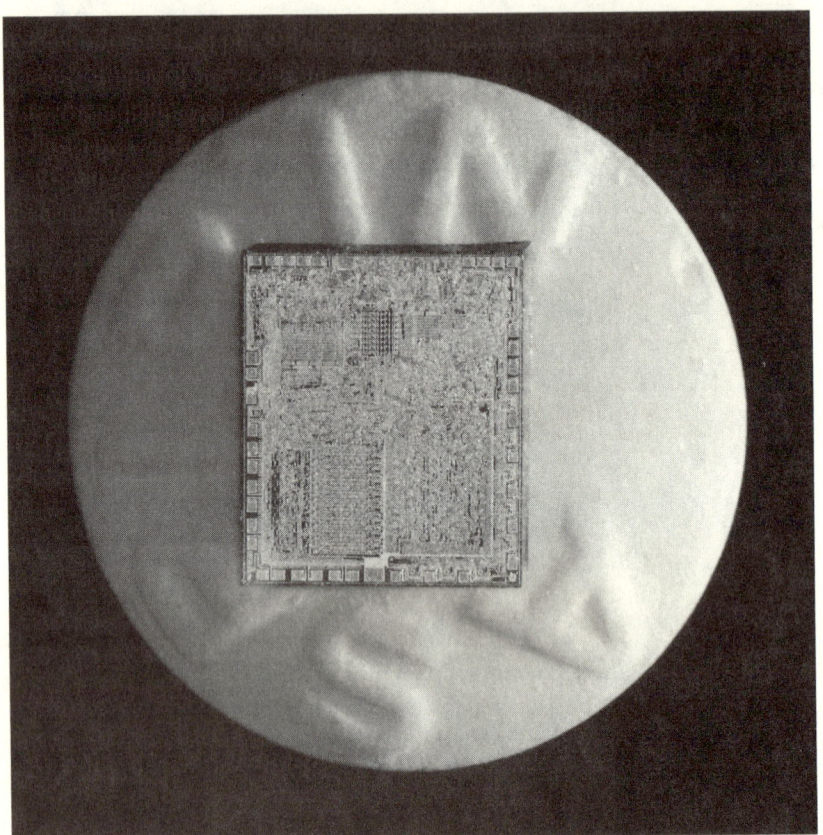

Courtesy of Intel Corporation

In the early 1970s, Atari used a microprocessor for the first video game, Pong, in which two players turned rotary knobs that controlled paddles in a computerized game of table tennis. Within a few short years, pinball's dominance in the arcade had ended, replaced by video games like Pac Man, Defender, Centipede, and Missile Command; by the early 1980s, game enthusiasts could play arcade-type games at home.

NOTE

It didn't take long for pinball manufacturers like Williams, Bally, and Data East to put microprocessors into pinball tables to control random payouts and scoring displays. As a result, silverball is making a strong comeback.

The creation of the microprocessor made Engelbart's vision of easy-to-use personal computers a reality. The first commercial microprocessor was available in 1971. The following year, there was a microcomputer on the market, although the first commercially successful personal computer—the Apple II, shown in Figure 3.7—wasn't released until 1976. By 1992, there were 65 million personal computers in use. The rest, as they say, is history (and the focus of Session 4). With the advent of the microcomputer, there were four generations of computers, and four sizes of computers: supercomputers, mainframes, minicomputers, and microcomputers.

Figure 3.7
The Apple IIE, one of the first in a family of commercially successful personal computers

Courtesy of Apple Computer, Inc.

The Fifth (and Future) Generation

Twenty years from now, computer students will learn about the fifth (and perhaps sixth and seventh) generation of computers. The technologies needed for the fifth generation of computers are being created and tested all over the world as you read this book. Computer scientists in many countries, including Germany, Great Britain, India, Japan, and the United States, are working on artificial intelligence—computer programs that can reason like human beings. This task may take years; because no one knows exactly how human intelligence operates, it's difficult to create programs that allow computers to work the same way. The work and discussions on artificial intelligence involve people from a number of disciplines, including anatomy, biology, computer science, education, mathematics, philosophy, and neuropsychology. Some of the preliminary findings are already being applied in expert systems (see Session 14) and a field called *fuzzy logic*.

Another area of research involves the way computers are constructed: computer architecture. Von Neumann's computer had only one processor, but there are many computer engineers who feel that the next generation of computers will be parallel-processing computers that use more than one microprocessor, allowing for greater speed and efficiency.

The processors of the future may be constructed with new materials. An exciting race in the field of computer and electrical engineering is the race for a viable superconductor. *Superconductors* are semiconductors that offer much less resistance to electrical flow. Less resistance means less heat, greatly increased speed, and better efficiency. Materials have been found that operate as superconductors, but only at very low temperatures that make a winter day in the Arctic seem incredibly warm. A superconductor that could be used at normal temperatures would not only be faster, but it would eliminate the bulky fans required in desktops to cool the heat created by semiconductor chips.

Another piece of fifth-generation technology is the optical storage device. Optical storage uses lasers to read and write information. Laser devices have two distinct benefits: capacity and durability. The compact disks already used for storage have incredible capacity and hold thousands of times more information than similarly sized tapes or magnetic disks. The laser never actually touches the surface of the disk, so optical disks aren't subject to the same wear and tear as other forms of storage. And optical disks are only the beginning: A prototype of an optical mass-storage cube has already been built. The cube, remarkably like the computer storage cubes used in Star Trek, holds thousands of times more information than the optical disks.

SECTION 3.2: PARTS OF A COMPUTER SYSTEM

Until recently, all the computers designed since von Neumann's paper on the EDVAC (in which he described a digital computer) have used his design. However, the design has seen minor modifications as his vision has been improved upon by others. Von Neumann's computer had five basic parts: input, a control unit, an arithmetic unit, memory, and output. The modern view of the computer combines the control unit and arithmetic unit into a processor, and acknowledges the fact that separate devices are used for memory and off-line storage. The five parts of the modern **conceptual computer** are input, processor, output, memory, and storage. Like von Neumann's computer, the conceptual computer isn't an actual computer, just a construct that allows people to think about and discuss computers and their functions without getting bogged down in brand names.

Input

Input devices have changed greatly since von Neumann's time. Keyboards were early improvements; today there are many other ways to enter data and instructions into a computer. Some of the most exciting work in input devices occurs in the world of microcomputers, as you will see in Session 5.

Memory

Memory is the working surface of the computer, and is directly connected to the computer's processors. When you want to run a program, the program is loaded into memory; when you use a computer to type a letter, the letter is kept in memory while it is being typed. Thus, the amount of memory in a computer determines the size of the programs a computer can run. Computers of the first and second generations used bulky magnetic drum memory. In 1961, Intel created the first RAM chips. **RAM** stands for random-access memory. There are many different types of RAM in use today. Figure 3.8 shows RAM chips on a SIMM or single in-line memory module.

DRAM, or dynamic RAM, is the type of RAM used in most computers. Information is stored electrically on DRAM chips. DRAM needs a steady flow of electricity to remain active. Because information stored in DRAM is erased each time the power is turned off, DRAM is known as volatile memory. Despite the variety of memory chips available, DRAM is the memory most often used in computers, and it's what people are referring to when they discuss computer memory.

Figure 3.8
RAM chips as part of a SIMM

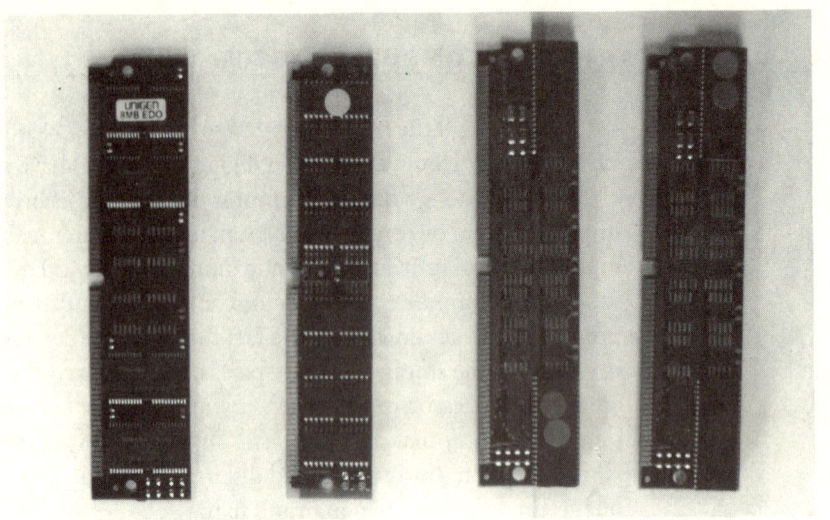

Courtesy of Twilight Technologies

SRAM, or static RAM, is faster than DRAM. SRAM chips are much more expensive than DRAM chips, so they are used sparingly. SRAM is used to create a **cache**—a designated area of memory that holds frequently used instructions and data so they can be quickly recalled by the processor.

There is more to life than increasing its speed.
—*Mahatma Ghandi*

VRAM, or video RAM, is exceptionally fast RAM, and is sometimes used on the video card (see Session 5) that a computer's monitor connects to. However, many video boards use DRAM rather than the more expensive VRAM.

RAM chips were originally called RWM—read/write memory—because a computer can read information from a RAM chip and write new information in its place. Another type of memory is **ROM**—read-only memory. The difference between RAM and ROM is that RAM chips are made to be easily written to, erased, and written to again, while ROM chips are not. ROM chips come with data or programs already on them that can only be read, and typically are used to hold instructions for what a computer should do each time it is turned on. ROM chips aren't volatile, so the information remains on the chips even after the computer is shut off.

There are four basic types of ROM chips: regular ROM, included in all computers, PROM, EPROM, and EEPROM. PROM (programmable read-only memory) chips are blank ROM chips that can be programmed once, and then can only be read. PROM chips are used by manufacturers of computers. EPROM (erasable PROM) chips can be erased with ultraviolet light and reprogrammed. EEPROM (electrically erasable PROM) chips can be erased with a strong jolt of electricity, then reprogrammed. Both EPROM and EEPROM have specific uses for information that must be updated, but only periodically. For example, EEPROM chips are sometimes used in sales systems to hold price information; when the information needs to be updated, the EEPROM is erased and reprogrammed.

Flash memory is a hybrid of RAM and EEPROM. Flash memory requires very little electricity to remain active. Although flash memory can be one hundred times as expensive as DRAM, it is being used for specialized tasks in microcomputers. Flash memory cards (which are really used as storage devices, not more memory) are sold for use in portable computers. However, this use of flash memory technology still needs improvements, particularly in regard to speed.

A Bit About Bytes

Capacity refers to the amount of data that can be held in memory at one time, and is measured in bytes. Before we look at bytes, it's helpful to think for a moment about the numbering system you are most familiar with: the decimal system.

In the decimal (base ten) numbering system, a digit can have one of ten values: 0, 1, 2, 3, 4, 5, 6, 7, 8, or 9. With one digit, you can represent any number smaller than ten; to write the number ten, you need two digits (10). You need three digits to write a number between 100 and 999, and four digits to write a number larger than 999. If you think of the decimal numbering system exponentially, you can represent values under 10^1 with one digit; two digits take you one number shy of 10^2; three digits can express numbers up to one less than 10^3; and four digits are required for 10^3 and beyond. Each additional digit allows you to represent numbers ten times larger, as shown in Table 3.1.

Computer data is stored electrically, or electromagnetically. The smallest piece of data that can be stored in a computer is called a **bit**—short for **binary digit**. With one digit, you can represent the numbers 0 or 1. This two-number system corresponds exactly to the conditions inside a computer. Either there is current flowing through a circuit (1), or there isn't (0). A magnetic spot on a disk is either positively charged (1) or negatively charged (0).

By combining digits, larger values than 1 can be represented, just like in the decimal system. To write a number larger than 1, you need a second binary

Table 3.1
Decimal Numbering System

Power of 10	Number of digits	"Place"	Numbers represented
10^0	1	ones	0–9
10^1	2	tens	0–99
10^2	3	hundreds	0–999
10^3	4	thousands	0–9,999
10^4	5	ten thousands	0–99,999
10^5	6	hundred thousands	0–999,999
10^6	7	millions	0–9,999,999

digit, just like you need two digits in the decimal system to write a number larger than 9. Each additional digit doubles the size of the number you can represent, as shown in Table 3.2.

Table 3.2
Binary Numbering System

Power of 2	Number of digits	"Place"	Numbers represented
2^0	1	ones	0-1
2^1	2	two	0-3
2^2	3	fours	0-7
2^3	4	eights	0-15
2^4	5	sixteens	0-31
2^5	6	thirty-twos	0-63
2^6	7	sixty-fours	0-127
2^7	8	one-twenty-eights	0-255

With eight bits, called a **byte**, you can write the number 255 in the binary system. This yields 256 possible numbers including the number zero. Digital computers send information a byte at a time, but to be really useful, the bytes need to be able to convey more information than the numbers 0–255. To do this, IBM engineers developed a data representation code called Extended Binary-Coded Decimal Interchange Code (EBCDIC, pronounced "ebb-suh-dik"), in which eight-bit combinations of numbers each represent a specific digit, letter, or symbol. (For example, the byte 11000001 represents the letter *A*.)

Other computer manufacturers found a need for a similar code. Because IBM patented EBCDIC, another code was developed—the American Standard Code for Information Interchange, or **ASCII**. ASCII (pronounced ask-key) only uses seven of the eight bits to represent a character; the other bit is used for error checking. (There is also an ASCII version that uses eight bits for character representation.) EBCDIC is almost exclusively used on IBM mainframe computers, while ASCII has become what its name implies: a standard code, used by all manufacturers. Table 3.3 shows some EBCDIC and ASCII codes.

Table 3.3 EBCDIC and ASCII Codes

Letter or Symbol	ASCII	EBCDIC
space	0100000	01000000
A	1000001	11000001
a	1100001	10000001
=	0111101	01111110
0	0110000	11110000
1	0110001	11110001
5	0110101	11110101

The codes are simply conventions—agreements about what letter, digit, or symbol a combination of numbers represents.

Measuring Memory

The **capacity** of a computer's memory is the amount of information that can be held in memory at one time. You can measure capacity in bytes, but it's inconvenient—imagine measuring the distance between New York and Miami in inches.

Computers have thousands, millions, or billions of bytes of memory. A **kilobyte** is roughly a thousand bytes: 2^{10}, or 1,024, bytes. Thus, one kilobyte of RAM can hold 1,024 characters of a program or data. A **megabyte** is 1,048,576 (2^{20}) bytes. A **gigabyte** is 2^{30} or 1,073,741,824 bytes. Modern microcomputers have between 4 and 64 megabytes of memory; supercomputers often have gigabytes of memory. Kilobyte, megabyte, and gigabyte come from the Latin prefixes for thousand, million, and billion, and are abbreviated **KB**, **MB**, and **GB**.

Processors

Von Neumann saw computers as tools to do math problems. Turing's vision of universal machines meant that computers needed the ability to handle logical problems as well as mathematical problems: an arithmetic logic unit. Arithmetic problems include addition, subtraction, multiplication, and division. Logical problems deal with comparisons: equal to, not equal to, greater than, less than, AND, OR, and NOT. A computer's arithmetic capabilities let it calculate a payroll from hours and hourly rates; its logical capability lets it sort the paychecks in alphabetical order.

The technology of the fourth generation combined von Neumann's arithmetic and control units into one chip: the microprocessor. Today's **central processing units (CPUs)** include two major parts: the arithmetic logic unit (ALU) with its connected registers, and a control unit that contains a clock, a program counter, an address decoder, and an instruction decoder.

The ALU performs calculations and comparisons; its **registers** are small memory areas that temporarily hold the data the ALU is working with and will require for the next operation. The **control unit** manages the flow of data to the registers and ALU. Together, the program counter, address decoder, and instruction decoder keep track of the separate pieces of work being done by the ALU. The control unit clock, a crystal that vibrates at a specific frequency, keeps the other five parts of the CPU synchronized. The speed of the CPU is determined by the clock speed, which is measured in **megahertz (MHz)** (millions of cycles per second) and is often referred to in the computer's description. For example, a Pentium 133 has a clock speed of 133MHz.

Computers include other processors in addition to the CPU. These other **coprocessors** are dedicated to specific tasks. By handling some of the work of the CPU, coprocessors speed up the overall performance of the computer. Math coprocessors are designed for increased speed in arithmetic. I/O processors handle information moving to and from input and output devices without disrupting the work of the CPU. DMA (Direct Memory Access) processor chips route information from DRAM to other parts of the computer, bypassing the CPU.

A recent innovation in computing is the idea of *parallel processing*—using more than one CPU at the same time. Parallel processing is much faster than a single processor, because two or more processors are dedicated to a task. Designing parallel-processing computers is difficult, because processing tasks have to be divided between the individual CPUs. The CPUs then have to be coordinated to accomplish the tasks assigned to them. Parallel-processing computers are the first non–von Neumann computers since the 1950s.

Storage

Computer storage is not a new concept. Even Hollerith's tabulating machine had data storage: the punched cards used to enter data. Both Turing and von Neumann's conceptual machines stored programs as well as data.

A perfect computer would have unlimited amounts of fast memory—enough to hold all the programs you ever use. When you ran a program, it would already be in memory, and therefore would run quickly. When you turned the computer off, all your work would be saved in the non-volatile memory, ready for the next time you need it. This ideal computer has two important attributes: fast memory and permanent memory. But it still can't be constructed today: the fastest of the permanent memory, flash memory, is still too slow. Computer engineers have arrived at a compromise that provides speed for computing, permanence for data and programs, and affordability. In today's computers, programs being used at any given time are loaded into memory; other programs and data reside in a separate area called **storage**.

Von Neumann's computer system classifies storage as a part of memory: RAM memory is called *main memory*, and storage is called *secondary memory*, *auxiliary memory*, or *peripheral memory*. Older terminology called memory *main storage* and storage *secondary storage*, or simply *storage*. In the age of microcomputers, these terms are being replaced in common usage with the terms *memory* and *storage* (none too soon, since the earlier terms are incredibly confusing). Fast, volatile RAM is used for memory. Slower, non-volatile devices are used for storage. When you need to use a program, the operating system copies the program from storage to memory so it can be used.

Types of Storage

There are several ways to classify storage based on construction and design.

Removable versus Nonremovable Media

One way to classify storage is to differentiate between removable media storage and nonremovable media storage. With removable media storage, a tape or disk or some other type of storage **media** is placed in a storage device like a tape or floppy disk drive. Removable media storage allows you to store information on media—like a diskette—and take it to another computer, or add programs to your computer from disk or CD-ROM. In nonremovable media storage devices, the media is permanently installed in the device and cannot be removed. A hard drive is an example of a storage device with nonremovable media.

Magnetic versus Optical

Storage is also classified by read/write method: magnetic, optical, or other. A hard drive is a type of **magnetic storage** composed of a stack of disks called *platters*. Both sides of each platter have been coated with an oxide-based material that can hold a magnetic charge. Arms between the platters have read/write heads similar to the heads used in video and cassette recorders that impart a negative or positive charge. When you write information on a disk, the head passes over the disk and writes information magnetically.

The second type of storage frequently used in computers is **optical storage**. When you write to an optical storage disk, a laser is used to "rough up" the surface of the optical disk by burning small pits in the disk material. When the disk is read by another laser, the rough pits absorb light; the smooth surfaces in between the pits reflect light back to the laser. Light and the absence of light (dark) represent data the same way positive and negative magnetic charges store data on a magnetic disk or tape.

Magnetic and optical storage methods have distinct advantages and disadvantages. Magnetic media is inexpensive, and can be repeatedly erased and reused. However, magnetic media is also comparatively fragile. Heat, dust, and magnetic fields all damage magnetic media. Over time, even carefully stored magnetic media loses its charge and wears out—and when it does, the data stored on it is lost. While stored magnetic media may last up to 30 years before it wears out, magnetic media in constant use (such as the system tapes of a mainframe computer system) may have a much shorter life span and need to be regularly replaced. Optical disks, on the other hand, are predicted to last up to 300 years with careful use, but are more expensive and cannot be erased and reused.

Even though most computers today use magnetic or optical storage, there are other methods. These include older methods, like paper tape and punched cards, and experimental methods, such as bioelectrical storage.

Direct Access versus Sequential Storage Methods

The fastest storage devices allow the computer to go a specific piece of information directly—take, for example, an audio CD player. When you press a button to go to track 5, the read head goes there directly, without having to first move through tracks 1–4. This type of access is called **direct access**, and is used in disks, diskettes, and CD-ROM drives. Direct access is also called **random access**, because information can be stored in any specific location on a drive, rather than having to fill a disk in order from beginning to end. Here, the sense of *random* is not "chaotic," but "not in sequence." (RAM chips are called *random access memory* for the same reason.)

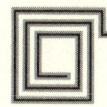

> **NOTE**
>
> The *ROM* in CD-ROM drives means you can only read information from the drive, not write information to the CD. You can get read/write CD drives that allow you to write information on CDs, but they are still expensive, costing ten times as much as CD-ROM drives.

Magnetic tape storage, usually associated with mainframe computers, is an excellent example of a sequential access system. Information is stored on tape sequentially, like individual tracks on a music cassette tape. For example, if a song you want to play is in the middle of a cassette tape, you must fast forward through the first half to get to your song. Even with very fast magnetic tape drives, **sequential access** storage methods take longer to retrieve data than direct access methods, because of the time it takes to rewind or fast forward the tape.

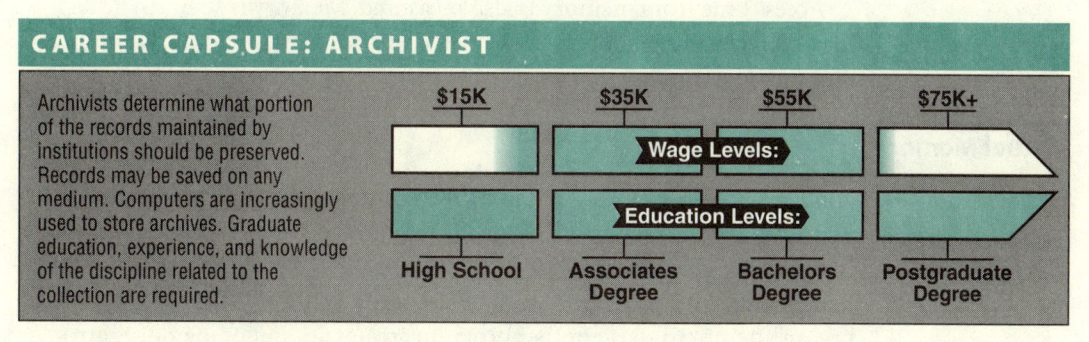

CAREER CAPSULE: ARCHIVIST

Archivists determine what portion of the records maintained by institutions should be preserved. Records may be saved on any medium. Computers are increasingly used to store archives. Graduate education, experience, and knowledge of the discipline related to the collection are required.

Wage Levels:
- $15K — High School
- $35K — Associates Degree
- $55K — Bachelors Degree
- $75K+ — Postgraduate Degree

Education Levels:
- High School
- Associates Degree
- Bachelors Degree
- Postgraduate Degree

Comparing Storage Devices

Regardless of type or storage methods used, all storage devices are compared based on two criteria: capacity and access time.

Storage Capacity

Storage capacity is measured using the same measurement as memory: bytes. This is often confusing to computer novices, and leads to misunderstandings about the capacity of memory and storage on their computers. But bytes, kilobytes, and megabytes are measures of capacity, just as inches, feet, and miles are measures of length. You can use feet to express the length of a room or the distance from a camera's lens to the subject being photographed; you use bytes to measure RAM or storage capacity.

Access Time

Access time is the average length of time that passes between the moment a computer requests information from a storage device and the moment the computer finds and starts to read the information. Access time is measured in thousandths or millionths of a second. One thousandth of a second is called a **millisecond** (ms); one millionth of a second is a microsecond; and one billionth of a second is a nanosecond. Access time for disk drives is measured in milliseconds. For example, a 13 ms drive means that, on average, it takes 13/1000 of a second from the time the CPU requests information from the disk until the disk's read/write heads are hovered over the information and ready to begin retrieving it. A drive with 26 ms access time is only half as fast as the 13 ms drive (and, therefore, should cost less).

Access time from memory is also measured. Memory is so much faster than storage that memory access speed is measured in millionths of milliseconds: **nanoseconds**.

Virtual Memory

Some computer operating systems (like Windows) allow a computer to use part of storage as memory; this is called **virtual memory**. Without virtual memory, if a computer has 8MB of RAM, only 8MB of programs—and data being used by the programs—can be in use at one time. When all 8MB are in use, an attempt to start another program creates an "out of memory" error. However, if a computer's operating system enables the use of virtual memory, the operating system sets aside part of a storage device (usually a hard drive) to hold parts of programs when there is no more space in RAM. When you start a program that would exceed the 8MB of RAM, the operating system takes an infrequently used portion of one of the current programs out of RAM and places it on the hard drive in a virtual memory **swap file**. If that program portion is needed later in the session, it is reloaded in RAM and some other program piece is moved to the swap file.

The advantage of virtual memory is that it allows a user to run two or more programs that, together, exceed the computer's available memory. The disadvantage is that both programs will run more slowly. If a user is frequently exceeding a computer's available RAM, the permanent solution is to purchase more DRAM memory chips.

Output

The final component of the conceptual computer is output. Printers were the primary devices used for output in the first generation of computers; computer screens (monitors) were later additions. Printed output has a lot of advantages. You can carry it around, put it in a physical file, or duplicate it to hand out at a meeting. Monitors give you instant output: you type text on the keyboard, and within milliseconds the text appears on the screen. Other output devices have been invented since the monitor and are described in Session 5.

What You Have Learned

Four major shifts in technology are reflected in the generations of computers. The first generation used vacuum tubes for processing; the second generation used transistors; the third generation used integrated circuits; and the fourth generation uses microminiturized circuits. Improvements in programming languages and storage also help define the four generations of computers. Today, we are on the leading edge of the fifth generation.

Computers of every generation include five basic parts: input, memory, process, storage, and output. Input and output devices allow the computer to accept instructions from and return information to users.

There are two types of memory chips: RAM (including DRAM, SRAM, and VRAM) and ROM (including ROM, PROM, EPROM, and EEPROM). Each type of chip is used for a different purpose. Memory is measured in bytes, kilobytes, megabytes, and gigabytes.

Processors have two parts: an arithmetic logic unit and a control unit. Processor speed is measured in megahertz.

Storage devices can be classified by media type (removable versus nonremovable), read/write method (magnetic versus digital) and storage method (direct versus sequential only). Storage capacity, like memory, is measured in multiples of bytes. Storage speed is quantified by measuring access time. Some computer operating systems use part of a storage device as virtual memory, a substitute for RAM.

Focus Questions

1. What are the generations of computers?
2. What primary technology was used in each of the four generations?
3. Sketch and label the five parts of the conceptual computer.
4. What is a bit? What values can a bit have?
5. How is memory measured?
6. What are the two primary types of memory?
7. What are the three systems used for classifying storage?
8. What are the two parts of a CPU?

Knowledge Reinforcement

A. How do memory and storage differ? How are they similar?

B. What are the advantages of optical storage? What are the advantages of magnetic storage?

C. Many organizations still use sequential storage devices. What kinds of information might be kept on tape or other sequential media? What types of information would organizations not want to store sequentially?

Further Exploration

Asimov's Biographical Encyclopedia of Science and Technology (2d rev. ed.). Isaac Asimov. Doubleday & Company, 1982, 0-385-17771-2. Brief biographies of significant scientists and inventors, including Babbage, Napier, and others.

Asimov's Chronology of Science and Discovery. Isaac Asimov. Harper & Row, Publishers, 1989, 0-06-015612-0. History of discoveries and inventions in science.

The Dream Machine. Jon Palfreman and Doron Swade. BBC Books, 1991, 0-563-36221-9. The rise of technology to the present.

Grace Hopper:
http://www.norfolk.navy.mil/chips/grace_hopper
http://web.mit.edu/afs/athena.mit.edu/org/i/invent/www/inventors

IEEE Computer Society:
http://www.computer.org/50/history

Past Notable Women of Computing (Kay Mauchly, Adele Goldstine, and many others):
http://www.cs.yale.edu/homes/tap/past-women.htm

Understanding Computers. Nathan J. Shedroff, Sterling Hutto, and Ken Fromm. Sybex, 1993, 0-7821-1284-6.

PART 2

PCs Take Center Stage

SESSION FOUR

Vocabulary

- architecture
- backups
- bus
- command-line interface
- DMA channel
- expansion slot
- external
- floppy diskette
- graphical user interface
- Bill Gates
- handheld computer
- hard disk
- hypertext
- internal
- Steve Jobs
- laptop computer
- links
- Microsoft Windows
- notebook computer
- palmtop computer
- pen computer
- personal computer
- personal digital assistant (PDA)
- ports
- Steve Jobs
- subnotebook computer
- system board (motherboard)
- terminal
- user interface
- wide area networking
- Winchester disk

The Personal Computer Revolution

UNTIL THE MID-1970S, TALK OF COMPUTERS conjured up images of a room full of equipment with huge reels of tape, lots of lights and switches, and white guys with white shirts, bad ties, and pocket protectors. **Personal computers** became a reality only after a few visionary people ignored those who said it couldn't be done. At the end of this session, you will be able to

- Discuss the events that led to the development of the personal computer
- Describe the role of a microprocessor
- Identify several types of storage devices
- Differentiate storage and memory capacities

75

SECTION 4.1: THE DREAM OF PERSONAL COMPUTING

In the 1960s, television cartoon shows like *The Jetsons* predicted space-age worlds where people would complain of sore fingers from pushing too many buttons. Telephones were replaced with two-way video screens and homework was completed with the aid of computer storehouses of information available in children's bedrooms. But *The Jetsons* was just a cartoon. Very few people could actually imagine that computers would ever really become that pervasive.

Bill Gates, shown in Figure 4.1, is the president and founder of Microsoft Corporation, the world's largest software company. He was 16 years old in 1971, the year historians site as the beginning of the fourth generation of computers. Two years earlier, Gates had begun to take classes in computer programming. At 15, he started getting paid for programs he wrote. He started Microsoft with his friend Paul Allen when he was 21.

Figure 4.1
Bill Gates, President, Microsoft Corporation

Courtesy of Microsoft Corporation

In 1995, less than 20 years after he founded Microsoft, Bill Gates was ranked by Forbes Magazine as the world's richest private citizen with an estimated worth of $18 billion. Gates topped the list again in 1996, and he is not the only person who has amassed a fortune in the personal computer revolution. What happened in the computer industry in the years between 1971 and today that provided such opportunity? What advances changed computers from room-sized giants available only to a few, to portable powerhouses ready to travel anywhere? To answer these questions, we have to look to technological developments in computer hardware and to a grassroots movement of computer hobbyists and hackers that changed the course of computer history and made personal computers a reality.

In the 1950s, it was widely believed that computers were too technical to be used by people outside the scientific and research communities. Additionally, their size and cost put computers out of the financial reach of everyone except government and big businesses. But then the time-sharing plans of the 1960s—which allowed businesses to buy time on mainframe computers—broadened the availability of computers, and, subsequently, interest by the general population. Small businesses, schools, health care institutions, and even individuals were able to make use of computing power by buying access time. Many of the big computer companies saw this distribution of computing power as the ultimate answer. In reality, though, accessibility only fueled a growing hunger for ways to manage the ever-increasing amounts of data that needed to be recorded, tabulated, reported, and analyzed. People began to glimpse the potential of computers, and the stage was set for the personal computer revolution to begin.

■ Companies Take Up the Challenge

In order for computers to become widely available, they had to become smaller, easier to use, and less costly. Xerox and Intel were two of the first corporations to take on these challenges. Xerox's role in this new and undefined field is especially interesting, since they had built a business on the importance of paper in an office—copies, copies, and more copies. But they were quite intrigued when they saw Douglas Engelbart's word processing presentation at the Fall Joint Computer Conference in San Francisco in 1968. Using a keyboard and the newly invented mouse, Engelbart's demonstration included an early **hypertext** system—a method of presenting information on a computer screen that allows the user to move from topic to topic in a nonlinear way, by clicking on **links** that connect documents. (Twenty-five years later, hypertext has become the hallmark of the Internet's World Wide Web.) To top it off, Engelbart communicated with another computer 30 miles away, giving his audience a glimpse of what would later become **wide area networking** (see Session 11).

By 1970, Xerox had established the Palo Alto Research Center (PARC) to develop a paperless office based on Engelbart's vision. In less than three years, PARC developed hardware and a software interface for a personal computer. In 1973, they released the Xerox Alto Workstation Computer, the first fully functional personal computer with a monitor and a keyboard. Not only did the Alto use a mouse, its **user interface**—the means by which a user communicates with a computer—included menus, icons, and pointers, and allowed users to make selections by pointing to objects on the screen. The Alto's user interface was similar to Microsoft Windows and the Finder used on Macintoshes. PARC developers even used the term *windows* to describe the interface.

Despite its foresight and ingenuity, Xerox never marketed the Alto. Distracted by stiff Japanese competition in the copier business, Xerox decided they could not risk their profitability on the Alto. Consequently, Xerox is not a big player in the computer hardware market today. As other companies took up the torch from Xerox and began building personal computers, PARC researchers continued their work toward the paperless office. Within a few years, they had devised laser printing, advanced word processor software, and Ethernet cards that allow computers to be connected together to form computer networks.

Bringing Down the Cost and the Size

Intel's involvement in the personal computer revolution focused on development of the microprocessor, the central processing unit of a personal computer, shown in Figure 4.2. By 1971, Intel had developed a working model of the microprocessor to use in **terminals,** combination keyboard/monitor workstations for mainframes and minicomputers. Terminal manufacturers weren't interested in the Intel 8008 microprocessor, so in 1972, Intel began looking for other possible uses.

The large hardware vendors of the time were not convinced that anyone would want a personal computer. A business that needed computing power could already access computers through a number of time-sharing systems, so what would someone do with a computer on their desktop? There were others, however, who didn't share the same views, including some technically

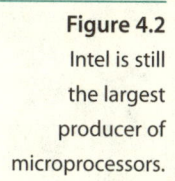

Figure 4.2
Intel is still the largest producer of microprocessors.

Courtesy of Intel Corporation

oriented hobbyists who couldn't wait to get their hands on Intel's microprocessors to build their own computers.

■ An Act of Desperation

Ed Roberts, owner of MITS, a failing calculator business in Albuquerque, New Mexico, dreamed up a plan to fuel the imaginations of technology enthusiasts, and in doing so, kicked the personal computer revolution into full gear. Robert and his friend Les Soloman designed a small computer, the Altair, based on Intel's new inexpensive microprocessor. The Altair, shown in Figure 4.3, came unassembled and without a keyboard, monitor, or software, but it had one thing the big companies had yet to achieve—a price tag computer hobbyists could afford. For less than $500, a person could assemble a computer with 1 kilobyte RAM and use switches on the front of the box to program it to accomplish different tasks. (Today's typical PC includes 16 *mega*bytes of RAM.)

Thanks to the cover article in *Popular Electronics* magazine on the Altair (named by Soloman's daughter after a *Star Trek* episode), Ed Roberts went from near bankruptcy to having a quarter of a million dollars in the bank in one month's time. A far cry from the personal computers of today, the Altair computer became the cornerstone of a new industry.

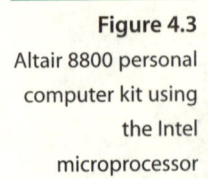

Figure 4.3
Altair 8800 personal computer kit using the Intel microprocessor

Copyright 1996, James R. Willing

And the Revolution Begins

Revolutions may be started by one or two people acting individually, but to succeed they need the energy of a mass of people. The Altair was the catalyst for a group of 22 people to gather in a garage in San Francisco in 1975 and form the Homebrew Computer Club. Within a very short period of time, the group grew so large it started meeting in an auditorium at Stanford University. The combination of highly-skilled techies and visionary entrepreneurs was all the microprocessor industry needed. A number of small companies, some spun off the Homebrew Computer Club, were formed to develop add-on devices for the Altair, including storage devices and circuit boards to increase the Altair's memory.

One Homebrew member, **Steve Jobs**, began to see that computers could have applications beyond the narrow interests of hobbyists. He teamed up with a technical wizard, Stephen Wozniak, to build a computer, which they debuted at the Homebrew Computer Club. Jobs named it the Apple I, shown in Figure 4.4.

Figure 4.4
The Apple I computer started the personal computer revolution.

Smithsonian Institution Photo No. 92-13442

To finance production of Apple I circuit boards, Jobs sold his Volkswagen, and Wozniak sold his Hewlett Packard programmable calculator. Together they raised $1,350, which they used to begin production in Jobs's parents' garage.

Other computer clubs started appearing around the country, and in 1976, the Atlantic City Computer Convention brought them all together. Ed Roberts was there with the Altair, and Wozniak and Jobs were there selling their Apple I circuit boards. By the end of 1976, 10 retail stores were marketing Apple I computers.

A little further north, in Washington, Paul Allen and Bill Gates were also fascinated with the Altair. Although they didn't have enough money to buy their own kit, they read the descriptive article in *Popular Electronics,* and based on that, used a computer language called BASIC to write a BASIC interpreter for the Altair. With the interpreter, Altair owners would be able to write programs for their computers in the popular, easy-to-use BASIC programming language. Even though they had never actually seen the Altair, Allen and Gates contacted Ed Roberts, and Allen flew out to New Mexico to meet with him. They found that the interpreter they had written—the first for a PC—worked flawlessly. In 1976, Bill Gates and Paul Allen renamed their company from Traf-O-Data to Micro-Soft. The hyphen was later removed.

SECTION 4.2: THE DREAM TAKES SHAPE

Other groups and companies sprouted up to service this growing industry. Large companies like IBM, Hewlett Packard, and Atari watched this movement carefully. Stephen Wozniak proposed that Hewlett Packard create a personal computer; Steve Jobs proposed the same for Atari. Both companies rejected their offers to help them build a personal computer; however, other companies began to position themselves to respond to the growing interest. In 1975, IBM released its first portable computer, Project Mercury, a briefcase-sized minicomputer with BASIC, 16KB RAM, tape storage, and a built-in 5-inch screen. It weighed 55 pounds and sold for nine thousand dollars. IBM also introduced its first microcomputer, the IBM 5100. Although it was less expensive than Project Mercury, retailing at five thousand dollars, sales and marketing were unsuccessful. The vision was becoming clearer, yet personal computers still had little to offer the general population. One of the biggest problems was the unavailability of fast, inexpensive devices to store computer data and the programs that generate them.

Storage for the Rest of Us

Prior to the 1970s, computer data was stored on reels of magnetic tape and, eventually, on magnetic disks. In 1971, IBM introduced an 8-inch **floppy diskette,** shown in Figure 4.5. These "memory disks," as they were called, were plastic disks coated with iron oxide. Data on floppy diskettes were accessed through the use of read/write heads that read the rotating diskette.

An even more significant development occurred in 1973, when IBM introduced the first hard disk. This hard disk drive with recording heads that rode on a cushion of air 18/1,000,000 of an inch thick could originally store 16KB of data on each platter. (It is not uncommon for today's hard disks to hold 1–2GB of data.) The first hard disks had 30 data tracks and 30 sectors per track, so IBM gave them the model number 3030. They were quickly dubbed **Winchester disks** after the Winchester 30-30 rifles. The nickname stuck, and is still used today for some hard disks.

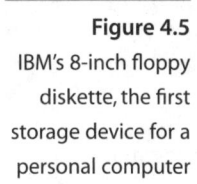

Figure 4.5
IBM's 8-inch floppy diskette, the first storage device for a personal computer

Courtesy of International Business Machines Corporation. Unauthorized use not permitted.

The first personal computers used a cassette tape recorder to store data. This was an inexpensive option but was very slow. Even the rudimentary software programs of the day took several minutes to load, making users long for floppy disk drives and hard drives for PCs. In 1976, the 5¼-inch *mini* floppy diskette was introduced by IBM. The drive, which came in both internal and external models, sold for $390. **Internal** models were installed into the computer system case. **External** models attached to the back of the computer by a cable.

Wozniak and Jobs wanted to find a way to bring down the cost of disk drive storage to make it a practical solution for personal computers. Wozniak's technical abilities shone through again as he designed a disk drive that only needed five chips instead of the typical fifty. This gave Apple the most reliable and least expensive drive available on the market and solidified Apple's position as a leader in the burgeoning personal computer industry.

Today, there are many devices and media available to store data and programs. Among the most common are 3½-inch floppy disks, CD-ROM disks, other optical disks, Zip disks, and tape cartridges (see Section 4.3).

■ Apple Takes the Lead

With the help of Armas "Mark" Markkula, the former marketing manager at Intel and Fairfield Semiconductor, Jobs and Wozniak, shown in Figure 4.6, incorporated Apple Computer in 1977 and introduced the Apple II computer. The Apple II included a keyboard, power supply, and a case, had 48KB of RAM, and could generate color graphics. The world was starting to take notice.

Figure 4.6
Steve Wozniak and Steve Jobs developing the Apple II

Courtesy of Apple Computer, Inc.

Apple continued to develop the Apple computer, with an emphasis on making the computer a useful tool. In 1979, Apple joined forces with a Harvard Business School student, Daniel Bricklin, and his friend Bob Frankston, who had designed a financial spreadsheet program called VisiCalc. Approximately one-fourth of all Apple Computers sold in 1979 and 1980 were purchased by businesses to run VisiCalc. Other software programmers began writing software for the Apple II, and it wasn't long before word processing programs, educational programs, and a whole host of games were available. The personal computer had come of age.

In December of 1980, Apple went public, offering 4.6 million shares of Apple common stock at $22 a share. The shares were sold within minutes, and many of Apple's 1,000 employees were instantly rich. Jobs, Wozniak, and Markkula each made $100 million, and in a single day, over 40 other employees became millionaires.

The Computer Wars Heat Up

In the same year that Apple went pubic, IBM contracted with Bill Gates at Microsoft to develop the operating system for an IBM personal computer that was to be released in 1981. Gates responded to this challenge by developing MS-DOS (Microsoft Disk Operating System). MS-DOS allocates system resources, such as the disk drives, the printer, and the monitor. MS-DOS has a **command line interface**, which means users type in one-line commands to give instructions to the computer. When IBM released the IBM Personal Computer, the IBM PC and MS-DOS were instant successes. In the years that followed, Microsoft focused on software, while Apple, IBM, and other companies continued to devote their energies to hardware.

In 1981, 300,000 personal computers were sold. The following year, that number increased ten-fold to 3,275,000. Apple Computer became the first PC company to reach $1 billion in sales. Other companies—including Radio Shack, Osborne Computer Corporation, and even Xerox and Atari—jumped into the personal computer market. Osborne Computer Corporation's Adam Osborne introduced the Osborne 1 Personal Business Computer, shown in Figure 4.7, in April of 1981. It featured a 5-inch display, 64KB of RAM, keyboard, modem, and two 5¼-inch disk drives for $1,795. Weighing only 24 pounds, it is considered the first successfully marketed portable computer. The Osborne also came packaged with tons of software, just like many of today's computer systems. Expecting to sell a total of 10,000 systems, Osborne found they were selling 10,000 systems every month.

But an industry that mushroomed overnight had some tough lessons to learn. By 1983, Osborne Computer had gone bankrupt, and both Apple and IBM had released new models that were dismal failures. Consumers weren't satisfied with expensive, hard-to-use machines and limited software choices. They wanted computers that were powerful, easy to use, and flexible enough to meet the needs of businesses, homes, and schools.

Apple's Lisa computer, introduced in 1983, was closer to the type of computer consumers were looking for, but its $10,000 price tag put it out of their reach. The Lisa was the first commercially available microcomputer with a **graphical user interface** (GUI, pronounced "gooey"), the display format that

Figure 4.7
The Osborne Personal Business Computer—the first successfully marketed portable computer

Copyright 1996, James R. Willing

allows users to use a mouse to point and click on objects to launch programs, open files, and issue commands.

Even though the Lisa was not successful, it did set the stage for the development and release of the Macintosh (Mac) computer in 1984. Consumers were thrilled with how simple the graphical Macintosh interface was to use, especially after their frustrated attempts to learn Microsoft's text-based MS-DOS operating system. Because MS-DOS-based microcomputers and Macintosh computers did not share compatible operating systems, users who wanted a graphical interface abandoned IBM's computers and embraced Macs.

In November 1983—at the same time Apple was preparing to release the Macintosh—Microsoft announced that they were developing a GUI called Windows, designed for computers that could run MS-DOS. A GUI for the IBM PCs would provide real competition to Apple's play for dominance in the graphically based microcomputer market. Because of problems with development, however, Microsoft didn't release its first version of **Microsoft Windows** until 1985. The Macintosh was well-established by this time, and since the first version of Windows had a number of problems, it received a less than warm reception. Computer purchasers had to make a choice between graphical Macs and MS-DOS-based IBM-compatibles—and none of them chose lightly. The differences between the two were so clear that arguments over the superiority of one system or another provided happy hour entertainment until the early 1990s. It wasn't until the release of Windows 3.0 in 1990 that Microsoft began to take users with heavy graphic requirements away from the Macintosh.

SECTION 4.3: THE DREAM BECOMES REALITY

During the last half of the 1980s, the software industry boomed, and computers continued to get smaller and more powerful with faster CPUs, more memory, and increased storage capacity. Desktop computers were augmented with more portable personal computers like laptops, notebook and subnotebook computers, pen computers, palmtops, and other handheld computers.

The terms **laptop computer** and **notebook computer** are often used interchangeably. Both refer to computers, such as the one in Figure 4.8, that can be carried in a briefcase or small carrying case and usually include all of the components of a desktop computer in a more condensed package. Notebook computers weigh 4–8 pounds and may be slightly less powerful than laptops. Laptop computers weigh 8–15 pounds and often have larger screen displays and more storage capacity than their smaller counterparts.

Figure 4.8
Notebook computers provide mobility and power, all in a lightweight package.

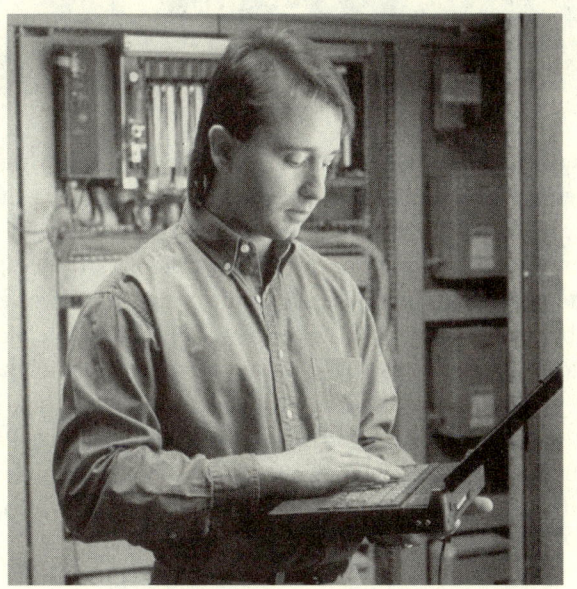

Photo by Glen Triest, courtesy of Valassis Communications, Inc.

Subnotebooks are the babies of the personal computer family. They are extremely lightweight and have smaller displays and keyboards. They often use external disk drives or special cards for storage. Other small computers range from **pen computers** that allow users to enter data using a special pen-like device to special-purpose **handheld computers** used by meter readers and delivery people. The Hardbody Handheld PC from Texas Microsystems (shown in Figure 4.9) is advertised as a computer for users who've "had their fill of cream-puff PCs." The Hardbody uses a pen-based interface, and you can drop it or use it in the rain and know that it will still work. In the next few years, expect to see an increased number of new, field-quality PCs like the Hardbody.

Figure 4.9
The Hardbody Handheld PC is for users who've "had their fill of cream-puff PCs."

Courtesy of Texas Microsystems, Inc.

Personal digital assistants (**PDAs**), like the Apple Message Pad 130 shown in Figure 4.10, are small, handheld computers that are gaining in popularity. These powerful devices have a growing variety of built-in tools: modems for communication with other computers, calendars, to-do lists, and appointment books. PDAs often use electronic pens that allow users to enter information by pointing at or writing on the screen. The Apple Message Pad 130 includes a special version of Quicken personal financial management software, can send and receive electronic mail and faxes, and connects to a desktop computer to share information. One of the Message Pad's more exciting features is that it recognizes 94,000 handwritten words, as well as a number of graphics and symmetrical objects, and converts them into printed text.

Figure 4.10
Apple Message Pad 130 with Newton 2.0

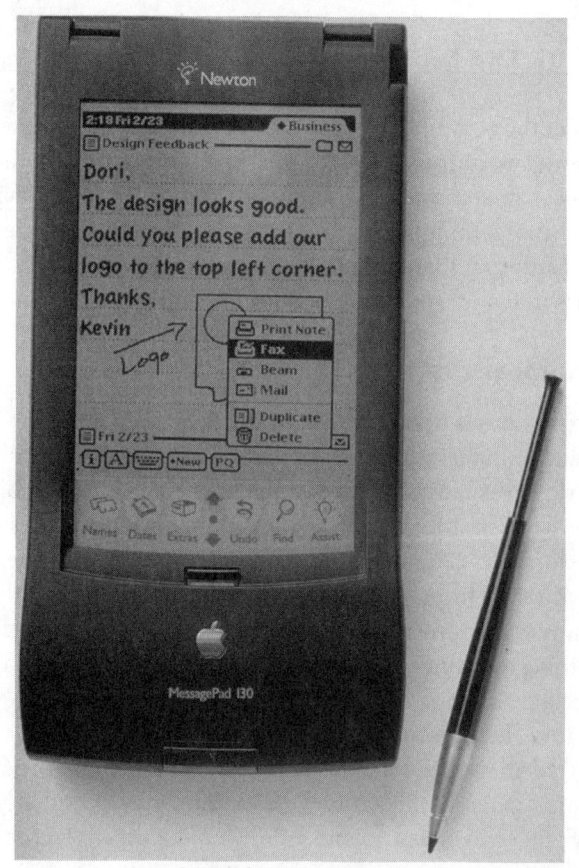

Courtesy of Apple Computer, Inc. Photo by John Greenleigh.

Another type of handheld computer, a **palmtop computer**, has much of the same functionality as a PDA but uses a miniaturized keyboard for data entry. Palmtops are often used as personal information managers to track appointments, record to-do lists, keep address books, and monitor expenses. The latest palmtops have a new version of Windows called Windows CE, scaled-down versions of Word (word processor) and Excel (spreadsheet), and Internet Explorer. Another new innovation is the Timex DataLink Watch, which allows users to download appointments, to-do lists, and phone numbers from an IBM-compatible desktop computer to a wristwatch. The watch holds between 50–70 entries at a time. Even Dick Tracy never dreamed of wearing a computer on his wrist!

SECTION 4.4: PIECES OF THE DREAM

Whether the computer you are using is a subnotebook, tower, or desktop, it has input and output devices, a microprocessor, memory, and storage components—all interconnected by a system board. But these devices are not the same as those found in larger computers. The compact size and affordability of PC hardware differentiates PC components and systems from their counterparts in mainframes, minicomputers, and supercomputers.

Microprocessors

The expectations of businesses for smaller, faster, and more powerful personal computers spurred the development of faster and powerful microprocessors. The original PC microprocessor, the Intel 8080, was an 8-bit processor, able to handle 8 bits of information at a time. Intel's 80286 processor is a 16-bit processor. In 1987, Intel released the 32-bit 80386 chip, the first chip to compete with mainframe computers for processing power. Only two years later, Intel was in the forefront again with the release of the 486 chip, the first chip containing over one million transistors. The 80486 is also a 32-bit processor, but includes support for virtual memory.

In 1993, Intel introduced the 64-bit 586 processor. After losing a court battle to trademark the designation 586, Intel named their 586 processor the Pentium. Other manufacturers, including Cyrix, produce 586 processors. Today's 586 and 686 processors, shown in Figure 4.11, contain more than four million transistors on a single chip.

NOTE

A large part of Intel's success is based on the company's ability to make their processor chips available more quickly than other manufacturers' chips, like releasing the Pentium before Cyrix's 586 chip was released. Being first in the market with a new processor has become an Intel trademark.

Table 4.1 summarizes information about PC microprocessors and the computers they are used in.

Figure 4.11
Cyrix 200 chip

Courtesy of Cyrix

Table 4.1
Processors and Computers

Processor	Type	Speed Range	Computers
8088	Intel 8-bit	4.77–8MHz	IBM PC, PC-XT
80286	16-bit	8–16MHz	PC-AT
80386	32-bit	16–33MHz	386-SX, 386
80486	32-bit	25–50MHz	486-SX, 486, 486-DX, DX2
Pentium (80586)	64-bit	66MHz+	Pentium, 586

■ The PC System Board

The speed of a computer depends not just on the speed of the processor, but on the speed of other components and the pathways between the components. The microprocessor and other components are connected to the computer's **system board**, also known as a **motherboard**, mounted in the bottom of the computer's case. Computer **architecture** refers to the design of the motherboard and the components connected to the motherboard.

The components on the system board are

- The microprocessor
- Coprocessors

- Chipsets for video or other specialized functions
- Spaces for RAM
- ROM chips
- Expansion slots for expansion cards
- Internal and external **ports** (connections for other devices)
- The system bus that connects the other components

Buses

Wiring pathways are laid in the system board to carry data and instructions, which travel as low-voltage electricity, between the CPU and components. These pathways are collectively called a **bus.** Like the processor, a bus can be 8-bit, 16-bit, and so on. A bus usually has three separate pathways, called *channels*, for different types of electrical signals: an address channel carries the memory locations for data; a clock channel transmits the clock pulses that keep the components synchronized; and the data channel moves data between components. Many computers have multiple buses to increase the amount of data that can be moved at one time.

System boards also have channels that are not part of the bus; these are called **DMA channels** (direct memory access channels). DMA channels transmit data from the disk drives to memory without passing through the CPU, speeding up both the CPU and data retrieval to memory. The speed and capacity of the system board's buses and DMA channels affect overall system speed.

Memory

A computer comes with ROM chips and some RAM chips that are soldered directly to the motherboard, as well as additional removable DRAM. You can add even more DRAM until you reach the limit that can be managed by the CPU. The expandable DRAM is the memory listed in computer advertisements. For example, a computer may be advertised as having "16MB memory, upgradeable to 64MB." This means that there are 16MB of DRAM installed, but the CPU can accept an additional 48MB.

RAM chips are mounted on circuit boards called memory modules. Most PCs use modules called SIMMs: single inline memory modules. The motherboard has SIMM slots where additional modules can be installed so that RAM in the SIMMs is directly connected to the bus and DMA channels.

Slots

System boards include **expansion slots,** which are used to directly connect other kinds of cards and modules to the system board. You can add cards to speed up the video display on your monitor, plug in game devices like joysticks, connect to a phone line for fax/modem services, or output PC information to a VCR. Like SIMM slots, expansion slots are limited. Once you have filled every slot, you can't add more devices directly to the system board. There are four generations of expansion slots: ISA (Industry Standard Architecture, a 16-bit bus), EISA (Enhanced ISA, a 16/32-bit bus), VLB (Video Local bus, a 32-bit bus), and PCI (Peripheral Component Interconnect bus, a 64-bit bus).

Ports for Input and Output Devices

Any device that isn't wired or plugged into the system board through an expansion or memory slot has to be connected to an outlet in the system board called a **port**. Ports connect directly to the system board, or are part of an expansion card. A system board includes internal ports for connections to internal devices like hard drives and floppy drives. Internal ports are part of the system board, and allow devices mounted inside the case to be easily connected. Typically, a computer will include ports for two disk drive controllers, each of which may control one or two storage devices. External ports are provided for a keyboard, mouse, printer, and other external devices.

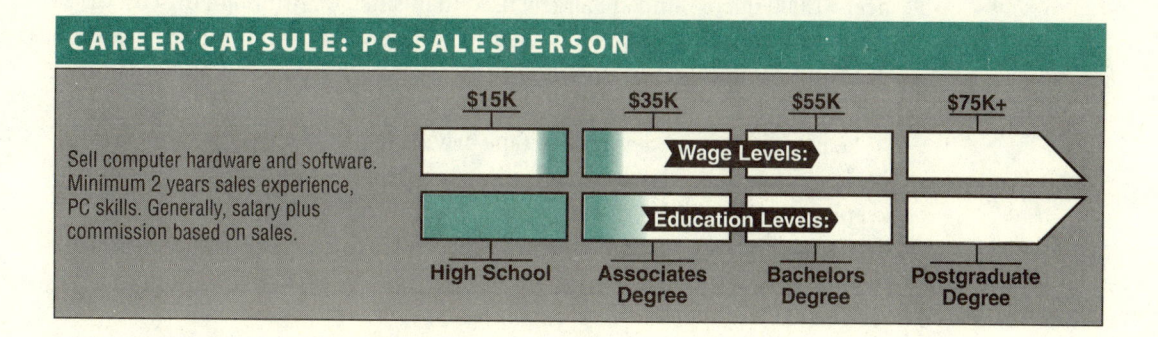

CAREER CAPSULE: PC SALESPERSON

Sell computer hardware and software. Minimum 2 years sales experience, PC skills. Generally, salary plus commission based on sales.

Wage Levels: $15K – $35K – $55K – $75K+

Education Levels: High School – Associates Degree – Bachelors Degree – Postgraduate Degree

■ Storage Devices

Most PCs include some type of large, internal, nonremovable read/write storage device like a hard drive. The typical hard drive in a new PC holds over 1GB of data. CD-ROM drives are becoming a standard storage device on many PCs. It isn't unusual for an application to be so large that it is shipped on 20 floppy disks—or one CD. Thus, CD-ROM drives provide users with an added level of convenience when installing or using programs.

Removable media PC storage devices include both sequential and direct access devices. Diskettes, or floppy disks, are the most popular storage media. Floppy disks are cheap and can hold over 1MB of data. Newer technologies include Iomega's Zip drives, with more expensive removable disks that hold 100MB of data, and fast, high capacity Jazz drives, with 1GB removable disks.

Table 4.2 lists removable disk sizes and capacities.

Table 4.2 Removable Media

Type	Physical Disk Size	Capacity	Cost
floppy disk	5.25"	720KB	less than $.25
floppy disk	3.5"	1.44MB	less than $.30
floppy disk	2"	3MB	less than $1.50
Zip disk	4"	100MB	less than $20.00
Jazz disk	4.5"	1GB	less than $200.00

Optical disks are becoming a preferred method of storage, due in part to their extreme durability. Optical disks come in varying sizes, but the audio CD size is used in PCs. CDs have a capacity of over 600MB and a physical size of only 4.72 inches. The disks are relatively inexpensive (under $10), and CD-ROM players are also affordable. Read/write optical disk drives still hover near $1,000 in cost, and are largely used in businesses. Although the cost of the read/write drive seems high, it still compares favorably with the costs of printing, binding, and distributing thousands of copies of employee training materials.

Sequential storage devices like tape drives are used for making archival copies of data called **backups**. A backup tape can be stored off-site for safekeeping and restored to the original drive if the original data is lost. Tape drives use high-speed, high-capacity tape.

What You Have Learned

In 1971, when Intel invented the microprocessor—a complex central processing unit on a single chip—the computer industry did not immediately embrace the idea of a computer that would sit on a desktop. Industry leaders still felt that mainframe computers provided all the computing power that anyone would ever need. The personal computer revolution came about because a few visionaries—such as Douglas Engelbart and a group of computer enthusiasts that included Steve Jobs and Bill Gates—made it a reality.

The first personal computers were essentially hobby kits for the technologically minded. With the introduction of new types of storage devices, including the floppy disk and hard disk drives, personal computers began to take shape. After Apple Computer released the Apple II in 1977, the world began to recognize the potential of personal computers. IBM jumped on the bandwagon, and with the help of Bill Gates's operating system, MS-DOS, the IBM Personal Computer came into being in 1981.

Focus Questions

1. What innovations found on today's PCs were used by the Xerox Alto?
2. What is the significance of the Homebrew Computer Club?
3. Why weren't large computer firms instrumental in the early life of PCs?
4. What is an internal device? An external device? Give an example of each.
5. What does the description "8-bit microprocessor" mean?
6. What are the components of a system board?
7. What is a port?
8. What types of removable storage are available for PCs?

Knowledge Reinforcement

A. What was the significance of the Altair 8800 to the development of PC software?
B. Has the microcomputer revolution ended? Provide reasons to support your answer.
C. Compare and contrast the development of the personal computer with the development of ENIAC.

Further Exploration

Aaron's World Famous Virtual Computer Museum:
http://www.quiknet.com/~abond/museum.html

Chronology of Events in the History of Microcomputers:
http://www.islandnet.com/~kpolsson/comphist.htm

The Dream Machine: Exploring the Computer Age. Jon Palfreman and Doron Swade. BBC Books, 1991, 0-563-36221-9. Two nice chapters on the Microcomputer Revolution, including the Homebrew Computer Club.

The Electronic Labyrinth—Douglas Engelbart:
http://jefferson.village.virginia.edu/elab/hfl0035.html

IEEE Computer Society's History of Computing:
http://wwww.computer.org/50/history

Information Age: People, Information, & Technology:
http://photo2.si.edu/infoage.html

Jim's Computer Garage (photos and information about the first personal computers): http://agora.rdrop.com/users/jimw

Jones Telecommunications and Multimedia Encyclopedia (MITS):
http://jefferson.village.virginia.edu/elab/hfl0035.html

Lexikon Service Publishing (history of computing):
http://www.apollo.co.uk/a/Lexikon/

The PC User's Pocket Dictionary. Peter Dyson. Sybex, 1994, 0-89588-756-8. Definitions from a PC slant of over 2,000 computer terms.

Xerox PARC:
http://www.parc.xerox.com/

SESSION FIVE

Vocabulary

- baud
- cathode ray tube (CRT)
- compression
- dot-matrix printer
- extremely low frequency (ELF) radiation
- facsimile (fax)
- file compression
- gas plasma
- impact printer
- ink-jet printer
- keyboard
- laser printer
- liquid crystal display (LCD)
- MIDI
- modem
- monochrome
- mouse
- optical character recognition (OCR)
- PCMCIA card
- peripheral
- pixel
- resolution
- scanner

The Ins and Outs of Personal Computer Hardware

THE PERSONAL COMPUTER REVOLUTION HAS created an insatiable market for faster, easier-to-use, and more powerful components and peripherals. This session provides an overview of personal computer input and output devices and focuses on the amazing developments in hardware that make personal computing unique. At the end of this session, you will be able to

- Classify each type of peripheral appropriately as input, output, or input-output (I/O)
- Delineate reasons for using a particular input or output device
- Compare impact and nonimpact printers
- Name three types of monitors currently in use
- Discuss several different methods for entering data in a computer
- Name and explain several devices that retrieve information from a PC

SECTION 5.1: AN OVERVIEW OF INPUT AND OUTPUT

Input, output, memory, and storage devices are called **peripherals,** because they are peripheral, or outside of, the processor. An input device allows a user to enter programs or data into a computer and issue commands—in short, to tell the computer what to do. An output device provides a way for people to view the results of computer processing and for other computers to use computer-generated information for additional tasks. Some peripherals, such as a fax/modem, are input *and* output (I/O) devices, because they both receive and send data.

SECTION 5.2: INPUT DEVICES

A vast array of input devices are available for entering text and graphics, issuing commands, inputting audio and video, and inputting data. Some of these devices have multiple functions, but, generally, a particular device is specially designed for the type of input a task requires. Several input devices are shown in Figure 5.1.

Figure 5.1
Common input devices

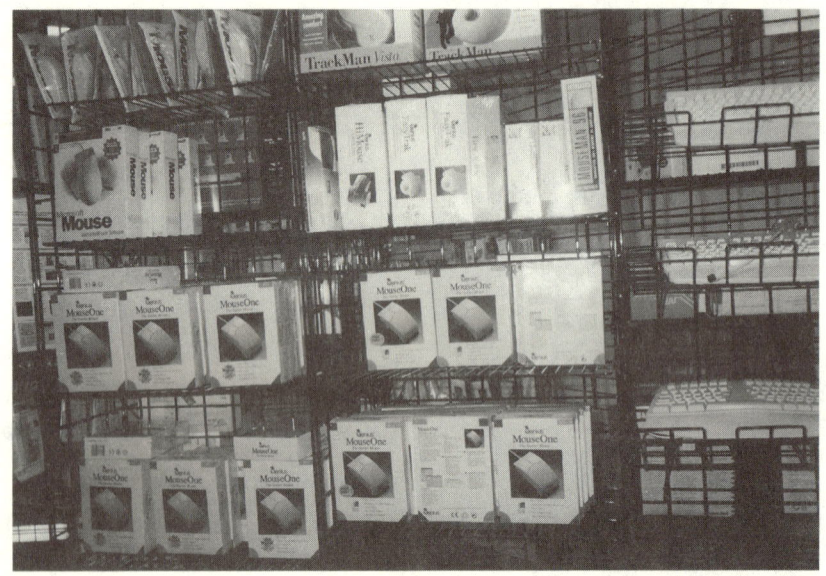

Courtesy of Twilight Technologies

Text-Entry Devices

Much of the input a computer receives originates as text-based data. A keyboard is most commonly used for entering text into a computer. A **keyboard** allows users to enter text by pressing alphabetic and numeric keys (see Figure 5.2).

Keyboards differ from typewriters in a number of ways. Computer keyboards contain special keys not found on a typewriter, including the Caps Lock and arrow or directional keys which are used to move within a document. The Caps Lock key (usually located to the left of the letter *A*) is called a *toggle* key—press Caps Lock once and it's on, press again and it's off. The Caps Lock key was originally included on computer keyboards for programmers using programming languages that required uppercase letters. Command keys can be customized by programmers for entering commands in programs. The Esc (Escape) key is often programmed so it can be used to cancel a command or to exit an undesirable situation. The Ctrl (Control) and Alt keys, located in the bottom row of keys next to the spacebar, are used in combination with other keys to enter commands. The function keys (F1, F2, and so on) are located across the top of a keyboard.

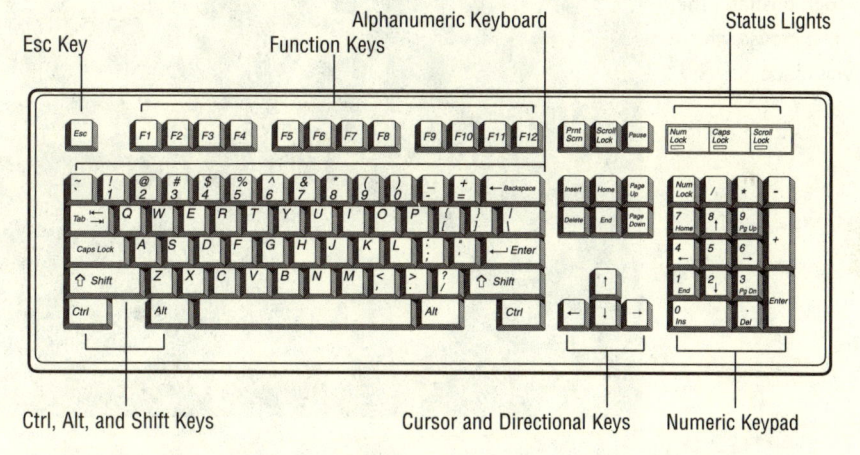

Figure 5.2
A computer keyboard

While keyboards work well for typists, they provide a barrier for other users. To use a keyboard, you must be able to read in the language used to label the keys and have a certain amount of physical dexterity. Other input devices have been designed to simplify computer use and reduce errors. Many of these devices fall into the category of pointing devices.

■ Pointing Devices

Pointing devices come in many varieties but have essentially the same objective, which is to allow users to control the movements of a small pointer on the screen. Rather than having to type commands, users can point to different areas of the screen and click to enter commands. Some pointing devices allow users to issue a command by touching an area of the screen with a finger; others allow users to create drawings or graphics by drawing on a tablet.

The Mouse

The most popular pointing device is the **mouse**, a small device that fits into your hand. The first mouse, shown in Figure 5.3, was invented by Douglas Engelbart in the early 1960s. Engelbart experimented with a variety of input devices, including foot pedals and knee controls, before settling on the mouse.

Figure 5.3
Douglas Engelbart demonstrates the first mouse, which was made of wood.

Provided by Douglas C. Engelbart and the Bootstrap Institute

Generally, the mouse is connected to a port by a cable; however, wireless mouse devices, which use infrared technology to send messages to the computer, are becoming common. Moving the mouse on the desktop rotates a small ball on the underside of the mouse. Sensors register the movement of the ball and send an electronic message to the computer about the mouse's position. The mouse pointer on the screen moves to correspond with the movement of the mouse.

Mouse devices, like those shown in Figure 5.4, are so easy to use even very young children can master them. By moving the mouse, users can point to objects on the computer screen, then click on a mouse button to send a command to the computer. Users can also hold down the mouse button and drag objects around the screen to reposition them. Dragging is an especially valuable skill when working with graphic images.

Figure 5.4
Surfing the Web with a GyroPoint

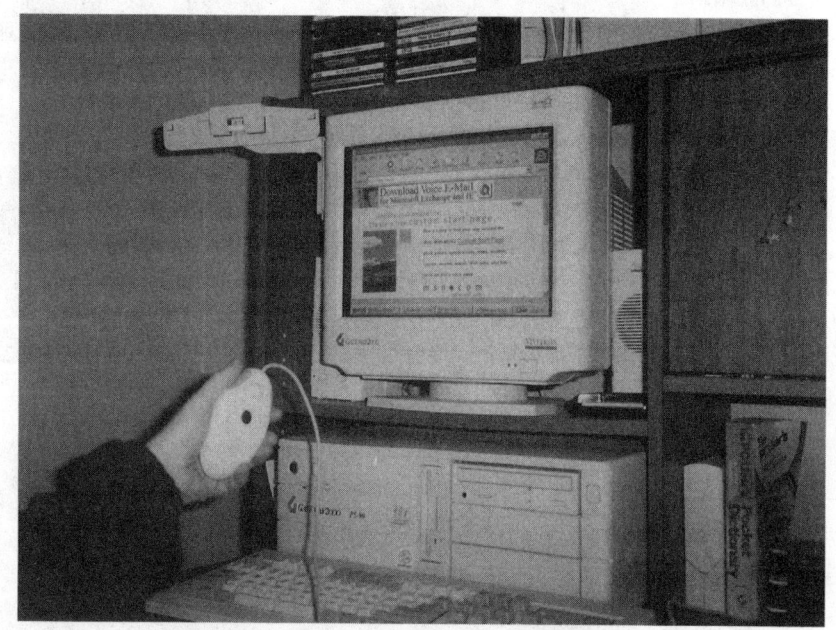

GyroPoint from Gyration, Saratoga, CA

One of the newer mouse-type devices on the market is designed specifically for surfing the Internet. The GyroPoint by Gyration, shown in Figure 5.5, uses gyroscope technology so users can point, click, and scroll without rolling the mouse on the desktop. The GyroPoint has a lengthy cord so you can sit back and relax while cruising around.

Pointing Devices for Laptop Computers

Some users, especially those who use laptops, find mice inconvenient because they require desktop space. Users who find mice a nuisance often prefer trackballs, which are essentially upside-down mice. The trackball stays stationary, and the ball is rotated with the thumb. Trackballs are built into some full-sized keyboards and laptop computers and are also sold as external pointing devices, such as the ones shown in Figure 5.6.

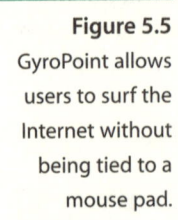

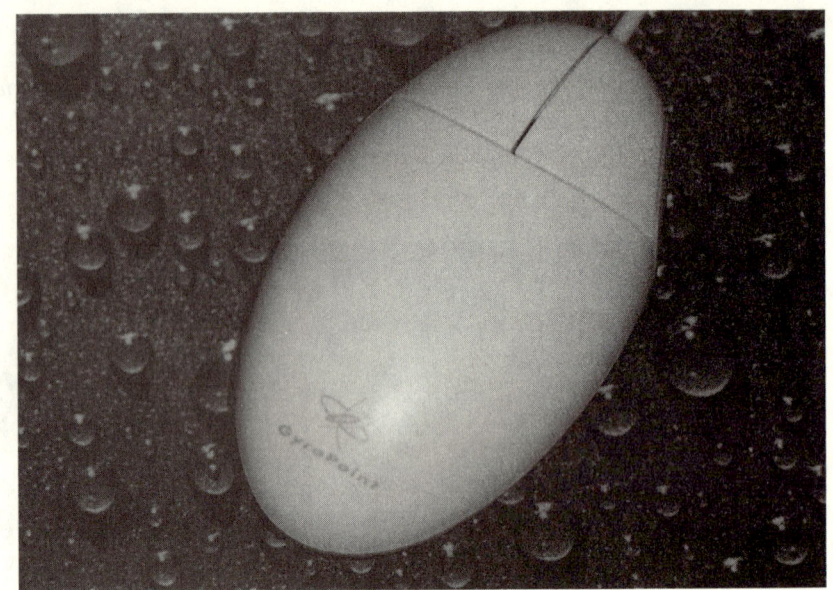

Figure 5.5
GyroPoint allows users to surf the Internet without being tied to a mouse pad.

GyroPoint from Gyration, Saratoga, CA

Figure 5.6
Logitech trackballs

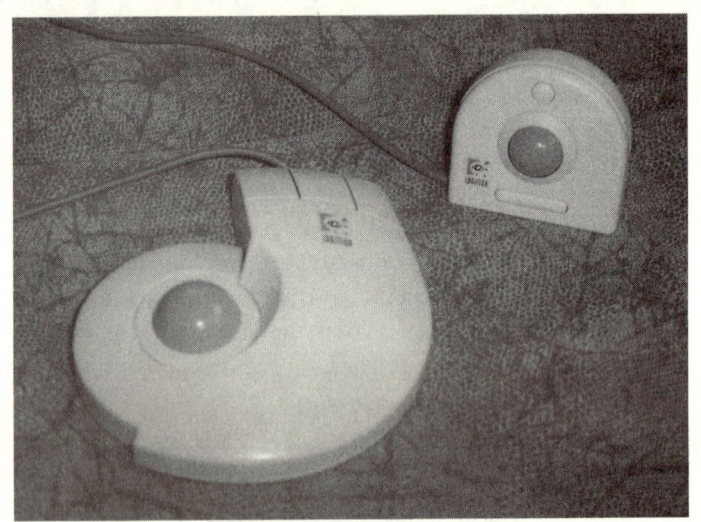

Used by permission of Logitech

Laptop manufacturers are experimenting with a number of other pointing devices. Some laptops have a trackpoint or GBH button (so named because it is mounted at the intersection of the G, B, and H keys on the keyboard). Trackpoints are commonly referred to as *eraser-heads* because they resemble pencil erasers. You manipulate an eraser-head with your index finger like a miniature joystick; the trackpoint's command buttons are built into the laptop case. With other portable computers, your index finger actually becomes the pointing device. To move the pointer on screen, you drag your index finger across a small square pad called a *touch pad*. To click, you simply tap your finger on the pad. All of the pointing devices take a little getting used to, and you'll find that once you try several, you'll develop a definite preference.

Touch Screens

Another pointing device that lets your fingers do the walking, a *touch screen*, is most commonly seen at tourist information areas, malls, museums, and airports. Users touch areas of the screen with their fingers to issue commands or call up information. An example of a touch screen application is located in a kiosk at Circle Centre Mall in downtown Indianapolis. By pressing different buttons or icons on the screen, users can discover what's happening in Indianapolis and the different things there are to do around town. Touching one button may take the user to another series of buttons where they can narrow down their choices according to their particular interests, budget, age group, and other criteria. Results are displayed on the screen. Another touch screen application is found in restaurants where employees touch a screen to enter patrons' orders. In some fast-food restaurants, you can enter your own order on a touch screen.

Joysticks

A joystick is a common pointing device used with computer games. Based on the controls found in airplanes and helicopters, joysticks are hand-sized sticks mounted on a base unit. The sticks can be pulled and pushed in all directions, making the joystick a very versatile pointing device for flying futuristic spacecraft through enemy territory, playing a game of basketball, or controlling the "point-and-kill" movements of adventure game characters. Joysticks have a number of buttons programmed to control different activities—such as firing a weapon, shooting a ball, or picking up a secret message—depending on the game being played. The boy in Figure 5.7 is using Microsoft's SideWinder 3D Pro joystick to play MegaGames' Tyrian.

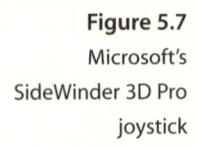

Figure 5.7
Microsoft's SideWinder 3D Pro joystick

Other Input Devices

Light pens are pen-like devices. When a light pen is touched to the computer screen, a light cell in the tip of the pen senses light from the screen and indicates the pen's location. The pen can be used to draw on the screen, or it can be tapped on the screen to register choices or issue commands. Light pens are a common input device for personal digital assistants.

Graphic tablets and digitizers are pointing devices used by graphic designers, architects, and artists to create images that appear on the computer screen. The images created on the tablet are converted to digital signals and transmitted to the computer. Other occupations require even more specialized input devices. For example, an engineer might use calipers to input the dimensions of a physical object into a computer-aided design (CAD) program.

All of the pointing devices listed in this section have the advantage of making certain types of input easy for users. However, they also have the disadvantage of taking the user's hands away from the keyboard. Speed typists complain that pointing devices slow them down; many would prefer to use keyboard commands whenever possible. Pointing devices also have the added disadvantage of creating muscle strain if reaching is involved. When using any input device, change positions periodically and do arm and hand exercises to get the blood flowing again and relax the muscles.

Audio, Video, and Graphics Input

Advances in technology have led to multimedia-capable computers that can produce dynamic sound, crisp graphic images, and full-motion video. Accordingly, peripherals dedicated to multimedia input are becoming more common and of higher quality.

An example of an audio input device is a small, inexpensive microphone you can use to talk into your computer and have your voice converted to digital sound waves. These digital sounds can be attached to documents or multimedia presentations or be transmitted through the Internet to a loved one around the world. Voice input is becoming a more common form of medical and legal dictation. Rather than having tape-recorded notes typed by a transcriptionist, a good microphone and speech-to-text software allow users to have their words immediately converted to text. Voice technology is also being used on a limited basis in other ways. Voice recognition is used as a security tool to prevent unauthorized entry to high-security locations. By matching a person's voice pattern to a previously recorded sample, it can be determined if the voice of the person requesting entry is authorized. Command applications allow users to control the computer through the use of specific words like "open," "save," "print," "close," and "exit." This technology is especially valuable when the user does not have use of their hands, either because of a disability or because the user is operating some other equipment at the same time in an industrial setting. Voice input may also be used for data entry. Users can complete a form verbally, responding to questions usually using preestablished number or letter responses.

NOTE

Voice technology is used instead of motion sensors on the doors of many urban storefronts in Japan. As you approach a door, say "Open, Please" in English or Japanese to open the door. If you forget to say "Please," you run into a closed door—Miss Manners goes high tech.

Speech technology is one of the most talked about computer-related developments on the horizon. Since people can talk much faster than they can type, it might not be long before the computer keyboard becomes completely obsolete. Not only do microphones and other voice input devices hold promise as the most convenient input device, they offer a new type of freedom. A simple phone call to a computer would be all it would take to get information, place an order, or conduct a myriad of other operations.

Although voice input devices provide exciting ways to input facts into a computer, we are also a visual society. There are devices you can use to enter graphic images easily. With a digital camera, you can take photos and input them directly into your computer. A digital camera uses no film; instead, images are recorded on the camera's SRAM, then uploaded (transferred electronically) to a computer. The photographs can be used as graphic images in documents or displayed on the computer's monitor.

There are two types of video input devices: fixed image video, and full-motion video. The fixed image (or still image capture) devices are connected between a video camera or VCR and a computer. The still image capture device converts the video signal into a graphic image much like a photograph. Video capture boards, installed in an expansion slot, have a port that a VCR or camera can be plugged into. Capture boards support full-motion video by digitizing and storing the video and audio signal to create a video "movie" that can be played on a PC.

■ Source Data Automation Input Devices

Much of the data we want to computerize already exists as hard-copy (paper) source documents. Rather than retyping all of this data, which not only takes time but introduces the risk of errors, several input devices have been developed that scan (read) hard copy into the computer. **Scanners** have become increasingly popular with businesses and individuals.

If you want to scan full pages of information, *flatbed* scanners allow you to feed in source documents like a copy machine. *Handheld* scanners are useful when the data you need is not on a sheet of paper. For example, you might need to scan inventory labels attached to all of the equipment in your office. You could move from chair to filing cabinet, just carrying a handheld scanner and a laptop or handheld computer. Handheld scanners are frequently used in industrial settings to scan labels in warehousing and manufacturing.

Scanned documents are stored as graphic images and cannot be manipulated without special software. **Optical character recognition (OCR)** was a process developed to enable a scanner to recognize text printed in special block type styles. With OCR, the scanned text could then be edited, reformatted, and stored by a computer. Although character recognition software does not always recognize 100 percent of the text, it converts most of it and then identifies the unrecognizable characters.

Two other types of character recognition, Optical Mark Recognition (OMR) and Magnetic Ink Character Recognition (MICR), are used for very specific purposes. OMR is used to process the #2 pencil marks on all those standardized tests you've had to take in your life. (The forms used in these tests are often called "bubble forms" because the user fills in circles.) Similar forms are also used for other types of questionnaires, including health histories in physicians' offices and customer surveys sent through the mail.

MICR is most commonly used on turn-around documents (documents that are returned to the source with additional information on them) like checks. Special magnetic ink is used when checks are printed to record the check number, bank number, account number, and check amount. When the check is processed, the check amount is also magnetically printed on the face of the check. All of this data is then scanned into the bank's computer system through special MICR scanners. With MICR, banks have greatly improved the speed, efficiency, and accuracy of check processing.

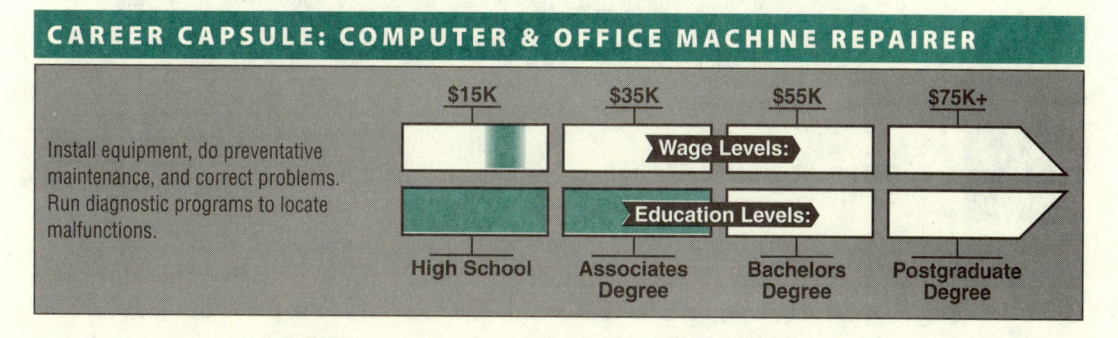

CAREER CAPSULE: COMPUTER & OFFICE MACHINE REPAIRER

Install equipment, do preventative maintenance, and correct problems. Run diagnostic programs to locate malfunctions.

Wage Levels: $15K — $35K — $55K — $75K+

Education Levels: High School — Associates Degree — Bachelors Degree — Postgraduate Degree

Flatbed or handheld scanners can be used to scan photos taken with traditional non-digital cameras. But some manufactures are building special photo scanners into their personal computers. To scan a photo, you just insert it into a photo reader mounted in the computer case. The photo is scanned, and the image can be then be used as a graphic, perhaps in a company newsletter or an electronic presentation.

Bar codes are a type of optical code that represents data through different thicknesses of vertical lines and spaces. Between retail stores and the U.S. Post Office, bar codes have become quite commonplace. Bar codes can represent numbers, or numbers and letters, depending on which bar code system, or symbology, is used. One of the most familiar symbologies is universal product code or UPC, the bar code you see on retail products that identifies the manufacturer and the product number. Typically, these numbers are scanned into computers using bar code readers, devices designed to interpret these symbols into characters. Bar code readers come as handheld guns, pen-like devices called wands (see Figure 5.8), and flatbed readers like those seen in most grocery stores. A combination of a reader and a computer terminal or PC is called a point-of-sale (POS) system.

Figure 5.8
Bar-code wand reader

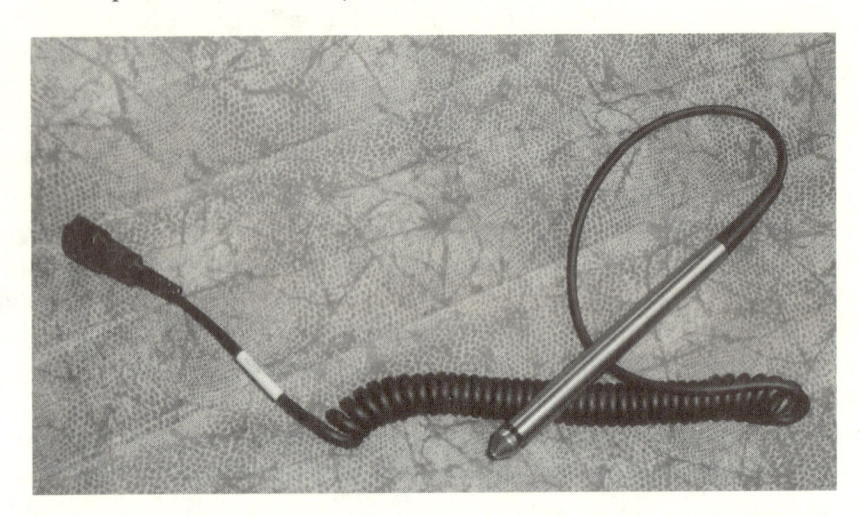

SECTION 5.3: OUTPUT DEVICES

Inputting a bunch of data into your computer won't do you any good unless you have some sort of output device that allows you to retrieve the information your computer has processed. The most common forms of output are produced by monitors and printers. Monitors and their video cards display text, graphics, and still video. Better video cards can send full-motion video to the monitor. Printers produce text and graphic output—everything from clip art (non-copyrighted graphic images available for use in documents) to highly specialized computer-aided design. Speakers—considered a standard peripheral device on multimedia personal computers—output music, human voice, and electronic sounds.

Monitors

The first output you encounter when you use a personal computer is what you see on the video monitor. A monitor is part of the computer's interface, and is integral to human interaction with computers. Monitors include

monochrome monitors, which display a single color on a lighter or darker color background, and gray-scale monitors, which display various shades of gray. But as the price of color monitors decreases, monochrome and gray-scale monitors are less common. Most video monitors and cards used today are capable of producing at least 256 colors. However, because they use less power, cost less, and require less capable (read: "cheaper") video cards, monochrome and gray-scale monitors still serve a valuable purpose in some business applications.

The size of monitors is measured diagonally, just as a television is. Fifteen-inch monitors are the standard on most desktop computers. But because of the growing interest in computer-generated graphics and videos, 17-, 19-, and 21-inch monitors are becoming more popular. Monitors are typically wider than they are tall. However, some of the larger monitors are designed so that they are, in effect, standing on their sides. This allows users to clearly see full-page documents on one screen, making design and publication work much easier.

CRT Monitors

Most desktop monitors are similar to televisions in that their pictures are produced using a cathode ray tube. A **cathode ray tube (CRT)** has a vacuum tube that forms the screen display at one end and a socket at the other end. The monitor image is produced by electron beams (which are invisible, by the way) that are generated in the neck of the CRT and shot against colored phosphors on the face of the CRT. When the invisible electron beam strikes a colored phosphor (red, green, or blue), the corresponding color is liberated. Using three synchronized electron beams to excite each color phosphor in the desired proportion, almost any color can be produced.

There are also some significant differences between CRT monitors and television sets. For one, monitors are capable of producing much higher resolution than most television sets. **Resolution** determines the clarity, quality, and detail of the picture displayed on a screen. Resolution is discussed in terms of **pixels**—individual spots on the screen that can display a particular color. Higher resolution not only makes images clearer but reduces the possibility of eyestrain that could occur after long periods of time looking at a monitor. In the computer industry, monitor resolution is often defined as the total number of pixels in height and width. For example, a 15-, 17-, or 21-inch monitor can be set to a resolution of 1024 pixels wide by 768 pixels high, or 1024×768. Scanners and printers still define their resolution in pixels per inch, as opposed to the total number of horizontal and vertical pixels displayed at one time.

Resolution is not the only measurement of image quality—color is the other defining characteristic. For example, a 1024×768 image at 256 colors can be much more detailed than a 1024×768 image at 16 colors, and a 1024×786 image at 16 million colors is virtually indistinguishable from a photograph.

CRT monitors also differ from televisions in how they draw pixels on the screen. Televisions draw every other line of pixels, and when they reach the bottom of the screen, they begin again at the top and fill in the missing lines. This process is called *interlacing*, and the staggered redrawing can cause a visible flicker. Non-interlaced computer monitors draw lines of pixels one at a time from the top of the screen to the bottom, a process that is repeated multiple times per second. The actual number of redraws is called the *refresh rate*. Faster refresh rates result in crisper, more fluid images.

CRT monitors and televisions also produce some undesirable output—low-levels of radiation, called **extremely low frequency (ELF) radiation**. As with many forms of radiation, the long-term impact of ELF radiation has yet to be determined. However, monitor manufacturers are beginning to incorporate safety standards into new monitors. Interestingly enough, American FCC standards for monitors are considered to be the least stringent in the world, while the MPR II Swedish standards are the toughest. To protect yourself from ELF radiation, you can purchase an ELF radiation guard that fits over the front of your monitor to block some of the emissions. It is also considered safer if you stay an arm's length away from your monitor and view the monitor directly rather than from the side, since most ELF is radiated from the sides and rear of the monitor. If you sit near several computers in an office, sit at least 4 feet away from the sides of other users' monitors.

Video Cards

A video adapter, or video card, provides the output to a computer monitor. Originally, video cards were special expansion cards. Today, basic video adapters are generally built into the system board, although you can purchase better boards to enhance video output. These adapters, which conform to standards developed by the Video Electronics Standards Association, control the resolution and number of colors that can be displayed by a monitor.

The most common video cards in use today are VGA (video graphics array) and SVGA (super video graphics array). Traditionally, VGA is

640×480×16 colors. SVGA is loosely defined as any resolution or color depth higher than that; namely, 640×480×256, or 800×600×16, or 800×600×16M, and so on.

Other Video Displays

In addition to CRT monitors, two other types of visual output devices are commonly used: LCD and gas plasma displays. Most laptop computers today use a **liquid crystal display** (**LCD**). There are two types of LCD panels: active matrix, and passive or dual-scan matrix. Active matrix uses more transistors to generate an image, making active matrix displays easier to read, and much more expensive.

A **gas plasma** display consists of three sheets of glass separated by a gas called plasma. When electricity is sent through a point in the display, it charges the plasma and the plasma gives off energy in the form of orange colored light in the same way a fluorescent light bulb emits white light. Gas plasma displays are occasionally used in laptops because they are very thin and are easy on the eyes. Because they do not have a size limit, glass plasma displays can also be used for large wall-sized displays. However, plasma displays use a large amount of energy, and can't display multiple colors.

LCD Projectors and Panels

If you're asked to give a presentation for a group of people today, using an LCD panel or projector will set you apart from the crowd. An LCD panel is an output device that sits on top of an overhead projector (where a transparency would go) and connects to a personal computer. Whatever is displayed on the computer is displayed on the LCD and projected onto a screen by the overhead. Using special presentation software, you can display images or video. An LCD projector works like an LCD panel, except it contains a built-in projector. Either device combined with a laptop computer makes a practical and useful tool for the occasional presenter or full-time lecturer.

▪ Printers

The market for printers has changed dramatically in the 1990s. Until recently, high-quality printing was expensive, and color printing was out of the question for most PC owners. Today, more and more home computers users are purchasing excellent quality color printers at affordable prices. As computers have moved into the mainstream, the caliber of printers has increased and prices have continued to drop. Printers for personal computers fall into two categories:

- Impact printers—dot-matrix printers, letter-quality printers, and plotters
- Nonimpact printers—laser printers, ink-jet printers, thermal printers, and dye-sublimation printers

Impact Printers

Impact printers, printers that make an image by hitting a print head or key against a ribbon, were the most common type of printer available for personal computers until the early 1990s. There are three major types of impact printers: dot-matrix printers, letter-quality printers, and plotters. Today, impact printers, such as the HP 5000 shown in Figure 5.9, are largely used to quickly print paychecks, invoices, and other reports generated by a network or mainframe computer.

Figure 5.9
High-quality print for high-volume production print applications is available in the HP 5000 family of printers. These printers can produce from 100 to 210 printed pages per minute (ppm) on fan-folded (continuous forms) paper.

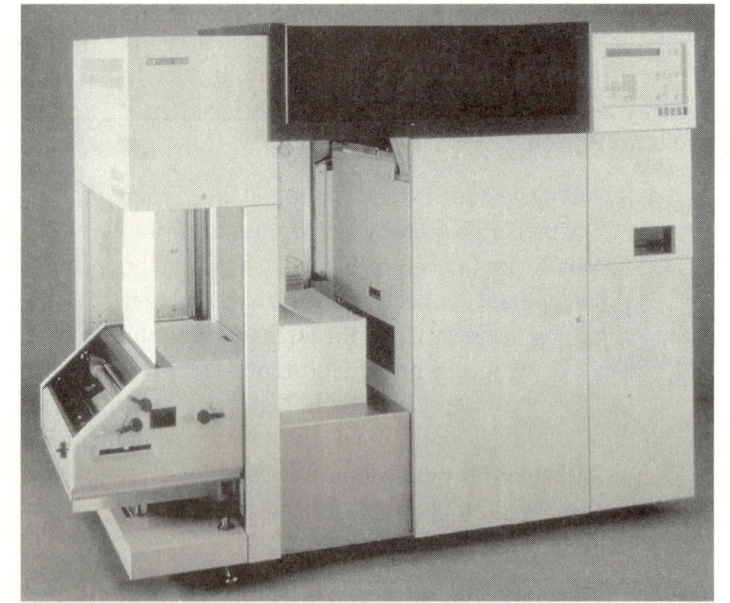

Photo courtesy of Hewlett-Packard Company

Dot-matrix printers form an image by using columns of small pins in 9-, 18-, or 24-pin configurations that strike a ribbon to form a pattern of small dots on a page. Because dots are used to create the image, dot-matrix printers can easily create both characters and graphics; however, the print quality of these printers is relatively low. Because impact printers actually strike the paper, they are primarily used today to print multiple-part forms.

Letter-quality printers, which are closely related to the typewriter, use a daisy wheel or a thimble hitting against a ribbon to produce text. Letter-quality printers are not capable of producing graphic images, and available type styles are dependent on the availability of different, interchangeable print heads. Letter-quality printers produce a better quality type than dot-matrix printers. Both dot-matrix and letter-quality printers are slow and noisy, making them unattractive in business settings.

Large architectural or engineering drawings may be printed on another type of impact printer called a *plotter*. A plotter is a printer that uses a series of pens filled with ink that switch on and off to reproduce an image. Drum plotters have pens that only move horizontally and use two drums to move the paper vertically against the pens. Electrostatic plotters are drum plotters that use a row of electrodes rather than a pen to create images on specially charged film or paper. Flatbed plotters resemble Etch-O-Sketch machines with pens mounted on a set of arms so that they can move both horizontally and vertically. The larger flatbed plotters, used in the automobile industry, can draw a full size drawing of a vehicle.

CAREER CAPSULE: COMPUTER & PERIPHERAL EQUIPMENT OPERATOR

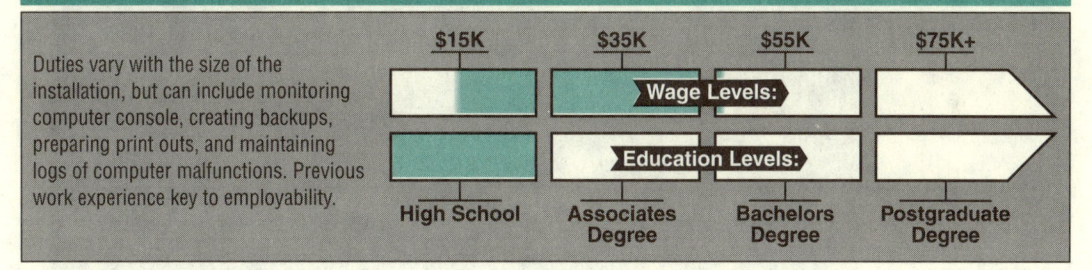

Duties vary with the size of the installation, but can include monitoring computer console, creating backups, preparing print outs, and maintaining logs of computer malfunctions. Previous work experience key to employability.

Wage Levels: $15K — $35K — $55K — $75K+

Education Levels: High School — Associates Degree — Bachelors Degree — Postgraduate Degree

Nonimpact Printers

Nonimpact printers, with their high-quality output, speed, low noise, and graphics capability, have quickly taken over the printer market. **Laser printers** generally produce the best output and, as a result, are commonly used in business settings. Laser printers produce an image the same way a copy machine does—by directing a laser beam onto a round drum. This charges a pattern of particles on the drum. As the drum rotates, it picks up an electrically charged powder called *toner*. The toner adheres to the paper and creates the text or graphic image. Laser printers print an average of six to ten pages per minute (ppm).

However, high-speed laser printers used in commercial applications can print up to five hundred pages per minute.

Printer resolution quality is measured in dots per inch (dpi). Extremely high quality laser printers can print in resolutions of up to 1200 dpi. Most laser printers print at 300 dpi; however, 600 dpi laser printers are coming down in price and becoming more common. Color laser printers like the HP Color LaserJet 5 shown in Figure 5.10 continue to be quite expensive. In order to print in color, the paper has to pass through the printer once for each different color. This requires the paper feeding mechanisms to be extremely accurate so the paper is precisely lined up on each pass.

Figure 5.10
Low cost per page and industry leading network-printing capabilities make this HP Color LaserJet 5 printer ideal for workgroups.

Photo courtesy of Hewlett-Packard Company

Fortunately, color printing is not limited to high-cost laser printers. Another type of nonimpact printer, called an **ink-jet printer**, is quite affordable for home use. And the quality of ink-jet printers isn't bad either—many produce high-quality, nearly photographic images.

Ink-jet printers, like the HP DeskJet 660C shown in Figure 5.11, print by spraying a fine jet of ink onto the paper; this ink can be black, or a combination of black, yellow, red, and blue. Like laser printers, black ink-jet printers are rated by the number of pages they print per minute. Color printers may be rated by *minutes per page* (mpp) rather than pages per minute, because whole numbers are more convenient than fractions. With ink-jet printers, users choose the quality of the print they want by selecting between draft, normal, and high-quality output. The quality of the output directly influences the speed of the printer—the higher the quality, the longer you wait for it.

Figure 5.11
HP's DeskJet 660C printer is designed for convenience. Black and color cartridges sit side by side, making it easy to print in true black and color on the same page without swapping cartridges.

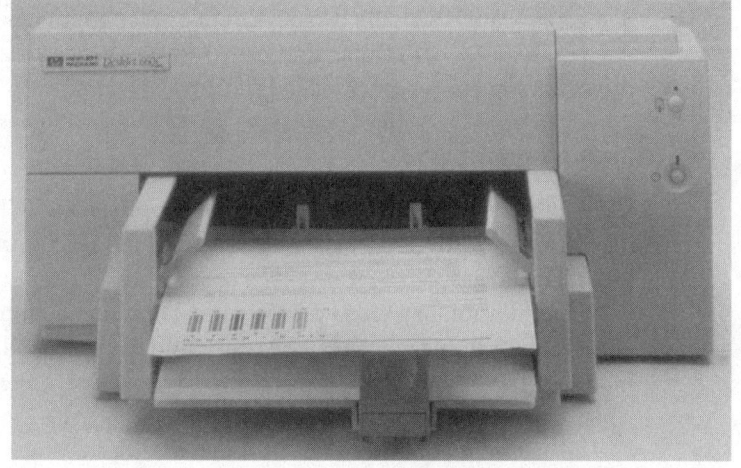

Photo courtesy of Hewlett-Packard Company

Thermal printers use heat to transfer an image onto specially treated paper. The early thermal printers used a shiny paper most commonly seen in calculators, and the quality of the printing was generally poor. Newer models of thermal printers, which use a process called *thermal wax transfer,* are of a much higher quality. Ink is injected into wax on a ribbon, and then heat is applied to the ink-filled wax so that it melts onto the paper at 66 dpi. *Dye-sublimation printing* works the same way as thermal wax transfer except that it smoothes the dots of ink once they are placed on the page; this changes the tones and produces photo quality images. Both thermal wax transfer and dye-sublimation printing are much faster than color laser printing and produce a better quality image at a lower cost. These printers are generally used for full-color publishing, including magazine publication.

■ Sound Output Devices

Voice, music, and other sounds produced by computers are amplified and projected by speakers, or through external jacks that can be connected to headphones or recording devices. Most PCs include small, cheap speakers like those found in the worst of clock radios. Multimedia PCs and multimedia kits that you add to your existing PC usually come with speakers of reasonable quality. But speaker quality varies, just as it does in home audio systems. For truly dynamic sound, consider purchasing a separate audio card and speakers or a multimedia kit manufactured by a major audio company like Altec Lansing, Yamaha, or Sony.

SECTION 5.4: INPUT/OUTPUT DEVICES

Some hardware is actually two devices in one: an input device, and an output device. This class of peripherals is called *I/O devices*. Storage devices like disk drives are sometimes included in lists of I/O devices.

■ Sound and Motion

Video cameras and camcorders with video input jacks, VCRs, and optical disk players are used to transfer graphic images to and receive images from a computer. The images can be transferred as static images or as moving pictures. With the addition of a video capture card, computer actions can be stored on video tape, or home videos can be edited and have text added to them. Animation software and supporting hardware allows users to create "movies" which can also be transferred to tape.

The biggest roadblock to full-motion video becoming commonplace is the size of the files video requires. The Disney movie *Toy Story*, the first fully animated feature-length movie produced entirely by computers, is an example of the difficulty video creates for computers. Each of the 114,000 frames of the 77 minute movie consumed 300 megabytes of hard drive space: a total of 34.2 terabytes.

NOTE

Here's an example that translates video's storage requirements into terms easier to understand: In May, 1996, there were 265,022 U.S. citizens. You could solicit a 63-page autobiography from each American citizen and store all the biographies in the 34.2 terabytes of storage required for *Toy Story*!

Because video is such a storage hog, developers are focusing on developing better methods of file **compression**, where repetitive and unnecessary bytes are removed before video files are stored, resulting in smaller, more compact files. As compression improves, we will see an explosion of video use in computer applications.

Specially designed electronic music keyboards, wind, string, and percussion instruments can be attached to a computer as input devices. Through the use of a standardized interface called **MIDI** (Musical Instrument Design Interface), computers, synthesizers, and instruments can communicate. With the addition of specialized software, whatever is played on an instrument can appear as sheet music on the screen. MIDI compositions can be created on screen with software, then output to an instrument through a MIDI port.

Musicians have found computerized instruments have other advantages, too. Because MIDI is a universal standard, sounds input from one MIDI instrument can be played back with the sound of another instrument so that the computer becomes a sophisticated synthesizer to create new and different kinds of music. MIDI provides composers with the ability to develop up to 16 tracks (16 sequences of code) that can be played simultaneously. A high-quality sound card can support enough tracks to create the effect of a full orchestra. Since MIDI code is very compact, it can be stored using significantly less space than the same recording in high-fidelity, digital sound. Surprisingly, MIDI sounds do not sound electronically produced. They accurately reflect the characteristics of the instruments they represent, and consequently, MIDI is regularly used by the recording industry to enhance or even originate musical compositions.

NOTE

The first music played on a computer was the tune "Daisy," played by a computer at Bell Labs in 1957. This bit of computer "musical trivia" is subtly referenced in the film *2001: A Space Odyssey*. Astronaut Dave Bowman sequentially removes memory modules to shut down HAL, an artificial intelligence computer. As the modules are removed, HAL loses more of its capabilities until, finally, HAL sings a few lines from "Daisy," then lapses into silence.

Fax Machines and Modems

When Douglas Engelbart first revealed his vision of personal computing in 1968, he demonstrated a computer communicating with another computer located at his laboratory 30 miles away. In his mind, computers were meant to talk to each other. Never has this been more evident than in the explosion of online communication in the 1990s. Commercial online services and the Internet have become a primary reason that many people are buying personal computers. Businesses are connecting satellite offices to headquarters with wide area networks and customized versions of the Internet called *intranets*.

> *A personal computer without a telephone line attached to it is a poor, lonely thing.*
> —*Stewart Brand, founder,* Whole Earth Catalog

A significant amount of traditional postal service delivery, commonly referred to as "snail mail," has been replaced by electronic mail. All of this communication is made possible by a device called a modem. A **modem** allows computers to communicate with each other by connecting through regular telephone lines.

Phone lines transmit analog signals—signals that travel as a wave, like sound. Computers generate digital signals. Analog devices are capable of handling varying values of signals within a certain range, or set of frequencies. Digital devices can only handle two values: 0 and 1. In order for a computer-generated digital file to be transmitted over analog phone lines, it must first be converted or modulated. When a digital signal is modulated, 0s and 1s are replaced with low- and high-frequency tones. When the analog signal is received by the remote computer, the signal must be demodulated, or reconverted back to a digital signal. The term *modem* comes from a combination of the two terms, *mo*dulate and *dem*odulate. Different types of modems are shown in Figure 5.12.

> **NOTE**
>
> Incredible as it sounds, fax machines are actually older than telephones! The first patents on fax machines date back to 1843. Of course, they couldn't use telephone lines, and the technology was quite a bit different, but the purpose was essentially the same. A French news report with a photograph was first sent by fax in 1914. By 1924, faxes were a regular part of the newspaper business.

Facsimile or fax technology is the transmission of images over telephone lines by converting text, characters, and graphics into a pattern of small dots. Fax modems combine the technology of modems with the technology of facsimile transmission to create a multifaceted device capable of sending documents to other computers or to facsimile machines at another location. Recent improvements in technology have produced multipurpose machines that include a fax, a scanner, and a copier all in one package.

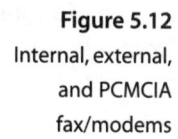

Figure 5.12
Internal, external, and PCMCIA fax/modems

Modems and fax modems are available on expansion cards as internal modems. External modems are connected to the computer's serial port. The phone line is connected directly to the modem, and lights on the modem indicate the status of the modem at all times.

A **PCMCIA card** is a plug-in card for laptop computers, about the size of a credit card, that is based on standards developed by the PC Memory Card International Association. Laptops include a PCMCIA port that can receive the cards. PCMCIA cards provide a variety of add-on options for laptop owners, including sound adapters, flash memory, network cards, and fax modems.

The most important factor in evaluating a fax modem is the data transmission speed. Early modems transmitted at a speed of approximately 300 bits per second (bps). Using a unit of measure for signal speed called **baud**, this was referred to as 300 baud. It's important to note, however, that since more than one bit can be sent per second, baud does not always correspond to the number of bits per second. Modern modems encode a signal using changes in several aspects of an audio analog signal. As an example, a 28.8KB modem is capable of sending and receiving around 115,000 (115K) bits per second. To access the Internet without frustration, modems need to transmit a minimum of 14,400bps or 14.1Kbps. Modems of 28,800bps (28.8Kbps) or faster provide users with less wait time and greater reliability in data transfers.

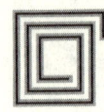

> **NOTE**
>
> The ultimate vision of the "information superhighway" is the creation of a complex network of digital communication lines that would allow computers to communicate without the use of modems.

What You Have Learned

Some of the most important innovations in the world of personal computers have been in the arenas of input and output devices. Although the keyboard is still the most common input device, there are a number of pointing devices, such as the mouse, trackball, trackpoint, joystick light pen, and graphics tablet. Other forms of input devices include digital cameras, scanners, and bar code and other types of data readers. Output devices include printers and monitors.

All monitors require output from a video card. Monitors have similarities to televisions but also have distinct differences in the technology used to create images. The quality of monitors is measured by the number of horizontal and vertical pixels, referred to as resolution. The number of colors that can be displayed also determines picture quality.

Printers are generally classified as impact and nonimpact printers. Nonimpact ink-jet printers are growing in popularity because of their quality, speed, low-cost, and ability to print color.

Modems and fax modems are input-output devices because data can be sent and received through telephone lines. Modems convert the digital signals created by computers into analog signals for transmission using telephone lines. The signal is then converted back to digital for the receiving computer.

Focus Questions

1. Why were pointing devices developed and what advantages do they have over keyboards?
2. Given the current state of technology, what is a major drawback with using the human voice as a form of input?
3. What is the purpose of file compression?
4. What is the difference between OMR and MICR?
5. How is resolution measured and what is it used for?

6. What are bar codes, and what is the advantage of using them?

7. Describe a situation in which you might use a fax machine instead of a fax modem. Describe a situation in which you might use a modem instead of a fax.

Knowledge Reinforcement

A. If you were only allowed to use one output device, which would you choose? Why?

B. How have advances in PC printing devices increased the opportunities for home-based businesses?

C. "Computer output technologies have been a driving force for improvement in television technologies." Do you think this is true? Why or why not?

Further Exploration

They All Laughed. Ira Flatow. HarperPerennial, 1992, 0-06-092415-2. The development of the facsimile and other great inventions.

HotWired Online Magazine (information about the making of the movie *Toy Story*):
http://www.hotwired.com/wired/3.12/features/toy.story.html

Vocabulary

- 4GL
- application
- assembly language
- BIOS
- business software
- business systems software
- code
- compiler
- development tool
- device driver
- DOS
- entertainment software
- environment
- executable program file
- high-level language
- icon
- information engineering
- install
- interpreter
- kernel
- knowledge software
- machine language
- menu
- object code
- operating system (OS)
- productivity software
- programming language
- prompt
- Rapid Application Development (RAD)
- software piracy
- shell
- system software
- Systems Analysis and Design
- utility
- Windows 95

SESSION SIX

Personal Computer Software

NO MATTER HOW TECHNICALLY SOPHISTICATED computers have become, they would never have become a mass market phenomenon without useful and understandable software. Software transforms the computer from a highly technical electronic device into an immensely practical and productive tool. This session introduces you to what software is and how software works with your computer. At the end of this session, you will be able to

- Define the major classifications of software
- Explain the basic functions of an operating system
- Differentiate between text-based and graphical user interfaces
- Define major types of applications software
- Describe the steps in the software development life cycle

125

SECTION 6.1: INTRODUCTION TO PC SOFTWARE

As you learned in Session 1, software is one or more programs (or sets of instructions) that the computer can understand. Computers resemble the multipurpose Universal Turing machines, because one computer can use many different types of software. With the flexibility software creates, you can use the same pieces of hardware to create documents, analyze numbers, answer the phone, or design a home. When you are finished working, you can relax with your PC by creating art, flying a jet, or building a simulated city.

If the hardware is the "body" of the computer, then software is its soul. All computers require software—without it, a computer is nothing more than a large paperweight, as useful as a tape player without tapes or a CD player without CDs.

Some software fits on a single removable disk, like a floppy disk, and can be used directly from the disk. Increasingly, users are having to **install** software—copy it to the computer's hard drive—either because the software is larger than a single disk, or because it must always be directly available to the CPU. Computers use two types of software: system software and applications, as shown in Figure 6.1. **System software** allows the computer to carry out basic operational functions, including input and output. **Applications** enable users to complete specific tasks.

Figure 6.1
Types of software

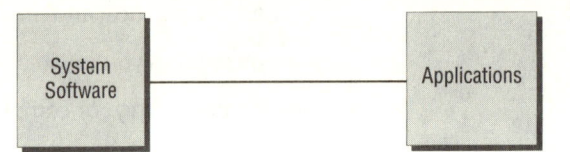

SECTION 6.2: SYSTEM SOFTWARE

There are four types of system software, shown in Figure 6.2: operating systems, including operating system environments; device drivers; utilities; and programming languages.

Figure 6.2 Types of system software

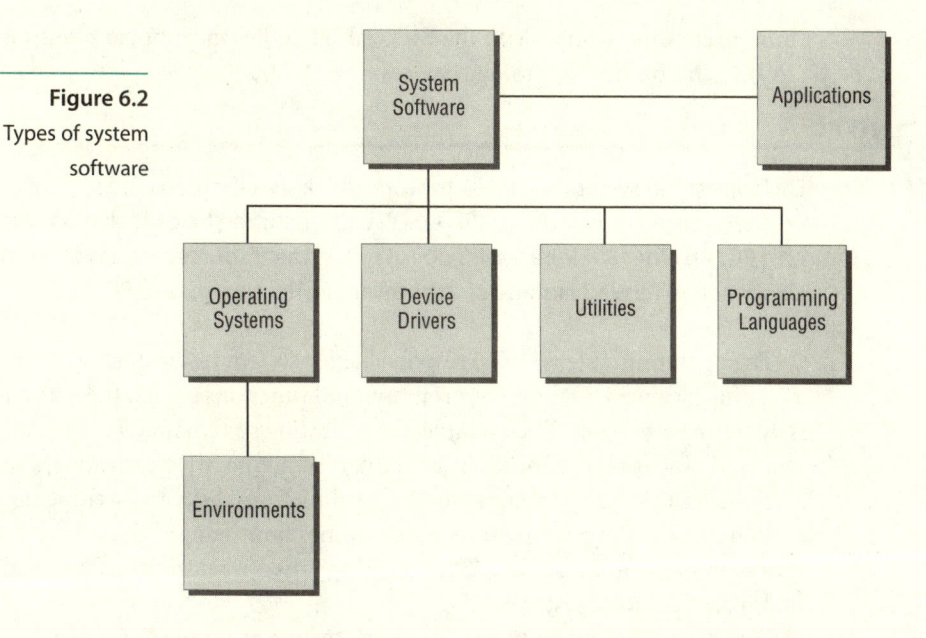

Operating Systems

When you turn on a PC, the computer conducts a power-on self test that tests the computer's RAM, identifies each of the storage devices connected to the computer, and checks to see if a printer is connected and turned on. The instructions for the self-test are stored in the computer's ROM as part of the system's **BIOS** or Basic Input Output System. The BIOS is the interface between the personal computer hardware and the operating system. An **operating system (OS)** is one or more programs that interact with the system's BIOS to control a computer's hardware. The operating system provides a standard set of functions that applications can draw upon to communicate with the BIOS. While the computer is in use, the operating system is responsible for letting you know when devices are not working properly (such as when a disk has been removed from a drive, or when a printer is not connected). Operating systems control input and output by monitoring and controlling the flow of data and other programs. Input is taken from the keyboard, mouse, or other input device and channeled to memory and the CPU. Output is sent to the screen, printer, or other output device. The operating system, through communication with the BIOS, also handles the input and output (I/O) operations for the storage devices.

> **NOTE**
>
> Each operating system is written to work with a specific hardware system architecture (including the BIOS). An OS written for the Macintosh won't work on a PC. An older 8088-based PC doesn't have the resources required to run an OS written to take advantage of the power of a Pentium-based PC.

The operating system is also responsible for system resource allocation—assigning hardware to different programs and functions so that the computer is operating efficiently. For example, the operating system may set aside part of a hard disk as virtual memory, or use part of memory for cache operations. The operating system manages storage, reading from disks and writing new files on disks. The operating system determines how many users can access the computer simultaneously. There are single-user operating systems, and multiuser operating systems.

Each operating system has a user interface: one or more ways that a user can enter commands. The operating system's **shell** is the program that takes commands from the user and passes them to the heart of the operating system, the **kernel**. Depending on the operating system on your computer, the user interface shell will either be text based or graphical.

Text-Based Operating System Interfaces

With text-based user interfaces, the user types commands to give instructions to the computer. Early operating systems required all the commands to be loaded at one time from a storage device. PC operating systems use command line text interfaces, where the user can enter one instruction at a time from a keyboard. The first PC operating system, the Control Program for Microcomputers, or CP/M, was a text-based operating system. CP/M was written by Digital Research, who were later approached to write another operating system for the first IBM PC. (This job was later given to Microsoft.) You can still find groups of CP/M users in university communities.

IBM PC-DOS was written in 1981 by Microsoft for the IBM PC personal computer. Microsoft's own version, named MS-DOS, is similar to PC-DOS. Both operating systems are referred to simply as DOS. **DOS** stands for disk operating system, so named because the operating system was stored on a floppy disk. The DOS command line includes a **prompt**, which tells the user that the PC is ready to accept instructions. Instructions are typed after the prompt. After each instruction, the user presses the Enter key to process the instruction; DOS accepts and processes the instruction based on a library of instructions included in the DOS operating system. The DOS command line below is used to copy all the files from a floppy disk (in the A drive) to the hard drive, C.

```
COPY A:*.* C:
```

Recent versions of DOS include a program called DOS Shell that lets users enter commands using a mouse.

UNIX (pronounced "you nicks") is another text-based operating system developed in the early 1970s by AT&T's Bell Labs. UNIX is a multiuser PC operating system that has been improved upon by many different groups in the past 20 years. There are different versions of UNIX, including BSD UNIX (improvements on the version of UNIX developed by the University of California at Berkeley), XENIX, AIX (IBM UNIX), and A/UX (UNIX for the Macintosh computer). Some versions of UNIX include a graphical user interface. There are various UNIX shells, including the C shell (as in "She sells C shells down by the UNIX shore").

Graphical User Interfaces

Early Apple computers used a text-based interface called Apple DOS or ProDos. The Lisa, which used a GUI, cost over $10,000, so it was not a commercial success. However, microcomputer users were excited by the easy-to-use interface. Apple adapted the Lisa operating system for use in its Macintosh computers. The Macintosh operating system, Mac OS, has been revised several times and is usually referred to by its version number. For example, the seventh version of Mac OS is called *System 7*. The Mac OS shell is called *Finder*; its graphical interface is shown in Figure 6.3.

A graphical interface like Finder uses small pictures called **icons** to represent programs or instructions. The user points to an icon and clicks the mouse to give an instruction to the operating system. Other instructions are given by making choices from **menus** that are part of the shell.

After the release of Mac OS, microcomputer users had a dilemma. On the strength of Mac OS, the Macintosh quickly established a strong hold in specific areas of the microcomputer market, including publishing and education. PC users adopted an air of superiority based on their abilities to use DOS or UNIX, and derided Macintosh users as WIMPS: users of windows, icons, maps, and pixels. It was generally agreed that the IBM PCs were more powerful for numerical operations, but many DOS users longed for an easy-to-use GUI like that found on the Apple Macintosh. Microsoft's Windows, released in 1985, was not an operating system, but an **environment**—a program that is used in addition to the operating system. An environment is something less than an operating system, since it requires an underlying OS to operate. Windows, essentially a shell for DOS, took instructions given by mouse and changed them into commands that could be accepted and carried out by DOS.

Figure 6.3
Macintosh window

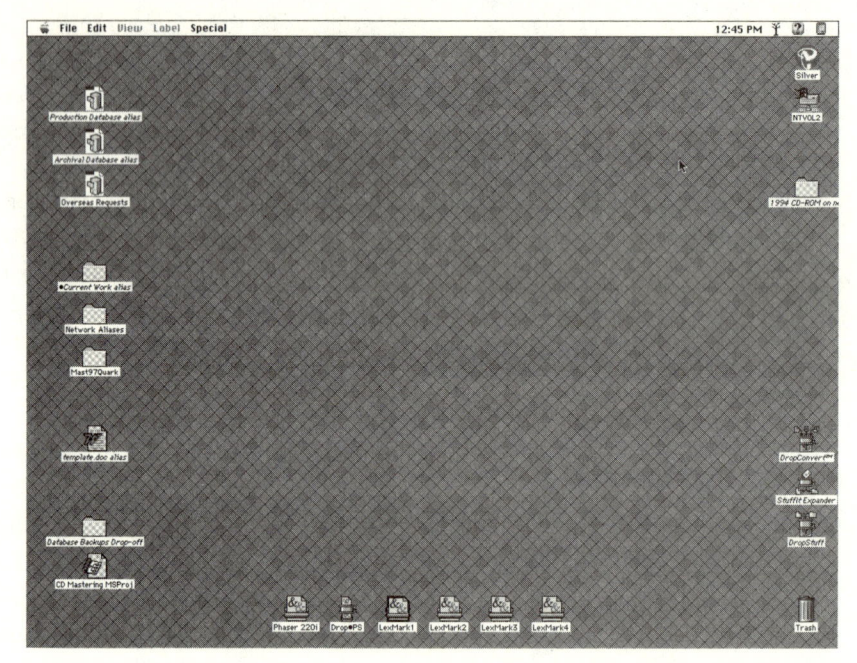

The earliest versions of Windows were not successful. In 1987, IBM and Microsoft began working on a graphical user interface that was intended to replace DOS and Windows. The new operating system, named OS/2, was released in December of that year. Microsoft was also still working on Windows, and released Windows 3.0, a drastic improvement over Windows 2, in May of 1990.

Rather than being replaced by OS/2, Windows 3.0 was a direct competitor with OS/2. Windows 3.1, an improved version, promptly followed. Today, Windows 3.1, shown in Figure 6.4, is considered an industry standard, and is used on more computers than any other environment program. Eventually, Microsoft pulled out of the OS/2 joint venture and concentrated only on Windows. Although IBM continues to sell OS/2, most new PCs manufactured by IBM are sold with a Microsoft operating system and/or environment.

> **NOTE**
>
> When a product is updated, it is often given a new version number. If the update is a major update, then the integer portion of the number is changed. For example, DOS 4.0 was a major change from DOS 3.0. If only minor changes are made, then the decimal following the number is changed: DOS 3.0 to DOS 3.1. When referring to software, the designation "3.*x*" means any version 3 (3.0, 3.1, 3.22). "3.*x* or higher" means any version of the software with a number equal to or greater than 3.0.

Figure 6.4
Windows 3.1

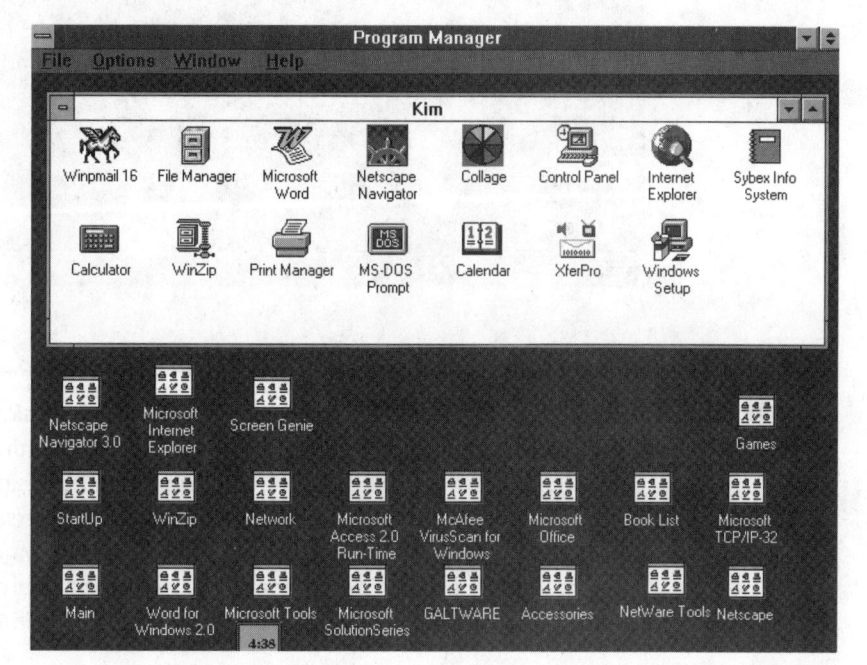

Windows 95, released (not coincidentally) in 1995, is the first version of Windows that is more than an environment. Windows 95 is an operating system. The OS functions formerly handled by DOS have been included within the Windows environment, so Windows 95 users don't require a separate operating system (see Figure 6.5).

Microsoft also has a multiuser version of Windows, Windows NT. Windows NT 3.1 uses the Windows 3.1 graphical interface. Windows NT 4.0 is modeled after Windows 95.

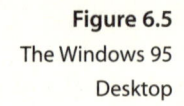

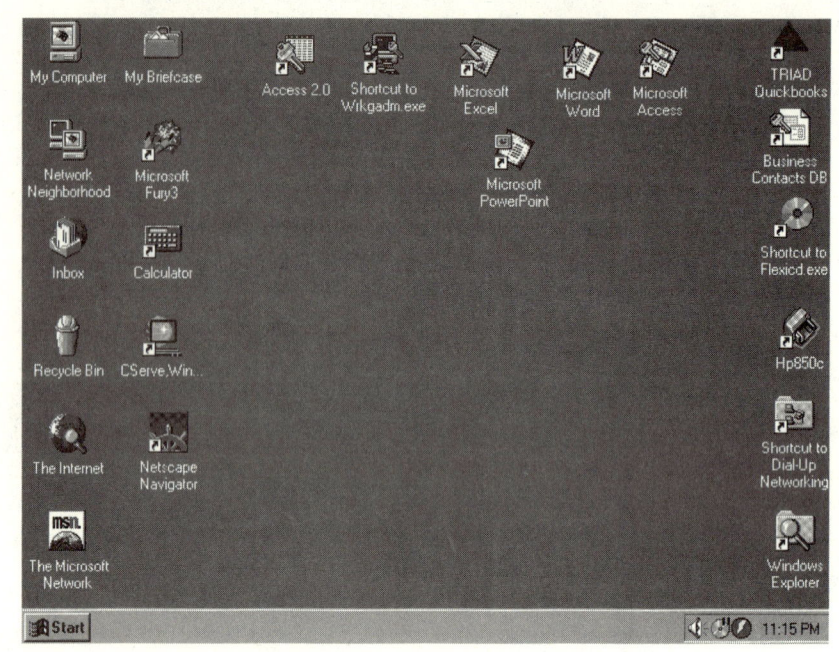

Figure 6.5
The Windows 95 Desktop

> **NOTE**
>
> As a rule, businesses are reluctant to purchase the first version of a program. Microsoft named the first version of their multiuser operating system Windows NT 3.1 instead of Windows NT 1.0 to avoid the 1.0 designation an to tie it to Windows 3.1 in the minds of potential purchasers. With the release of Windows 95, Microsoft has initiated a change in the way new versions are numbered. The new methodology relies on the year a product was first released—or the promised year of release, which is sometimes the same year.

In most operating systems, the program code for the OS is separated into multiple files. For example, DOS used three files that contained operating system commands, input and output commands, and the text-based user interface. These files form the core of the operating system. Other programs are also included with an operating system, such as tutorials on operating system use, system documentation files, device drivers, and utilities.

■ Device Drivers

The operating system includes general information about devices that can be connected to the computer. **Device drivers** are programs that provide specific information to the computer about a particular piece of hardware. When you attach new hardware to a PC, you also install the device driver for the hardware on the computer's hard drive. The device driver is used by the operating system to communicate with the new hardware.

Some device drivers are generic because the devices they control were built to a particular specification. For example, there are a small group of mouse drivers that work with most mice. Where there is a great deal of variation in devices, device drivers must be very specific. Nearly identical printers built by the same manufacturer will have different, individual drivers that take advantage of the features of each printer. If you don't have the proper driver for a device, the device may work, but may produce partial or unsatisfactory results: for example, a printed page where all the text is underlined.

Utilities

Utilities are programs that are used in conjunction with the operating system to control and use a computer's hardware, or manage data and program files. For example, you might use a utility to copy all the information on one disk to another disk. Most utilities assist with file storage and management operations. Utilities are used for a variety of system tasks, including

- Formatting a disk so it can be used to store programs and data
- Managing data and programs—copying, moving, renaming, or deleting data and program files
- Securing data by checking for computer viruses, or creating a backup copy or encrypted copy of important work
- Recovering lost data or programs
- Performing diagnostic tests on computer hardware

Operating systems include the utilities required to minimally manage storage devices. For example, the DOS operating system includes the following utilities:

- FORMAT, used to prepare a disk for use as storage media
- COPY, so files can be copied from one storage location to another
- RENAME, used to change a file's name
- DEL, the file deletion utility
- BACKUP and RESTORE, used to make a copy of files on another drive
- UNDELETE, to help recover files mistakenly deleted

Some of these utilities, like COPY, are actually part of the program code of the operating system's program files. Others, like FORMAT, are separate files that are included as part of the operating system. Utilities such as First Aid 95 (shown in Figure 6.6) can be purchased as additional products. Some popular utility programs are shown in Table 6.1.

Table 6.1
Popular Utility Software Programs

Utility Software	Publisher
Virus detection and removal	
PC-cillin	Touchstone Software Corp.
ThunderBYTE Anti-Virus	ThunderBYTE, Inc.
Norton Anti-Virus	Symantec
McAfee Virus Scan	McAfee, Inc.
File compression	
PKZIP	PKWare, Inc., widely available shareware
WinZip	Nico Mak
System protection and performance optimization	
Norton Commander	Symantec
FirstAid 95	Cybermedia, Inc
System backup and restore	
Microsoft Backup	Microsoft Corp.
Uninstall and disk cleaning	
Remove-It	Vertisoft Systems, Inc.
CleanSweep	Quarterdeck

■ Programming Languages

Computer **programming languages** are used to write computer programs, which are then translated into **machine language,** binary code the computer can implement. The programming language allows the user to enter instructions that are more easily understandable than machine language. The finished program is called **code**. Most computer programming is done by programmers, who are also called software developers or software engineers.

Figure 6.6
Utility software programs such as First Aid 95 perform a variety of system tasks.

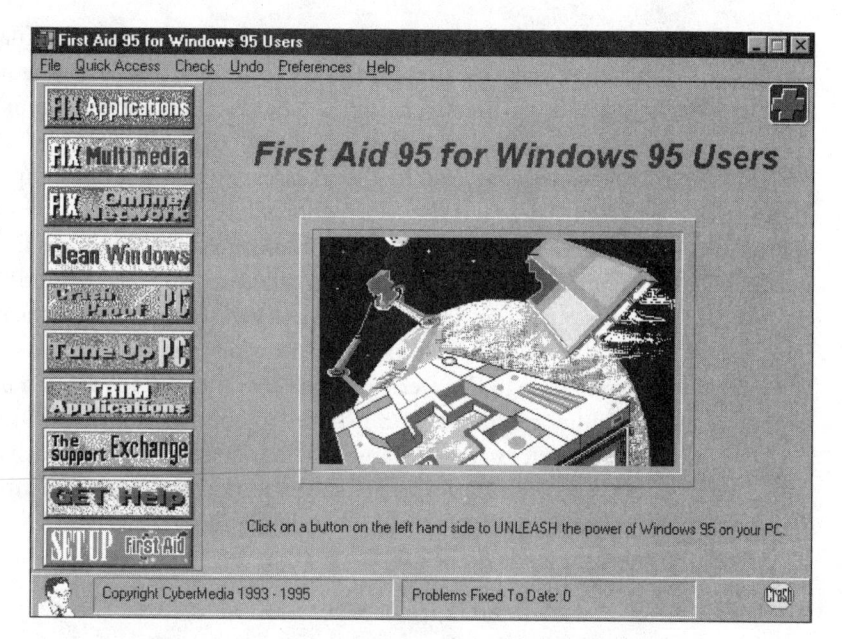

Early personal computers included a programming language (usually BASIC) with the operating system files, because users frequently wrote programs to handle specialized tasks. With few personal computers in the hands of users, there was little or no demand for specific programs to give tests to students, track a family genealogy, or calculate freight discounts. The increased number of microcomputers in homes and businesses has created a market for many specialized programs. Today, most computer users purchase programs they need rather than writing the code themselves. Some computers still include a version of the BASIC programming language, but other languages need to be purchased separately.

There are many computer languages. Some are designed for work on a specific computer, such as a graphics animator. Most languages are more general, and will run on a number of computers. The more the commands of a programming language resemble a "natural language" like English, the easier it is to learn, and the more popular it becomes. So why don't all programming languages resemble natural language? Languages that are far away from natural language are, by definition, closer to machine language. And although they are harder to use, they are more powerful tools.

There are five generations of programming languages, just as there are five generations of computers. (The generations of languages don't coincide exactly with the generations of computers, however.) The first generation of programming languages began with the first machine language program. Machine language uses the 0s and 1s of binary code, and requires programming code to directly manipulate hardware like specific spots in memory, storage, and the CPU registers.

Second-generation low-level **assembly language**, an improvement on machine language, uses short abbreviations like MUL (for multiplication) and ADD (for addition). The completed assembly code is then translated into machine language by a program called an *assembler*. Assembly language makes programming easier, but still gives programmers the power that comes with the ability to directly access memory and storage areas. Many older assembly languages were machine-specific, so code written for one type of computer could not be transferred to another computer. Today, more general assembly languages are largely used to write programs, such as operating systems and high-performance software, that communicate intimately with hardware. Assembly language code to print "Hello, world!" on the computer monitor is shown below.

```
          .radix   16
          .model   small
          .data
hello     db       "Hello, world!", 24
          .stack   100

          .code
main      proc
          mov      DX, DGROUP      ;set DS to point to data
                                    seg
          mov      DS, DX

          mov      AH, 9           ;call DOS print service
          lea      DX, hello
          INT      21

          mov      AX, 4C00        ;call DOS terminate service
          INT      21
main      endp
          end      main
```

The third generation of programming languages are called **high-level languages**. High-level languages have commands that replace several lines of assembly language code, so code written in high-level languages is more concise. The first high-level language was the Formula Translator language,

FORTRAN, written in the late 1950s for scientific use. COBOL (see Session 3), a general business language, followed quickly thereafter.

> **NOTE**
>
> Once a programming language has been widely used, it will stick around for quite a while. IBM's Report Program Generator (RPG) language was used extensively in the early 1960s to write programs for IBM mainframe and mini-computers. RPG fell out of favor as easier-to-use languages were created. However, all the programs written in RPG were still out there, requiring periodic updates and changes as business conditions changed. Eventually, RPG programmers began to retire, and there was (and is) a need for a new generation of RPG programmers.

A number of high-level programming languages were invented in the 1960s: BASIC, designed to make computers easier for nontechnical people to use; ALGOL, which premiered a theoretical concept called *structured programming* that changed the way all programs were written; LOGO, written for the educational market; and LISP, used in artificial intelligence programs. In these and other high-level languages, the assembler has been replaced with an interpreter or compiler. Some high-level languages use a program called an **interpreter** to translate a program into machine language line by line. Interpreted languages give immediate feedback if a programmer enters commands incorrectly. Each time the program runs, it is translated by the interpreter. The "Hello, world!" program looks like this in Microsoft QuickBASIC:

```
10 PRINT "Hello, world!"
```

Some languages use a compiler rather than an interpreter. With a compiler, all code is entered and saved on a storage device, then processed by a **compiler** program which reports any errors. When the code entered by the programmer is free from technical errors, the compiler generates a version of the program in what is called **object code**. Object code is then run through yet another program, called a *linker,* which creates a final machine language version called an **executable program file**.

It's easier to write a program using an interpreter than a compiler. However, since the interpreter must be used each time the program is run, programs that have been compiled run more quickly than interpreted programs. In compiled programs, the executable program file created by the linker is saved for future use. Some languages include both an interpreter and a compiler, combining both ease-of-use and rapid execution. When a programmer is finished creating code with the interpreter, an object code version is compiled for future use.

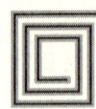

> **NOTE**
>
> Compilers and interpreters check program code for technical errors, including typing errors and the incorrect use of the language's programming commands. They cannot check for logical errors in the program, such as using the wrong sales tax rate or an incorrect formula. It is the programmer's job to make sure that program logic is error free.

The fourth-generation languages are considered very high level languages. Some fourth-generation languages, called **4GLs**, are used for a very specific purpose: to allow users to enter natural-language commands to work with a collection of information called a *database*. (Databases are described in more detail in Section 6.3.) There are different types of 4GLs, including

- Report generators like Impromptu that produce a written report from the information in a database

- Query generators like English Wizard (see Figure 6.7) and SQL, that search for information that meets a specific criteria, such as all the customers who live in Mississippi

- Application generators that are used by programmers to create separate programs that use the information from a database

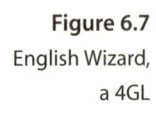

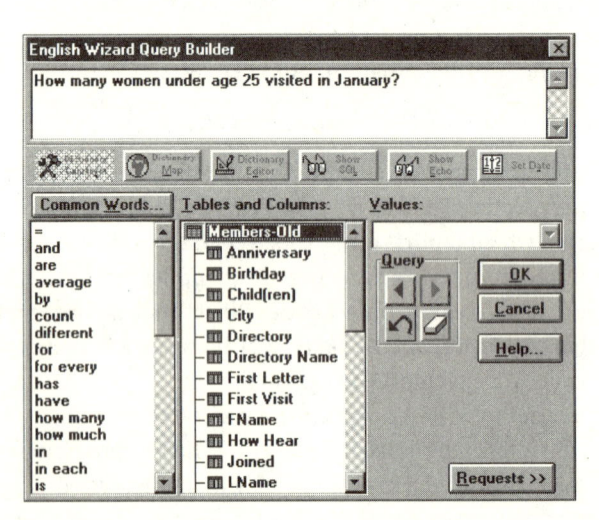

Figure 6.7
English Wizard, a 4GL

Some 4GLs only work with one database; others work with a variety of databases. For example, ABAP/4 is a 4GL designed specifically for use with

SAP R/3 databases and program code. Products like English Wizard, SQL, and Impromptu work with a number of different databases.

Not all fourth-generation languages are 4GLs. There are fourth-generation languages, such as Turbo Pascal, that can be used for creating databases and other general programming, rather than simply for accessing information in one or more databases.

Fifth-generation languages use object-oriented programming (OOP). With object-oriented programming, program code and the data used by the code are wrapped together in a single object. Each object is part of a class of similar objects, and has *attributes* (properties) and *behaviors* (methods, or actions carried out by the object). A fifth-generation program is a combination of objects. One advantage of OOP is that a programmer can code an object and reuse it within the same program or in another program. The first OOP language, SmallTalk, was created at Xerox PARC in 1972. Ada 95, OO-COBOL, Visual Basic, and C++ are other extremely powerful OOP languages.

Development Tools

Development tools are used by programmers to create large software programs. Some development tools include a programming language, and others are simply add-ins used with languages like C++ and Visual Basic. Borland's Delphi (which uses the Object Pascal programming language) and Powersoft's PowerBuilder are two frequently used application development tools.

Internet Languages

With the increase in Internet use, languages have been developed specifically for use with the graphical portion of the Internet, the World Wide Web. The Hypertext Markup Language (HTML) is a simple language that programmers use to describe how the contents of an Internet home page should be displayed on a computer screen. You can buy Web editing programs that help you use HTML easily, even if you're not a programmer; some word processors even include HTML editors. For dazzling effects, you need another of the new Internet-friendly languages, Java, which can be used to add animation and other effects to the text-only Internet pages created with HTML only. The "Hello, world!" program code written in Java is shown below.

```
Class HelloWorld {
   public static void main (String args [ ]) {
   System.out.println ("Hello, world!");
   }
}
```

There are reasons to learn a computer language, even if all the programs you want to use already exist. Computers respond to instruction in predictable ways, and programmers learn how to make the computer respond by following a set of instructions to complete a specific task. Knowing how programs are constructed also helps you to learn new software more easily and learn why software may "behave" (or "misbehave") in a certain way. There is no better way to understand computers than to take a good course in a programming language.

SECTION 6.3: APPLICATIONS SOFTWARE

All application software (or applications or, less formally, apps), requires an operating system. Many applications only run on one operating system. Other applications are available for more than one operating system—one version for the Macintosh, another for UNIX, another for DOS and Windows 3.1, and a fourth version for Windows 95 and Windows NT. The operating system required for a product is often included in the application name, as in Microsoft Office for Windows 95 or PageMaker for the Macintosh. Applications are broadly classified as business software, knowledge software, or entertainment software (see Figure 6.8).

■ Business Software

Business software includes two types of software: business systems software, and productivity software. **Business systems software** is designed to support the basic functions of a business, including financial functions, manufacturing functions, and client tracking functions. Business systems software is available in three different forms:

- Retail software, referred to as "off-the-shelf"

- Products developed for a specialized purpose and available through an authorized vendor or "solution provider"

- Custom software developed by an individual or firm

Off-the-shelf products are increasingly used in business. A businessperson can visit a computer store and buy QuickBooks for managing financial information and Gold Mine for tracking clients. Such products can generally be customized by adding company information. Off-the-shelf software has several distinct advantages: it's less expensive, it has already been tested on other

Figure 6.8
Application software diagram

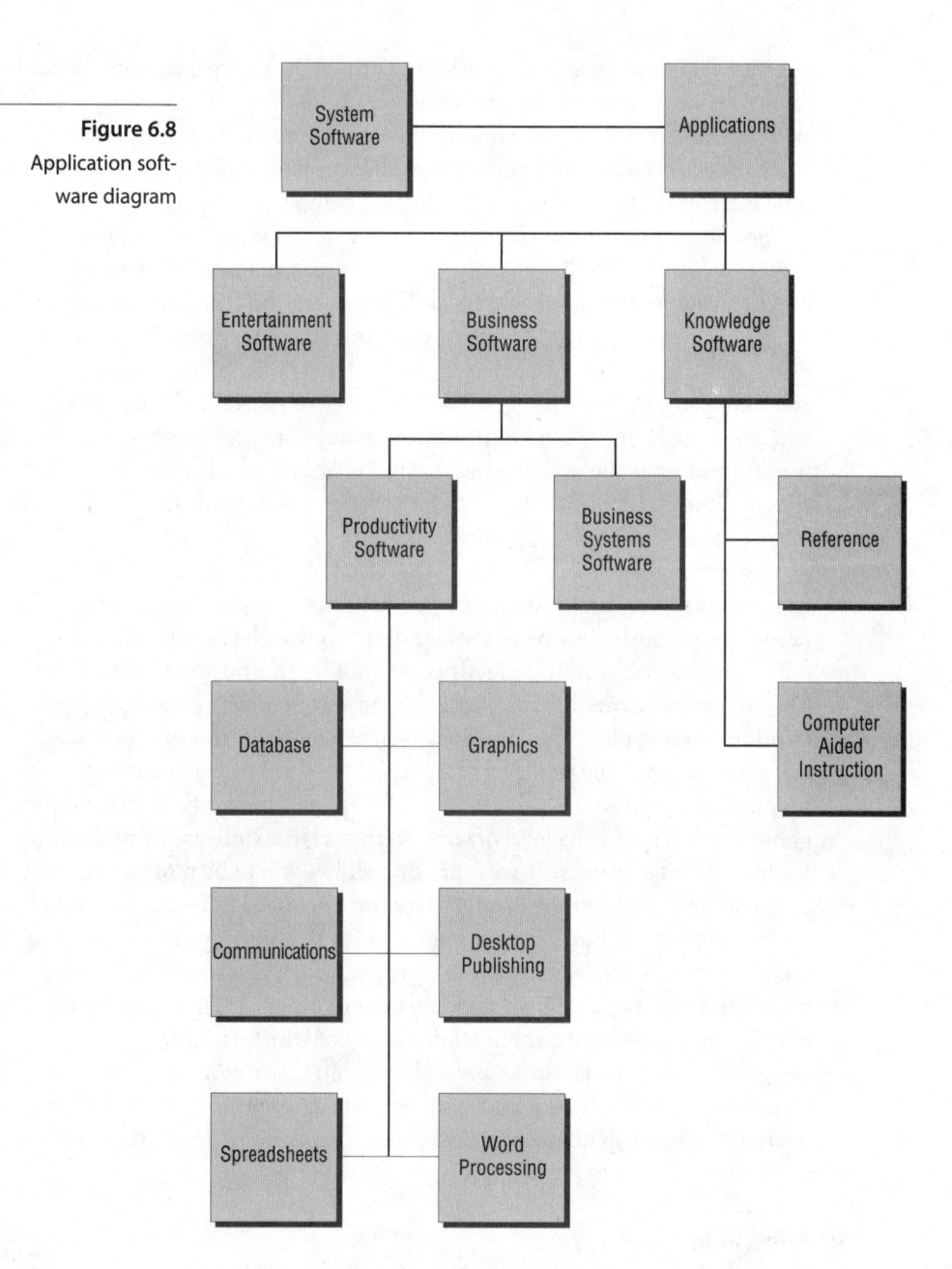

customers, and if the software is popular enough, supplemental materials like manuals and training disks may be readily available. The disadvantage of off-the-shelf software is that it lacks flexibility because it is written for businesses in general, not for a particular business. Ultimately, an organization is forced to "do business" in a way that the software supports, or get by without full software functionality. For example, if the payroll software a company purchases doesn't track compensatory time, the company will have to track comp time manually—or simply quit authorizing comp time.

Specialized products are like off-the-shelf products but allow a greater degree of customization. Typically, this software is installed by a trained installer, who interviews managers and employees and changes software settings to achieve a greater degree of customization. Solomon Software, a PC accounting software firm, has trained partners that sell and install Solomon's accounting packages. The advantage of specialized business systems software is that it can be customized to support the business rules and workflow of a particular company. But there are two disadvantages—higher cost, and the possibility that, even with customization, the software still won't fully support the way a company works.

Business managers can also hire programmers or computer consulting firms to create business system software designed specifically to meet the needs of their business. The advantage of this is that the finished software, properly designed, will be perfectly compatible with a business's functions. The disadvantages are the cost, both human and financial, of designing and creating a new application. A business will pay more for this one-of-a-kind software, and staff and managers can expect to spend time in meetings with programmers and analysts to identify software requirements. Also, most programmers can't offer the level of support that a large software company can.

Productivity software is software that allows you to be more productive and work more efficiently. Productivity software used to be the domain of the business office, but is increasingly used in the home environment. You use productivity software to create a product, such as a newsletter, an electronic presentation, a budget, a video, or a mailing list. There are thousands of different productivity applications, many of which fall into one of six categories—word processing, spreadsheets, databases, desktop publishing software, graphics software, and communications programs. The use of productivity software in homes and businesses is explored in depth in Sessions 8, 9, 10, and 11.

Knowledge Software

Knowledge software covers a range of applications, from tutorials on computer use to dictionaries and encyclopedias on CD-ROM or disk. You'll take a look at knowledge software in Session 7.

■ Entertainment Software

Entertainment software is, perhaps, the fastest growing segment of the software market, particularly when you realize that game machines are special use computers. Millions of dollars are spent on Sega and Nintendo cartridges each year. But many of us use our PCs as stress-reduction tools, playing games to unwind at the end of a busy day. Entertainment software is examined in Session 7.

The lines between the categories of software can easily become blurred. Increasingly, for example, games aimed at young children also include educational components, to encourage parents to purchase the software. A spreadsheet program may include graphics and database capabilities. A word processor might include communications software, so completed documents can be sent to coworkers through electronic mail. As software becomes more sophisticated, it has become quite common for single products to accomplish a variety of tasks.

SECTION 6.4: SOFTWARE DEVELOPMENT

While the terms *program* and *software* can be used interchangeably, there is a distinction between the two. A short piece of code that does one specific task is generally referred to as a program, while a package of programs that work together, like the programs that combine to form an operating system, is generally referred to as software. Using a programming language to write code is only one part of developing a comprehensive software package.

■ Development Teams

The early history of software development was characterized by the lone programmer working in a dark basement to create a best-selling PC software package. Today, almost all software development work is done by teams. Small development teams work to create games. Large teams, which can utilize hundreds or even thousands of programmers, create applications and operating systems. Development teams are formed to create systems using a particular system design methodology.

■ Systems Analysis and Design

There are different ways to approach software design, based on the intended use of the finished software. **Systems Analysis and Design** (Systems A & D) methodologies are often used to construct business software systems, including hardware and software. The Systems A & D methodology is a professional methodology; development teams using Systems A & D include analysts and programmers, and rarely include users.

Systems A & D uses a formal system development life cycle that is often modified for use in other, nonbusiness software development. The system development life cycle specifies a sequence of steps that are used to develop an information system:

- Problem recognition—the realization that there is a need to create a new information system or modify an existing system.

- Analysis—studying the existing manual or computerized system to determine the requirements for a new system.

- Design—researching and specifying hardware, programming languages, and tools that will be used to create the new system.

- Coding—writing programs for the new information system.

- Documentation—creating written materials for reference and user training.

- Testing—using the coded programs to ensure they comply with design specifications. Testing is often done by *piloting*, which means using the software and hardware on a limited basis and documenting and correcting design and coding problems.

- Implementation—installing the new system and, if necessary, converting existing data or systems.

- Maintenance—upgrading or repairing the new information system as required. If major changes are required, a new system development life cycle begins.

Programmers who specialize in Systems A & D are called system analysts or programmer analysts.

NOTE

There are different versions of the systems development life cycle that combine steps or break main steps into sub-steps. One international computer design firm uses a system development life cycle with over 50 steps.

Information Engineering

Another software development methodology is called **information engineering**. Developed in the 1980s, information engineering uses a four-step process to develop information systems:

- Strategic planning—reviewing the mission, goals, and objectives of the organization and determining the overall information system needed to support the plan

- Business analysis—analyzing the available data and current work practices

- System design—designing a comprehensive information system and communicating that design to users

- Implementation—creating and implementing the individual components of the information system

Unlike the system development life cycle, information engineering involves the new system's users in every step of development. Information engineering's strong ties to strategic planning make it attractive to business managers, and help ensure the final product will meet the actual strategic goals and objectives of the business.

Rapid Application Development, or **RAD**, uses the methodologies of information engineering to quickly create and implement new systems. A team that includes users is created to design the new system. Based on the skills of the users on the team, programmers and analysts may also be included, but some RAD systems have been created without the help of programming professionals. Development tools like Delphi that specifically support RAD are used by the team to create the system within a specified time frame.

SPECIAL TOPIC: SOFTWARE ETHICS

As you have learned in this session, software doesn't "grow on trees." Individual programmers or development teams invest time creating new software products for home and business use, and can copyright the results of their efforts. When a software product is completed and ready to be released, the developers have four different ways to make the software available to the public—as commercial software, shareware, freeware, or public domain software.

Most software is *commercial software*. When you purchase commercial software, you don't own the software; instead, you own a

SPECIAL TOPIC: SOFTWARE ETHICS (continued)

license to use the software under conditions specified in the license. Usually, the license is printed on the outside of a sealed envelope that contains the software CDs or disks. The envelope seal encourages you to read the license and states that you accept the conditions of the license when you break the seal to remove the software. The rights granted by the license vary, so you should read the license to make sure that you understand how the software may be installed and used.

Business software often grants an employee the license to use software at work or at home. For example, Visio Corporation's single user license lets you install Visio on one computer, but the primary user of that computer is allowed to make "a second copy for his or her exclusive use on either a home or portable computer." Personal software like games and instructional software is generally licensed for use on one machine, period.

Shareware is software that you can install and try out for a fixed period of time, generally 30 days. At the end of the trial period, you purchase a license to be able to continue to legally use the product. WinZip, a popular compression utility by Nico Mack, is available through the Internet for a trial period. Shareware is a good way for users to check out new software, and a convenient way for individuals and smaller software companies to make their products available to end users.

Freeware has been copyrighted by its developers, but anyone is allowed to use the software without paying a fee. Freeware has strong historical roots in the early history of microcomputers, when some programmers believed that all software should be free. (It helps to remember that this movement began just after the 1960s.)

Public domain software has no copyright, and is available for free use. The majority of the public domain software was developed by institutions like university computer departments. Some public domain programs are utilities that programmers can use in program development.

Software piracy is the making of illegal copies of commercial software or shareware. A Business Software Alliance (BSA) survey in 1994 estimated that software piracy worldwide cost software developers over $15 billion annually, with losses of nearly $3 billion in the United States alone. The survey reported that 35 percent of the software used in the United States is pirated software. Every time individuals make copies of software to give to their friends, they are pirating software.

Software manufacturers build safeguards into their products to make illegal installation more difficult, but they are increasingly relying on legal remedies. U.S. and international copyright laws provide stiff penalties (up to $100,000 per infringement) for copyright violation, and the BSA has 65 centers to investigate copyright violations. With so much at risk, many businesses and educational institutions have designed their information systems and personnel policies to insure compliance with copyright enforcement.

What You Have Learned

Software is one or more programs that a computer can understand. Application software allows users to complete specific tasks. Computers require system software to run; system software includes operating systems, devices drivers, utilities, and programming languages. Operating systems can be either text-based, such as MS-DOS, or graphical, like Windows 95. Device drivers help computers understand the specific needs of a peripheral hardware device. Utilities perform system tasks, such as formatting disks and managing files. Programming languages are designed to help programmers write instructions computers can understand. Systems analysis and design and information engineering are two methodologies used to develop software. When someone buys software, they are really buying a license to use the software and must comply with the restrictions of the license, including how many copies can be legally made.

Focus Questions

1. Identify the major classifications of software.

2. What is an operating system and what are two of an operating system's major functions?

3. What is the difference between a text-based OS and a GUI?

4. List one example from each of the five generations of programming languages and describe at least one of its characteristics.

5. List the three classifications of application software.

6. What is productivity software?

7. What are the eight steps in the system development life cycle?

8. What are the four ways to distribute software? Which way does software piracy most affect and why?

Knowledge Reinforcement

A. Should all software be in the public domain? Provide at least three reasons to support your position.

B. Find and read the license agreement of at least two commercial software products. What are their similarities and what are their differences? How many copies could you legally make of the software?

C. Why do you think some people prefer a text-based environment to a graphical one?

D. What operating systems are running on the computers at your school or your workplace? See if you can find out why they were chosen and if there are plans to change them.

Further Exploration

Blue Mountain Home Page (RAD technologies design):
http://www.bluemtn.com

Borland Corporation Home Page (RAD tools, including Delphi):
http://www.borland.com

Business Software Alliance Home Page (software piracy):
http://www.bsa.org

Fast Track to Visual Basic 4. Arthur Tennick. Sybex, 1996, 0-7821-1900-X.

Microsoft Corporation Home Page (Microsoft operating systems and programming languages, including Visual Basic and Visual C++):
http://www.microsoft.com

PART 3

Up Close and Personal

Vocabulary

- add-on
- computer-aided instruction (CAI)
- drilling-down
- hypertext link
- online help
- options
- search
- search results
- sims
- tutorial software
- zoom control

SESSION SEVEN

Family Computers: Knowledge and Entertainment

HOME COMPUTERS ARE FAST BECOMING the latest addition to the list of necessary home appliances. Whether the proliferation of home computers is a passing fad or a benchmark of the changing times will be largely dependent on how beneficial personal computers prove to be in the home environment. The focus of this session is knowledge and entertainment tools for the home computer. At the end of this session, you will be able to

- Identify the key issues related to the role of computers in the home
- Distinguish the types of reference resources available to home users
- Describe the characteristics of quality software for the home market
- Identify types of entertainment software

151

SECTION 7.1: NOT A COUCH POTATO ANYMORE?

The average North American watches between 15 and 30 hours of television per week. Watching television is, by definition, a passive pastime. (That is, of course, unless you classify channel surfing as activity.) But home computers threaten to change TV's passive dominance of our lives. Computers require a higher level of interaction than televisions. Whether you are playing a game, preparing for an exam, or researching your favorite hobby, computers require you to make choices, to become involved in directing the action, to think about what is happening and what you want to do. Many people are finding that spending time in front of their home computers is more rewarding than spending the same amount of time glued to a television. As these people add new games, reference tools, and educational packages to their computers, they fuel the growing market for many different types of home-based software.

Capturing an Audience

The home computer software market is quite competitive. Just like a television show, a software package designed for home use must be entertaining if it is going to survive. Best-selling software titles have a number of common features:

- *They are easy to install.* It can no longer be assumed that a computer user has a technical orientation. The instructions accompanying successful software are written for the new, nontechnical user—the users who still can't program their VCRs. The software's setup or installation routines are easy to follow, and it is easy to execute (run) the software after it is installed.

- *They have a well-designed user interface.* If the screen is crowded and hard to figure out, users lose interest quickly. A well-designed user interface is interesting to look at, graphically appealing, and understandable.

- *They use graphics and animation effectively.* Because people are easily bored with lots of text, the software must have graphics. Animation and video are becoming more common in home software, and they are welcome additions (as long as the hardware can support the amount of system resources the software demands).

- *They make effective use of audio.* Software can be enhanced through the use of sound and music. Of course, it can be overdone. Well-designed software will not use sound for the sake of sound; instead, it will use sound that enriches and energizes the software.

- *They have a quality help system.* Software used to be accompanied by printed manuals several inches thick. Dedicated users might plow through them, but most users were simply intimidated. Today, most software uses what is referred to as **online help**, help that can be accessed on-screen. Well written online help has easy-to-find answers that can get the user back to the task at hand quickly and efficiently.

SECTION 7.2: EDUCATIONAL SOFTWARE

We are used to learning by listening to someone give a lecture or by reading a book. Some people learn easily by these traditional methods, but many people need to approach learning differently. Visual learners are deeply affected by stunning visual displays, and absorb information most readily when it is demonstrated. Auditory learners respond quickly to sounds and music, and remember information easily when it has a catchy "soundtrack." Kinesthetic learners are drawn to movement—the movement of objects, or personal interaction with new information. Educational software is designed to teach learners of all types by engaging the learner interactively, and on their own terms.

Educational software is not limited to software used in schools, although there are a large number of products designed specifically for school use. Included in the category of educational software are

- Reference tools, including dictionaries, encyclopedias, medical references, and atlases.

- Computer-aided instruction or tutorial software, including tutorials to help you prepare for a standardized exam, learn a foreign language, or master skills you need to navigate the Internet.

- Educational simulations—software in which users manipulate a computerized model to see the impact of their choices. Common applications include urban planning scenarios, medical care, and science experiments.

A significant and growing number of the educational software titles available for the home market are being produced as CD-ROMs. The primary reason for this is that CD-ROMs have a large storage capacity. At about 600MB, one CD-ROM holds the equivalent of approximately 417 floppy disks!

Reference Tools

Thinking about using *reference tools* often conjures up memories of researching a topic for a school paper at the local library—visiting the card catalog, finding a Dewey decimal number, then searching through the stacks. If instead of books you wanted articles, you might head for the *Guide to Periodic Literature* and end your search by experiencing the joys of working with a microfilm reader.

Today, computerized reference tools have opened up a whole new world for the intellectually curious. And the exciting thing is that many of these tools are available for home users. Whether you need to complete a class assignment or plan your next vacation, there is a software product designed to meet your needs.

Encyclopedias the Easy Way

Since the fourth century B.C.E., when the Greek philosopher Speusippus, a disciple of Plato, assembled the first encyclopedia, people have turned to these massive storehouses of knowledge to explore subjects of interest. It is no wonder that one of the most popular reference tools available today is the electronic version of the encyclopedia. Electronic encyclopedias weigh less than their 21-volume bound counterparts, and they make even the most complex research an unabashed pleasure.

Electronic encyclopedias and other reference tools use three primary methods to help users access data. The most common method used to access data is the **search** method. Searching a computerized encyclopedia takes minimal effort and the rewards are significant. To search (or *find*), you enter keywords or phrases; within seconds the **search results** appear, providing a list of all references to your topic. Click on the reference you want to see, and the article will appear.

Many references provide graphic illustrations, audio, and video to accompany the text. As shown in Figure 7.1, rather than just reading about the women's suffrage movement, you can actually see the women of the 1920s marching to demand their right to vote. This multimedia approach to information makes history come alive in new and exciting ways.

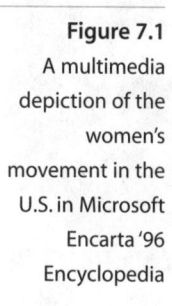

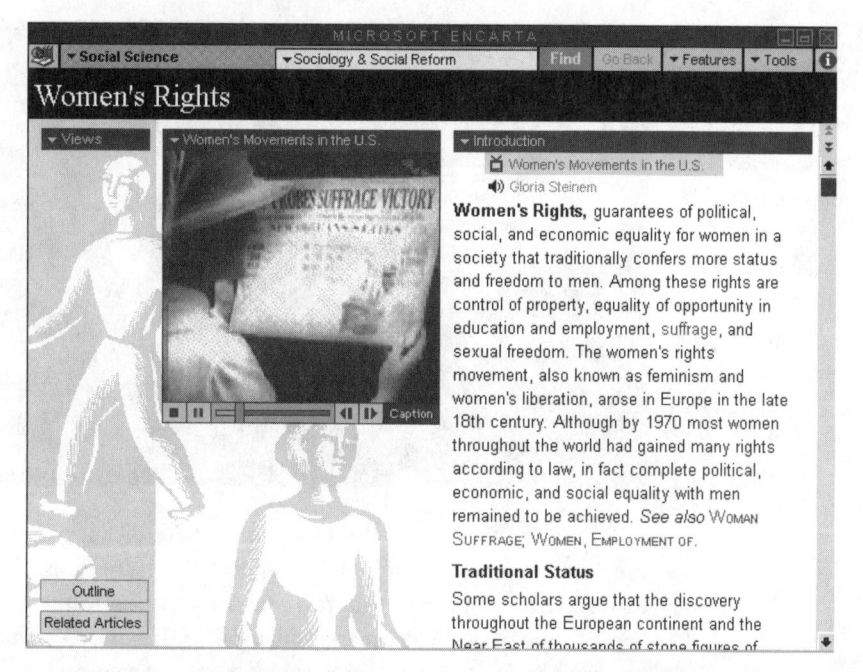

Figure 7.1
A multimedia depiction of the women's movement in the U.S. in Microsoft Encarta '96 Encyclopedia

As you're reading an article, you may find a word or phrase that is underlined and/or a different color than the rest of the text. For example, the word "suffrage," shown in Figure 7.1, is red in the Encarta article, indicating that it is a hypertext link.

A **hypertext link** (sometimes called a *hot link*) is a word or phrase that takes the reader to a related topic. Hypertext links are useful because, as human beings, we tend to think in nonlinear ways, and when we see something that catches our interest, we want to be able to pursue that topic immediately. Hypertext is a convenient way to provide nonlinear access to highly organized linear material.

Most encyclopedias and reference tools also have at least one additional method of accessing data—a list of major categories you can delve into. This approach is useful if you need help narrowing down your topic. For example, let's say you need to do a report for a zoology class, but you're not sure what topic to write about. If you have access to the New Grolier Multimedia Encyclopedia, you could use Grolier's Knowledge Explorer Index to explore the different parts of the natural world. From the Nature section of the Index, you could choose the Animal World, the Human Body, or the Plant World. If you choose the Animal World, as shown in Figure 7.2, you can watch a video on the animal world.

Figure 7.2
The Animal World video in the New Grolier's Multimedia Encyclopedia's Knowledge Explorer shows the evolution and interdependence of animals.

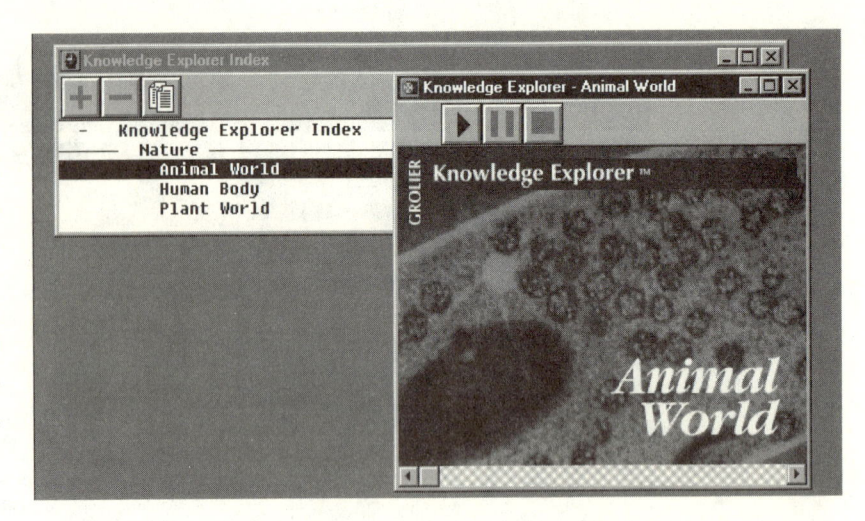

Similarly, if you wanted a look at global events happening at the time that the Sumerians were developing cuneiform, you could use Encarta's Timeline feature, shown in Figure 7.3. You can scroll through the timeline until you come to the period you are looking for—in this case, 3500 B.C.E. Then, you can click on the topic area you are interested in to see a brief article on that topic, or click on the hypertext links to see more extensive articles.

Figure 7.3
Use Encarta's Timeline feature for an overview of past civilizations: the greatest hits of 3500 B.C.E.

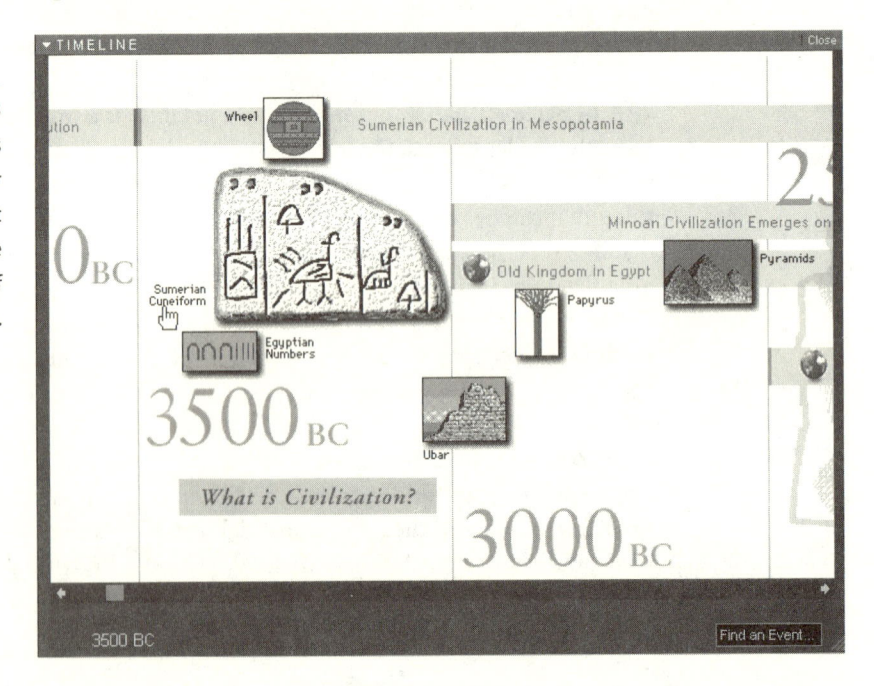

A Vast Library of Reference Tools

Electronic reference tools are not limited to encyclopedias. Software titles available for the home market include references for history, geography, science, biblical studies, national parks, birds, animals, cookbooks, health, and medicine.

The quality of information in these guides makes their paper counterparts seem a trifle lacking. For instance, identifying a bird using a traditional field guide usually requires a lot of guess work, but the National Audubon Society Interactive CD-ROM Guide to North American Birds lets you search for the bird by life zone, location, shape, color and size.

When you find the bird you are looking for, there are several photographs, a detailed description of the bird and its habitat, and recordings of bird songs and calls. This certainly beats the traditional field guides' attempts to describe bird sounds. (Did you know that an eastern meadowlark makes this sound—"tee-yah, tee-yair"? Or how about a yellow-bellied flycatcher—"pse-ck, pur-wee"?)

And what if you find the bird is renowned for its tender and succulent flesh? Preparing dinner is no problem with an electronic cookbook—just pull up your favorite recipe or search for something new and different. Enter a meal plan and the number of people you are feeding into software like Better Homes and Gardens Healthy Cooking CD Cookbook, and it automatically prepares a shopping list for you. And if you're concerned about nutrition, you can see the nutritional make-up of your dinner as well as the number of calories and grams of fat per serving.

Other types of electronic reference tools include telephone directories; guides to movies, music, and writing styles; and dictionaries. The American Heritage Talking Dictionary is a good example of the power of multimedia reference tools. How many times have you looked up a word in a dictionary and tried to figure out the pronunciation codes? If you use The American Heritage Talking Dictionary, not only would you find a definition and the complete etymology (root) for the word, but you can also click a button and have the dictionary pronounce the word for you.

Or what about those times when you can't remember what something is called—you know it's some kind of duck, but you can't remember its name. By using the Talking Dictionary's Word Hunter feature, you can see a list of all the words that have your search words in their definition. The more general the search text, the more choices you'll have. Figure 7.4 shows the results of a search on the word *duck*. Word Hunter found 72 definitions that contain *duck*—everything from *cold duck* to *Muscovy Duck* (the latter is known for its succulent flesh). Click on a term to see its definition.

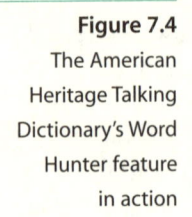

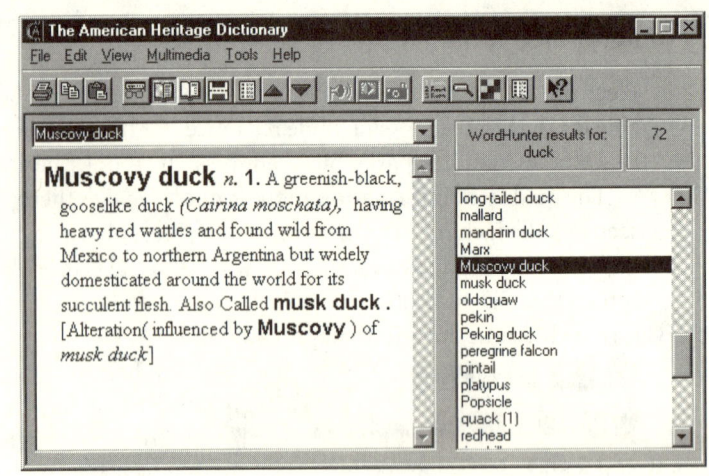

Figure 7.4
The American Heritage Talking Dictionary's Word Hunter feature in action

Another category of reference software gaining in popularity is atlas software. Atlas software is similar to two types of geographic productivity software: trip-planning software and mapping software. All three types generally present users with a large map. By clicking on an area of the map, users are allowed to see greater and greater detail. This technique, called **drilling-down**, is an effective point-and-click tool used in a variety of software packages. Another tool, called **zoom control**, allows users to adjust how much of the map they are seeing and the level of detail at any given time.

You can use the atlas to explore various countries. In the Rand McNally Quick Reference Atlas, you can drill down to a specific country, like Guatemala, and then see detailed information about the country including its history, politics, land, people, economy, and statistics, as shown in Figure 7.5.

Interactive Learning

The computer is also a great tool to help you to learn a new craft. Interactive learning tools come in many formats, one of which is **computer-aided instruction (CAI)** or **tutorial software**. CAI is software that helps the user learn a particular skill by having them interact with the computer. A primary characteristic of CAI is that it requires the user to enter information as they work toward mastering a skill. Although there are vast differences in particular CAI programs, most CAI tracks the user's progress through a series of drills, exercises, or assignments.

Mavis Beacon Teaches Typing is an example of CAI software for home use. After you "enroll" in Mavis's classroom, she puts you through a series of drills that teach you correct keyboard finger placement and improve your typing speed and accuracy. The software constantly analyzes how you are doing and

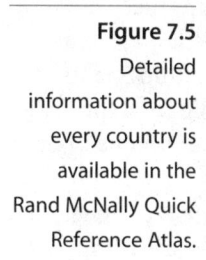

Figure 7.5
Detailed information about every country is available in the Rand McNally Quick Reference Atlas.

where you are experiencing problems, and custom-designs exercises that will address those problems. A typical classroom session is shown in Figure 7.6. Words appear on the screen that the student must type before time runs out. Meters on the left side of the screen measure accuracy, speed, and corrected speed. A clock keeps time while a metronome ticks, setting a rhythm. The results are saved and compiled into a report card that contains a number of graphs and charts, showing your progress over time.

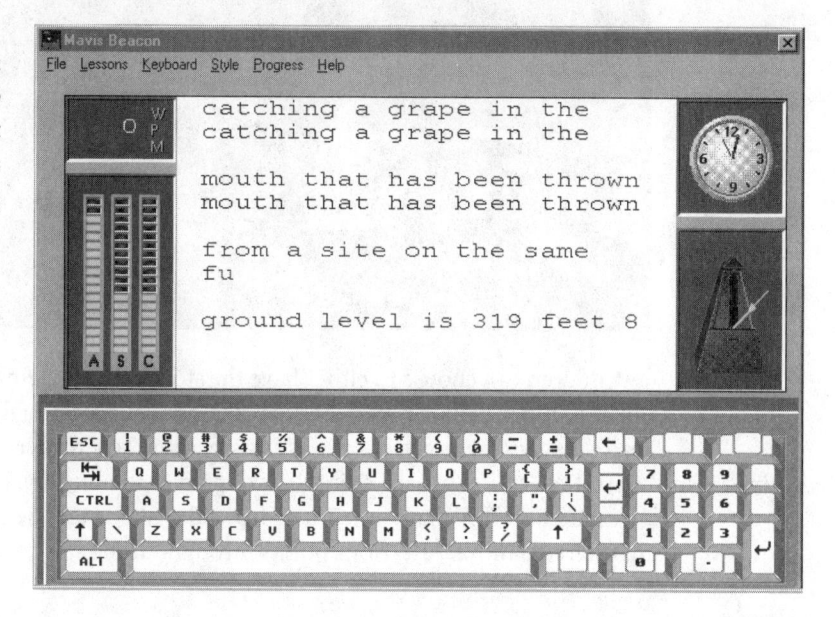

Figure 7.6
Taking a typing test with Mavis Beacon Teaches Typing

CAI software is also available for students studying for standardized tests like the SAT or the GMAT. These packages provide sample tests that are scored just like the real thing, helping students practice skills they are deficient in *before* taking the actual test. CAI products teach languages from Spanish to American Sign Language to computer languages. Each is designed to provide extra help for those who need it outside of the classroom, and in some cases, they can actually replace the classroom.

A completely different kind of interactive learning software is designed to help children practice basic reading and math skills while they are being entertained by computer animation. One of the finest examples, Disney's Toy Story Animated Storybook, shown in Figure 7.7, is a whole new type of children's story. Designed to help young children develop word recognition skills, build vocabulary, practice strategic thinking, and solve problems, Toy Story Animated Storybook is a book that has come alive.

Figure 7.7
The Toy Story Animated Storybook brings the story to life.

Children can choose to either have the story read to them by Hamm, the talkative piggy bank, or read the story themselves. Encouraging children to read the story themselves is an easy task because self-readers are allowed to control the action in each scene. Clicking on each object on the page produces a new trick—a toy that dances, a bedspread that changes designs, a mobile that starts to move. At various points throughout the story, users are presented with games and puzzles they must solve for the story to move on. In one scene, they must match a toy with a shadow of the same shape; in another, users follow verbal directions to identify toys by their color and size and then put them away in the proper location. All of the activities are intentionally designed to get children so involved in the game that they don't even realize they are learning. And Disney's animation is so sophisticated that you don't have to be a child to be attracted to Toy Story's visual appeal.

Other similar activity-oriented learning tools are designed to support specific elementary and junior high school subjects. The Oregon Trail and The Amazon Trail are designed for young people studying social studies. In both products, students are sent on an adventure steeped in historical facts and geographic information. They are given problems to solve and decisions to make while interacting with the local people, historical figures, and flora and fauna of the region.

In The Amazon Trail, adventurers head down the river with a cache of supplies, which they then trade for the things they need to get them through the dangers of the jungle. Guidebooks like the one shown in Figure 7.8 provide additional information as the adventure unwinds. This combination of adventure game and reference book makes software like The Amazon Trail popular among students and teachers alike.

Figure 7.8
The Amazon Trail guidebook helps students learn history, biology, and geography during an imaginary Amazon trip.

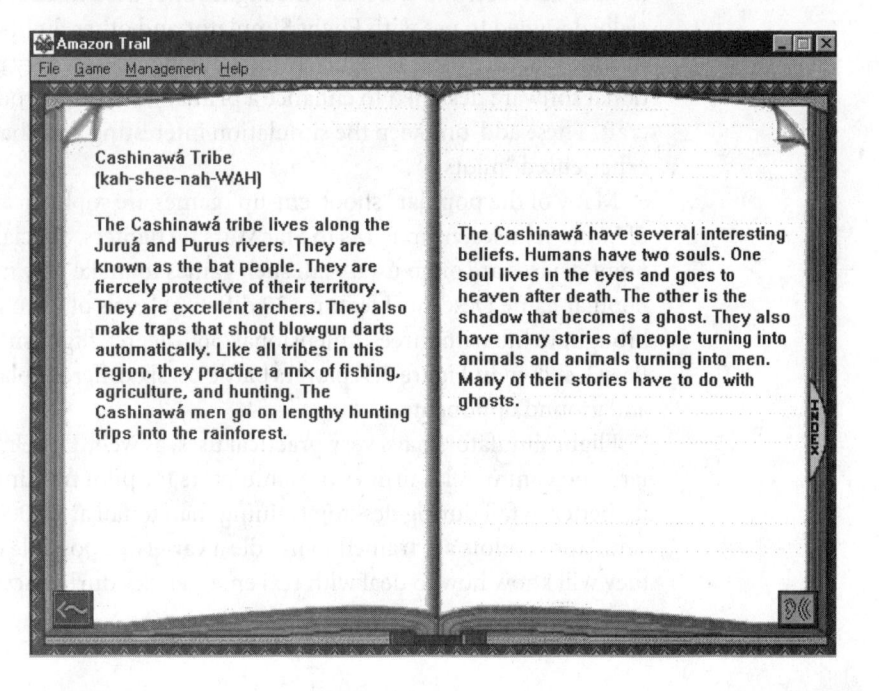

Educational Simulations

Educational simulations attempt to simulate a real-world situation, giving students an opportunity to see the impact of decisions, learn a skill, or experiment in safety. A growing number of educational simulations have been designed for use in school computer labs. These range from software that safely simulates chemistry experiments to biology software that allow students to "dissect frogs" without having to kill living creatures. Surgery simulations are gaining in popularity in medical schools for obvious reasons.

For home use, there are two popular simulation products that provide both fun and interactive learning: Microsoft Flight Simulator and Sim City 2000 by Maxis. While their merits may be debated by some, educational experts consider simulators valuable training tools for real-life situations, even if they are found in the games section in the software store.

Originally introduced for the Apple II, flight simulators are one of the oldest types of simulator software products on the market. In Flight Simulator, you fly a plane from one airport to another using all the controls and navigational tools of a real plane. Actual airport designs from major airports around the world, aerial views of real cities, and true-to-life implications of pilot decisions make Flight Simulator as close to the real thing as you can get. Input devices that look and work like the flight yokes used in aircraft have been specially designed to use with Flight Simulator and other flight-based software. In addition, Microsoft is regularly introducing new scenery **add-ons** (additional software designed to enhance a primary software product) and new aircraft. These add-ons keep the simulation interesting and challenging for experienced "pilots."

Many of the popular "shoot-em-up" games are sophisticated simulations of battle vehicles, from F-14s to Star Wars tie fighters. Special virtual reality input devices are often used with such games to make play more realistic. The popular game Descent II features 30 different levels of alien mine mazes brought to life with three-dimensional, 360-degree flight simulation. In Fury3, shown in Figure 7.9, players battle on six different planets, facing air and ground opponents.

Flight simulators have very practical uses, as well. The United States military and commercial airlines use simulators for pilot training, reasoning that it's better to fail during desktop training than to fail at 10,000 feet. Through simulation, pilots are trained to handle a variety of possible emergencies, so they will know how to deal with real emergencies during actual flights.

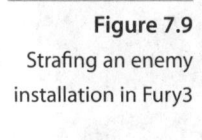

Figure 7.9
Strafing an enemy installation in Fury3

Another line of simulators is designed to show users the impact of decisions as they work to build suitable environments for people and other living creatures. SimCity 2000, shown in Figure 7.10, is an updated version of the classic Maxis product. Here, you assume the role of the mayor and city planner. You must make decisions about zoning, when and where to build hospitals, schools, police and fire stations, power plants, recreational facilities, roads, and public transportation, and a host of other elements of a city's infrastructure.

As mayor of a simulated city, you have to decide when the city needs an airport and how to fight crime. What is the impact of a military base near your city? Should you build a nuclear power plant? How can you improve exports to neighboring cities? All of these questions must be answered while you are dealing with unexpected disasters: fires, tornadoes, floods, and hurricanes. And you must build your city with the resources available. You make decisions about raising and lowering taxes on businesses, industry, and on the Sims themselves (the citizens of your fair city), and determine how much money each city department receives in its annual operating budget.

Figure 7.10
Planning and managing a community in SimCity 2000

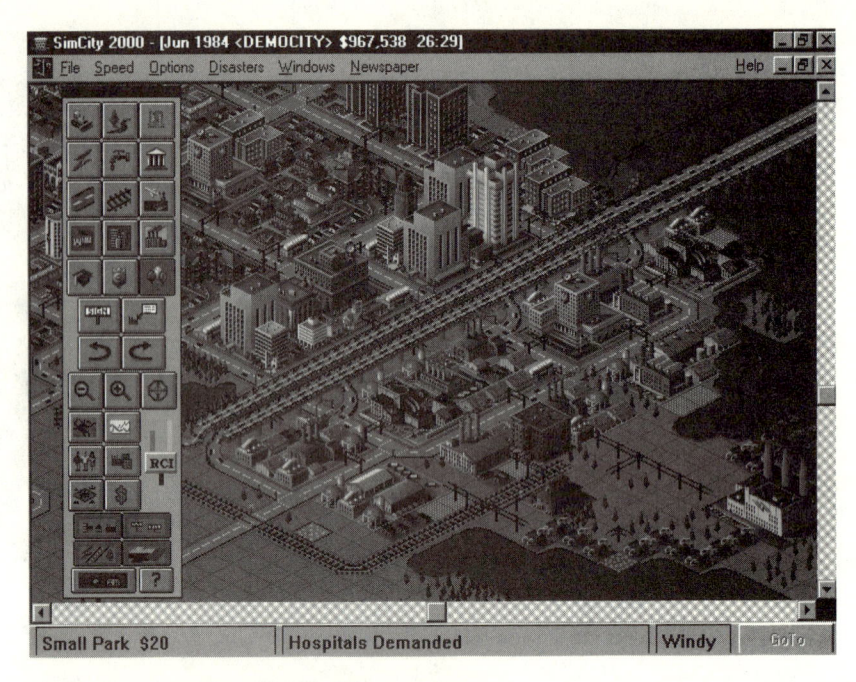

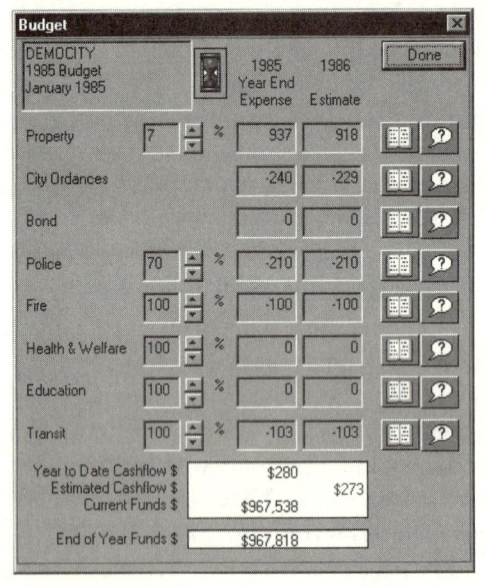

SimCity is so complex and realistic that it is used in environmental and city planning schools throughout the world. SimCity and other modeling simulators, often simply called **sims**, are appealing for several reasons. They are open ended, so you can work on your model city or ant farm for hours or months. And simulator time is adjustable, so you can make a year last for an hour—or ten seconds. If you're action oriented, you can turn up the speed and watch as new skyscrapers are constructed in seconds and neighborhoods deteriorate in the blink of an eye. But there's no hurry; you can also pause the simulator and spend infinite amounts of time building an infrastructure.

> *SimCity 2000 really brings your city—and its resident Sims—to life. If this game were any more realistic, it would be illegal to turn it off.*
>
> —Maxis

The original SimCity set a humor standard for sims, including touches like the scenario where Godzilla trashes Tokyo. Other successful sims work hard to meet this standard, including the latest sim, Afterlife: The Last Word in Sims, where users become "regional spiritual directors" of two synchronized sim realms: heaven and hell. Poor performance results in a visit from the Four Surfers of the Apocalypso. Other Maxis simulators include Sim Earth, Sim Farm, Sim Ant, Sim Isle, Sim Life, and Sim Tower. These products offer both casual and serious users hours of fun and challenge in this complex world of simulated planning.

There are also medical simulations, which have been popular since the battery operated surgery game, Operation. With the software program Theme Hospital, you become the administrator of a hospital, trying to balance patient care with hospital profits. Real-life medical simulations let you experience situations you can't experience in real life, like conducting open heart surgery. In the simulated operating room, no one asks if you're qualified; even if you've never driven past a medical school, you can pick up a scalpel and go to work. (The simulated patient screams if you forget anesthesia.)

Simulation software has both educational and entertainment value, which makes it particularly valuable as a model for both types of software. Good educational software always makes learning enjoyable, and meaningful entertainment software provides users with new challenges and skills.

SECTION 7.3: ENTERTAINMENT SOFTWARE

It may not be surprising that the number one use of a home computer today is entertainment: playing games. And games aren't just for youngsters. After a long day at work, adults like to come home, take their minds off of the stresses of the world, and be entertained. Computer games provide people with that option.

> *I wrote my first software program when I was thirteen years old. It was for playing tic-tac-toe.*
>
> —Bill Gates, The Road Ahead, 1995

From a programmer's point of view, computer games are the most difficult type of software to code. Best-selling games include action-triggered sounds, thematic music, intense graphics, and video. Many advanced computer courses use game programming projects to teach higher-level programming techniques. Entertainment software developers regularly have to solve problems most traditional programmers rarely encounter. For example:

- How do you make an object "explode" realistically? (For slow motion explosive excellence, see Microsoft Fury3.)

- What characteristics make an object look friendly? Intimidating? (Descent II uses a warm light blue for the friendly "Gobot" and vivid reds, greens, and navy blues for enemy robots.)

- How do you provide feedback and instructions for users who are too young to read? (Disney's Toy Story uses voice and easy-to-understand icons.)

- Can you create a game that has no instructions at all and still make it playable? (Yes. See the adventure game Myst.)

For many programmers, games are the ultimate challenge to their programming abilities. The next time you use entertainment software, take a moment to appreciate the programming skill displayed in the product.

Games also have a financial appeal for programmers. The business software market is dominated by large software corporations, making it difficult for individuals or small companies to launch a successful new word processor or spreadsheet. Gaming software can be created by small development teams, and successful games sell hundreds of thousands of copies. Programmers can still make a personal fortune creating games.

There are as many ways to categorize games as there are software stores. For ease of discussion, we'll divide games into six broad categories:

- Simulators, discussed in the previous section

- Arcade-style games

- Traditional games

- Puzzle games

- Adventure games, including 3-D "walkthrough" games

- Strategy games, including military strategy

- Sports games

As with movies, some software contains violence and mature themes. In 1994, the software industry established the Entertainment Software Rating

Board (ESRB) to avoid the imposition of an external rating system. The ESRB previews entertainment software and assigns a rating ranging from EC (suitable for early childhood) to AO (adults only) and includes content descriptors like "Mild Animated Violence" to explain the rating. While membership in the ESRB is voluntary, in its first two years the board rated over 1,500 pieces of software produced by more than 140 companies, and it has been widely praised by legislators, educators, and psychologists. If you're wondering about the rating of a particular piece of software, look for the ESRB label on the product's package, or call the ESRB at 800-771-3772.

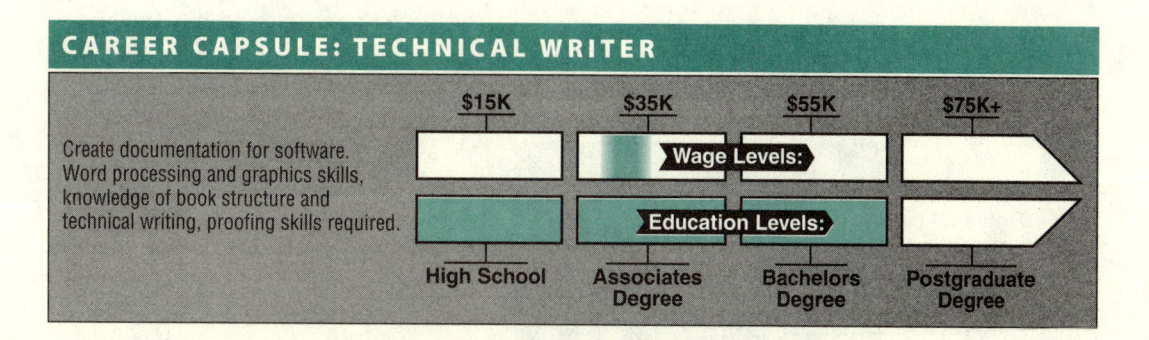

CAREER CAPSULE: TECHNICAL WRITER

Create documentation for software. Word processing and graphics skills, knowledge of book structure and technical writing, proofing skills required.

Wage Levels: $15K – $35K – $55K – $75K+

Education Levels: High School – Associates Degree – Bachelors Degree – Postgraduate Degree

■ Arcade-Style Games

During the 1980s, the "arcade decade," arcade games made use of powerful, special-use microprocessors to provide sound and graphics action. Games like Centipede, Defender, Missile Command, Donkey Kong, and Q-Bert were available for home computers or gaming systems, but the versions with realistic sound and graphics were housed in arcades. The improved hardware in home PCs has moved arcade games into the family room. Recently, game manufacturers have begun reviving 1970s and 80s arcade games and releasing them on CD-ROMs with improved graphics and sound. PC Pinball games like Pinball Arcade are also increasing in popularity. In the meantime, the number of arcades declines each year as more game players prefer to play in the comfort of their homes on their own PCs.

■ Traditional Games

Before computers, there were board games and card games. These traditional games have been adapted for PC play. Microsoft Solitaire, included with all versions of Windows, is thought to be the single most played game on personal computers. (It's there, it's free, why not?) Many other card games are available as well, including other versions of solitaire, hearts, bridge, blackjack, and poker, as are PC versions of popular board games like Scrabble, checkers, and Monopoly.

Some traditional PC games merely resemble their traditional counterparts; others include animated pieces or other special effects. The first microcomputer chess machine, Chess Challenger, was released in 1977. The characters were recognizable: black pieces, white pieces, and a black-and-white checked board. Other PC chess games followed, including Chess Master and Battle Chess, an animated chess game with fantasy characters including giants and trolls. Chess Wars: A Medieval Fantasy features three-dimensional pieces, digitized sound, and full-motion video. In Figure 7.11, the Black King battles a White Pawn as the result of a user move in Chess Wars. For more information on the history of computerized chess, see the Special Topic at the end of this session.

Figure 7.11
Chess pieces battle for board dominance in Chess Wars.

Puzzle Games

Puzzle games for the personal computer include crossword puzzle software, on-screen jigsaw puzzles, and more active games like Pipe Dream and Minesweeper. Puzzle games rely on the ability to form relationships between words, puzzle pieces, shapes, or numbers—the software equivalent of Rubik's Cube.

One of the best-selling puzzle games of all time is Tetris (see Figure 7.12). The goal of Tetris is to completely fill a row on the screen so it will be removed from the playing field. As shapes drop from the top of the screen, the Tetris player rotates the shape and moves it into place, then drops it to try to fill a row. Since Tetris uses shapes, no reading skills are involved, making this a game for all ages. Unlike many games that only require response to an easily

Figure 7.12 Puzzle games like Tetris can help users improve their spatial and decision-making skills.

memorizable sequence of events, Tetris drops pieces in a random fashion, so players must learn to respond to each piece—a higher level skill than simple memorization.

Adventure Games

Do you long to travel to new and interesting places on a quest for knowledge or treasure? Travel to your closest computer software store and ask for directions to the adventure games. There are adventure games that take place in the United States, Europe, Asia, on moon colonies of the future, in dungeons and caverns, in worlds that only exist in the imagination, and in places you'd be fairly sure were adventure free—like modern bureaucracies.

Every adventure game has a goal: rescue the princess, free the hostages, discover the hidden treasure, or escape to yet another world. In some games, players adopt personas or characters that have special attributes of strength, intelligence, or guile. Players choose how they will interact with the objects, characters, or creatures encountered in the scenario as they work toward the goal.

These games are the direct descendants of Dungeons & Dragons. Some of these fantasy adventure games can be played on the Internet or computer networks, becoming multiplayer adventure games where players' characters meet and join forces to complete a quest. Despite the fact that many multiplayer adventures still use a text-based interface, these games have a special appeal, because they involve interaction with other players' characters, adding unknown human elements to the game.

Myst is real. And like life, you don't die every five minutes. In fact you probably won't die at all.

—*Myst Documentation*

The adventure game Myst, created by Cyan, Inc. and marketed by Broderbund, has been a best-selling game since it was released in 1994. Designed by brothers Robyn and Rand Miller, Myst is visually rich and intellectually stimulating. The Cyan development team spent months creating the worlds of Myst, using Stratovision software to create a specialized terrain for each world. Although nothing in Myst would offend young players, this is clearly an adult adventure, rewarding reasoned action with yet another artistically amazing world to explore. A scene from the island is shown in Figure 7.13.

Figure 7.13
Island boardwalk from Myst

■ Military and Strategy Games

Strategy games, including military games, have seen increasing popularity in the past few years. New standards for strategy and conquest games have been set by the games Warcraft, Conquest of the New World, and Civilization I and II. Military strategy games are a combination of simulation and adventure games. Players command battalions or armies within a scenario, usually drawn from history. TalonSoft's critically acclaimed Battleground series includes software for famous battles from U.S. and world history like Shiloh,

Gettysburg, and Waterloo. Close Combat uses a string of battles from the Second World War, beginning with Omaha Beach. These and other best-selling military strategy games are reviewed by historians for accuracy of characters, movement, chronology, and terrain.

Not all strategy games are historically accurate, but that doesn't make them any less engaging. In Civilization II (successor to the best selling Civilization software), players build cities, command armies, send and receive diplomats, construct the Hanging Gardens and other wonders of the world, and devise new technologies. Players choose a personal empire and control its development. Neighboring empires may declare war or trade alliances, and after a few hours of play you cease to be disturbed by the fact that your Aztec empire's closest neighbors are the Mongols and the Babylonians.

Sports Games

Sports enthusiasts can find software for almost every professional and amateur sport, with the possible exception of the Scottish caber toss. Since professional sports draw the largest audience, there are a bevy of NBA, NFL, NHL, and major league baseball games where players choose teams and individual players to control during game play. Some game packages are updated annually following a sport's draft and free agency period so team rosters are accurate. Some sport games include brief tutorials to help the player with their game, teaching them, for example, how to become a better golfer or improve a tennis serve.

What You Have Learned

Quality software packages share some common characteristics, including ease of installation and use. Educational software and entertainment software are two types of programs created for the home market. Educational software includes reference software and computer-aided instruction software like tutorials. Entertainment software includes different types of games, many of which could also be classified as knowledge software.

Focus Questions

1. What are the common features of best-selling software packages?
2. How does CAI software differ from other educational software?
3. What are sims?

4. What is a search criteria? What type of educational software uses search criteria?

5. Why is entertainment software a challenge for programmers?

Knowledge Reinforcement

A. While membership in the ESRB is voluntary, some large chain stores like Wal-Mart now require an ESRB seal on all software they purchase for resale. What do you think are the financial implications of this decision for small software development companies? What effect do you think Wal-Mart's decision will have on the entertainment software industry?

B. What kinds of reference software would you be inclined to purchase? Why?

C. What types of skills can't be learned completely from educational software? Could software be developed to help build these skills?

Further Exploration

CD Magazine Online (reviews of CD-ROM-based entertainment software):
http://www.cdmag.com

Deep Blue vs. Kasparov:
http://www.chess.ibm.park.org

Entertainment Software Rating Board:
http://www.esrb.org

In-Vehicle Map Systems, International Map Trade Association:
http://www.maine.com/maptrade

The Road Ahead. Bill Gates. Viking Penguin, 1995, 0-670-77289-5.
Bill Gates's personal vision of what the future holds in store for us. An interesting and informative guide to computers of today and tomorrow.

SPECIAL TOPIC: MIND GAMES

Alan Turing used chess as an example of the type of activity that could be completed by a Turing Machine. The first computer chess program was coded in 1957. In 1966, scientists in the USSR and the U.S. pitted their chess programs in a one-on-one tournament. (The Soviet program won.) But, as Han Solo would say, "Good against the living?—that's another thing."

It would seem that a chess game would be an easy program to code, especially when you look at the flashy, high-speed games created today. After all, it's a small board, with only 64 squares and 16 pieces per team. But chess, unlike many other games, has infinite combinations of "winning moves" based on the strategies of the players and previous moves within a game. As programmers spent increased time on chess code, they realized that the complexity required for a program able to beat world class grandmasters was close to human intelligence.

Programmers continued to develop chess programs and enter them in chess tournaments, but it wasn't until 1977 that any computer chess program could beat a grandmaster in even one game. In 1988, the Deep Thought program shared the first prize at the U.S. Open chess tournament with a human grandmaster. The next year, Russian chess champion Garry Kasparov beat Deep Thought in both games of a two-game match.

For the next six years, programmers worked to create a chess program that could best Kasparov. In February, 1996, the Association for Computing Machinery held a seven-game tournament in Philadelphia. The half-million dollar purse included $400,000 for the winner, and the balance to the loser. Deep Thought's successor, IBM's Deep Blue, features eight CPUs and is capable of considering over 40,000,000,000 possible moves in the three minutes included in each turn. Despite Deep Blue's firepower, Kasparov won, four games to two.

SESSION EIGHT

Productivity at Home

Vocabulary

- cell
- cell address
- clip art
- communications software
- computer-aided design (CAD)
- database
- desktop publishing
- digital camera
- digital photograph
- editing
- field
- file extension
- filter
- formatting
- formula
- integrated
- office suite
- online bill paying
- personal financial management software
- query
- record
- render
- spreadsheet
- text insertion
- word processor
- word-wrap

Although increasing knowledge and reducing stress are two valuable uses for home computers, more and more people want to be able to accomplish something tangible with their computers. Whether you want to write a letter, keep track of your daughter's soccer team roster, manage household finances, create a flyer for a yard sale, or design a house, you'll use productivity software to do it. Productivity software for the home is a burgeoning market. At the end of this session, you will be able to

- Name the major categories of home productivity software
- Delineate the major tasks and common features of word processor, spreadsheet, and database software
- Define the role of personal financial management software
- Describe the hardware necessary to create multimedia documents

175

SECTION 8.1: THE BIG THREE

In 1979, WordStar, a word processing program, was developed by Seymour Rubenstein and his company MicroPro. WordStar, used to create letters and other documents, was an instant success and gave many people a reason to buy a personal computer for home use. The same year, Visicalc and SuperSort were released. Visicalc was a spreadsheet, used to work with numerical data. SuperSort was a data management program or database.

AppleWorks, developed for the Apple II, included a word processor, spreadsheet, and database sharing a common user interface—the first combination of the "big three" applications available to the personal computer user. **Communications software**, software which allows personal computers to interact with each other over telephone lines, eventually expanded the "big three" to four major categories.

Today, application software contains many categories and subcategories. Productivity software is one branch, usually classified under business software. (Refer to Figure 6. 8 for a review of the categories of applications software.) However, the desire to be able to produce home and family oriented products has created an entire (and very large) market for productivity tools specially designed for home use.

Word Processors

When most people look at a keyboard, they think "writing." A **word processor** is primarily a writing tool. In some ways, writing with a word processor is similar to writing with a typewriter; in other ways, it is quite different. The similarities begin with the use of a keyboard and end with the output of a printed document. The differences include everything in between.

There are two ways to write with a typewriter. Either you knows exactly what you are going to say because you wrote it out first in long-hand, or you tear page after page out of the typewriter, ending up with a wastebasket full of mistakes and previous drafts. On the other hand, a word processor is a dynamic writing tool. You can type whatever comes to mind and then edit, rearrange, and delete to your heart's content. You never have to print the document until you are completely satisfied with its contents.

Word processor programs have grown from simple text editors such as WordStar to full-featured software programs with many of the capabilities of desktop publishing software. One of the most common word processors for the home, shown in Figure 8.1, comes as part of the Microsoft Works software suite. It includes most of the features needed by home users, including spelling and clip art.

Figure 8.1
Microsoft Works 3.0 word processor

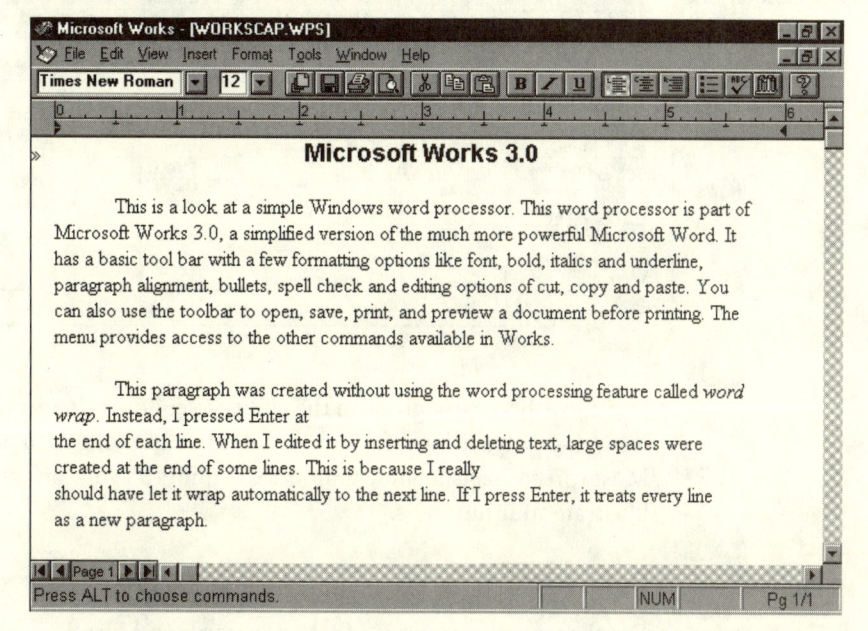

Spreadsheets

Spreadsheets are to numbers what word processors are to words. Adding, subtracting, multiplying, dividing, finding averages, calculating percentages, and even finding the future value of your money are things spreadsheets do best. A spreadsheet, shown in Figure 8.2, is the electronic equivalent of the accountant's ledger with columns and rows of figures, but its use extends well past the boundaries of accounting to science, engineering, and other fields that require numerical analysis.

The intersection of a column and a row is called a **cell**. Each cell has a **cell address**, the designation of the column and row the cell is in. Calculations are made by entering a **formula** into the cell where you want the results of a calculation. For example, in Figure 8.2, the formula for the total income is =SUM(D4:D8). Translated, that means "this cell equals the sum of cells D4 through D8."

Figure 8.2
A Microsoft Works spreadsheet

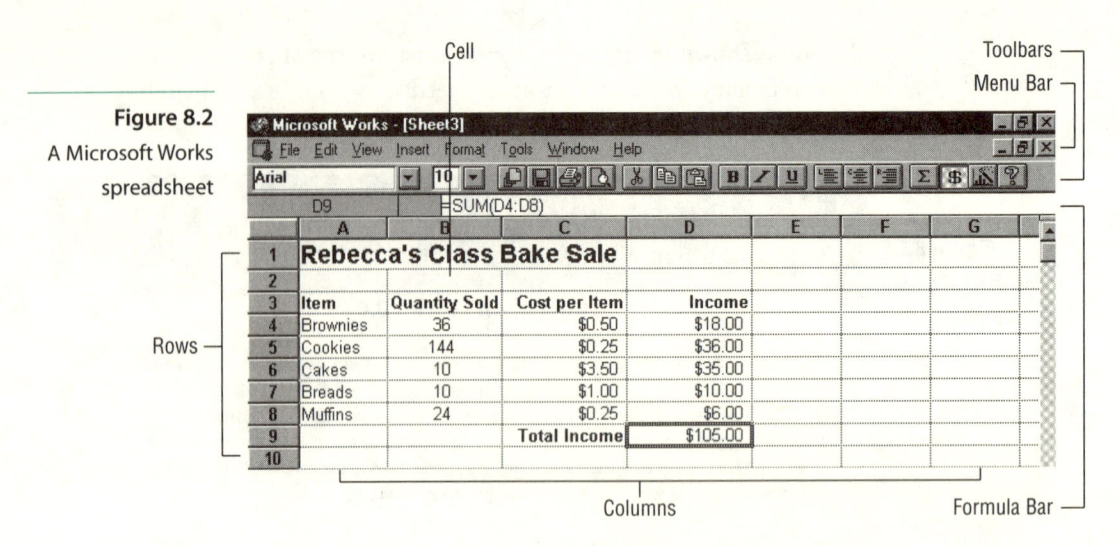

[Screenshot of Microsoft Works spreadsheet "Rebecca's Class Bake Sale" with labels: Cell, Toolbars, Menu Bar, Rows, Columns, Formula Bar. Data shows Brownies 36 $0.50 $18.00; Cookies 144 $0.25 $36.00; Cakes 10 $3.50 $35.00; Breads 10 $1.00 $10.00; Muffins 24 $0.25 $6.00; Total Income $105.00]

Spreadsheets also give you the ability to conduct financial and statistical analysis—helpful stuff if you're a student or applying for a home mortgage. Most spreadsheets include graphics capability so you can create charts that illustrate your numbers.

Databases

Databases are collections of related records and files. For example, a telephone directory is a printed version of a database. A category of data—such as first name, last name, street address, or city—is called a **field**. The complete telephone listing for one person is a **record**, which is all of the information related to one entity.

Databases can be used to keep track of any type of list or collection. You are quite familiar with paper-based databases: address books, recipe card files, and membership lists are all databases. And you saw a variety of electronic databases when you learned about knowledge software in Session 7. Encyclopedias, dictionaries, and other electronic reference tools are all databases, too.

Electronic databases allow you to not only keep track of information but to search for it in different ways. Let's say you were working on a campaign for a local politician and wanted to invite everyone in your neighborhood to a fund-raising party. You could go door-to-door and invite everyone personally (which actually wouldn't be a bad idea!), or you could sit down with the phone book and, page by page, select all the people who live on your street, which would be a trifle tedious. However, with electronic phone books such as Phone Disc or Select Phone, you can just enter your street address and zip code and instantly see a list of all your neighbors.

Databases provide you with incredible flexibility to put data to work for you in ways a paper record-keeping system never could. One of the biggest advantages of using a database application to record data is the ability to create forms for data entry, such as the home inventory form shown in Figure 8.3. If you have a lot of fields and a lot of records, it's significantly easier to focus on one record at a time if you can see it all on one easy-to-read form.

Figure 8.3
Home inventory database form

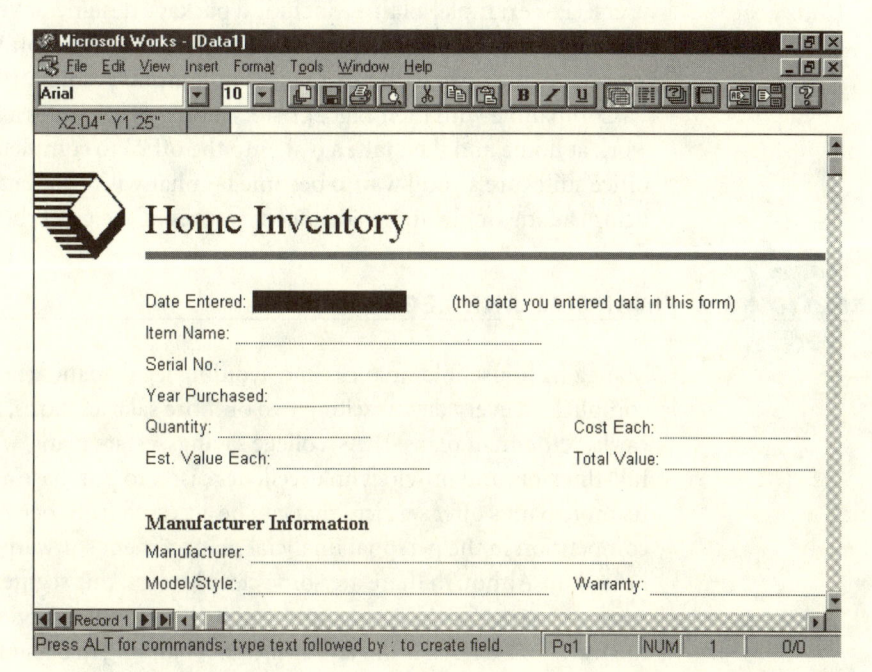

Once you enter the data into the home inventory database, you can sort the records by the year purchased, the value, or any combination of fields. You can also **query** the records so that you can develop a report showing only the items you purchased after 1995 or that cost over $1,000. Querying records means asking a question of the data so that only the data which meets established criteria is shown.

An Office Suite at Home

An **office suite** is a collection of office tools that includes a word processor, a spreadsheet, and other applications. Office suites are **integrated** products, which means they share a common user interface and are designed to work well together. For instance, if you create a list of names and addresses in a suite's database, the list can easily be combined with a document in the word processor to send out personalized letters. Once you learn one application in a suite, you are well on your way to knowing the fundamentals of all of the applications.

The three major office suites on the market today are Microsoft Office, Corel WordPerfect Office, and Lotus Smart Suite. Primarily designed for business use, these include many features that are not typically used by home users. (For example, all three include a package designed to create electronic presentations.) Scaled down office suites, such as Microsoft Works and Perfect Works, are included with most personal computers sold for home use.

Compatible with their bigger sisters, home office suites allow users to start work at home and then take a disk into the office to complete the job. Home office suites are a good way to become familiar with productivity software before taking on the more advanced features of the powerhouse suites.

SECTION 8.2: FINANCIAL AND LEGAL

Managing household finances and avoiding legal quandaries become more complicated every day. Tracking two or more salaries, taxes, mortgages, credit cards, retirement plans, IRAs, college savings, estate plans, wills, and trusts is a full-time job, and provides an excellent reason to purchase a home computer. As more banks offer services that can be accessed from personal computers, competition in the personal financial management software market has heated up. Although there are some clear leaders, this segment of the home software market is changing rapidly now that Internet services have entered the fray. (You'll learn more about Internet banking in Session 14.)

Financial Management

Financial management software is a type of database software. The first financial management packages were nothing more than glorified checkbooks. If you could add and subtract on your own, they served no real purpose. In contrast, today's **personal financial management software** is invaluable not only for tracking income and expenses but for analyzing where your money is going; paying your bills quickly, easily, and on time; and planning for your financial future.

Without a doubt, the most difficult part of using an electronic financial manager is remaining disciplined about using it. Many people start the year full of good intentions, but by March or April the commitment has died and so have the entries. For personal financial management software to be useful, then, it must make entry easy and relatively painless. Quicken by Intuit, shown in Figure 8.4, is by far the best selling and most comprehensive package on the market. Quicken's user interface is so well designed that programmers use it as a standard to measure the functionality of interfaces they develop.

Figure 8.4
Balancing your checkbook in Quicken

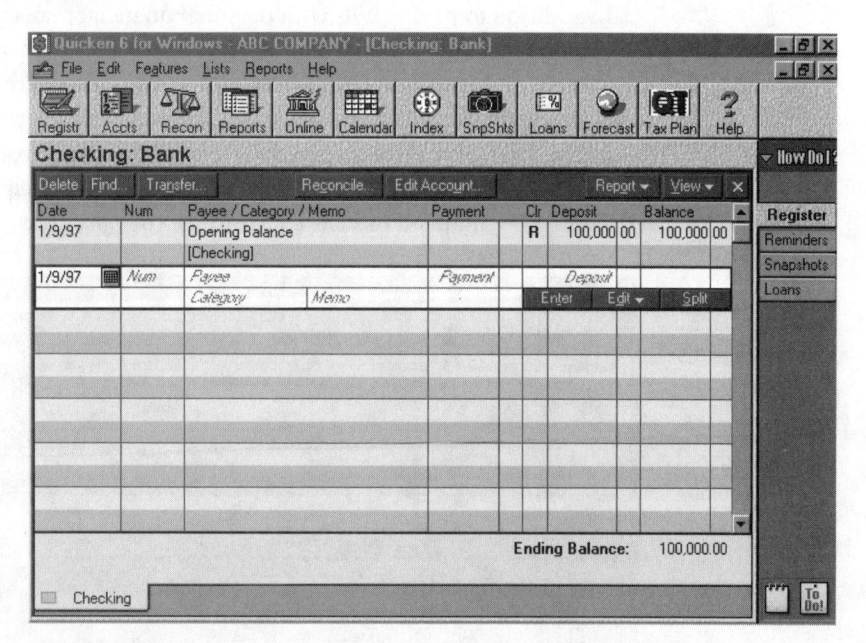

Personal financial management software allows you to set up a category list (or in bookkeeping terms, a chart of accounts) so you can track expenses by category. With a category list, you can assign expenses to a particular category: automobile, entertainment, clothing, groceries. You can even assign expenses to subcategories: gasoline, dining, and so on. At the end of the month, you can see how much you spent in each category, and can compare your totals to the previous month or the same month last year.

Although you can use personal financial management software simply to track your finances, you can also use it to print checks directly from your computer or to pay your bills online. **Online bill paying** is a banking service that allows you to connect via modem to a banking institution and pay bills with electronic transfers. If your creditors can't receive funds electronically, then the bank prints a check and sends it for you. There is a monthly fee for the service, but if you calculate the savings in checks and postage, it generally works out to your advantage. Some people are reluctant to use online bill paying services, feeling more comfortable knowing that "the check is in the mail." Despite this, financial institutions and financial software companies are positioning themselves to be ready when consumer demand for the service kicks in. Quicken and Microsoft Money, the two leading financial software packages, are already configured to make use of online bill paying.

In addition to paying bills with personal financial management software, you can track loans and interest, calculate mortgage payments, estimate retirement savings, set up household budgets, and compare actual expenses to budgeted expenses. You can also establish savings goals for your next vacation, a new car, or whatever else you intend to buy. Once you have entered all your hard-earned cash, you can then access a variety of helpful reports, shown in Figure 8.5, and print or view charts to see your progress.

Figure 8.5
Quicken's Report window provides users with options to customize built-in reports.

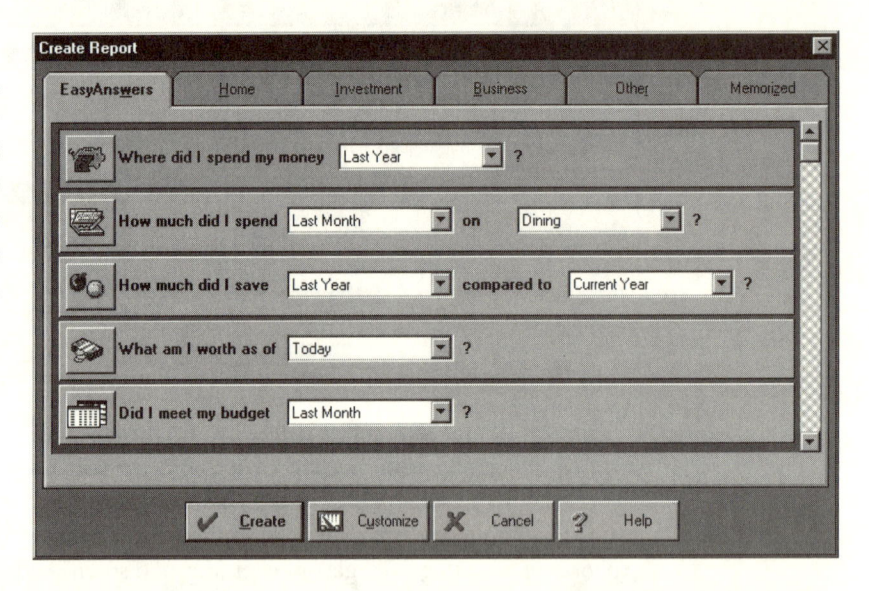

One of the most beneficial features of personal financial software is help with tax preparation. When you set up income and expenses categories, you simply designate if each item is tax related. You can even tie an expense to a specific line of a U.S. income-tax form. When tax time rolls around, you can print a report that shows all of your tax-related items by category—charitable expenses, medical expenses, mortgage interest, income tax withholding—and then enter the amounts directly on your tax forms.

■ Tax Preparation Software

Tax preparation software has become so common that the Internal Revenue Service allows you to file your return electronically. If you use Quicken throughout the year and then choose Intuit's tax preparation software, TurboTax, preparing your taxes is easier than ever. TurboTax imports all of your tax-related information directly from Quicken, so all you have to do is review it for accuracy, add anything you might have missed, and send it on its way.

Even if you haven't used personal financial management software throughout the year, electronic tax preparation software makes a lot of sense. Tax preparation packages are developed by financial and tax experts and help make sure you are getting all of the deductions you deserve. Many of the programs have built in audit flags to alert you to items for which you need to have adequate documentation. TurboTax even walks you through an interview process just as if you were meeting with a professional tax preparer. You just answer questions, as shown in Figure 8.6, and all the forms are filled out for you by the software. If your answer to a particular question means you need to complete an additional form, TurboTax lets you know and helps you prepare the form.

Figure 8.6
An interview with TurboTax

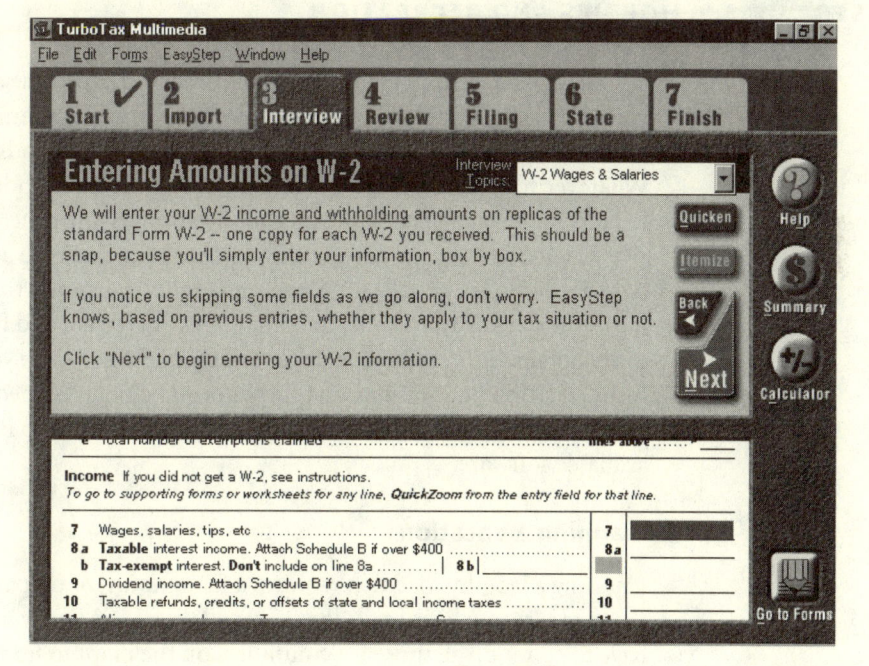

For most people, income tax preparation will never be one of the highlights of the year. However, using a personal financial manager throughout the year spreads the misery across all twelve months. All of a sudden, April 15th just becomes another beautiful spring day.

Electronic Legal Help

In addition to financial help, there are home software products that make common legal issues easier to handle. You can use software to set up a will or a living trust and draw up simple legal contracts, such as a personal loan agreement. Software such as WillMaker and Living Trust Maker by Nolo Press provide step-by-step instructions using an interview format similar to TurboTax.

Other software is available that contains predesigned forms and agreements for common legal contracts you can use when renting a home, hiring a contractor, or selling a piece of property. Even if you have an attorney review your computer-generated wills and legal agreements to ensure compliance with local, state, or provincial regulations, legal packages still lower your legal expenses by decreasing the time your attorney has to spend drafting documents.

SECTION 8.3: HOBBIES AND RECREATION

You've worked hard all day and now it's time to come home and do the things you want to do. For some people, leisure time is spent planning their next vacation. For others, leisure means figuring out how to landscape the yard. Whatever your interests are, a number of new software products are available to help you make the most of your hobbies and leisure time.

A lot of shareware and freeware is written specifically to address a specific hobby: baseball card collecting, arts and crafts, sports and fitness, dog training, or horseback riding, just to name a few. Shareware and freeware are most easily obtained through a special interest group devoted to your passion or through a club or organization to which you belong. Ask people who share your hobby, and you'll more than likely find someone who is familiar with available software.

Planning a Vacation

Planning a lengthy road trip requires a fair amount of preparation. You have to make sure you have maps that cover all the places you want to visit. You have to count up all those little numbers on the maps to find out how far you'll be traveling and how long it's going to take. You have to calculate how far you want to drive each day, research lodging options, and make reservations. You need to contact various travel bureaus to find out what special attractions are in the area that you may want to visit.

Once you realize that most accidents occur within 30 miles of home, every day starts to look like a good day for a long trip.

Trip planning software and a laptop computer are becoming essential items for many travelers these days. At any point along the way, you can recalculate your route, build in a side trip, or change your destination altogether—and your personal travel agent is right there to provide you with all the information you need. With trip planning software, you enter the starting and ending point of a trip to produce a map and detailed directions to your destination. In Rand McNally TripMaker, a popular trip planning software package, you can enter a driving profile that takes into account how fast you drive and the types of roads you prefer (interstates, divided highways, local roads). Once you've entered the trip information, TripMaker displays the route and complete directions, including distances and travel time. Figure 8.7 shows a trip from Flint, Michigan to Virginia Beach, via Rogers, Arkansas mapped out in TripMaker. You can print the map and directions for use on the road, as well as detailed information about lodging, restaurants, sports activities, and sight-seeing opportunities.

Figure 8.7
Rand McNally TripMaker develops a map that shows your route and any detours you want to make.

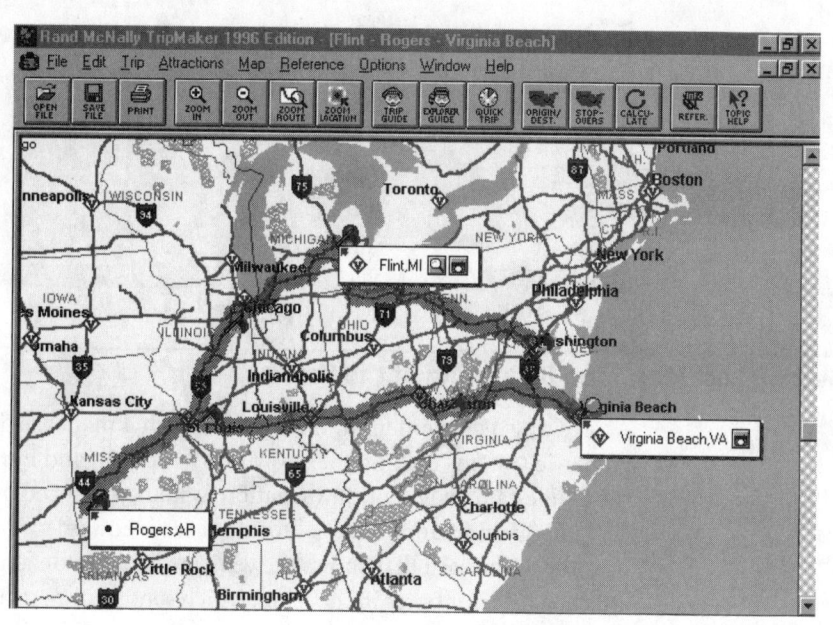

Finding Your Way Once You Arrive

Mapping software is designed to provide a greater level of detail, right down to street-level maps and information. Mapping software has many applications in business environments and is used to identify sales regions, delivery routes, store locations, and other critical business geographic data. In Rand McNally StreetFinder, the best-selling mapping software, you enter a street address to see where that address is on the map. Users can also place a number of "flags" at various places on the maps to identify specific addresses and their locations, as shown in Figure 8.8. Mapping software is especially useful when creating a street-level map to your home or business.

Figure 8.8
Rand McNally StreetFinder can show you how to get to a particular address in a new city.

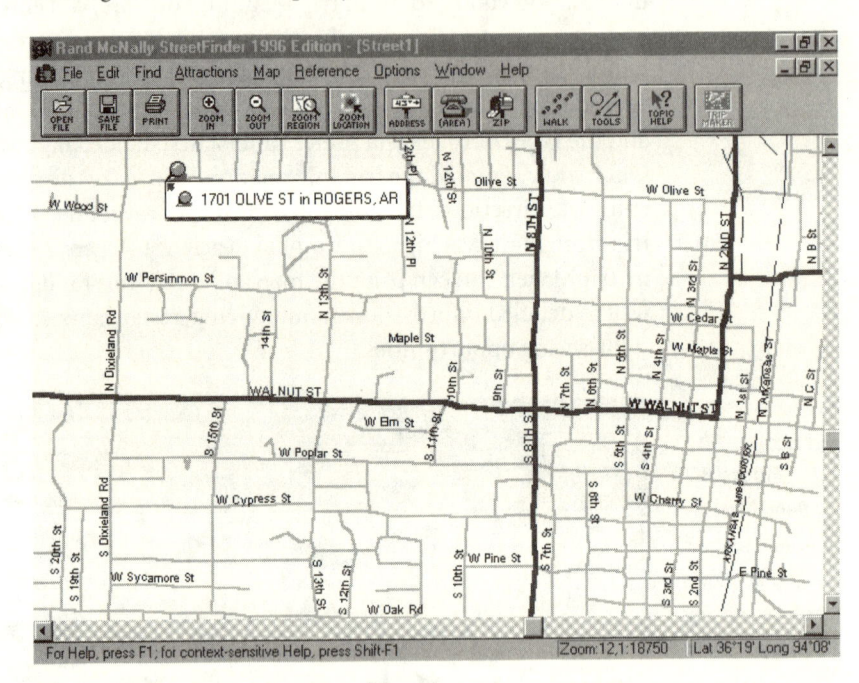

Getting Lost May Soon Be a Thing of the Past

An exciting development in the world of digital maps are the in-vehicle route guidance systems making their way into American and European cars. With the Guidestar Navigation Information System, produced by Navigation Technologies in Sunnyvale, California, a car is equipped with a video monitor near the dashboard that shows the vehicle's location on a map. The monitor is attached to a computer in the trunk which sends pulses to a global positioning system (GPS), linked to Defense Department satellites. The driver is given verbal instructions through small speakers.

The next wave of in-vehicle systems are called *autonomous route guidance systems*. With these systems, drivers are guided to their destination through a combination of extremely detailed maps, wheel sensors that measure how far the car has traveled, and an internal compass that keeps track of direction. Even one-way streets and streets where turns aren't permitted are included in the guidance system's calculations!

Genealogy and Family History

Interest in genealogy and family history has sky-rocketed since the 1977 airing of the television miniseries *Roots*. And once again, computers are providing fingertip access to huge amounts of relevant information. Genealogy research is rampant on the Internet, which provides computerized access to millions of records, from birth and death certificates to census and marriage records. And with thousands of other people out there searching, you're bound to run into someone who's related to you sooner or later.

Computerized software includes guides that walk you through the process of searching for ancestors, creating family trees, and recording family member information. Family Tree Maker, from Banner Blue Software, includes a CD-ROM that contains 100 million names. Although the records you need to search to find your relatives are too large to be contained on a single CD-ROM, the program tells you which indexes of public records contain the information you are seeking. You can then buy the appropriate indexes from the software publisher or head to the public library to locate the record sources.

Recording your own family stories will help your descendants discover their roots. Several of the software products available help you create a multi-media scrapbook and family history. Echo Lake, shown in Figure 8.9, is designed to help you capture your own history, and is a great tool for recording childhood and family memories in the form of stories and histories.

You may want to include photographs in your genealogical scrapbook. As part of your regular photo processing, you can get photos taken with any type of camera returned to you on disk; these are called **digital photographs**. Two companies that offer this service are Kodak and Seattle Filmworks. Another approach you can use is to purchase a **digital camera**. Digital cameras store images using a digital storage device such as a floppy disk or flash memory rather than traditional film. The digital images can be transferred to a computer for use with different software applications. Professional digital cameras costing $15,000 or more are used by news journalists and businesses who need high-quality photos in an easy-to-use format. Personal digital cameras, called *point-and-shoot cameras*, are available for less than $500.

Figure 8.9
Echo Lake incorporates multimedia to capture your family's history.

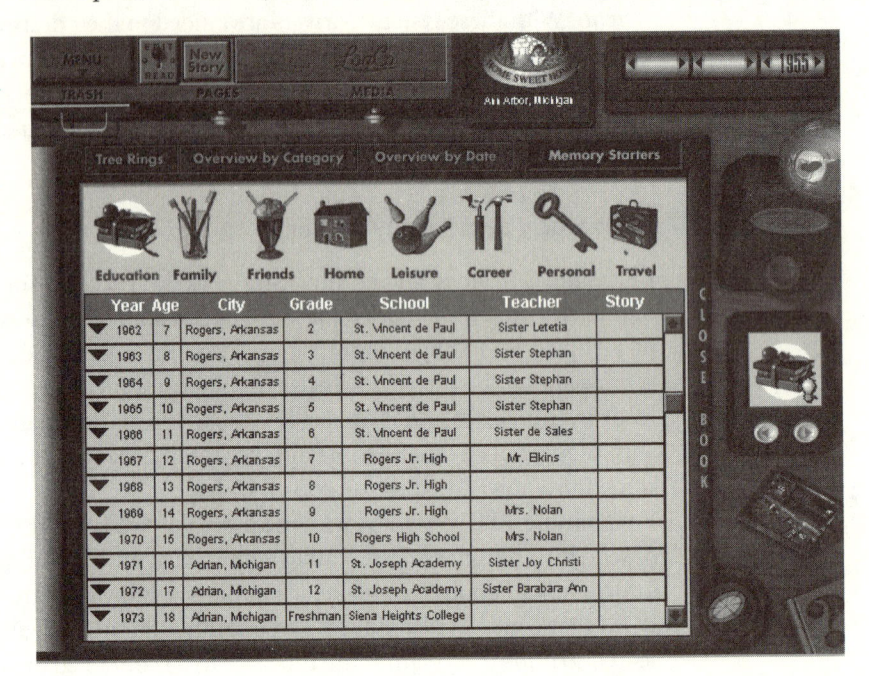

The primary difference between professional and personal digital cameras is the resolution of the pictures they produce. Generally speaking, the more pixels the better the image. Because pixels are lost during compression, the amount and type of compression used by the camera also affects picture quality. The better point-and-shoot digital cameras have a low compression ratio (3-to-1) and medium to high resolution (better than 300×300).

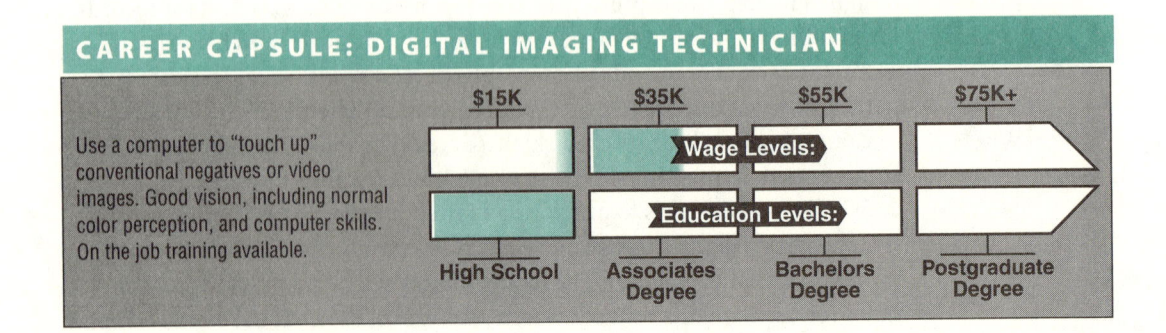

CAREER CAPSULE: DIGITAL IMAGING TECHNICIAN

Use a computer to "touch up" conventional negatives or video images. Good vision, including normal color perception, and computer skills. On the job training available.

Wage Levels: $15K | $35K | $55K | $75K+

Education Levels: High School | Associates Degree | Bachelors Degree | Postgraduate Degree

Design Tools

Whether you are building a new home, remodeling your old one or just want to landscape the yard, design software can help you draw professional-looking plans to guide you on your way. **Computer-aided design** (**CAD**), the use of specialized design software in the drawing of a product's specifications, has been used in manufacturing for several years. CAD programs are used in the design of automobiles and airplanes, buildings and landscapes, mechanical parts, and printed circuit boards. Professional CAD programs produce three-dimensional wire frame outlines of the product and some actually **render** the image, converting it to a fully-formed graphic with colors and shading.

Design software for the home user is based on this sophisticated CAD software. And in fact, some products, such as Planix Home Architect 3D (shown in Figure 8.10), actually produce images that are CAD compatible. Once you are finished sketching out your ideas, you can take your plan on disk to your architect and have professional drawings made. Design software is available for home design, kitchen and bath remodeling, landscape design, and interior design.

Figure 8.10
Planix Home Architect 3D includes a number of home designs that you can modify to your specifications.

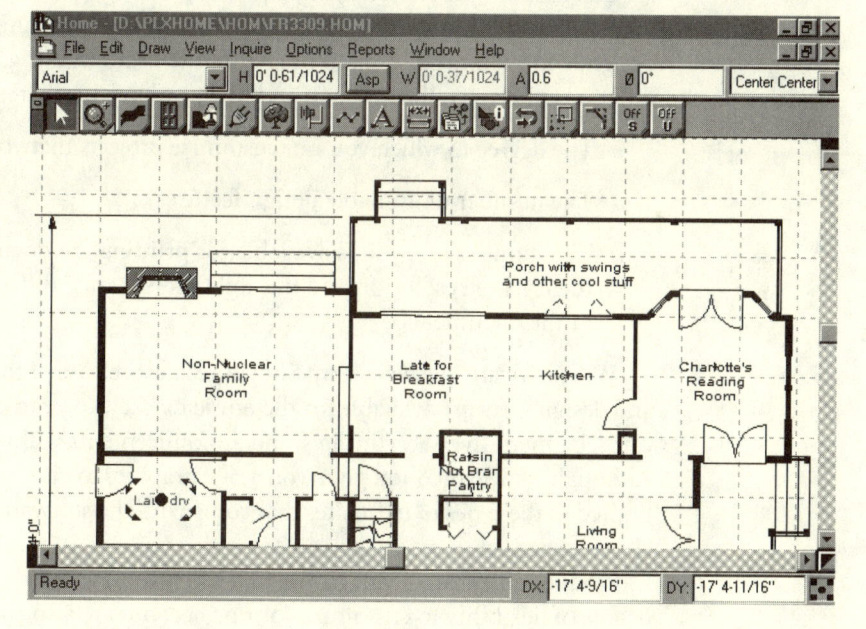

SECTION 8.4: PRINTING AND PUBLISHING

Since the release of the Apple II in 1977, computer-generated graphics have been a source of immense excitement among home computer users. In the mid-1980s, Apple released the Apple IIGS and the Imagewriter II printer, the first personal computer and printer capable of producing color graphics. Although the Imagewriter II was only a dot-matrix printer and the color quality was tenuous at best, it marked the beginning of an insatiable consumer hunger for color and graphics.

Desktop Publishing

Desktop publishing, the use of a personal computer and page-layout software to produce printed materials, incorporates text and graphics in an aesthetically appealing way. Desktop publishing software is available for all levels of interest and ability. There are a number of desktop publishing software products on the market, like Adobe PageMaker and Quark Xpress, that are designed for professional, high quality printing—this book, for example, was produced using Quark. At the other end of the spectrum are products designed for young children to use with little or no training. The primary differences between the low-end and high-end products are:

- The degree to which you can customize projects that you are working on
- The number of available design features
- The number of options available for printing the document, such as the level of resolution and the ability to separate different color layers of the document

With software like New Print Shop, the latest release of the oldest graphics and design software available for the home market, you can create greeting cards, banners, flyers, certificates, and announcements within minutes. Although New Print Shop gives you 4,500 graphics to choose from, you are limited to the types of templates that come with the software (or can be purchased separately).

Products like Corel Print House and Microsoft Publisher provide a greater degree of flexibility to customize your project but are also able to do most of the layout work for you if you prefer. Both products come with a large number of predesigned templates and a ton of graphics. Microsoft Publisher, shown in Figure 8.11, comes closest to a professional desktop publishing package, because it allows links to be created between pages so articles can be continued on subsequent pages.

Figure 8.11
Desktop publishing project using Microsoft Publisher

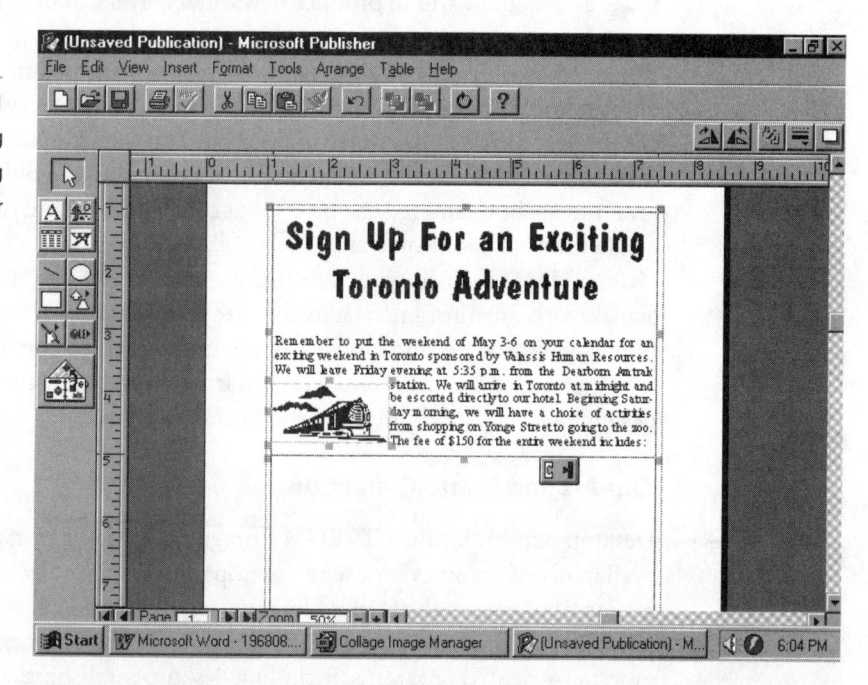

When deciding on desktop publishing software, there are several things to consider:

- Does the software include templates for the types of projects you intend to create? If you want to create multiple-page newsletters, buy a higher-end product with good text editing features or the ability to import text from your word processor.

- Will children be using the software? If so, you may want a product with less flexibility and more guidance so children don't become frustrated.

- How much time do you want to spend learning a product? Products like New Print Shop and Hallmark's Card Studio can be used right out of the box with little effort. Other products require some practice time to understand their features.

Why Not Use a Word Processor?

Why not just use a word processor to produce your printed materials? The simple answer is, "You can." Word processing programs include a number of features that allow you to produce newsletters, flyers, booklets, and other materials. The primary distinction between word processing software and desktop publishing software is that word processing software is focused on text while desktop publishing software is focused on page layout. In word processing software, text is entered onto a page and then graphic images are inserted as objects for the text to flow around. In desktop publishing, text and graphics are both entered as objects that can be resized and repositioned to create the exact look you want to achieve.

Regardless of which type of software you choose to use, it's possible to achieve virtually the same results for many projects. However, with desktop publishing software, once you learn the software, you'll complete design and layout tasks more quickly and with less frustration because of the special design tools and aids built in.

Clip Art and Photo Collections

Desktop publishing and CD-ROM storage have caused an explosion in the availability of graphics for use in desktop publishing projects. **Clip art** is a collection of images in the form of line images, maps, drawings, or photographs available in digital form for use in publications and documents. Today, most graphics-oriented programs, including desktop publishing software, come with their own clip art collections. For example, the Microsoft Clip Art Gallery (see Figure 8.12) comes with all Microsoft productivity software. Images can be added from other clip art collections to make them available for use in your documents. Some, but not all clip art comes with a license to use the images royalty-free. Read the clip art license to understand restrictions on how you can use the images.

Graphics programs save images using different file formats. Each format uses a unique **file extension**, three digits attached to the end of file name. Before you can use a graphic image in a document, you must be sure the software you are using can accept or translate the file format into a format it can work with. The higher-end desktop publishing and word processing programs include **filters** which can translate images saved in specific file formats to formats the software can use. Table 8.1 shows the most common graphics file formats.

Figure 8.12
Microsoft ClipArt Gallery 2.0

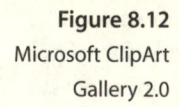

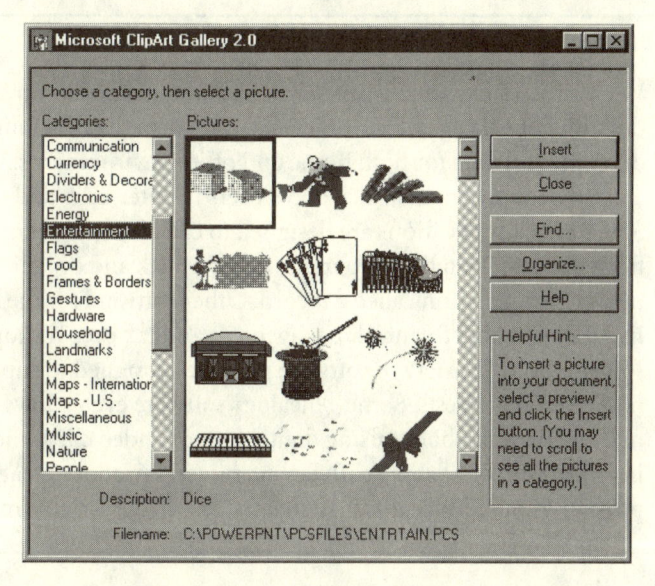

Table 8.1
The Most Common Graphics File Formats

Graphics Format	Three-Digit File Extension	Accepted By
Tag Image File format	TIF	Most Windows and Macintosh applications
Windows Bitmaps/ Windows Paint	BMP	Windows only
WordPerfect Graphics	WPG	Different file formats between Windows and Macintosh versions
Macintosh PICT	PCT	Macintosh and some Windows applications
Windows Metafile	WMF	Windows only
JPEG File Interchange format	JPG	Many Windows and Macintosh applications

Before you buy clip art or photo collections, read the label to make certain the clip art is in a file format your software can accept (or has an appropriate filter for). To determine what format your software can accept, consult your software's document or help files.

What You Have Learned

Word processors, spreadsheets, databases, communication software, and desktop publishing and graphics software form the new foundation of productivity software for both home and office environments. Word processors are software programs which allow users to enter, edit, and format text. Spreadsheet applications are designed to calculate numbers and create charts from the data. Database programs help to track and organize a collection of fields of information called a record. Other software for the home market includes personal financial management and tax preparation software, legal software, and a variety of software packages designed to support people's hobbies and interests. Some genealogy software even allows for the creation of multimedia scrapbooks using digital photos, video clips, and sound recordings. Desktop publishing software helps users produce creative publishing projects—including cards, newsletters, and flyers—right from home.

Focus Questions

1. List the major categories of home productivity software.

2. What is the major task of each of the following types of software: word processor, spreadsheet, and database?

3. List three features of personal financial management software.

4. What is online bill paying, and what is one of the major impediments to its success?

5. If you wanted to buy desktop publishing software that your 7- and 10-year-old children could use, what features would you look for in a software product?

Knowledge Reinforcement

A. Bill Gates' dream is for every home to have a personal computer. Do you think this is a realistic dream? If so, how long will it be before it is a reality? If not, what are the roadblocks to fulfilling Bill's dream?

B. Since 12-year-old Thomas is the only one in his family to use the family's computer, his parents decided to move it into his bedroom. Do you think this is a good or a bad idea?

c. Find out if your bank offers online banking services. If so, would you consider using them? Include the reasons for your decision.

Further Exploration

Apple Computer Corporation:
http://www.apple.com

Everton Genealogical Helper (genealogy resources):
http://www.everton.com/

Intuit Corporation:
www.intuit.com

Microsoft Corporation:
http://microsoft.com

Nolo Press Self-Help Law Center (self-help legal software):
http://140.174.208.58/index.html

SPECIAL TOPIC: PURCHASING COMPUTERS AND SOFTWARE

Whether you are purchasing a computer for home or business use, it's helpful to have a method for selecting a computer to meet your needs. For the past decade, a good quality desktop PC has cost around $2,200—but every year, that $2,200 buys more features, more speed, and more power. No matter what system you purchase, you'll find it for less within half a year. If you shop carefully, you'll get a good deal out of your computer in those six months, which helps minimize post-purchase regret.

1. Begin by making a list of things you want to be able to do. Do you want to keep track of your finances? Surf the Internet? Create colorful publications? Play games? If other family members or employees will be using the computer, involve them in this process. Make a list, then prioritize the list so you know what the computer must be able to do, and which tasks are optional. Transfer the prioritized list to the Task column of the Computer Purchase Worksheet on page 199.

2. Think about your own personality and the personalities of other intended users. Do you learn new hands-on activities by experimenting, or do you like

SPECIAL TOPIC: PURCHASING COMPUTERS AND SOFTWARE (continued)

lots of user manuals? Does taking a course speed your learning? The results of this assessment will guide your software selection and purchase. If you prefer to take classes on new software or purchase manuals, you'll want to select popular software so courses and supplemental materials are readily available.

3. Take your task list to the store and begin shopping for software. As you shop, note that extra software features cost extra money. If you don't need the features of a business quality word processor, look at a word processor designed for home use. Some computer stores have software installed on-site that you can take for a "test drive."

4. Select software for the tasks you listed in step 1. Fill in the Software, OS, Processor/RAM, Hard Drive, and Other columns for each piece of software you selected. Each software package lists specific requirements for hardware and operating systems. For example, Visio, a drawing package, is only available for Windows. It runs under Windows 3.1 with 8MB of RAM or Windows 95 with 4MB of RAM, and requires at least a 386-25 processor. The amount of hard drive space required for installation isn't indicated on the package, so you can use 35MB as a safe, liberal figure. Visio also requires a VGA or SVGA monitor and graphics card.

5. Now, examine the OS (operating system) column of the Purchase Worksheet. If any of your priority software requires a specific operating system, then you need to make sure you purchase a computer that supports or comes with that OS. If you have two pieces of priority software that work exclusively with different operating systems, you need to abandon one choice and choose new software for its task. If all the software you selected is available for multiple operating systems, then you get to choose. Go to a computer store and spend time using each potential OS and asking questions: "How do you compare Windows 95 with Windows 3.1? Which is easier to use, System 8 or Windows?" Talk to other users. You'll need to use the OS every time you start an application, so ask good questions and choose carefully. Add your operating system choice and its system requirements to the Purchase Worksheet in the Operating System Requirements section.

6. Now you can begin filling in the Hardware Requirements section of the Worksheet. The processor and RAM listed on software packages are the minimums required for the software to run. To determine the minimum amount of RAM your new computer should have, find the highest amount of RAM listed for any individual piece of software, then add at least 8MB to find your required RAM. For example, Microsoft Office for Windows 95 requires 8MB to run at all, so you'll want 16MB so it will

SPECIAL TOPIC: PURCHASING COMPUTERS AND SOFTWARE (continued)

run well. If you intend to multitask (run multiple applications simultaneously) or work with complex database or graphics files, you'll require even more RAM than is indicated and a faster processor. Add another 8MB if you intend to multitask large (8MB or better) applications. Fill in the RAM you'll want in the Hardware Specifications area.

7. Next, find the most capable processor listed, and move up one entire model. If, for example, all of your software will operate on a 486 processor, you want a 586 (Pentium). Even though this version of your software is designed for a 486, the next version will have more features and require more power. Buying a more capable processor now means you won't be disappointed next year. Fill in the processor you'll want in the Hardware Specifications area.

8. The programs you initially purchase represent a fraction of your total storage requirements. You'll want to purchase additional software later and store files you create on the hard drive. To choose a minimum hard drive size, total the megabytes from the Hard Drive column of the Purchase Worksheet, making sure you include the operating system's requirements. Then, multiply the result by five. If your software list includes drawing, animation, desktop publishing, or CAD software, multiply by ten. For example, if your hard drive requirements total 120MB, your hard drive should be at least 600MB; it should be 1200MB (or 1.2GB) if you plan to use a drawing or desktop publishing package. Fill in the hard drive size in the Hardware Specifications area.

9. With the amount of software that comes on CD-ROM, you'll probably want to add a CD-ROM to your list of hardware specifications. Good CDs cost less than $200, and make installing software hassle free. You'll probably also want to add an entire multimedia kit, which will include quality speakers. The standard, internal PC speaker produces poor sound quality and is totally inadequate for today's multimedia software.

10. Now, it's time for the $2,000 question: do you need a portable computer? How often will you need to take your computer to another room, on a trip, to work or school? Portable PCs cost between $1,500 and $2,000 more than desktops for the same power, features, and functionality, so don't answer hastily. If a portable is a real option, make a note under Additional Features.

11. If you have any desire to send and receive e-mail and faxes or connect to the Internet, add a fax/modem card (a PCMCIA fax/modem card for a portable computer) to your hardware specs. The minimum tolerable modem speed for Internet use is 28.8Kbps. For e-mail and faxes only, you can get by with 14.4 kbps.

SPECIAL TOPIC: PURCHASING COMPUTERS AND SOFTWARE (continued)

12. There are several factors to consider when selecting a printer. (If you purchase a portable computer, you'll want to look at portable printers.) Do you want to be able to print in color? How many pages do you project you'll print in a month? What quality of output do you need? Printers are rated by anticipated usage and print quality. The more printing you intend to do, the more you'll need to spend on a printer. Computer and discount stores usually have several printers to choose from, and can print a sample so you can see the print quality. If you plan to do a lot of printing, compare the price and page count for the cartridges or toner used in the printer. Hewlett Packard, Canon, and Epson have been manufacturing printers for years, and toner and cartridges for these brands are readily available and competitively priced.

13. Select the type of seller you want to work with. If you or a good friend has a fair amount of technical sophistication and can follow written instructions, you could purchase directly from a manufacturer, a discount or department store, or order through a mail-order distributor. *Computer Shopper* magazine, available at computer and book stores, includes ads from dozens of computer manufacturers and distributors. If you want someone to set up and test your system, install the software you purchase, and even provide some help to get you started, you'll want to purchase your computer from a local computer store. Your computer may cost a bit more, because you're paying up front for service and support. However, it's better to spend an extra $100 for a functioning computer and a knowledgeable salesperson than to save money on a computer you don't know how to set up or use. Keep in mind that everyone knows someone who knows someone else who builds computers in their spare time and can give you a bargain. But unless you're able to handle all your troubleshooting and support issues on your own, just say "No."—your friend's hobby is building computers, not supporting them.

14. Two purchase criteria are left, warranty and price. There are several types of warranties: on-site, carry-in, mail-in, and replacement. You'll want to choose a warranty based on how long you'll be willing to be without your computer. Now take your Purchase Worksheet to computer stores or browse catalogs to compare the price and warranty of computers that meet your specifications. Many computer vendors will be willing to review the specifications on your worksheet and give you a price for the total package. Remember that companies always treat you better *before* they get your money; if a seller isn't helpful before the sale, make your purchase somewhere else.

Computer Purchase Worksheet

Software Requirements

Task	Software	OS	Processor/RAM	Hard Drive	Other

Operating System Specifications

Hardware Specifications

RAM		CD-ROM	
Processor		Multimedia Kit	
Hard Drive		Printer	
Monitor		Fax/Modem	
Other Storage		Additional Features	

SESSION NINE

Vocabulary

- ARPANET
- Tim Berners-Lee
- browser
- commercial online information service
- connect time
- domain
- domain address
- download
- e-mail
- electronic bulletin board
- FAQ
- File Transfer Protocol (FTP)
- Gopher
- home page
- host
- Hypertext Markup Language (HTML)
- Hypertext Transfer Protocol (HTTP)
- Internet
- Internet service provider (ISP)
- IRC
- listserv
- mailing list
- search engine
- site
- spider
- streaming technology
- subdomain
- TCP/IP
- Telnet
- thread
- universal resource locator (URL)
- Usenet newsgroup
- Virtual Reality Modeling Language (VRML)
- WAIS
- Web page
- World Wide Web

Doorway to the World: Online Services and the Internet

EARLIER IN THIS CENTURY, THE TELEPHONE changed the way we communicated with other people and, as a result, brought the world closer together. Those same telephone lines are now providing instant access to every conceivable type of information and communication between people worldwide. At the end of the session, you will be able to

- Trace the history of the World Wide Web
- Identify the differences between commercial online services and the Internet
- Describe the major services of the Internet
- Identify the major roles of browsers and search engines

201

SECTION 9.1: THE BIRTH OF ONLINE COMMUNICATION

In the United States in the 1960s, concern about a nuclear attack by the Soviet Union was on everybody's mind. People were building bomb shelters in their back yards and stocking them with provisions in case the unthinkable ever happened. The U.S. military wanted to find a way to ensure that communications networks would not be destroyed, even if some of their sites fell victim to attack. So, the Advanced Research Projects Agency (ARPA) of the U.S. Defense Department funded a project to connect university computer scientists and engineers together via their computers and telephone lines. This project, called **ARPANET**, allowed researchers to share each other's computer facilities over long distances. Immensely more popular, however, was the use of ARPANET to exchange electronic mail with other users.

The next logical step from person-to-person electronic mail was to find a way to broadcast the same message to multiple users. In this way, large-scale dialogues could occur with everyone reading and responding to everyone else's messages. ARPANET **mailing lists**, lists of users who all expressed interest in receiving e-mail about a particular general topic area, were developed, and a distribution system was established for the mail messages. One of the first large mailing lists was for science fiction aficionados, called SF-Lovers. With the combination of electronic mail, file transfers and mailing lists, this network of networks, dubbed the **Internet**, was beginning to take shape.

Standardized Protocols

In 1975, Stanford University's Vinton Cerf developed a communication protocol called Transmission Control Protocol (TCP) and an addressing protocol called Internet Protocol (IP). TCP divides messages into streams of packets that are sent and then reassembled into messages at their destinations. IP addresses each packet and routes the packets across different nodes and through different networks before they arrive at their ultimate destination. By 1983, **TCP/IP** was established as the dominant standard for connecting computer networks. The TCP/IP standard allowed the Internet to grow from the original four **host** computers (the central computers in networks) in 1969 to almost 600 hosts by the end of 1983.

In 1983, the U.S. military segment of ARPANET was separated out and became known as MILNET. The Defense Department discontinued

ARPANET's funding in 1989. By that time, the Internet had taken on a life of its own and no longer needed government support. Universities, laboratories, and private industries from around the world had developed essential communication links. With or without government funding, the Internet would survive.

Electronic Bulletin Boards

It was during the life of ARPANET that computer technology advanced from the era of enormous mainframes to desktop-based microcomputers. It didn't take long before personal computer owners began to show an interest in connecting with other computers from their homes and businesses. As modems and communications software were introduced into the market, the same people who championed the development of the personal computer began setting up ways to communicate with each other.

Because the Internet was developed for UNIX-based computers, it was primarily only available to users in university and research settings. To address their own needs to connect with other users, personal computer owners of the late 1970s and early 1980s began to create a communication system that could run on DOS-based and Apple microcomputers. **Electronic bulletin boards** allowed anyone with a computer, a modem, and some relatively inexpensive software to set up a file system where other users could dial in and post messages, play games, and exchange files. People soon began to connect "on the boards." Unlike mailing lists, messages could be accessed by anyone subscribing to the bulletin board service. One person would leave a message and another would respond, then someone else would respond to the later message and on it went. (This type of conversation, called a **thread**, often continues endlessly, long after the subject of the first message has lost its relevance.)

By the mid 1980s, electronic bulletin boards had become a popular way to "meet" other computer users, voice opinions, receive technical help, and download shareware and freeware. Today, electronic bulletin boards are still a communication option for many computer users despite or maybe because of the growth of the Internet. Many of the approximately 30,000 bulletin boards in existence in the United States are run by hobbyists who do not charge other users fees to access their computer. There are many national bulletin boards in existence today, but most boards tend to be local (so users don't have to incur long distance charges), and are often focused on a particular subject area. Boards are more intimate and more personal than the Internet and provide an easy way for people with similar interests to congregate and interact.

Commercial Online Services

As bulletin boards were growing in popularity, commercial organizations began to see the value in providing computer users with online access to information. They reasoned that if people found value in bulletin boards systems, surely there was a way to make online communication appealing enough that people would want to pay for additional services.

Two of the first **commercial online information services**, the Source and CompuServe, provided subscribers with a number of services for a fee based on **connect time**, the amount of time a user was actually connected to the service. The commercial information services were able to offer a wider range of services and easier access than the local bulletin boards. While many bulletin boards only had one incoming phone line to handle calls, commercial online services offered 24-hour access on hundreds of phone lines. The commercial services encouraged the involvement of the major hardware and software vendors so that computer owners could get up-to-date information about their favorite products. Soon, businesses outside the computer realm saw a value in establishing an online presence.

Although quite a few online services are in existence today, CompuServe (which eventually purchased the Source), America Online (AOL) and Prodigy are generally considered the top three commercial online information services. They each minimally offer the following types of services:

- Up-to-date news, weather, and sports information
- Electronic mail
- Computing support
- Entertainment and games
- Financial and professional information
- Travel information and reservations
- Reference and education resources
- Forums or special interest groups on specific topics
- Chat rooms for meeting people online
- Access to the Internet

CompuServe, the oldest of the remaining commercial online services, started as a data storage company in 1969 and began its online information service in 1979. From the early days, CompuServe was considered a top source for stock information, business news, professional organizations, and access to reference materials. One of CompuServe's greatest strengths is that it has access numbers in 185 countries, so business travelers can always connect to the service, receive e-mail, and have reference information at their fingertips. Figure 9.1 shows the Windows-based CompuServe Information Manager.

Figure 9.1
CompuServe Information Manager

A partnership between Sears, Roebuck and Company and IBM, Prodigy (shown in Figure 9.2) began operations in 1984 with a clearly identified marketing focus. In the beginning, Prodigy boasted lower connect time rates because it was supported by advertisers who would flash messages across the bottom of the Prodigy screens. If a member was interested in any of the products listed, all they had to do was click on the ad and they would be taken directly to that advertiser's information. Prodigy's competitors watched this experiment with keen interest and Prodigy's success eventually influenced the role of advertising in the other online services.

Figure 9.2
Prodigy was the first online service to include advertisements.

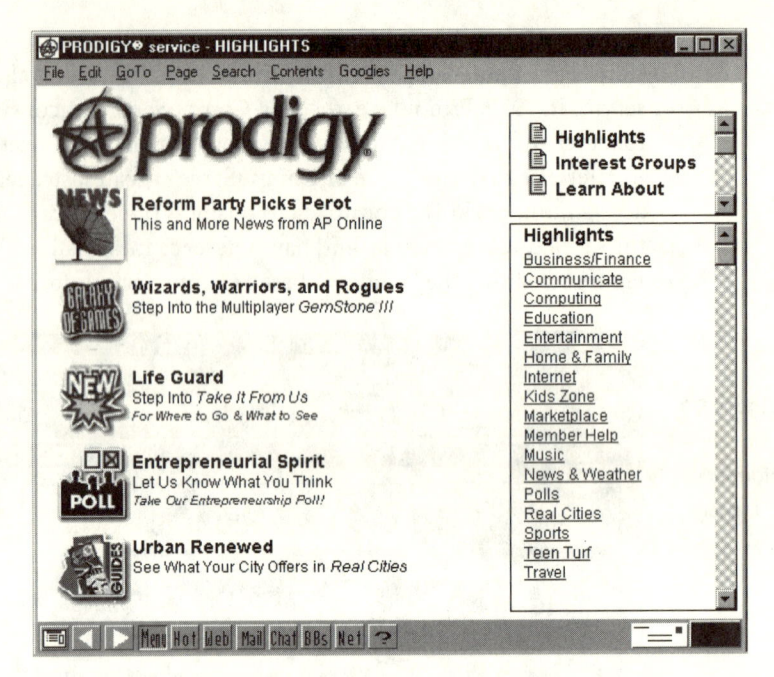

When America Online (AOL), shown in Figure 9.3, was launched in 1985, it promoted itself as the service for social users: a place where people could meet, participate in live chats and get to know each other. AOL's People Connection and Life, Styles, and Interests sections have always been two of the most popular destinations for online socializers. In the 1990s, AOL reached out to the business sector, and today it is successfully positioned in both markets.

The World Wide Web Takes Control

The Internet continued expanding during the 1980s, as more networks were connected and more people were able to access those networks through universities and businesses. By the end of 1990, there were over 300,000 hosts connected to the Internet, a growth rate of 2000 percent in 10 years. Despite this rapid growth, the commercial online information services—with their graphical user interfaces and friendly, organized approach to accessing information—had nothing to fear from the text-based Internet. The Internet had little appeal to inexperienced users, and attracted correspondingly little commercial interest. The Internet was seen as just another source of information for those who were brave enough to enter its entangled web of UNIX, text-based commands.

Figure 9.3
America Online's main switchboard

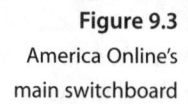

What has happened in the 1990s could not have been predicted by even the most savvy business analysts. In 1992, Swiss software engineer **Tim Berners-Lee** introduced a graphical, hypertext navigation tool called the **World Wide Web** to the Internet. The World Wide Web provided the potential for the Internet to become as graphically interesting and easy to use as the commercial online services. Berners-Lee developed the Web as a convenient and efficient way to access documents stored on a number of different computer systems at CERN, the European particle-physics laboratory in Geneva where he worked. He had no intention of changing the course of human history, but within only a few short years, the World Wide Web has become an international phenomenon.

By the beginning of 1996, just four years after the introduction of the World Wide Web, the number of Internet hosts had risen to over 9 million and is predicted to double every year into the next millennium. IntelliQuest, a market research firm in Austin, Texas, estimates that 21 million individual new users in the United States alone will begin using the Internet or an online service by the middle of 1997.

> *You can't rest on your laurels, because there is always a competitor coming up behind you.*
> —*Bill Gates,* The Road Ahead, *1995*

In response to the incredible expansion of the Internet, all of the commercial online services have had to undergo a dramatic shift. CompuServe and Prodigy are both planning to abandon their proprietary software and become more closely integrated with the Internet. Moreover, all three services provide direct access to the Internet through their software. Whether the commercial online information services will survive into the second millennium depends on how they redefine their corporate missions and realign their services with those exploding on the Internet.

SECTION 9.2: THE INTERNET TODAY

Today's Internet is a collection of computer networks from all over the world which provide access to a number of information sources and services. While several of the services have their roots in ARPANET and early electronic bulletin boards, others have only been made possible by the development of the World Wide Web and the multimedia capacity of today's computers. All types of software and hardware companies are jockeying for the competitive advantage that can be obtained by developing new products that interface with the Web. With each passing day, a new service or innovation makes its debut on the World Wide Web. The only winners in this breakneck competition, besides consumers, are those companies that are able to take risks, develop flexible products and services, and keep the door open to new ideas.

■ Services of the World Wide Web

The World Wide Web is the fastest-growing marketplace, research facility, and communication tool in the world. It's possible to find information about almost any subject imaginable—from today's sport scores and stock prices to the dietary habits of an endangered Amazonian insect. You can watch movie previews, hear sound clips from the latest music CDs, listen to the news, research a subject for a paper, go on a virtual tour of the White House, explore Disney World, get the lyrics to all the Monty Python songs, go shopping, make airline reservations, even hold conversations with people from all over the globe.

All types of companies are recognizing the value of worldwide exposure to their products or services. Some of these businesses see the Web as an effective place to advertise, others see it as an opportunity to set up a new kind of business where consumers can actually shop and order products online.

What makes the Web most interesting, however, is the diversity of information that is available at no charge to anyone who logs in. You can download free software, read online newspapers and magazines, price a used car, and research any topic under the sun. It's virtually impossible for someone to access the Web and not find something intriguing. And because the content is changing all the time, there is always something new to browse or a new site to explore.

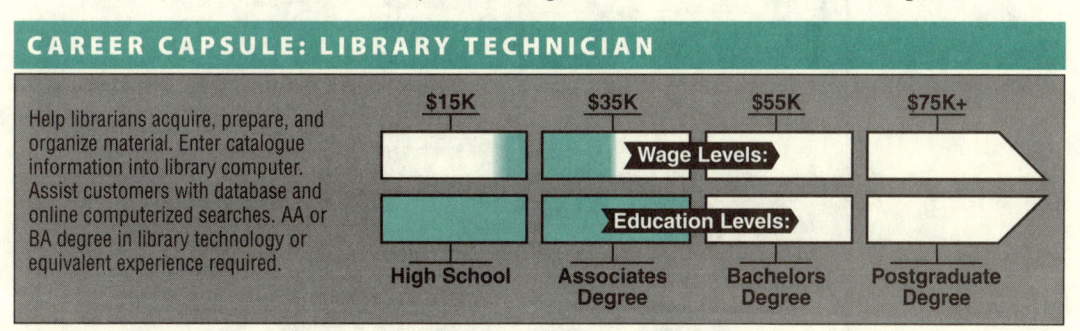

CAREER CAPSULE: LIBRARY TECHNICIAN

Help librarians acquire, prepare, and organize material. Enter catalogue information into library computer. Assist customers with database and online computerized searches. AA or BA degree in library technology or equivalent experience required.

	$15K	$35K	$55K	$75K+
Wage Levels:				
Education Levels:				
	High School	Associates Degree	Bachelors Degree	Postgraduate Degree

Other Common Internet Services

Prior to the existence of the World Wide Web, Internet users had access to a number of tools to help them make use of computers on the Internet. The graphical World Wide Web has successfully incorporated many of these text-based services. As a result, it is possible to use these services without even realizing that you have left the Web. Three of the most-used Internet services that exist in both text-based and graphical forms include e-mail, mailing lists, and Usenet newsgroups.

E-Mail

Electronic mail or e-mail is probably the best know of all the Internet services. **E-mail** is a service that allows users to send electronic messages to other users with electronic addresses regardless of the system they are using. E-mail has provided the ability to almost instantaneously send written documents from one side of the globe to another, and has changed the way people think about correspondence.

A typical Windows-based e-mail application is Netscape Mail, shown in Figure 9.4. Both incoming and outgoing mail can be filed in mail folders. The right side of the screen shows who sent the mail, the subject, and the date it was sent. The contents of the e-mail itself appear at the bottom of the screen.

Figure 9.4
Netscape Mail

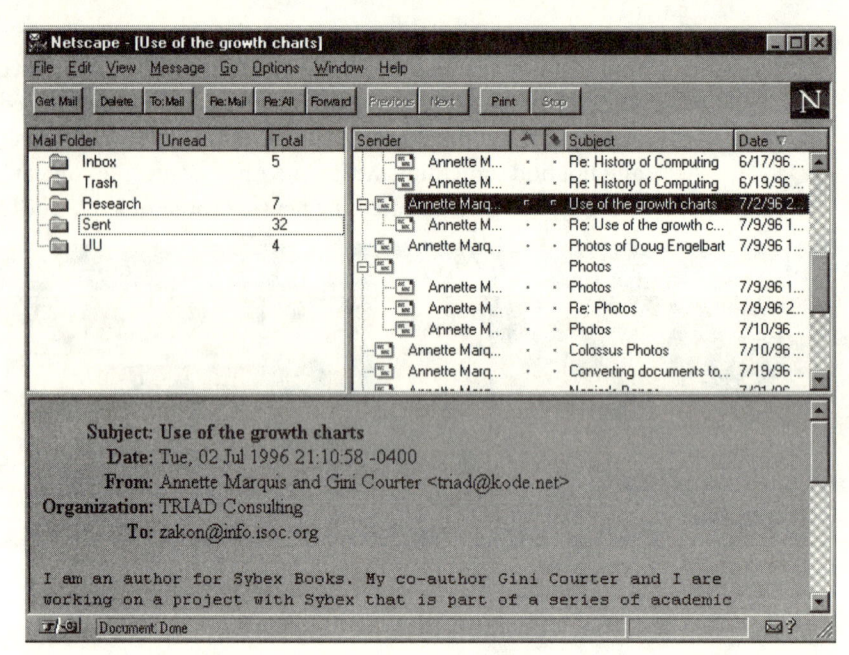

One the most significant advantages of e-mail over traditional forms of correspondence is the ability to easily reply to mail received. The recipient can click the reply button, write their response, then click the send button; the response is on its way in minutes. Many people find that they correspond more efficiently and more promptly using e-mail than when using traditional forms of mail (referred to as "snail mail").

Mailing Lists

Today's mailing lists, also called **listservs**, are the direct descendants of the ARPANET mailing lists. There are literally tens of thousands of mailing lists in existence on every conceivable topic—from computer-related subjects to Voodoo. Mailing lists are a form of group e-mail. One person writes a message, which is broadcast to all the subscribers of the mailing list. Then, anyone who receives the message can reply to it, and their reply is broadcast in the same way. Because of this system, mailing lists can become overwhelming very quickly—it is not uncommon to receive 80 to 100 e-mail messages in one day. When that happens every day of the week, very few people can find the time to read them, much less respond to them. Some mailing lists archive the messages each day and send them out as packets of messages. This certainly helps in managing the e-mail avalanche, but mailing lists can still get out of control without great diligence. Although they are quite useful if you want to stay informed about a particular topic, lists should be chosen carefully to avoid having to dig out from under mounds of e-mail.

Usenet Newsgroups

Usenet newsgroups are text-based discussion groups on every topic imaginable—a more public form of mailing lists. Newsgroups are technically not a part of the Internet because they use the UNIX to UNIX Copy Protocol (UUCP) rather than the TCP/IP of the Internet. However, newsgroups have become such a popular service that most Internet providers include access to newsgroups. Anyone in the world with Usenet access can participate in a public newsgroup at any time (some groups are privately maintained and are not available to the general public). It's possible to read one or two messages (called articles) or all of them as time and interest allow.

NOTE

Because newsgroups are maintained on UNIX computers, their names reflect the UNIX naming conventions. For example, the newsgroup discussion for members of the Gumby fan club is alt.fan.gumby. The Alternate Trek Reality newsgroup is alt.games.atr.rpg.

Finding a high-quality newsgroup can sometimes be a challenge. Word of mouth is often one of the most effective methods. To find out about a newsgroup, you can read the **FAQ** (Frequently Asked Questions) article found in the newsgroup called news.answers. This article generally describes the newsgroup, its purpose, members, and what topics are typically discussed. Figure 9.5 shows a list of some of the 25,000 Usenet newsgroups.

Figure 9.5
Usenet newsgroups using America Online

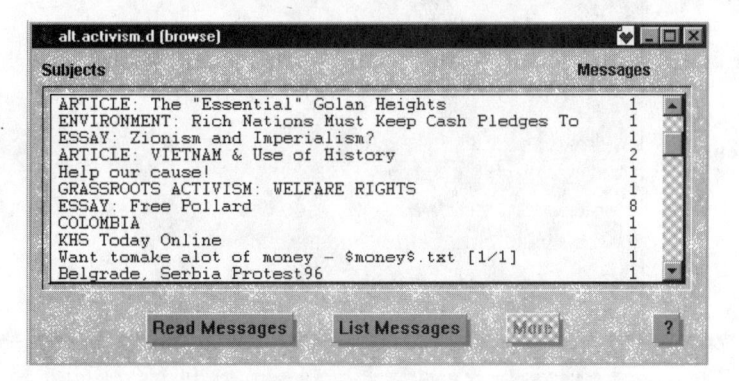

Other Internet Services

In addition to the mail-related tools, there are text-based tools used to exchange files and communicate with other computers on the Internet. Users of the Web can access these services from various Web sites. These include:

- **FTP**—A system that lets users transfer files from one computer to another. Software programs, multimedia files, or documents can all be sent using **File Transfer Protocol**.

- **Gopher**—A search tool that allows users to search through computers on the Internet through the use of a menu, it is largely being replaced by the World Wide Web. Figure 9.6 shows a typical Gopher menu.

- **IRC**—A worldwide chat system, Internet Relay Chat allows users to type messages and receive immediate live responses from other users.

- **Telnet**—A system that allows users to access other computers, then run applications or access files that are housed there. Library card catalog databases are often setup using Telnet.

- **WAIS**—Wide Area Information Servers provide a full text indexing system for documents searched in specific databases.

Figure 9.6
Typical Gopher menu accessed through the World Wide Web

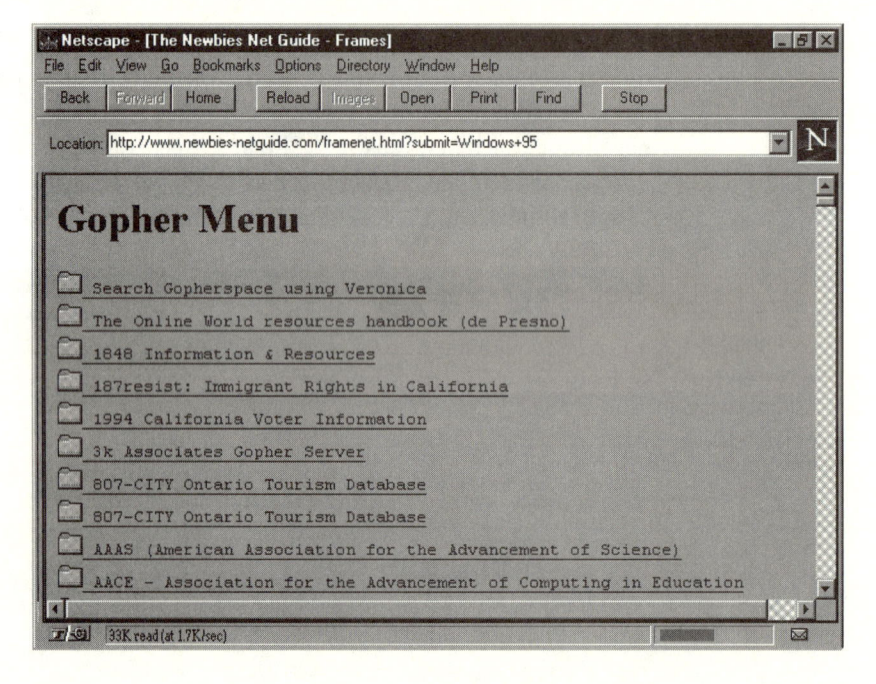

Accessing the Internet

As the demand for access intensifies, establishing an Internet and World Wide Web connection continues to become easier. There are three primary ways to gain access to the Internet:

- Students and staff of colleges and universities can gain access at no cost through their school. They may not have access to the World Wide Web, but can usually use e-mail, FTP, and Telnet services.

- You can subscribe to a commercial online information service like CompuServe, Prodigy, or America Online, which allows you to explore the Internet as part of the monthly fee.

- You can subscribe to an **Internet service provider (ISP),** an independent business that provides subscribers access to the Internet for a monthly fee.

A major consideration in deciding which type of access to choose is how many hours you expect to be online each month. Subscriptions are typically based on the numbers of online hours. You can purchase plans which include from five to twenty hours per month, with an additional fee for each hour over. Many of the services also offer unlimited use plans and include a discount if you pay for a year in advance. Because of the intense competition for subscribers, pricing plans rarely remain constant in today's market. It's important to examine the pricing structure of the commercial online services and then compare them to a couple of ISPs before making a decision about which to choose.

Other questions you should consider in selecting a provider are

- What services do they provide access to (e-mail, Telnet, Usenet)?

- What access rates can they support? A fast modem does no good if your service provider only supports slower ones.

- How many incoming lines do they have—how often can you expect a busy signal?

- Do they have access numbers in other cities so you can connect when you travel?

- Who do you call if you have a problem with the service? What hours is technical support available?

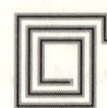

> **NOTE**
>
> Since the Internet is no longer funded by the U.S. government, alternative methods have been developed to pay for its growth. At the current time, most ISPs and other organizations who want direct Internet access pay the telephone company a flat rate of $20,000 and a fee every month to lease a special type of telephone line called a T-1 line. Because it's a flat fee, users do not generate additional costs if they stay online. Most of the content on the Internet is placed there by volunteers, or is paid for by businesses who desire a presence on the Net.

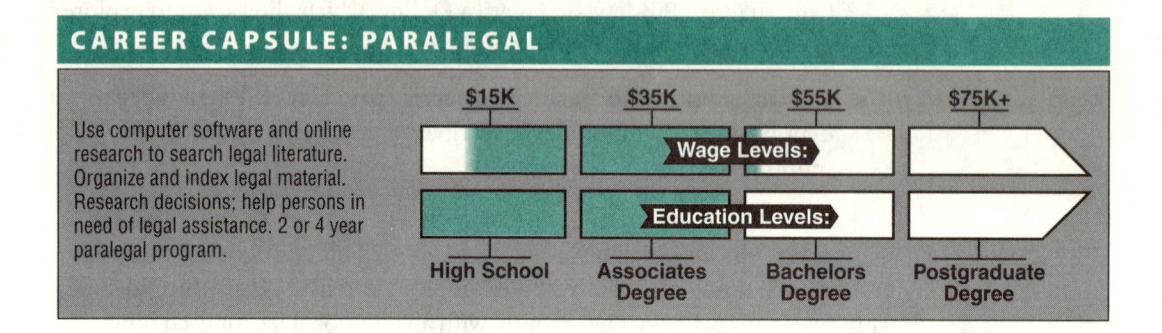

CAREER CAPSULE: PARALEGAL

Use computer software and online research to search legal literature. Organize and index legal material. Research decisions; help persons in need of legal assistance. 2 or 4 year paralegal program.

Wage Levels: $15K – $35K – $55K – $75K+

Education Levels: High School – Associates Degree – Bachelors Degree – Postgraduate Degree

■ Internet Addresses

Although the World Wide Web is technically only a portion of the Internet, there are fewer services each day that cannot be accessed through the structure the Web provides. The Web combines TCP/IP, the protocol for sending documents across networks, with an entirely new method of locating and accessing documents on different networks. Berners-Lee created a simple coding mechanism involving a string of characters called a **universal resource locator (URL)** that identifies the name and address of each document available to the Web. The URL identifies

- The type of server protocol used where the document is located. A server set up specifically for Web documents uses **Hypertext Transfer Protocol (HTTP)**.

- The type of site: generally, World Wide Web (WWW); File Transfer Protocol (FTP), a protocol used specifically to transfer files from one computer to another; or Gopher, a client-server application that organizes the files on a server so users do not need to know or enter exact file names.

- The address of the host computer (**domain address**). The domain address consists of the name of the major server or **site**, the **subdomain** (usually the network, university, or company name), and the **domain** (a two or three letter designation of the type of institution).
- The specific location of the document on that computer's network (folders and subfolders and then the document's name).

Domain Names

Domain names are typically two- or three-character designations of the type of institution or organizations that own the domain. There are six common domain names used in the U.S.:

- MIL—military
- GOV—government
- COM—commercial companies
- EDU—educational institutions
- NET—companies and groups who administer the Internet
- ORG—other organizations

Countries outside of the U.S. use a two-letter country code as their domain name.

Here's how the address http://www.microsoft.com/msoffice/train_cert/word.htm, where you'll find information regarding Microsoft certification, is constructed:

Protocol	Type of site	Subdomain	Domain	Folder	Document
http	www	microsoft	com	msoffice/train_cert	word.htm

By assigning an address to each document that can be accessed on the Web, documents can be accessed directly from other documents using Hypertext Markup Language (HTML) code. A link is created from one document to another. Clicking on the link sends a message to that document's host computer and the document is retrieved. Figure 9.7 shows a typical hypertext link from a search tool to a document. Underlined words designate links to other documents.

Figure 9.7
Example of hypertext links

50% The Nature Conservancy [Find Similar]
URL: http://csde.aces.k12.ct.us/friends/ccsi/csusa/enviro/naturcon.html
Topic:
/Life_and_Style/Environment/Groups_and_Organizations/By_Region/United_
Review: The beauty of the Nature Conservancy is that to protect habitat, they just buy up property. You can find chapter links here and info on the Great Lakes Biodiversity Project, the East Maui Watershed Partnership and other programs.

Berners-Lee never intended for people to type in URL addresses directly. As improved methods of accessing files are developed, Berners-Lee expects that URL addresses will soon become invisible to users. In the meantime, Web users have the option of entering a URL address directly or clicking on a hypertext link that can direct them to the desired document.

People will have to learn who they can trust on the Web. One way to do this is to put what I call an "Oh, yeah?" button on the browser.

—Tim Berners-Lee, creator of the World Wide Web

SECTION 9.3: TOOLS TO EXPLORE THE WEB

The World Wide Web has stimulated the development of numerous new ways to navigate the Web, to find all of the Web's buried treasures, and even to design your own exciting Web sties. You can spend all day browsing through the content on the World Wide Web (surfing), or you can target your search and have your results in just minutes. Whatever your approach, the World Wide Web provides an easy way to travel the globe without leaving your home.

Browsers

A document on the Web is called a **Web page**. The first page in a series of related documents or a site is called a **home page**. A **browser** is a software program designed to provide a friendly interface on the Web, display Web pages, and move between Web sites. A browser plays an important role in managing your interaction with the Web. Among other things, a browser lets you review Web content; save, download, copy, or print what you find; mark an address with a bookmark so you can return to the same site later; read and send mail; and record a history of where you've visited.

Competition between companies who make browsers has been fierce at times. By 1996, Netscape Navigator, shown in Figure 9.8, emerged as the clear leader in the browser wars, capturing over 85 percent of the market. Microsoft's Internet Explorer, shown in Figure 9.9, is positioned to go head to head with Navigator, and it is unclear as this book goes to press which of the two will be declared the winner. Both products provide integrated e-mail and news services, bookmarks to save the locations of worthy Web sites, security features to prevent unauthorized access to information about users, and a number of other features to make browsing the Web easier.

Figure 9.8
Netscape Navigator and Netscape's Home Page

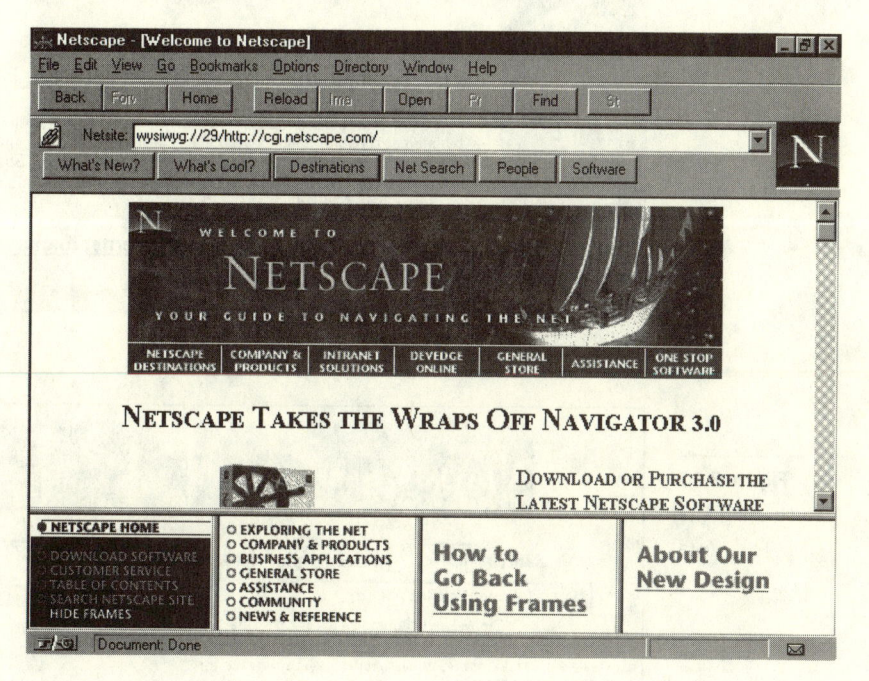

Search Engines

A **search engine** is an application on the Web that allows you to search for particular Web sites based on key words or concepts. There are a growing number of search engines found on the World Wide Web, and each one produces somewhat different results. One of the largest search engines, Alta Vista, shown in Figure 9.10, was created by Digital's Research Laboratories in Palo Alto, California. Each day, Alta Vista indexes over 30,000,000 Web pages and 3,000,000 Usenet newsgroups and processes over 12,000,000 requests.

Figure 9.9
Microsoft's Internet Explorer

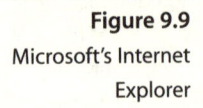

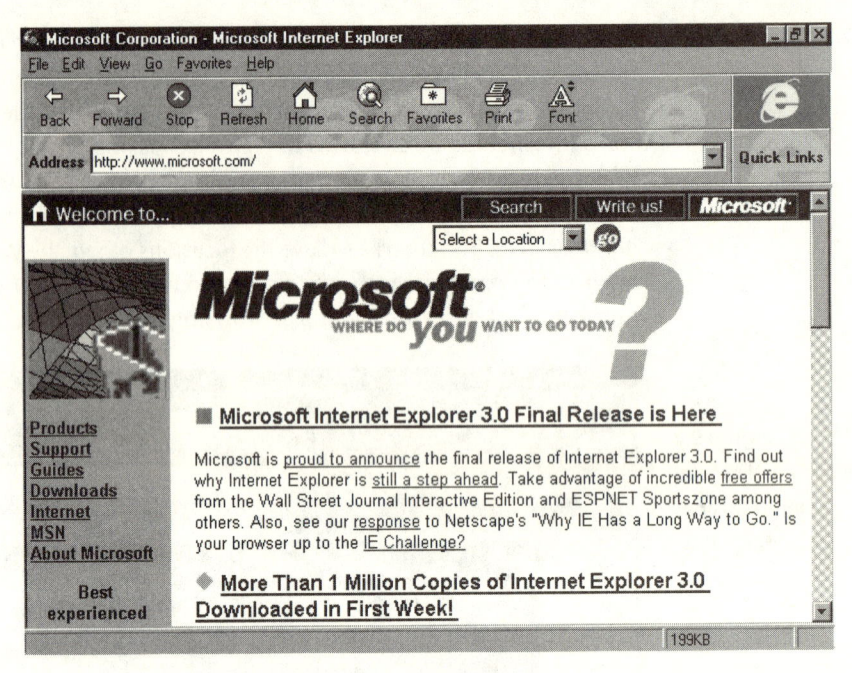

Figure 9.10
Search using Alta Vista

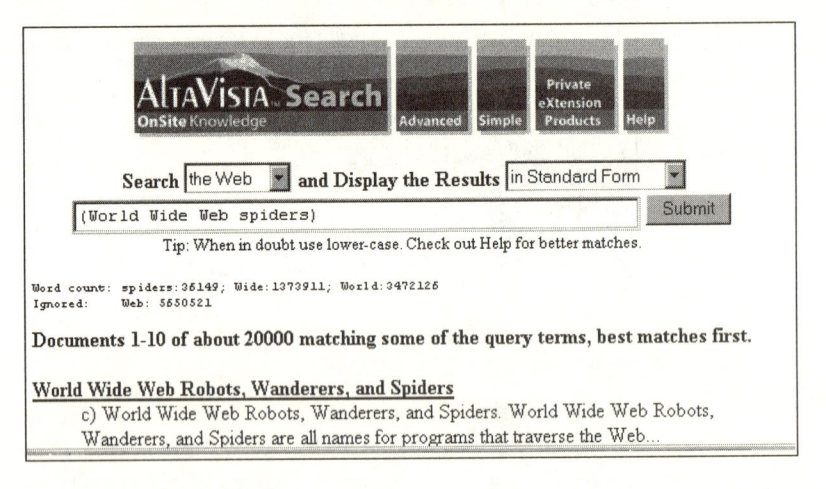

Alta Vista and other similar comprehensive search engines use a software program called a **spider** (also called a *robot*) that automatically travels through the Web's hypertext structure, retrieves a document, and then retrieves all the documents referenced by the first document. Once the documents are retrieved, they are reviewed by index software that can analyze 1GB of text an hour. Then when users enter a search word or phrase, the index directs them to appropriate Web pages.

Learning to navigate the Web requires learning about the various search tools available and what their specialties are. For example, Yahoo is organized by subject matter, so if you're looking for collections of resources related to a single topic, it is a great place to start (see Figure 9.11). Other search engines, such as The Internet Sleuth, only reference databases that are found on the Web and the articles in them.

Figure 9.11
Yahoo organizes searches by category.

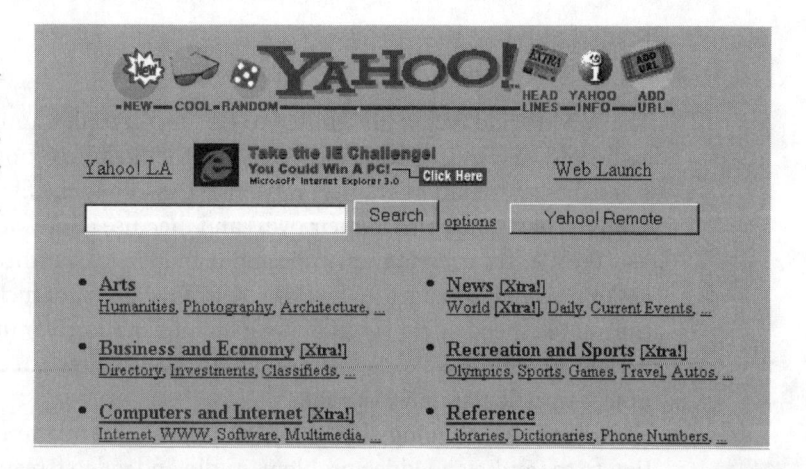

Each search engine has its own rules for how to conduct an effective search using that particular engine. To learn how to narrow down your search to pages directly related to your topic, it's important to read the Help files that are available on the search engine's home page. For example, if you choose to search on the word *spiders* to find out about how spiders are used on the World Wide Web, many of the search engines will return references to the six-legged creatures as well as to the software versions. But you can narrow down the search so that only software references appear, if you know the rules of the search engine you're using. Many people figure that they can sort through the results of a broad search, but when your search returns 30,000 references, this can be a daunting task.

People have no fundamental right to be able to discover everything instantly.

—Tim Berners-Lee

CAREER CAPSULE: PRIVATE DETECTIVE OR INVESTIGATOR

Assist governmental units, businesses, and the public in obtaining information. Use online databases. No formal educational requirements; licensing requirements vary by state.

Wage Levels: $15K / $35K / $55K / $75K+

Education Levels: High School / Associates Degree / Bachelors Degree / Postgraduate Degree

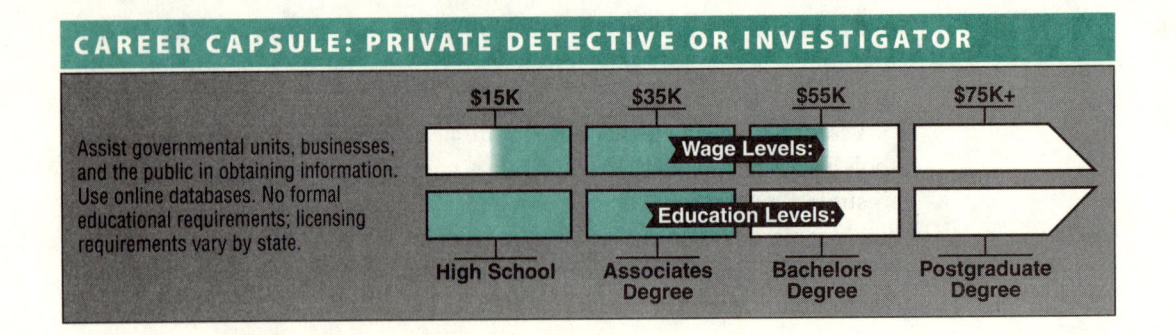

■ Audio and Video

The World Wide Web is not limited to text and graphics. You can also listen to audio and view video files on the Web. In order to access most audio and video files on the Internet, users must first **download** the file (transfer the file from the host computer to their own) and then use a software application to play the file. Transferring real-time audio and video over the Internet continues to present challenges to developers. TCP/IP does not include any ability to control the speed or consistency at which information is transferred. Some packets may move quickly, while others are slowed down because of congestion at a particular network's site.

Streaming technology has provided an adequate but far from ideal solution to the audio and video problem. Audio and video streaming applications begin playing the file as it is being downloaded, rather than waiting until the entire file is received. This means that the user does not have to wait for the file to be completely downloaded. Audio streaming is being used successfully to "broadcast" the content of radio shows such as *Gina Smith's On Computers*, a weekly Saturday afternoon radio talk show, as shown in Figure 9.12. However, it's important to note that the quality of the transmission is still affected by the traffic load on the Internet and the user's modem speed.

New audio and video technology is being developed that will correct the transmission and quality problems. Within the next five years, audio and video on the Web will be as commonplace as text is today.

SECTION 9.4: BECOMING A CONTRIBUTOR TO THE WEB

One of the most exciting elements of the Internet is that everyone can participate. The Web is not only a tool for locating information, it is a tool for disseminating information. Anyone who wants to can become an Internet publisher, by creating their own Web pages and using hypertext links to connect them to other pages and other Web sites. A small business can have as

Figure 9.12
Gina Smith's
On Computers
Web Page

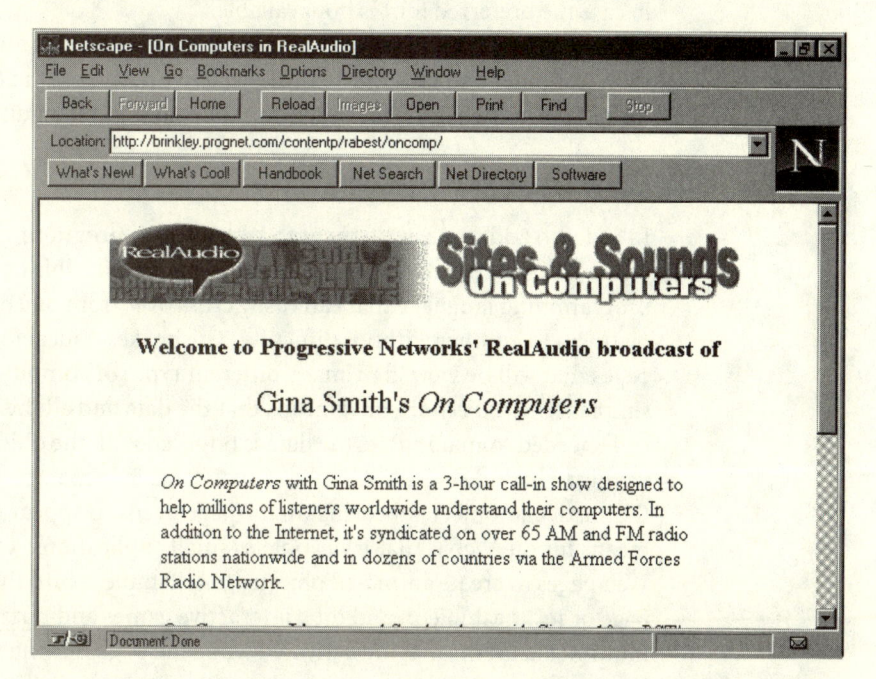

much of a presence on the Web as a major corporation. In fact, some of the most popular Web sites belong to innovative entrepreneurs who see the Web as an opportunity to compete with Goliath. Race, gender, age, and physical ability are no longer factors when the Internet becomes your communication medium. All you need is a some knowledge about how Web sites are created, a little ingenuity to make your site interesting, and a willingness to try something new.

Creating a Web Page

Hypertext Markup Language (HTML) is used to create Web pages and specifically to link one page to another on the Web. HTML is a set of text codes, called *tags*, that format a document so it can be read by a Web browser. Many applications exist that write HTML code for you while you use special design tools to create a Web page. Major word processing applications like Microsoft Word and Corel WordPerfect have HTML designers available for their products. These products are somewhat limited in the available design features but are improving with each new release. Fonts pose a special problem to Web page designers because the person viewing the document must have the font on their system that the designer used to create their page. Until this problem is resolved, good designers designate substitute fonts as backups in case the preferred font is not available.

Once your page is created and the links are verified, you can upload it to your ISP's computer and instantly become an active participant in the World Wide Web. (ISPs may charge a fee to activate your site and maintain it after it is up.)

Making a Web Page Come Alive

In order to add some excitement to Web pages, a programming language called Java has recently entered the scene. Java is a flexible object-oriented programming language that can easily cross over from one operating system platform to another without difficulty. This makes it ideal for use on Web pages that will be viewed by many different types of computer systems. In simple terms, *object-oriented* means that the data and all the programming code needed to manipulate the data is bundled with the object. Rather than having to include an entire application with each Web page, only the code for the particular object appearing on the page needs to appear there. What this means for the Web is that Java applets (small applications) can be attached to Web pages to create animated objects (for example, a bird flying across the page or text flashing on and off), interactive games and puzzles, and other multimedia events that are activated while the page is being viewed. Java has become a very popular way to draw attention to a particular Web page and make it stand out from the rest.

Many people predict that Java and other programming tools like it could ultimately mean the demise of large full-featured software applications. This is because with Java, the parts of the application you need become part of the document itself. This change from an application-centric to a document-centric approach may be down the road, but Java certainly opens the door to a dramatic shift in the way we interact with computer software.

Virtual Reality

The Web may just be in its infancy but already it's predicted that a new programming language, called **Virtual Reality Modeling Language (VRML)**, will change the graphical Web into a 3-D environment. Sites created with VRML will allow users to "walk through" a city, examine an object from all sides, or navigate through a virtual office. VRML promises to be an exciting advance in Web technology, but because it is dependent on processor and connection speeds, it may be a while yet before all users will be able to benefit from this innovation.

What You Have Learned

The Internet began as a U.S. military project to develop a way to protect the flow of information in the event of a nuclear attack. Electronic bulletin boards and commercial online information services were developed in parallel to the Internet. Today a variety of services are available through the Internet, including electronic mail, file and document exchange, mailing lists, newsgroups, and access to electronic databases. The development of the World Wide Web has been instrumental in bringing Internet access to anyone with a personal computer. The World Wide Web uses hypertext to guide users from one document to other related documents. Browsers and search engines help you navigate the Web. HTML, Java, and VRML are programming tools that help create dynamic Web pages.

Focus Questions

1. What is an electronic bulletin board?
2. Describe how TCP/IP works.
3. What is a major difference between newsgroups and mailing lists?
4. Identify the components of the following Internet URL:

    http://www.cis.ohio-state.edu/hypertext/faq-list.htm

5. What is the purpose of a search engine, and why does it matter which one you use?
6. How can you become a contributor to the World Wide Web?

Knowledge Reinforcement

A. Find three articles from recent newspapers or magazines about issues related to the Internet. Based on the articles, what do you think are the biggest concerns people have about the Internet? Choose one issue and indicate how you think the problem should be addressed.

B. Should minors be allowed to access the Internet without adult supervision? Why or why not? What controls should be put in place to prevent children from accessing inappropriate information on the Internet?

C. Recent incidents have pointed to the Internet as the source of bomb-making instructions and a child pornography ring. Should the content of the Internet be censored?

D. Contact a local computer store or public library and see if you can obtain a listing of electronic bulletin boards in your area. How many bulletin boards are there? Find out any information you can about what the purposes or special interests of the boards are.

E. Contact a local computer store or Chamber of Commerce and see if you can obtain a listing of Internet Service Providers in your area. If there are any local ISPs, call at least two of them and ask them to send you information about the services they provide. Compare and contrast the services. Which would you choose? What additional information would you want to find out before subscribing?

Further Exploration

All Known Internet Search Engines:
http://www.primenet.com/~rickyj/search/html

For recent additions to Usenet Newsgroups:
http://world.std.com/whatsnew/usenet.html

The Internet Society (history and information about the Internet):
http://www.isoc.org/
gopher://gopher.isoc.org/11/internet/history/

An Interview with Tim Berners-Lee:
http://web.mit.edu/afs/athena/org/t/techreview/www/articles/july96/bernerslee.html

To search for mailing lists, Usenet groups, and FTP sites of interest:
http://www.tile.net

Usenet Newsgroups Frequently Asked Questions:
http://www.cis.ohio-state.edu/hypertext/faq/usenet/FAQ-List.html

World Wide Web Robots, Wanderers, and Spiders:
http://info.webcrawler.com/mak/projects/robots/robots.html

PART 4

Computers in Business

Vocabulary

- batch system
- communication system
- conversion utility
- data mining
- data source
- data warehouse
- decision support
- delimited text
- detail report
- dynamic data exchange (DDE)
- electronic presentation software
- exception report
- expert system
- field code
- group scheduling software
- information system
- Information technology (IT) planning
- mail merge
- management information system
- object linking and embedding (OLE)
- office automation system
- open database connectivity (ODBC)
- personal information manager (PIM)
- real-time system
- relational database
- summary report
- transaction
- transaction processing system

SESSION TEN

Business Systems and Software

Prior to the 1970s, only large businesses that had access to a mainframe or minicomputer could computerize their operations. The PC revolution meant that small and midsize businesses finally had a way to automate many of their labor-intensive bookkeeping and financial management tasks. At the end of this session, you will be able to

- Identify the five types of information systems
- Explain the purpose of IT planning
- Describe advantages of management information systems
- Discuss contemporary office automation software
- Describe some of the steps in information technology planning

227

SECTION 10.1: INFORMATION SYSTEMS

Information technology (IT) planning—also referred to as strategic technology planning, information services planning, and enterprise technology planning—is a process by which organizations decide how computer systems can help them achieve their company's objectives. Most successful companies today have a formal technology plan. However, with the rapid pace of technological change, IT plans are often outdated before they have a chance to be implemented. Therefore, effective IT plans include flexibility for hardware and software selection and incorporate an openness to new technologies and innovations.

Types of Information Systems

IT plans are concerned with **information systems**—the combinations of software, hardware, and skills that support the mission and objectives of the business. There are as many information systems as there are businesses, but they fall into five broad categories:

- Transaction processing
- Management information
- Expert systems
- Office automation
- Communication systems

The following sections focus on the first four categories of information systems, all of which rely on communication systems. **Communication systems** connect computers, allowing employees to work collaboratively and access shared information easily. Networks, client-server databases, intranets, and other communication systems issues are discussed in Session 11.

SECTION 10.2: TRANSACTION PROCESSING SYSTEMS

Transaction processing systems capture information about the **transactions** (events) that occur in a business. For example:

- Point of sale systems capture information about sales transactions.
- Order entry systems record orders and customer data.

- Accounting systems track changes in income, expenses, assets, liabilities, and business equity.

- Inventory systems capture changes in inventory through sales or purchases.

- Registration systems record student and class information.

Transaction processing systems were originally developed as mainframe applications and have been operational in many large businesses for 30 or 40 years. For most businesses, implementing a system to process transactions is one of the first priorities when considering automation. Personal computers have allowed small businesses that would have never thought about having a computerized billing or inventory tracking system to implement transaction processing systems.

There are many *off-the-shelf* software products available for businesses of different sizes that include one or more types of transaction processing systems. Off-the-shelf software products are products that have been designed to meet general business needs and usually allow only a limited amount of customization to fit a particular business. For example, Quickbooks, shown in Figure 10.1 is a microcomputer-based off-the-shelf software product used to manage a small or midsize business's finances.

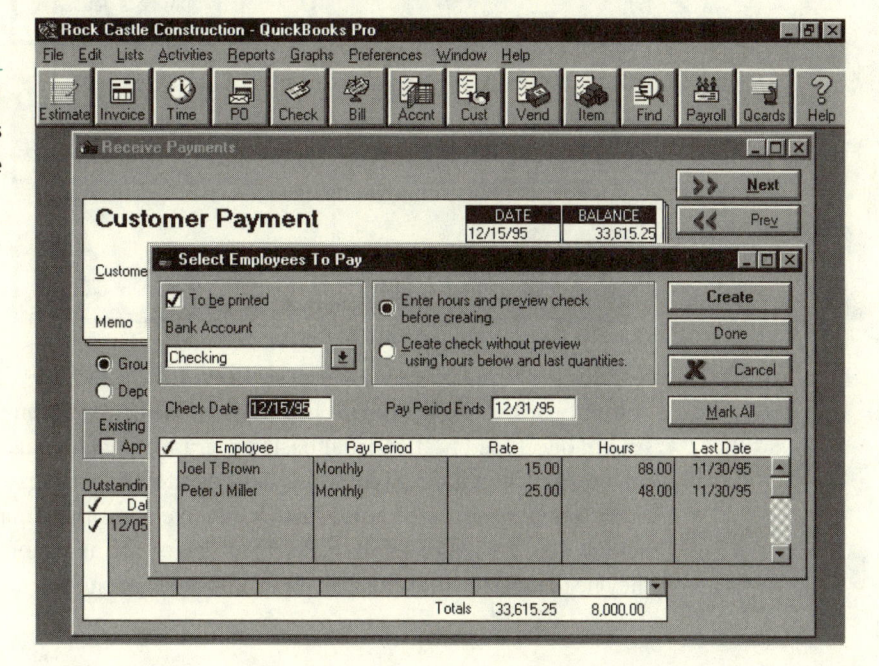

Figure 10.1
Quickbooks financial software

Quickbooks is the business version of the personal financial software package, Quicken. Although managing personal and business finances have some similarities (paying bills, tracking deposits, categorizing expenses), businesses also have unique needs. In Quickbooks, a businessperson can create an estimate for a job, order materials for the job, track employee time, create invoices to bill for the work completed, and track receivables (outstanding payments due the company). Figure 10.2 demonstrates the Quickbooks transaction processing system. Converting from a manual bookkeeping system to a computerized accounting system such as Quickbooks increases a company's efficiency and builds in controls and safeguards that are more difficult to ensure in a manual system.

Figure 10.2 Transaction processing

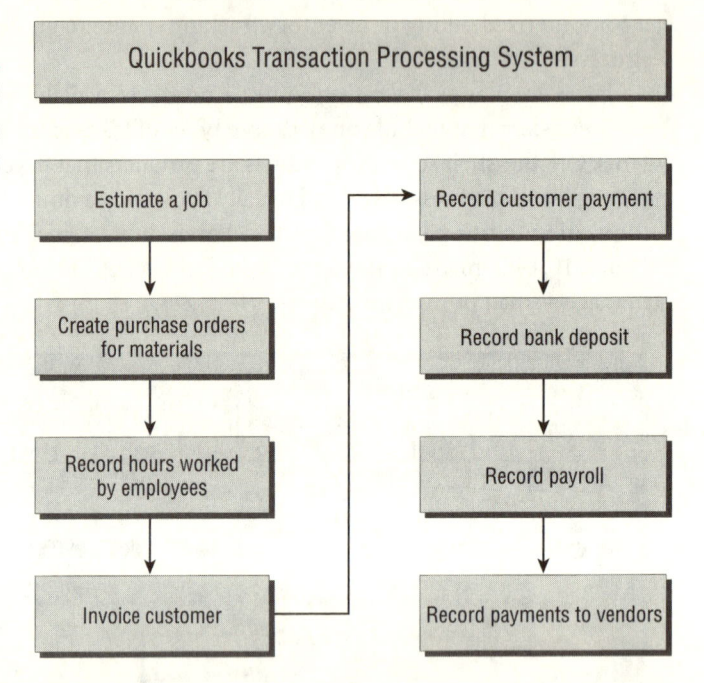

Quickbooks Transaction Processing System

Estimate a job → Create purchase orders for materials → Record hours worked by employees → Invoice customer → Record customer payment → Record bank deposit → Record payroll → Record payments to vendors

Another popular business accounting software package, Solomon IV from Solomon Software (see Figure 10.3), is a full-featured accounting information system developed in the Visual Basic programming language. Unlike other off-the-shelf products, Solomon is designed to be customized. Although many businesses may be able to use it just like it is, others may want to modify field names, design new forms, delete tables, create new modules—whatever they need to make it fit the way their business operates.

Figure 10.3
Sales Order form in Solomon IV accounting software

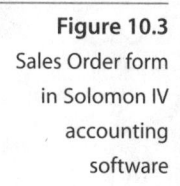

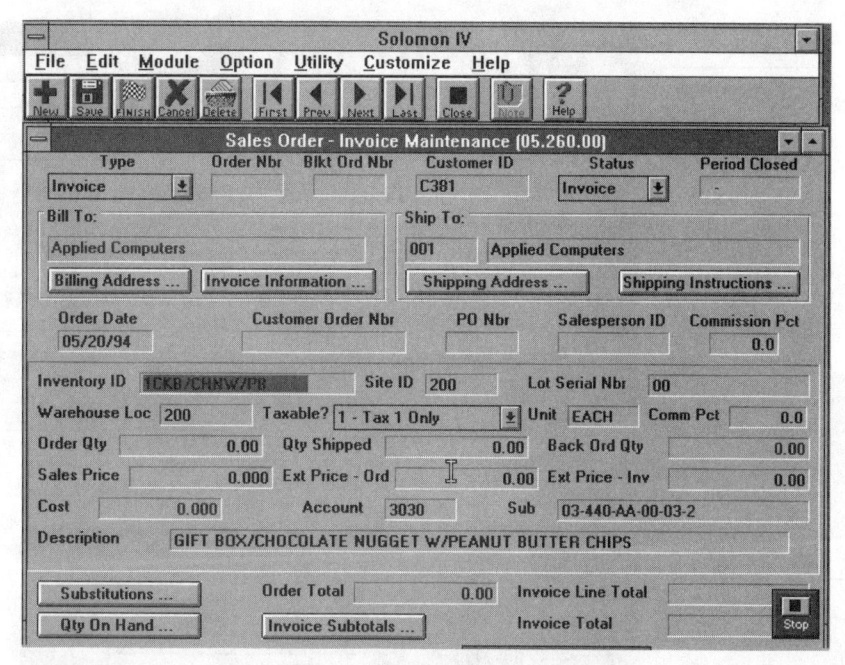

If a business is unable to find off-the-shelf software that meets its need, it may choose to hire a software development firm to design custom transaction processing software. Custom software is more costly, will generally take longer to implement, and makes the client totally dependent on the software developer for future upgrades. The ongoing costs of maintaining custom software are often as much as the initial development cost, but custom software provides the business with a product that more closely matches the flow of the business's transactions.

A third option exists for those businesses that do not want to purchase off-the-shelf or customizable software but also don't want to incur the time and expense involved with developing a totally customized product. Software products such as Microsoft Access for Windows 95, a database development tool, include a number of predesigned databases that can be customized using Access's friendly interface. Figure 10.4 shows an Orders by Customer form that is part of the Access *Orders Entry* database.

Each of the databases included with Access is developed using one of the Access Wizards, (see Figure 10.5), step-by-step programs in which users make choices to create a customized product. Even after the Wizard creates the database, the user can add fields and develop new forms. Wizards provide users with a starting point: a well-designed database structure that is open to modification and improvement.

Figure 10.4
Orders by Customer form

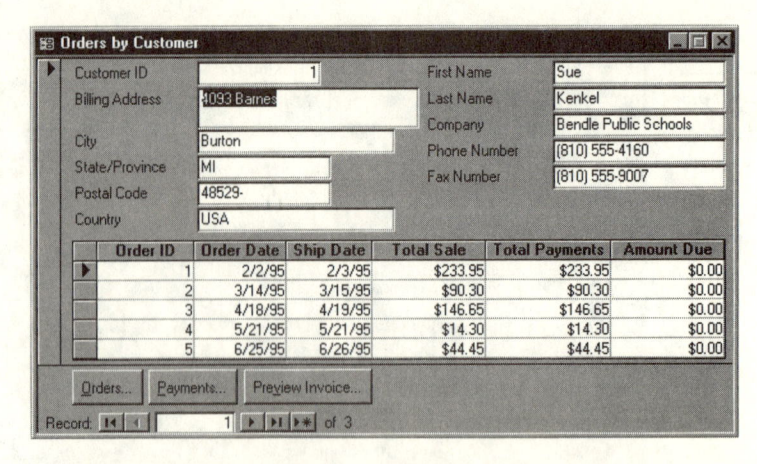

Figure 10.5
Microsoft Access Database Wizard

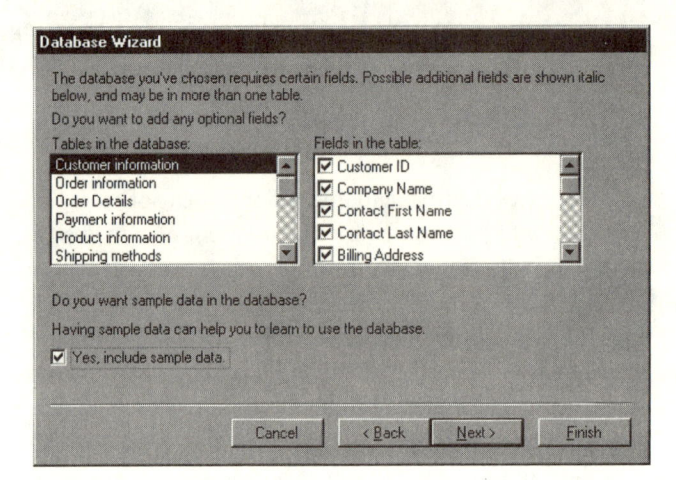

Whatever approach a business takes to developing their transaction processing systems, computers provide organizations with the ability to track large volumes of data conveniently, efficiently, and accurately.

SECTION 10.3: MANAGEMENT INFORMATION SYSTEMS

Management information systems provide reports based largely on data from a company's transaction processing system. For example, an accounting system provides income statements and balance sheets, but a manager may need other specific reports on the status of customer accounts or hours worked by employees. A **summary report** summarizes activities for a particular time period: for example, total orders from each sales region or total hours worked by a department during the last month. A management information system also supplies **exception reports**, reports which identify records that do not follow the expected process: only those customers who didn't place an order, or those departments with significant overtime hours. **Detail reports**, reports which list detailed data, are created for supervisors or lower level managers: inactive customers grouped by sales representative, or the hours each departmental employee worked during the last month.

Management information systems also provide analysis tools for **decision support**. Analysis tools allow managers to create additional reports and examine data in ways that weren't included in the managerial information system's reports. Fourth-generation tools, such as English Wizard, allow managers to directly query a database to find, for example, inactive customers over the age of 30.

Good transaction systems include a management information component. Users can create reports and charts, like those shown in Figure 10.6, which provide quick information to help make decisions and track the company's financial stability. Based on the accounts receivable information, a company may decide to make contact with customers who are more than 30 days overdue or may not agree to additional orders from overdue customers until their accounts are paid.

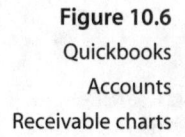

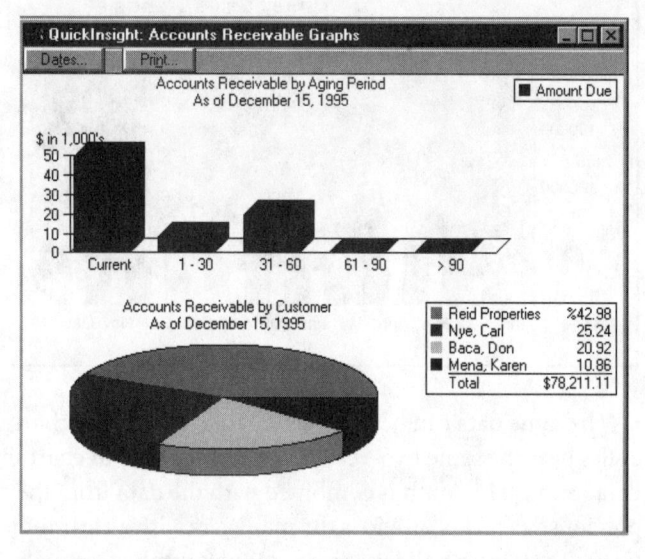

Figure 10.6
Quickbooks Accounts Receivable charts

Because computerized systems can easily store historical data, management information systems are able to track and report comparative data to show trends over time. This ability allows managers to evaluate areas of their operations that are showing improvement and other areas that may be showing a decline in performance. Spreadsheets like Excel are used to analyze trends and model future scenarios. In fact, spreadsheets were the first office automation tool designed specifically for managers. The first chart in Figure 10.7, created using Excel, shows a comparison of net turkey revenues for a two-year period. It's clear from the line chart that 1996 sales consistently exceeded 1995 sales, so managers can easily see that the sales department has successfully broadened its customer base.

Figure 10.7
Microsoft Excel charts

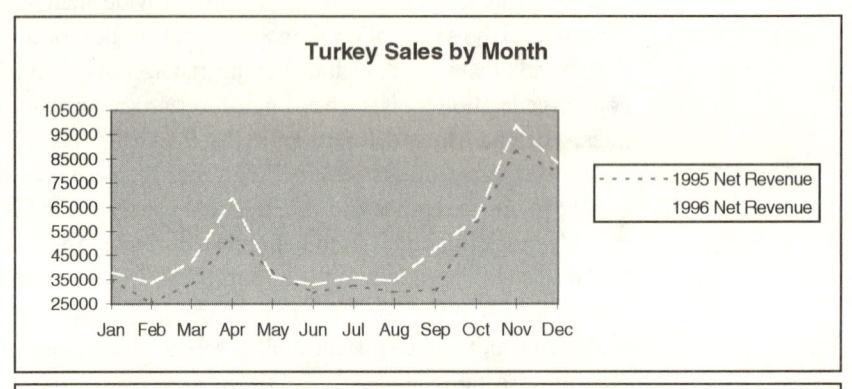

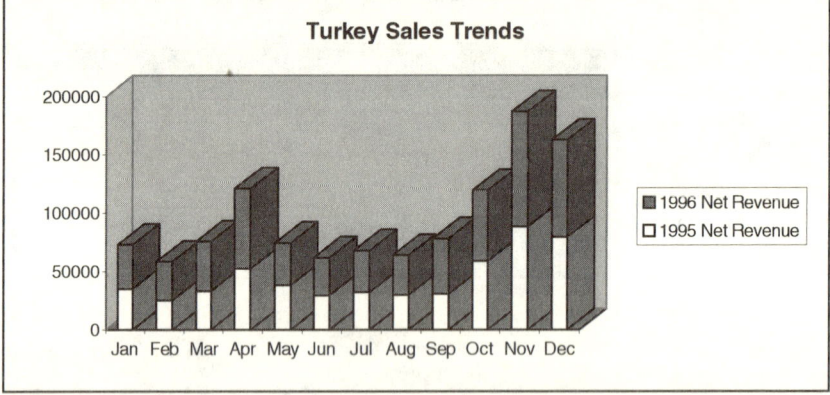

The same data can be represented in a stacked bar chart to show business cycles over the same two-year period. In the second chart in Figure 10.7, the data from each month is combined with the data from the same month in the previous year. This provides the managers with a clear indication of peak times (the winter holiday season from November through December and the early spring around Easter). Armed with this information, managers can appropriately schedule employees, intensify the availability of transportation systems, and manage cash flow. This information may also show that management efforts to level sales throughout the year have not been successful, and could serve as a catalyst for the company to research whether adding chickens to their product line might provide the company with more stability throughout the year.

Data Warehousing

Successful companies have developed methods to analyze historical data and put the information that is derived to use in furthering the goals of the business. As you have seen, spreadsheet applications are often used to provide this analysis. As transaction processing systems accumulate more and more data, businesses have recognized a need to pull the data together from different systems to be able to conduct more thorough analyses. **Data warehouses** are subject-oriented, central storehouses of electronic data that can be accessed by managers and other decision-makers within a company for data analysis and extraction. Data warehouses combine data from different databases into one warehouse (collection) and build relationships between the databases. For example, a bank's data warehouse might have data from customer savings and checking accounts databases, loan and mortgage databases, and credit card databases. Thus, a manager could query the database and locate all of the bank's information about a particular customer.

In addition to combining data about an individual customer, data warehouses have become popular tools for managers who previously might not have had access to aggregate data about customers. It might be valuable for a bank manager, for example, to learn the average savings and credit debt of customers who were given personal loans in the last 12 months. Without data warehousing, this question would be very difficult to answer, but querying a data warehouse provides the information in a matter of minutes. If trends are noted in the data, the manager can query deeper and determine whether particular loan officers accepted higher debt limits than others, or if there is a relationship between savings history and loan defaults.

Another advantage of data warehouses is that they can provide historical data that isn't subject to revisions and modifications. The operational data that resides in the active databases of the company changes with each new entry, and cannot present an accurate picture of the business across time. A data warehouse contains data that has, in effect, been frozen at the time of the most recent update. Although new data can be appended to the warehouse, it always reflects a fixed point rather than the moving target represented in operational data. This assures that accurate comparisons can be made.

Data Mining

The concept of data warehousing was introduced by IBM in the late 1980s. An even more recent development provides data warehouse users with new tools to analyze data. **Data mining** software examines data using a data mining engine to finds relationships in the data that no one might have suspected existed. Without the use of data mining, a typical analysis is based on human assumptions about what relationships might exist between the data elements. For example, a grocery chain might assume that customers who buy certain brands of spaghetti sauce also buy certain brands of pasta. With a traditional data warehousing query tool, they might discover that there is no real relationship between brands of pasta and brands of sauce, and assume that there is no way to predict who will buy a particular brand of spaghetti sauce. However, a data mining engine could examine the grocery store's transaction data and determine that the real predictor of which brand of spaghetti sauce someone buys is whether they own a dog or a cat.

NOTE

Don't laugh. A market research study determined that pet ownership preference is a prime determinant of pasta sauce purchase behavior.

With data mining, you can examine data when the sheer volume of facts makes it impossible for you to conduct successful spreadsheet analysis. A leading company in data mining technology, DataMind Corporation, makes software that examines the data in a database and develops a data model users can then explore. For example, users in an insurance company could start out by asking a question like "What are the characteristics of good drivers?" The data mining software will examine the company's database to identify the relationships within the data and develop a relationship model that can be used to answer a more specific question like "Who is a good driver?" Data mining tools make data analysis more thorough and ultimately more useful for forecasting and planning.

The Changing Role of Data Management

One of the most significant recent changes in business systems is the role that database applications are playing in today's offices. Data from large mainframe databases can now be extracted and imported into a desktop spreadsheet or database application. Departments can combine data warehouse data with department-specific databases that are maintained locally, a combination that makes data much more accessible to individual departments for review and analysis. Salespeople can take detailed customer data on the road in notebook computers to make well-informed sales calls. Many managers feel that as end users develop a sense of data ownership, data reliability becomes more important to them, and as a result, they take increased care while entering data.

CAREER CAPSULE: PRODUCT COST ESTIMATOR

Work in sales and job costing departments of large companies. Use spreadsheet and statistical software to determine appropriate product costs. Detail oriented, business and math background. BA in business or math preferred.

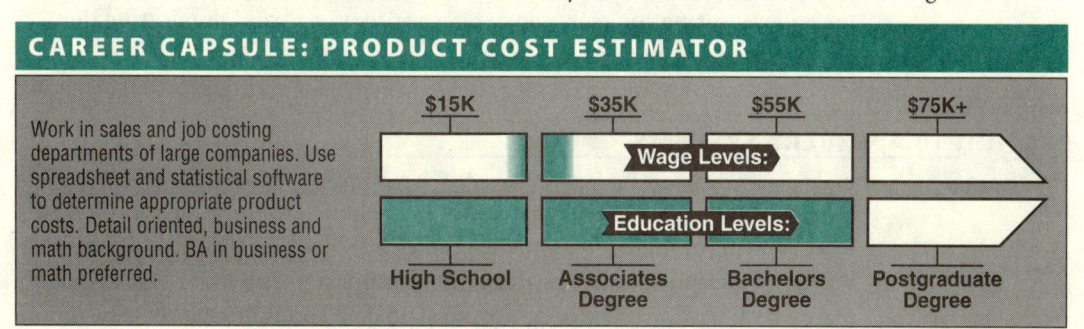

Wage Levels: $15K – $35K
Education Levels: High School – Associates Degree – Bachelors Degree – Postgraduate Degree ($55K – $75K+)

However, there are also dangers inherent in this new data availability. Information extracted from a data warehouse accurately reflects a particular point in time. When this information is combined with active data, users can lose track of which data is historical and which is current. An employee with access to mixed data may make an inappropriate business decision based on obsolete information. There is also a risk that departments will develop local databases that no longer have a relationship to the company as a whole. Each department can spend time and resources entering and managing data, not realizing that they are duplicating data that exists somewhere else in the company.

And finally, the notebook computers of traveling business people are stolen with increasing frequency by corporate spies who are stealing more than just a few inconsequential memos to company clients. In some cases, they are finding copies of the entire corporation's databases: all their customer and billing information, internal correspondence, product prototypes, and other company secrets. Release of this information could cause the early death of some companies in highly competitive markets.

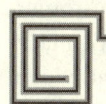

> **NOTE**
>
> Increased airport security has created a new way to steal portable computers during peak flight times. Two rip-off artists get in line in front of a person with a computer. After the owner has placed the computer on the x-ray belt, the first person moves quickly through the body scanner. The second person has pockets full of change and car keys, and is stopped by security at the body scanner, also holding up the computer's owner. This provides the first thief with the time required to steal the computer as it comes off the belt.

To minimize these problems, it's essential for various departments to work with their Information Services departments to develop data management protocols, security precautions, and confidentiality procedures. Each employee must take responsibility for learning how their data needs fit into the larger information technology plan and work to avoid duplicating the efforts of others.

SECTION 10.4: EXPERT SYSTEMS

Expert systems are software programs that help determine a correct solution to a problem (or make a reasonable prediction) based on the user's answers to a series of questions. Answers are used to eliminate possibilities, as in the game of Twenty Questions. The programs contain data about the subject area and use decision trees to direct the questions and guide users to answers. Since all the facts of a particular situation or question may not be known, expert systems may not be able to answer with certainty. They are designed to mimic a human expert who can make use of the known data and make an expert judgment call.

Early expert systems used examples from zoology to correctly identify animals. A user was asked: Does the animal live entirely in water? Does the animal bear live young? If the answer to both questions was "Yes," then further questions would help narrow the choice to a specific water mammal. Expert systems have been created and continue to be refined for use in medical diagnoses (Does the patient have a fever?) and legal research (Is a land contract involved in the dispute?). Very successful expert systems have been designed to determine where to drill for oil.

Expert systems can be applied to any field where the logic behind decision-making can be defined. Repetitive tasks that require a significant amount of data to be evaluated in a short time frame are good candidates for expert systems. IF-THEN scenarios are often used in rule-based expert systems, like the system American Express uses to approve charges being made by customers. Since American Express cards have no credit limit, decisions must be made about whether the charges are within an acceptable range for the individual customer. When a store calls American Express to approve a customer's purchase, an expert system determines if the purchase is outside of the customer's recent normal buying pattern. If it is, then the expert system reviews a number of American Express databases to evaluate past credit card usage, spending patterns, payment patterns, and other factors. Within seconds, the expert system makes a recommendation to the credit authorizer—an actual human being—who then gives the final authorization.

Many software companies use expert systems to help technical assistance personnel diagnose customers' computer problems over the phone. Figure 10.8 shows an expert system incorporated into the Windows 95 Help Troubleshooting system. In this example, if the user chooses the first option, "I can connect to the remote computer, but I do not see a terminal screen" (the IF statement), they are asked what kind of connection they are using. Depending on their answer to that question, they are then told what steps to take to correct the problem (the THEN statement). This system has limitations, however, and may eventually indicate that it cannot solve the problem and direct the user to a human expert, the administrator for the remote computer.

Figure 10.8
The Windows 95 Troubleshooter

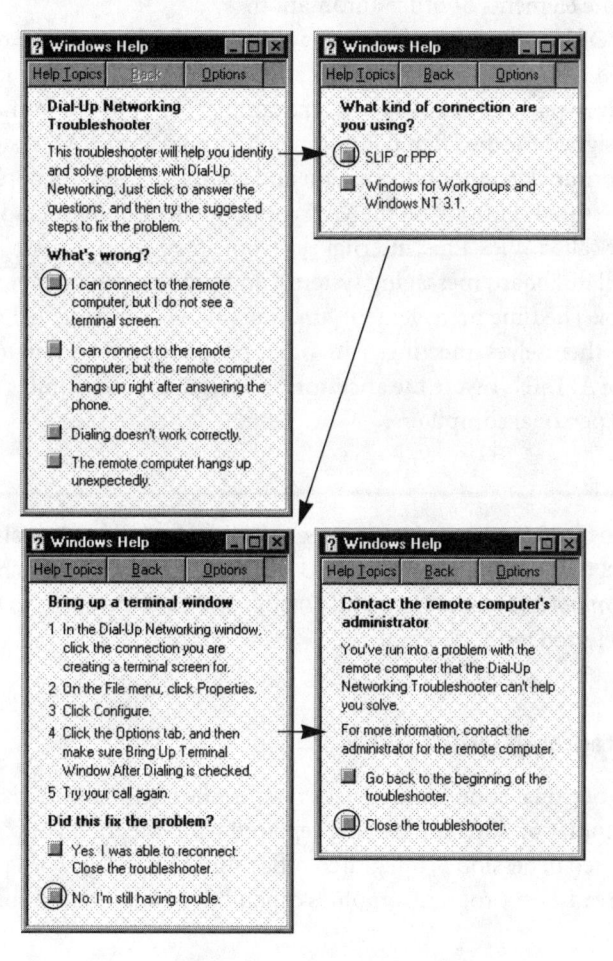

SECTION 10.5: OFFICE AUTOMATION SYSTEMS

Office automation uses a variety of technologies to streamline routine tasks involved in the processing and managing of work in an office. **Office automation systems** typically include word processing, data management, electronic mail, group conferencing, and group scheduling systems. Broadly defined, office automation also includes telecommunications (telephone systems), dictation equipment, and image processing (copiers, scanners, facsimile machines, and digital camera equipment). The term "office automation" evolved in the 1960s and 70s when offices moved from being paper-driven to machine-driven. Today, it is virtually impossible to find an office without some elements of office automation.

Office automation software was originally designed for mainframe and minicomputers and combined a number of applications into a single menu-driven package. ALL-IN-1 is an example of an office automation system designed for the Digital Equipment Corporation's VAX systems. Workers use a terminal to enter information and complete tasks. All applications and data are stored centrally on the VAX computer. ALL-IN-1 includes a word processor called WPS-Plus, internal electronic mail, group messages (an internal bulletin board messaging system), and time management or scheduling system. The time management functions allow users to schedule appointments for themselves, meetings with other people, and maintain to-do lists. Systems like ALL-IN-1 were the ancestors of integrated office suites designed to run on personal computers.

> **NOTE**
>
> The term *dumb terminal* has been used to describe terminals, to emphasize the fact that terminals have no CPU and, therefore, no processing ability. *Dumb terminal* is (1) redundant and (2) offensive to some users, so *terminal* is now the preferred term.

■ Integrated Office Suites

As personal computers replace mainframe terminals on many desktops, office automation software is being replaced with integrated office suites. As discussed in Session 8, integrated office suites include a word processor, a spreadsheet program, graphics capabilities, presentation software, a personal organizer, and other smaller applications. Some office suites also include a database development application such as Microsoft Access or Borland Paradox. The three best selling office suites, Microsoft Office, Corel WordPerfect Suite, and Lotus Smart Suite, offer powerful integrated features, which means that a document created in one application can be used in another application. Table 10.1 identifies the applications included with each of the three major office suites.

CAREER CAPSULE: ELECTRONIC PAGINATION SYSTEM OPERATOR

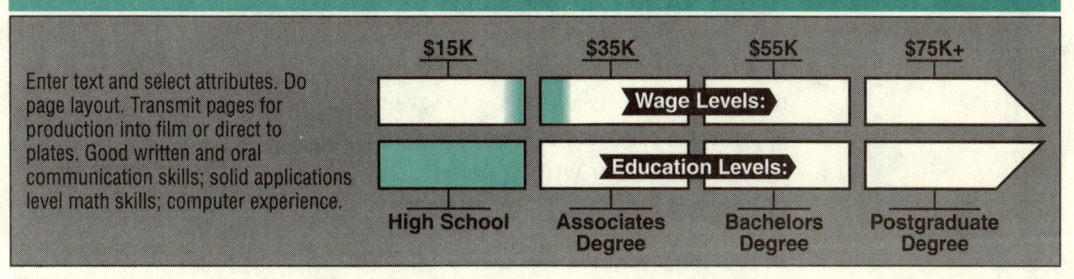

Enter text and select attributes. Do page layout. Transmit pages for production into film or direct to plates. Good written and oral communication skills; solid applications level math skills; computer experience.

Wage Levels: $15K–$35K
Education Levels: High School–Associates Degree

Table 10.1 Applications in the Major Office Suites

	Microsoft	Corel	Lotus
Word Processor	Word	WordPerfect	Word Pro (Ami Pro)
Spreadsheet	Excel	Quatro Pro	123
Presentations Planner	PowerPoint	Presentations	Freelance Graphics
Database Developer	Access	Paradox (Borland)	Approach
Scheduler/ Personal Information Manager	Outlook (Office 97)	Sidekick	Organizer
Additional Apps	Clip Art Gallery; Office Art; Office Binder; HTML editor	CorelFLOW (flowcharting); Internet connectivity; Envoy	ScreenCam

Because of the flexibility of today's office applications, documents can easily be converted from one application to another—rarely should anything ever have to be typed more than once. There are five primary ways in which data can be shared between applications:

- Most Windows applications are OLE 2.0 compliant. **OLE** (pronounced "O-lay") or **object linking and embedding** is a protocol that allows one application to exchange data with other Windows applications. For example, a table created in WordPerfect can be changed into an Excel worksheet using the Windows copy and paste tools.

- If you know you want to open a document in another application, many applications allow you to save the document in the destination application's format. A WordPerfect document can be saved as a Word document; a letter written on a PC can be saved in Macintosh format, or vice versa.

- Import tools are also available that allow, for example, an Excel worksheet to be converted into an Access database.

- Many applications have **conversion utility** programs that allow users to open a document created by another application and have it automatically converted to the format used by the active application. Conversion utilities are not always part of the standard installation, however, and may have to be installed later if it is discovered that they are needed.

- Database applications can exchange data with other database applications using a protocol such as **ODBC** (**Open Database Connectivity**) or OpenDoc. ODBC compliant databases have the greatest ability to migrate up to larger, more complex database management systems on a network (see Session 11 for more about networks) or down to simpler local databases for use within a department.

If you find yourself retyping, remember there's probably a better way!

Word Processing

The cornerstone of every office suite is the word processor. Even with all of the other technologies available, offices are still primary conveyors of text-based and, generally, printed documents. Even in the paperless office, the written word is the mainstay of every business. Word processors simplify the entry and editing of basic text. Virtually every other function word processors perform is designed to make documents aesthetically appealing. There is a general expectation in the business community that an effective company will present high-quality printed documents. Sloppy, poorly written, and poorly designed printed work is a good indication of a company's lack of commitment to quality.

Whether they are designed for home or business use, the major features of word processors differ only slightly. There are, however, some features which are used predominately in business settings. The most important of these is the **mail merge** feature. Mail merge allows companies to maintain mailing lists of customers and clients and send personalized letters to them and print mailing labels with minimal effort. The document on the left in Figure 10.9 is a Word merge document (called a main document) containing **field codes** from a **data source**. Field codes are markers that represent data in a data source; a data source is a database or data list containing fields and records. (See Session 8 for more about fields and records.) The document on the right shows one of the letters that resulted from merging the names and addresses in the data source with the main document.

Figure 10.9
Word merge document containing field codes from a data source

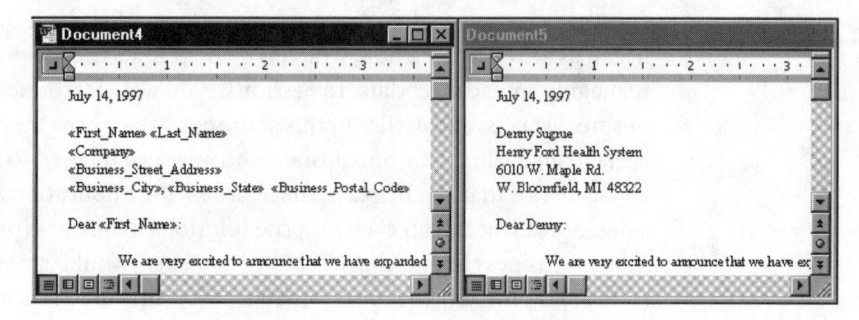

You can purchase labels in many different shapes and sizes, which makes it easy to use the mail merge features for a number of other uses. An inventory database can be merged with labels to create price tags. Employee names, job titles, and department names can be merged with name tag labels for the next company training session. Names and addresses can even be merged with Rolodex cards to fill a card filing system.

Moreover, your data sources aren't confined to lists created in a word processor. Word, for example, can use a database created in Access, Excel, Paradox, or even a **delimited text** file, a file created in any application which uses commas or other characters to delimit or separate fields and records. With Access and Excel, Word uses a feature called **dynamic data exchange (DDE)** to open the data file and "borrow" the records for the purposes of the merge. Mail merge is a powerful office automation tool, especially when the word processor has the ability to use varied data sources.

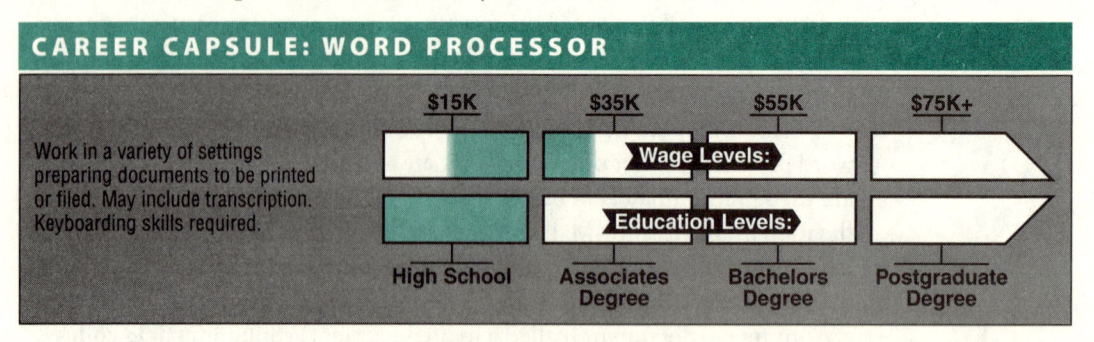

CAREER CAPSULE: WORD PROCESSOR

Work in a variety of settings preparing documents to be printed or filed. May include transcription. Keyboarding skills required.

Wage Levels: $15K – $35K – $55K – $75K+
Education Levels: High School – Associates Degree – Bachelors Degree – Postgraduate Degree

Spreadsheets

While Lotus 123 once controlled the spreadsheet market, Microsoft Excel has gained prominence as the most popular spreadsheet application. Lotus 123 and Quattro Pro (Corel's spreadsheet) began life as DOS-based products and eventually moved to the Windows environment. Excel, on the other hand, began as a GUI application, which is evident in its user-friendly approach to managing spreadsheet data. In Session 8, you were introduced to the concept of spreadsheets, and earlier in this session, you saw how they can assist managers in analyzing data. Spreadsheet software can be used to evaluate "What if?" scenarios that can help a manager assess the implications of different decisions. Spreadsheets can even propose solutions to business problems and help achieve business financial goals. Many managers would agree that spreadsheet software is probably the most valuable office software in their tool kit.

Database Development Tools

Database products such as Access and Paradox are generally only included in the professional versions of the office suites and are different from other suite applications. Although these products are often called database applications, in reality they are database development tools. Before users can enter data, they have to develop or design the database. Access and Paradox are both examples of relational databases. A **relational database** is a collection of fields which are organized into different tables of data. Each table represents a distinct part of the database. These tables are then linked together through a common field which forms a relationship between the tables.

For example, a business may have a table that contains customers' names, addresses, and phone numbers and another table that contains orders. The two tables are linked by a common Customer ID field. Figure 10.10 shows the tables and relationships that exist in an Access Orders Entry database.

Figure 10.10
Relationships in the Access Orders Entry database

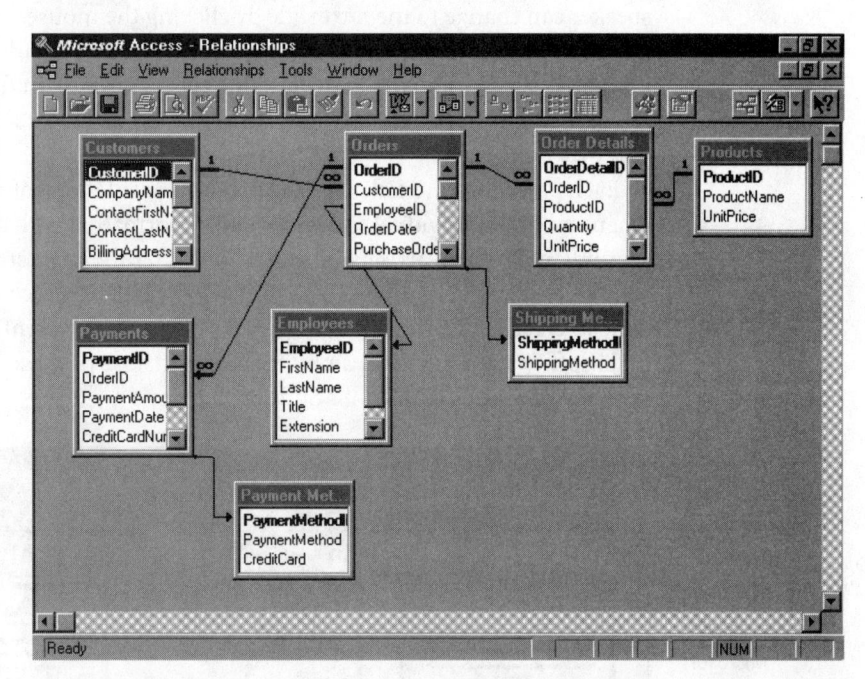

Relational databases are much more powerful than single-table or flat-file databases. Complex information regarding a single individual or item can be maintained without having to repeat data. Users can query the data and develop reports that cross tables and return all data related to a single individual or group of individuals.

Automating Presentations

A business wouldn't be a business without meetings. Employees get together to hash out company policies; they invite their customers in to hear their latest sales pitch; or company representatives go to client sites to present a new project proposal. White boards, flip charts, and overhead projectors have been the mainstay of business meetings for years.

Electronic presentation software can be used to create traditional overheads and slides. But the real power of this software becomes evident when it is used to create on-screen electronic presentations that are run from a computer and displayed using an LCD projector. No more fumbling around with overhead transparencies which always seem to be upside down or backward. An electronic presentation can be set up to run continuously, or if desired, the speaker can change to the next slide by clicking the mouse. Each screen can be projected in color, and unlike 35 mm slides, electronic slides can even be animated. Slides can fade in or out, lines of text can fly in from one side or the other, text characters can appear on the screen to the sound of machine gun fire.

Each presentation made with electronic presentation software is composed of a number of individual slides that can be formatted with custom backgrounds, colors, clip art, charts, and tables. After the basic structure of the slides is in place, then different actions can be added to each slide and its contents to create a lively, entertaining, and professional presentation. Each of the major office suites includes a presentation software package. Figure 10.11 shows Microsoft PowerPoint's Slide Sorter view.

Figure 10.11
Creating an electronic presentation with Microsoft PowerPoint

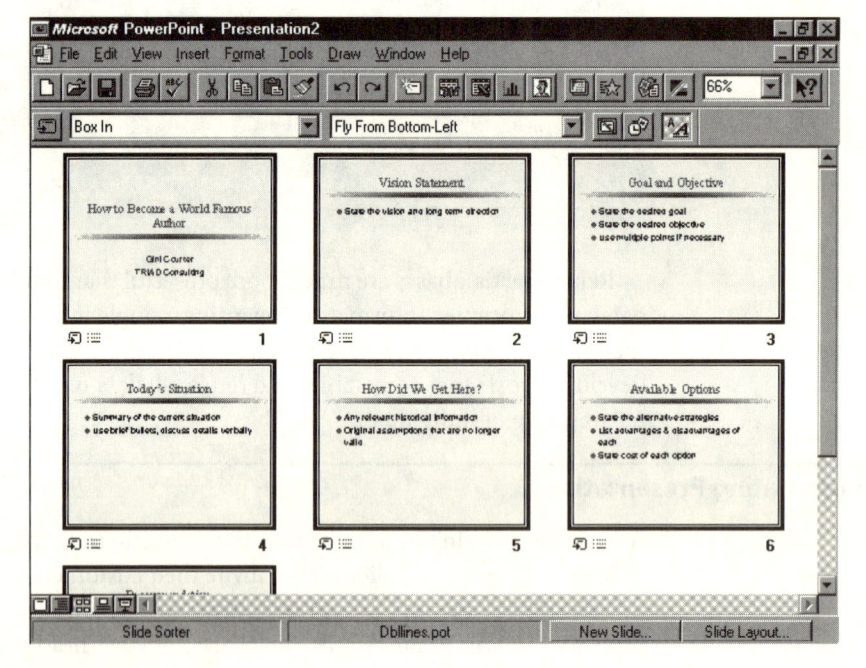

Tracking People and Schedules

One of the last applications to receive attention in the office suites is a combined application that includes an address book and a scheduling/time management program. These programs are referred to as **personal information managers** (**PIMs**). PIMs are typically the least well integrated applications in office suites. Exchanging data with other suite applications is difficult and in some cases impossible.

> **NOTE**
>
> Many people who are comfortable with electronic versions of traditional appointment and address books choose to carry hand-held PIM computers like a Sharp Wizard. Handheld PIMs are easy to slip into a pocket or briefcase, they don't required booting an entire computer system to operate, and are less conspicuous on the subway.

Several of the leading PIMs are independent applications that are not part of an office suite. Despite some of the drawbacks, PIMs are beginning to grow in popularity for a couple of significant reasons:

- As more companies are installing local and wide area networks (see Session 11) electronic scheduling is becoming a realistic alternative to the problem of trying to schedule meetings between groups of people.

- The software products themselves are becoming more fully featured, easier to use, and more integrated with other applications. This is partially a reflection of the growing demand and partially because the other office products have become mature enough for software companies to devote resources to what until recently have been regarded as accessories or sideline products.

- Microsoft released a new version of Windows in late 1996 called Windows CE that is specifically designed for handheld computers. Modeled after Windows 95, Windows CE allows users to access the Internet, use applications such as Word and Excel, and synchronize directly with their desktop PCs.

Contact Managers

Contact managers started out as electronic address books but have developed into applications that provide strong support for sales, marketing, and client management. Contact managers such as Symantec's ACT! and Janna Systems' Janna Contact '95 keep track of names and addresses, but also allow users to record the results of phone and personal contacts, write up to-do lists related to each client, and even indicate when certain clients need to be contacted again. In some cases, contact manager data can be used to generate mailing labels and letters using a word processor's mail merge tools. For anyone who has to keep track of sales and marketing calls, contact managers make a world of difference.

Group and Personal Scheduling

Secretaries, assistants, and executives spend countless hours trying to coordinate meetings with other people who also have busy schedules. All the attendees must first be polled to develop a list of feasible times. Even if a mutually agreeable time becomes immediately obvious, everyone must still be contacted again to confirm the date and time of the meeting. As soon as the meeting time is selected, someone invariably has to reschedule, and the process starts all over again.

When the personal schedules of key individuals are maintained using electronic **group scheduling software** on a network, these scheduling nightmares disappear. In order to schedule a meeting, all a busy department head has to do is open their group scheduling program and complete a meeting request form. This form generally includes a description of the meeting, a list of attendees, a location, and an approximate length. The program reviews each person's schedule and determines the next time slot in which everyone on the list is available. Electronic messages are automatically sent to those people asking them to confirm that the date and time are acceptable. When they reply to the message, the meeting is again confirmed by electronic mail.

Many personal scheduling programs will print out pages that fit into manual personal planner systems. (Common formats include Day-Timer, Rolodex, Day-Runner, and Franklin Planner.) This is especially helpful for assitants who maintain their employers' schedules. After entering all of the information in a scheduling program, they can just hand their bosses printouts of their schedules in a familiar format.

SPECIAL TOPIC: DEVELOPING AN IT PLAN

Developing an information technology plan is a critical part of any company's planning process. IntegrationWare, a leading information systems consulting firm in the Chicago area, recognizes the role of an IT plan in its work with Fortune 500 companies. IntegrationWare's mission states that "IntegrationWare is committed to establishing a new generation of extraordinary PC solutions to meet our clients' business needs, providing effective business content to an integration of proven computer and software products." The company's approach is unique in that they look for solutions that reuse and integrate existing software components, off-the-shelf products, and custom-designed products. This integration-oriented approach results in efficient use of resources, faster product development, and a more incremental change process for clients. IntegrationWare's Jim Flury developed the following proposal to model the IntegrationWare approach to helping a business develop an IT plan. The proposal outlines the objectives, scope, and outcomes of the IT planning process.

Information Technology Plan Project Proposal

Objectives

As XYZ Company continues to achieve a significant growth rate, the need for an information system is becoming increasingly evident. Consequential investments will be made in hardware and software to support business growth. The key issue is to determine what changes best support short-term and long-term needs. The Information Systems plan provides a long-term view of system requirements, short-term transition strategies, and overall investment requirements for matching Information Technology capabilities to the needs of the business. Through development of an Information System plan, we will

- Determine business goals, strategies, and risks where the impact of Information Systems is noteworthy

- Assess business applications to identify requirements for change, opportunities to improve performance, and potential software package solutions

- Assess technology architecture options, looking for high-performance and cost-effective options which can grow with the business

- Identify a strategy to achieve change, identifying high-priority projects and investments, a high-level timeline, and preliminary cost factors to achieving change

Scope

There are two approaches to this project. The standard approach is to develop a plan that addresses the development of the key business systems. This provides a better view of the long-term planning considerations and there is less concern that the project's scope will increase in the course of planning. An alternative approach is to focus only on the order entry and order processing systems, as this area is clearly the most crucial to XYZ

SPECIAL TOPIC: DEVELOPING AN IT PLAN (continued)

Company's business process. As strategic direction is set for this area, it then simplifies the approach for other related applications (which must be addressed later).

The project activities in general are the same for either scope scenario. Alternative #1 has a higher project cost but it provides a more complete result. Alternative #2 zeros in on the problem area with less project time and cost, although later efforts are needed to set the plan for other applications. This scope decision needs to be made as part of finalizing this letter of agreement.

The scope of the project, independent of the application scope alternatives, will also include assessments of application development options, technology requirements, data requirements, and Information Services organizational requirements relative to the future applications vision.

From an applications development perspective, we will consider three basic options for the key applications:

1. Redevelop or modify current software applications.

2. Custom development of new applications, particularly if there is a change in the technology platform.

3. Utilize software packages and modify or extend them as needed to ensure business requirements are met.

Each of the above has its own unique advantages and cost considerations. The analysis of the project will not address in-depth application requirements, but it will present the likely

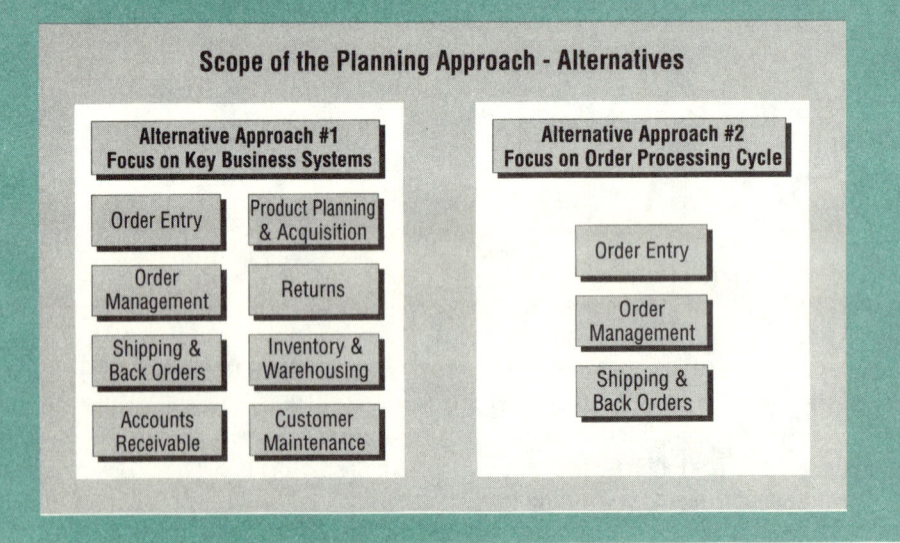

Scope of the Planning Approach - Alternatives

Alternative Approach #1 — Focus on Key Business Systems
- Order Entry
- Product Planning & Acquisition
- Order Management
- Returns
- Shipping & Back Orders
- Inventory & Warehousing
- Accounts Receivable
- Customer Maintenance

Alternative Approach #2 — Focus on Order Processing Cycle
- Order Entry
- Order Management
- Shipping & Back Orders

SPECIAL TOPIC: DEVELOPING AN IT PLAN (continued)

magnitude and pluses of each of the three options. In the case of software packages, we will identify representative leading products for the purpose of our planning analysis—a more exhaustive package search is left for later project efforts.

From a technology perspective, we will forecast a future view of the technology architecture to support continuing growth of the business. The options to be considered include

- Extensions and upgrades to the current technology environment
- Transition to a client-server architecture, leveraging leading server and database technology with user access through PC applications.

From a data perspective, we will identify and document requirements and performance factors including

- New data requirements (in terms of subject databases)
- Data volumes related to key application processing cycles
- Database management software requirements

From an Information Services organizational perspective, we will identify issues and requirements in terms of skills, organizational structure, the organization's approach to technology transition, and providing the internal capability to implement and support the future systems vision.

The next step in group scheduling is the introduction of software that will be able to schedule meetings between people from different companies using the World Wide Web. A calendar interchange protocol is being adopted that allows different scheduling products to share information. Netscape Corporation is working with various calendar vendors to develop software that can use the protocol.

What You Have Learned

Deciding how computer systems can help the organization achieve its objectives is called IT planning, and is part of the strategic planning process. IT planning creates broad specifications for five types of information systems: transaction processing, management reporting, communication, expert systems, and office automation. Transaction processing systems record and track business events. Management reporting systems provide managerial information from transaction processing systems. New tools in management reporting include data warehousing and data mining. Expert systems help users reach a conclusion based on their answers to the expert systems' questions. Office automation software is increasingly being replaced by office productivity software, including office suites.

Focus Questions

1. What is information technology planning?

2. List the five categories of information systems.

3. Name two types of transaction processing systems and what they do.

4. Define the three major types of reports from a management information system.

5. What's the difference between a database and data warehouse?

6. What is an expert system? Give one example of how an expert system is used.

7. Which type of office automation software could you use to make a proposal during a meeting?

8. What's the advantage of using group scheduling software?

Knowledge Reinforcement

A. What are some of the reasons that you think a business would choose to develop an information technology plan? How would you go about developing such a plan? What are some of the things you would want to know before you started the plan? What role do you think the skill level of the users plays in an IT plan?

B. Do you think employees should be able to download the company's database files to their notebook computers to take with them on a business trip? Should stealing a company's corporate database be legal or illegal?

C. Think of an expert system you would like to develop to help you solve a problem or make a reasonable prediction about something in your everyday life or something you would like to know about. What would you like the system to do? What would be some of the elements of the decision tree you would want to include?

D. Talk to someone you know who works in an office. Find out what kind of office automation software they are using. Does the software run on a PC or a mainframe? What types of applications are available to them? Do they use them all? Why or why not?

Further Exploration

Corel Corporation:
http://www.corel.com

DataMind Corporation:
http://www.datamindcorp.com

IntegrationWare:
http://www.integrationware.com

Lotus Corporation:
http://www.lotus.com

Microsoft Corporation:
http://www.microsoft.com

SESSION ELEVEN

Vocabulary

- asynchronous
- bus LAN
- client
- client-server application
- coax
- connectivity
- dedicated line (leased line)
- dial-up connection
- distributed system
- duplex (full duplex)
- enterprise network
- fax back service
- firewall
- groupware
- half duplex
- Integrated Services Digital Network (ISDN)
- intranet
- local area network (LAN)
- login
- network
- network administrator
- network communication protocol
- network standard
- node
- packet
- parity checking
- password
- peer-to-peer network
- platform
- private branch exchange (PBX)
- rights
- ring LAN
- server
- simplex
- star LAN
- synchronous
- thinwire
- token-ring LAN
- topology
- twisted-pair
- user ID
- voice mail
- Webmaster
- wide area network (WAN)
- wireless transmission
- workstation

Connectivity: From LANs to the Internet

A DECADE AGO, COMPUTERIZED CUSTOMER and vendor lists and small local area networks adequately handled the internal and external communications needs of most businesses. Some of the high-tech tools of the 1980s have now matured, and new tools have emerged that help a business maintain a competitive advantage in a world where the new standard is intense connectivity. At the end of this session, you will be able to

- Describe types of networks and LAN topologies
- Explain how electronic mail is used in a business
- Describe network communication protocols and simple transmission validation methods
- Compare and contrast client-server databases, groupware, and intranets

255

SECTION 11.1: CONNECTIVITY BASICS

The term **connectivity** includes all the methods used to build connections between computers, thereby connecting users. On the lowest level, connectivity involves hooking one computer to another so that users can share a printer or document files. At the high end, connectivity uses satellites to create live video connections for businesses with vendors or affiliates half a world away, as shown in Figure 11.1.

Figure 11.1
Connectivity

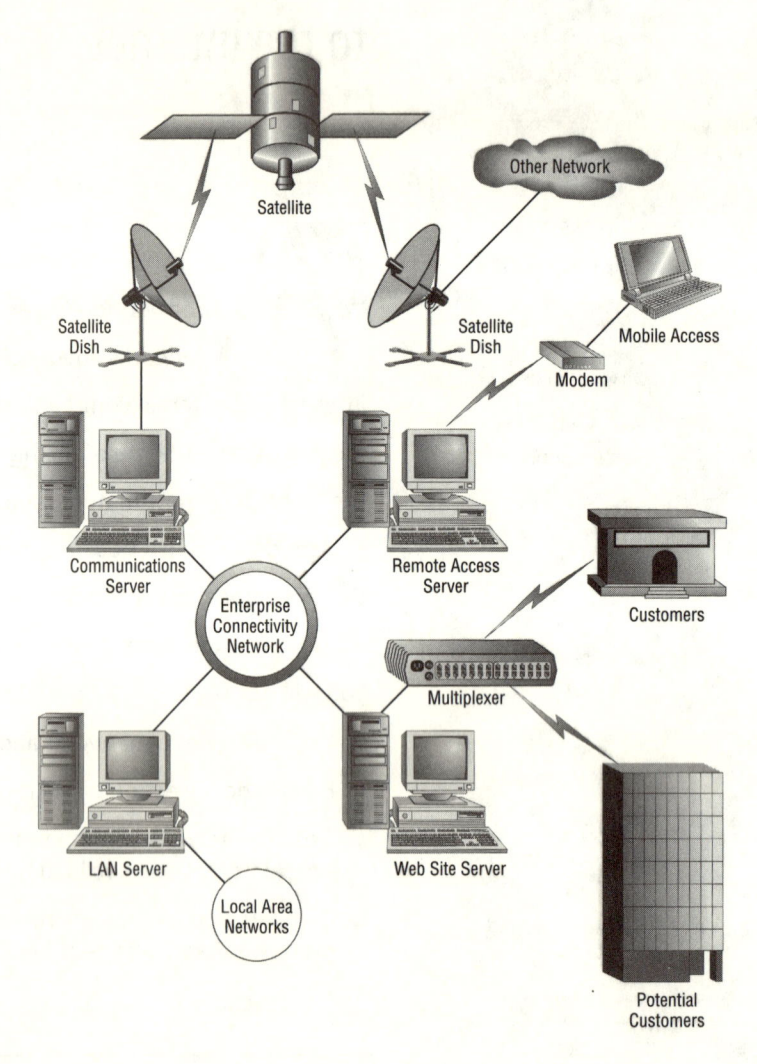

SECTION 11.2: COMMUNICATIONS SYSTEMS

The ability to effectively communicate information internally and externally determines whether a business will thrive, or even survive. Communications systems, composed of hardware, software, and a transmission medium, are designed to allow organizations to swiftly move data and information through the business environment. Most businesses utilize a multidimensional communications system: many separate communications systems capable of carrying sound or data. These communications systems may be public systems like the telephone system or private systems.

The telephone system has several advantages as a business communications system. For one, you can have a fairly high level of confidence in a technology that's been in place for over one hundred years. The system is reliable, and the number of users keeps the average cost per user quite low. In addition, attaching computers to the telephone system is easy with the addition of a modem. And telephony hardware is standardized and inexpensive in comparison to other, less standardized equipment.

The telephone system has disadvantages, as well. Your connection to the telephone system is only a temporary **dial-up connection**, severed when you hang up the phone. When you need to make a call, you risk not being able to connect to the system. For example, try calling across the continent on Mother's Day afternoon or at 11:59 p.m. on New Year's Eve.

Some of the transmission media used in the telephone system is old and is not capable of high-speed data transfer. The fastest public telephone lines can transfer slightly more than 30,000 bits of data per second—more than adequate for voice transmission, but much slower than the transmission rate capabilities of computers. And use of the public system results in monthly fees and long distance charges.

The myriad Baby Bells—the companies that comprise the telephone system—provide two alternatives to regular public lines: dedicated lines, and ISDN. **Dedicated lines**, also called **leased lines**, are permanent connections between two buildings—for example, between a corporate headquarters office and a manufacturing facility a mile away. Leased lines aren't shared with other users, so continual access is guaranteed. Businesses can invest in high-speed T1 and T3 dedicated lines, with a top speed of 45 megabits per second: 1,500 times faster than dial-up public lines.

AT&T's **Integrated Services Digital Network (ISDN)** standard was designed for high-speed transmission of digital data, and allows one line to carry up to three separate signals. This means that with one ISDN line you can hold a voice conversation and attach to a network at the same time. ISDN services are only available on a dial-up basis in major metropolitan areas. The conversion to ISDN is costly: Pacific Bell will spend $16 billion in California to upgrade conventional copper lines to ISDN.

There are other telephony alternatives to the public telephone system. A business can install their own telephone system for in-house needs, only using the public system for external communications. A **private branch exchange**, or **PBX**, is an internal telephone system, including hardware and cabling. PBX equipment can be purchased outright or leased, and the lines can be used for voice or data transmission without paying per-call fees to the telephone system.

■ Communications Modes

Because video and sound are data, too, public or private broadcast radio, television, and cable systems are also communications systems. The thousands of miles of television cable already installed could eventually provide an alternative to public telephone systems, although major modification to the system would be required due to the assumptions made about communication modes when cable was originally installed.

The television cable system wasn't designed to be a two-way system. Rather, it was based on a simplex communications model. **Simplex** communication is one-way communication—a monologue. Even though cable will physically allow signals to travel in either direction, you don't have a transmitter in your home, and the cable company isn't prepared to receive your incoming signal.

Half-duplex communication is a step up from simplex. Half duplex is two-way, non-simultaneous communication. Walkie-talkies use half duplex, either sending or receiving, but not at the same time. You press the walkie-talkie's transmit button and speak. Until the button is released, you cannot hear an incoming transmission.

Full duplex, also called **duplex**, is two-way, simultaneous communication like a telephone system. Both participants in a telephone conversation can transmit and receive at the same time, because the equipment can handle simultaneous communication. Computer communications are easiest over a system that was designed for a duplex communications mode.

■ Communication Verification

Voice transmission always includes a context. If one small portion of a spoken word isn't transmitted clearly, the receiver may still understand the word because of surrounding syllables and total context. When transmitting data, a change of one bit is the difference between one character and another, the difference between correct data and incorrect data. If the receiving device or computer doesn't receive the beginning of a transmission, the entire message may be misunderstood. Because the telephone system was originally designed for voice transmission, not communication by computer, telephone communications often result in "lossy transmission." Computer communications need verification systems to help handle some of the telephone system's inadequacies.

Communication protocols are standards that help coordinate transmissions and validate that the data received is correct. **Parity checking** is a simple protocol for data validation. Remember that ASCII uses only seven of the eight bits in a byte to represent a character; the eighth bit is used for parity checking. Eight bit codes (like EBCDIC) add a parity bit to the end of each word. Parity checking uses either of two possible settings: odd parity, and even parity.

Here's how it works. The ASCII representation of the letter H is 1001000; I is 1001001. If you were transmitting the word "HI," the ASCII code would look like this:

1001000

1001001

Your computer attaches a code to the beginning of the transmission that indicates whether parity for the transmission is odd or even. If it specifies even parity, then the sum of the 1s and 0s for each byte will need to be an even number. The computer adds a parity bit after the last data bit. The H is already even, so zero is added. One is added as the parity bit for I:

1001000+0= 2 (even)

1001001+1= 4 (even)

The receiving computer quickly totals each byte to make sure the total, including the parity bit, is an even number. If the total is not even, action is taken. The specific action depends on other aspects of the communications devices and protocols. The receiving computer may request the message again, or may notify the user that the transmission couldn't be validated and may be incorrect.

Odd parity works the same way as even parity, but the total of the data word bits and the parity bits must be an odd number. Parity checking is a low-level error-checking system. If two 0s or two 1s are lost from the message during transmission, the parity will still be correct, even though the byte received is wrong.

Parity is often omitted from serial data transmissions because there are other, more precise ways to help ensure transmission validity, such as the more reliable cyclical redundancy check (CRC). Transmitted data can be validated most easily when both the sending and receiving computer know the length and timing of transmissions. Errors in length or timing clearly signal a transmission problem, providing another level of reliability. With **synchronous** communications, data is transmitted at a set rate, timed by a common clock. Almost all the communication inside a computer happens synchronously, timed by the CPU clock. Synchronous communication between computers is difficult because of the need for a common clock device and separate signal line for the clock signal, but is used where data validity requirements are stringent.

With **asynchronous** communication, the computer or device at the transmitting end sends a start bit to signal the beginning of a message, and a stop bit at the end. If a device receives a transmission without a start bit, it signals the transmitting device (or the user) that an error has occurred. Dial-up communications are asynchronous.

Whether you use synchronous or asynchronous transmission, or even, odd, or no parity, both devices must use the same configuration. The transmission configuration is commonly called a data frame. For example, a computer is sending a transmission using this group of settings: 1 start bit, 5–8 data bits (almost always 7 or 8 bits), 1 parity bit (even, odd, or none—in which case the bit is omitted), and 1 or 2 stop bits. The computer on the receiving end must also be set to the identical configuration to successfully receive the transmitted data.

Communications Media

Communications media provide the links between transmitting and receiving devices. Cable is the most common communications media, and the least expensive for short distances.

Cable

Twisted-pair cable is used for short-distance data transmission, and for lower density voice transmission, even over long distances. Telephone wiring in residences uses twisted pair. Twisted-pair cable includes two, four, or more pairs of copper wire.

Coaxial cable, or **coax**, is the primary communications media for non-broadcast television. (That's why it's called "cable TV.") Coax consists of a copper wire, covered with a plastic insulator and wrapped with a metal mesh shield that prevents signal interruption by nearby communications wiring. When coax is used for computer networks, it is often called **thinwire**. (Even though coax looks thicker than twisted pair, the wire inside is one thin wire.) On both twisted pair and coax, transmissions are sent as low-level electrical charges.

> **NOTE**
>
> In the late 1970s and early 1980s, some of the older copper telephone wire in the United States was replaced with newer fiber-optic cable to provide the infrastructure for the Star Wars defense system. The copper wire was adequate for voice transmission, but fiber-optic cable supports the faster transmission rates utilized by digital signals.

Optical fibers are extremely fine glass fibers, smaller in diameter than a hair from your head. The exterior of each fiber is clad (coated) to reflect light inward, and clad fibers are then coated with plastic. Bundles of optical fibers surrounded with a protective plastic shell form a fiber-optic cable. Fiber-optic cables use light formed by a laser or LED (light emitting diode) rather than electricity for transmission.

> *186,000 miles per second. It's not just a good idea—it's the law.*
>
> —*Robb Morse*

Fiber should be cheaper than coax or twisted pair, because the raw materials for fiber optic cable are cheaper than copper. However, fiber is still more expensive, partly because the technology is relatively new, quality standards are rigid, and, therefore, manufacturing costs remain high. But even at a higher price, fiber provides an important advantage: speed. While both light and electricity travel at the speed of light, the metal in wire creates more resistance and slows transmission speed more than the fiber in fiber-optic cable.

Wireless Media

Wireless transmission methods are used for broadcast transmission (television and radio) and transmission where cabling is not practical. The least expensive wireless method is radio wave, used for cellular phones and cellular modems.

Microwave transmission is also used for cell phones and pagers. Microwave has its own disadvantages. Microwave transmissions must be sent in a straight line, and can't pass through buildings or other solid objects. On the ground, microwave is only good for distances of about 25 miles. At greater distances, the effects of the earth's curvature would require a tower hundreds of feet tall to maintain a direct line of transmission (see Figure 11.2). For longer distances, a series of microwave relay stations can be built, and a signal sent from one location to another through the relay stations. Alternately, microwave signals can be sent to a satellite, then transmitted to another satellite or a ground-based microwave station.

Figure 11.2
Microwave satellite transmission

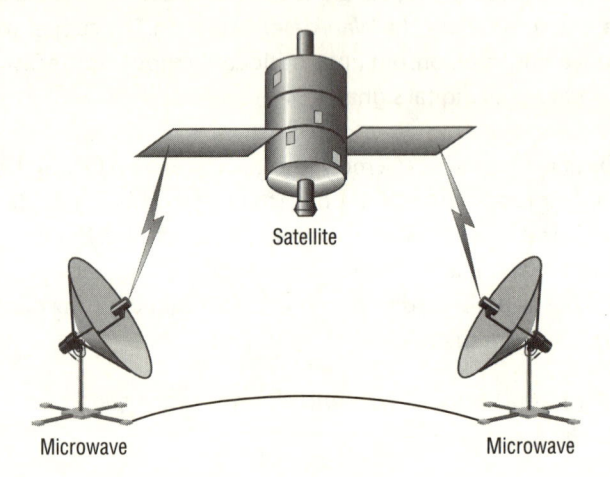

For satellites to be useful for microwave transmission, they need to be in a predictable position relative to earth-bound transmitters and receivers. For this reason, microwave satellites are placed in a Clarke orbit 22,237 miles above the earth's equator. At this distance, the satellite is in geostationary orbit, which means it orbits the earth at the same rate the earth rotates, effectively keeping the satellite in the same relational position.

SECTION 11.3: COMPUTER NETWORKS

In a general sense, a network is any system that allows individuals or machines to communicate. The telephone communications system is a public network. Computer **networks** are groups of computers and peripheral devices that are connected by cable or wireless communications media and able to communicate with each other. The existence of a network opens the door to endless possibilities, ranging from electronic mail (e-mail) sent from user to user to interactive work on a group project. There are three types of networks: local area networks (LANs), wide area networks (WANs), and the Internet. All networks require hardware and software, and common standards and protocols for communication.

■ Network Hardware Basics

Each network uses a **network standard** that specifies how a transmitted signal travels on the network. Network standards include methods for resolving the collisions that occur when one signal runs into another. Standards are designed to support one or two different data transmission speeds, which are limited or enabled by the network designer's choice of communications media. All computers on the network have to use the same network standard, which is accomplished by buying network standard expansion cards for each computer that needs to be networked. For example, all computers on an Ethernet network will use Ethernet expansion cards to connect to the network. Table 11.1 provides a comparison of some network standards.

Table 11.1 Network Standards Compared

Network Standard	General Use	Transmission Speed per Second
ARCNet	LAN	2 megabits or 20 megabits
ATM	WAN	100 megabits
Ethernet	LAN	10 megabits
Fast Ethernet	WAN	100 megabits
FDDI	WAN	100 megabits
Token Ring	LAN	4 megabits or 16 megabits

■ Network Software Tasks

The most important task of network software is to manage the transmission of data from one computer or device to another. When you transmit a file to another computer over a network, your network software intercepts the file and sends it as a series of transmissions called **packets**. Each packet contains your computer's network address, the address of the computer or device you're sending the file to, and one section of the file. The packet is then sent to the receiving computer by cable or wireless media. At the receiving end, the network software reconstructs the file from the incoming packets.

Specific networking software supports one or more **network communication protocols** that describe the structure of packets. You can send information between networks or computers that use different networking software, but they must use the same communication protocol. Table 11.2 compares widely used network communication protocols.

Table 11.2
Widely Used Network Communication Protocols Compared

Network Communications Protocol	General Use	Comment
AFP	AppleTalk and Macintosh Networks	Developed by Apple Computer
DECnet, or LAT	Digital minicomputer networks	Developed by Digital Equipment Corporation
IPX	Novell NetWare Networks	Internetwork Packet Exchange, developed by Novell
TCP/IP	Used on all networks and in the Internet	Transmission Control Protocol/Internet Protocol, developed by the Department of Defense as the standard for ARPANET

SECTION 11.4: LOCAL AREA NETWORKS

When a small number of users needs to be interconnected frequently or for long periods of time, the cost-effective way to connect them is with a **local area network,** or **LAN.** There are two types of LANs: peer-to-peer, and client-server LANs. Peer-to-peer networks connect users' computers directly or through a device called a hub. Client-server networks use one or more larger, specialized computers, called **servers,** to hold special network software and applications and data that more than one user needs to access. Computers other than the server are called **clients** or **workstations**. The computers in the network (including the server) are called **nodes**.

Peer-to-Peer Networks

The simplest LANs, called **peer-to-peer networks**, directly connect computers and their peripherals. A user's computer can access the drives and printers attached to its peers (other computers) on the network. In Figure 11.3, users at all four computers can use either of the printers, even though the printers are directly connected to only two of the computers. The network also allows a user at any computer to access the storage devices on other computers if they have been given access to the drives by that computer's user. Peer-to-peer networks are generally Ethernet networks cabled with twisted pair, or infrequently, thinwire.

Figure 11.3
Peer-to-peer network

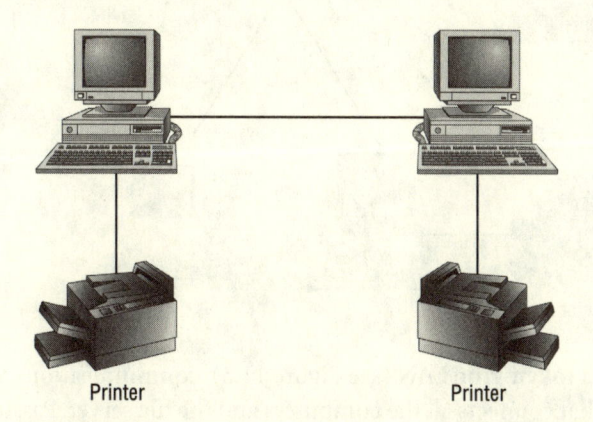

Peer-to-peer networks work well for a small group of users who need basic file- and print-sharing services. Depending on the network software used to facilitate communication between the computers, peer-to-peer networks can accommodate between 2 and 25 computers that are physically close together. Windows for Workgroups and Windows 95 include the network software a PC peer-to-peer network requires; or you can purchase separate network software.

Client-Server Networks

There are three types of client-server LANs. Each type has a different layout, or **topology**. The **star LAN**, shown in Figure 11.4, connects each computer directly to the server. Communications between two workstations, such as e-mail, flow through the server.

Figure 11.4
Star LAN

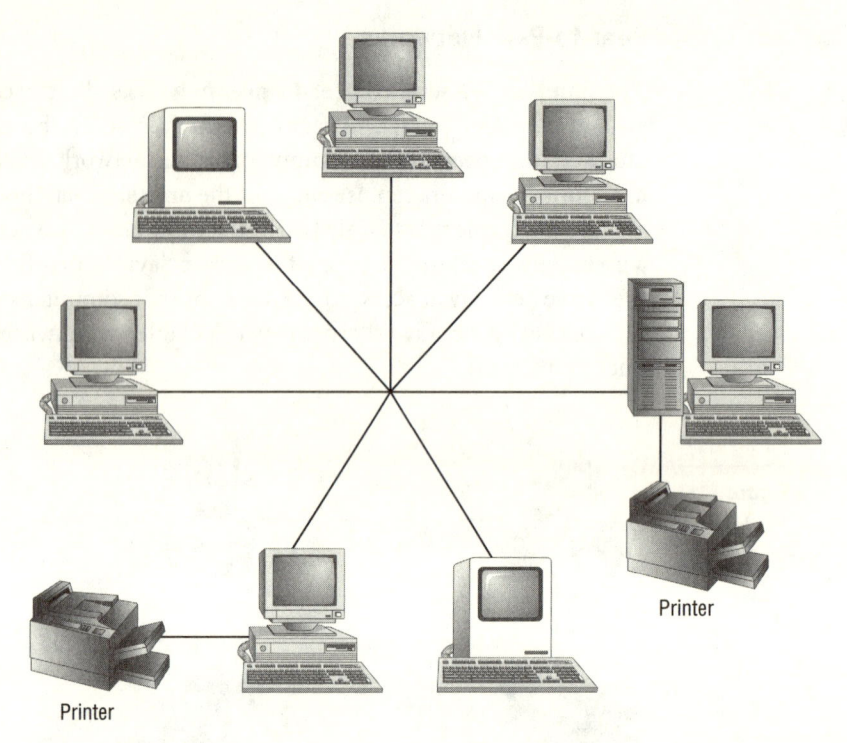

In a **token-ring LAN** (see Figure 11.5), communications are carried in a ring that connects all the computers and the file server. Passing messages from one computer to another can be faster in a token ring since communications don't necessarily have to pass through the server.

With the third topology, the **bus LAN**, computers are connected to a common communications line that originates at the file server. As you can see in Figure 11.6, the bus topology resembles a bus line, with each computer representing a bus stop. As in star LANs, information sent from one computer to another must first flow through the server. With the bus LAN, hundreds of users can be connected in one local area network in a small area (such as the same office building).

■ Networking Software

Most client-server LANs use Novell NetWare or Windows NT networking software. Until recently, NetWare was the LAN standard and all other software was regarded as second rate. Now, Microsoft and Novell are engaged in a market war for LAN dominance. Each software has different strengths, and the

Figure 11.5
Token-ring LAN topology

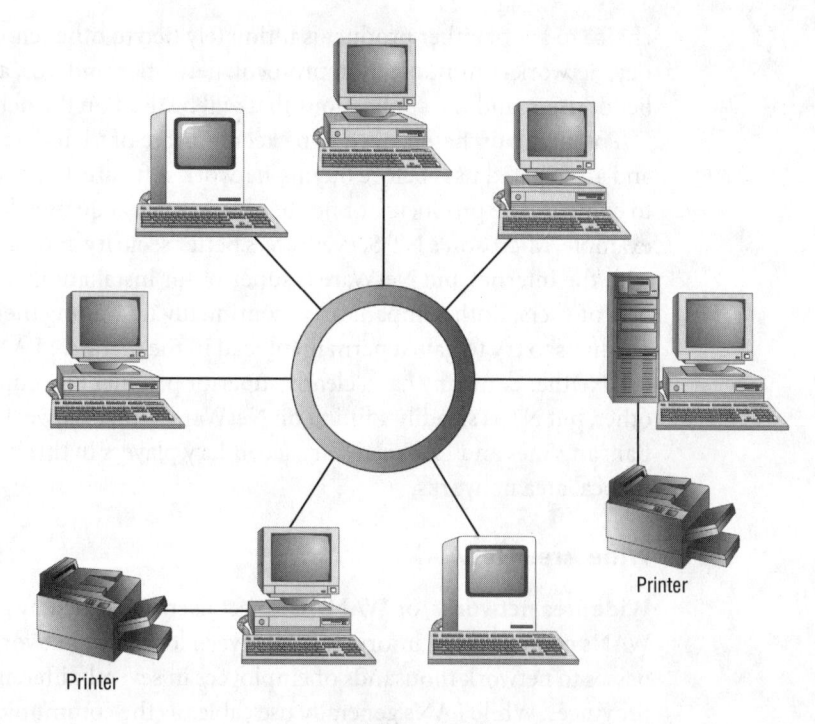

Figure 11.6
Bus topology

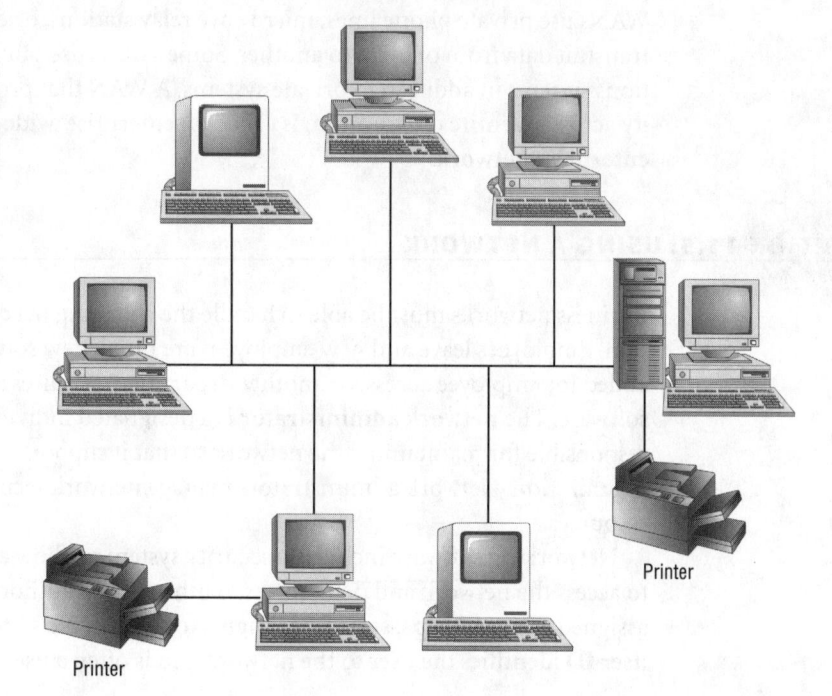

choice to adopt either product is ultimately tied to other choices about topology, network communication protocol, network standards, anticipated number of users, and the applications that will be used on the network.

Potential purchasers need to be keenly aware of their data requirements and anticipated uses before buying network software. Otherwise, it's too easy to compare the products but not be able to make a quality decision. For example, Microsoft's NT Server offers better security and easier connectivity with the Internet, but NetWare is superior for installations with large numbers of users. Both companies are continually upgrading their networking products to try to gain a permanent lead in the lucrative LAN software market. Neither company has a clearly superior product in comparison to the other, but NT is steadily gaining on NetWare. Other networking software, like Banyan Vines and LANtastic, are secondary players in this battle for the future of local area networks.

Wide Area Networks

Wide area networks, or **WANs**, connect users separated by great distances. WANs communicate information between local area networks, allowing businesses to network thousands of employees in several different states or provinces. While LANs generally use cables as the communication medium, WANs use private phone lines, microwave relay stations, or even satellites to transmit data from one site to another. Some WANs use public communications systems in addition to private systems. A WAN that provides connectivity across an entire organization is called an enterprise-wide network or **enterprise network**.

SECTION 11.5: USING A NETWORK

Business networks must be able to handle the changing needs of an organization. Employees leave and new employees are hired, new software needs to be added for employee access, or another department requires access to existing software. The **network administrator** is a designated individual who is responsible for maintaining the network so that it supports the work of the organization. Network administrators manage network security and network resources.

Networking software includes a security system to allow authorized users to access the network and deny access to others. Each authorized user is assigned a user ID, a password, and rights to use specific system resources. A **user ID** identifies the user to the network and is often a user's first initial and last name. A **password** is a code that the user must enter to gain access. The combination of a user ID and password is called a network **login**. Identifying yourself to the network by using your user ID and password is called *logging on* the network. (For example, if another user wants to know if you are connected to the network, he would ask "Are you logged on?") The network administrator sets up new user accounts, assigning user IDs and passwords and giving **rights** (access to specific network resources) to users.

User rights are assigned to files or groups of files in a directory. The types and names of rights that can be extended to a user account vary with the networking software, but, in general, include the ability to

- Read (look at a file)
- Write (create a new file or edit an existing file)
- Delete
- Use (a printer or other device)

When network user Sherry turns on her PC, she can automatically use local resources: her computer and attached devices, and software installed on those devices. If she wants to use network resources like a network printer, she has to log on the network. The network administrator told Sherry that her user ID is *sschmitt*, and her password is *eyeedit*. Sherry's login will look something like this:

```
login sschmitt

PASSWORD? *******

Welcome, sschmitt!
```

When Sherry entered *login sschmitt*, the network software prompted her for a password. Sherry typed *eyeedit*, but asterisks appeared on the screen in place of the letters to prevent people nearby from learning her password. After Sherry entered her password, the network software checked a list of user accounts and passwords, and verified that Sherry was a listed user, and that the password was correct before logging her onto the network. After she has logged on, Sherry will have access to the network resources that the network administrator has granted her the right to use. For example, Sherry works in accounts payable, so the network administrator gave her rights to the accounts payable system, productivity applications, and printers in the accounting department. An employee in payroll would have access to payroll software, productivity applications, and the accounting department's printers, but not the accounts payable system.

Network Security

The network administrator is responsible for establishing network security, but users are accountable for the security of their own passwords. A good security system is easily bypassed when users give their passwords to others, on purpose or accidentally. Users are supposed to memorize passwords, but it isn't unusual to see a sticky note taped to the side of a monitor with the user's password written on it, or find the password on a Rolodex card filed under the letter *P*.

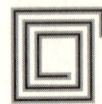

NOTE

Some users change their passwords to something easier to remember, like the name of their spouse or significant other. Unfortunately, this means that anyone who knows your wife's name also knows your password. For a password to be secure, it should be something that other people wouldn't easily guess.

Most organizations encourage, and some systems even require, employees to change their password on a periodic basis: the first day of every month, or at the beginning of each quarter.

SECTION 11.6: NETWORK APPLICATIONS

As you will see in later sessions, many businesses use a combination of networks to provide connectivity. The connectivity solutions chosen depend on the business needs that the systems have to support. For example, a mail order business may have a vital need to communicate with customers by telephone, while a manufacturer may need to receive customer orders electronically. There are two types of business applications that are often placed on networks, even if the networks were established for other purposes: electronic mail and scheduling. Networking software generally has e-mail and scheduling capabilities built in or readily available as add-on software.

Electronic Mail

Typically, a business network solution includes internal e-mail between users on the same network. Some businesses also include external e-mail by connecting their mail system to the Internet so employees can reach outsiders with ease.

Simply adding e-mail to the business environment changes the way people work. Without e-mail, employees who take a few days off return to a pile of pink "While You Were Out" messages. Hours can be spent trying to return these calls, and employees get used to spending as much time trying to contact each other as they do actually communicating. And when they finally get through to the person they're trying to reach, employees take handwritten notes to keep track of information exchanged and decisions made.

When Charlotte returns to work after a three-day vacation, she logs onto her computer and checks her e-mail. There are several notices of meetings and events that she adds to her calendar before deleting the messages. Some e-mail requires a reply, so she clicks the Reply button, then enters her return message rather than spending time playing "phone tag" to return messages (see Figure 11.7).

Figure 11.7
Sending an e-mail reply

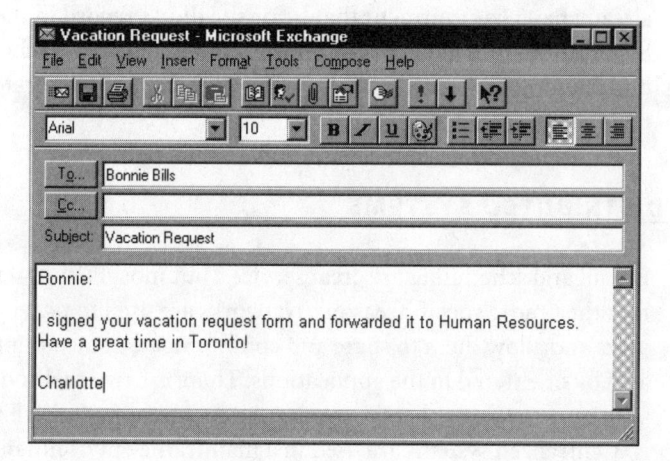

Two messages and one reply need to be kept for future reference, so Charlotte saves them on her computer. Later, she can print a copy if she needs one. She quickly schedules a meeting with a committee by typing a meeting notice and sending it to the list of group members. Networked e-mail allows Charlotte to work more efficiently and respond quickly to requests for information or decisions.

Like any technology, e-mail can be misused. Some users see e-mail as a way to distribute lots of information that no one wants. Rather than sending information to the three people who should see it, they send a copy to anyone who might be remotely involved in a project. Some companies have formal policies on e-mail use; others count on coworkers to gently notify individuals who abuse e-mail.

Scheduling

Scheduling software is used to create and communicate schedules for individuals, groups, and physical facilities. Simple scheduling software allows a small number of users to schedule rooms and equipment, but may allow other users to view the schedule of upcoming events or scheduled rooms. More complex software lets individual users maintain their schedule and access other users' schedules for group meetings or events. If, for example, you need to schedule a meeting with three other employees, you can instruct the scheduling software to find a time within the next week when all four of you have an open block in your individual schedules, schedule the meeting, and notify the other three employees.

This type of usage only works if all employees diligently maintain their individual schedules. Otherwise, meetings are scheduled when an employee already has a commitment that he or she didn't record in the scheduler. Some companies have successfully implemented group scheduling software but abandoned the effort when individuals failed to accurately maintain their calendars.

SECTION 11.7: DISTRIBUTED SYSTEMS

E-mail and scheduling are great services, but most businesses install networks for other, more specific reasons. Networks are used to provide applications to users and allow them to share and communicate data and information created by or entered in the applications. There are two methods to allow multi-user access to an application: centralized systems and distributed systems.

Centralized systems are used in a mainframe environment. With a centralized system, all users connect to a large computer that contains the data and applications they need to use. Users typically don't use PCs, but use terminals that include a screen, keyboard, and connection to the mainframe, but no processor. The mainframe CPU handles all the processing tasks for the entire system. In **distributed systems**, two or more computers are connected so that processing for system tasks can happen in multiple locations. Networks are, by definition, distributed systems, and open up new possibilities for application development. Two types of client-server applications, workgroup software and intranets, spring naturally from a network environment.

Client-Server Applications

A **client-server application** utilizes the processing power of local workstations and one or more central servers. Within the application, client workstations request data or information from a server. There is a direct parallel between client-server LANs and client-server applications: messages travel from the client to the server requesting data, information, or services, which handles the request.

Designing client-server applications is an art as well as a science, for developers must determine which tasks are most effectively handled locally by the workstation, and which tasks should be handled by the server. For example, a user needs to send a promotional letter to all the customers who haven't placed an order in the past six months. The promotional letter already exists as part of an order entry system. The user enters a request to generate the letters at the local workstation. Four separate activities need to be completed to handle the request:

1. A query asking for customers that meet the "haven't ordered in six months" criteria has to be generated.

2. The query has to be processed against the file of all customers.

3. Letters have to be generated by merging the query results with the letter.

4. The letters have to be printed.

Depending on the order entry system's design, the request can be handled in a variety of ways. For example, the query may be created locally, and the entire list of customers communicated to the workstation, which processes the query, merges the results, and prints. This arrangement has most of the work occurring at the workstation, while the server operates as a file server, responding to the request for data in the customers file. Another possibility is that the workstation sends the request to the server, which creates and processes the query, generates the letters, and sends them to a network printer.

Neither of these arrangements takes full advantage of the processing power of both the workstation and server. Client-server application developers use object-oriented programming tools to decide how to divide the tasks to provide the best efficiency and system responsiveness. In this example, development considerations will include the processing speeds of workstations and servers, network communications speed, physical storage location of letter templates and query tools, and a variety of other factors that influence system design.

Workgroup Software

Workgroup software, also known as **groupware,** is a document-based client-server database application that operates like a combination of a database and e-mail. A workgroup document can be any type of file—a word processing document, an electronic slide show, a chart, a worksheet, an e-mail message, or a record from a highly structured database. But unlike traditional productivity software, groupware is designed to allow many users to interact with the same group of documents. Documents are stored in one or more databases that users can access from their PCs.

Groupware allows users to interact with each other easily. Databases can be developed for notes and comments on a group project, or information on client requests. Workgroup software can also enforce workflow processes, so that a document is routed to a series of people in sequence or simultaneously. For example, a patient's file needs to be reviewed by a physician, then sent to a social worker, then forwarded to billing, and finally to the medical records department. With a workgroup application, when the physician is done with the file, it is automatically sent electronically to the social worker. The social worker and medical records technician can track the file's progress by checking its status.

Novell's GroupWise and Lotus Notes (see Figure 11.8) are well-established groupware packages. Notes is the world's best-selling workgroup software, but its dominance in the business market was recently challenged not by other groupware, but by a relatively new use for the Internet.

The Internet and Intranets

A major part of the Internet's appeal is its performance across all **platforms,** or all types of computers, using varied operating systems. Unlike many LANs, the Internet supports Macintosh computers, PCs, UNIX machines, minicomputers—any and all computing devices with dial-up capabilities. A recent development in the Internet is private Internet networks called intranets. An **intranet** is a World Wide Web site that is only accessible to an organization's employees. By June of 1996, nearly 20 percent of U.S. businesses were using intranets, and the percentage continues to grow rapidly, making Intranets the fastest-growing area of Internet development.

The cross-platform performance of the Internet means that intranets provide an affordable way to network computers and provide client-server capabilities in a mixed-platform environment. If the marketing department uses

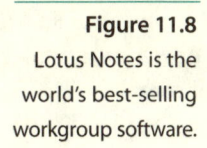

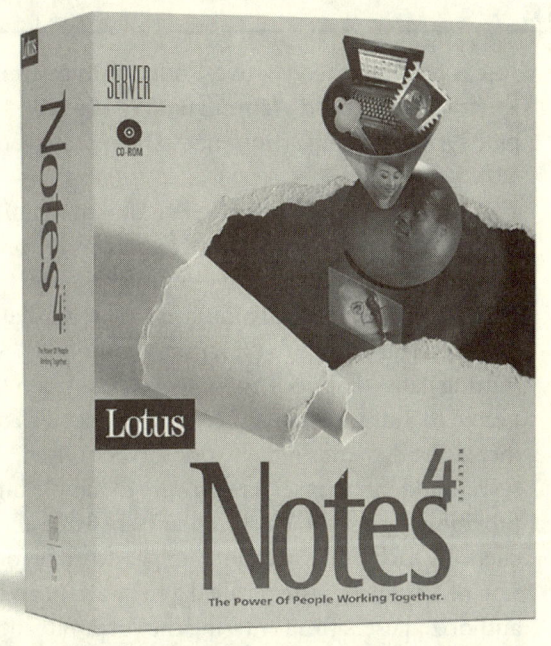

Figure 11.8
Lotus Notes is the world's best-selling workgroup software.

Courtesy of International Business Machines Corporation. Unauthorized use not permitted.

Macintosh computers, MIS and Human Resources use a UNIX system, and Sales is running Windows 95, they can connect with an intranet. Intranets enable companies to

- Provide employees with easy access to employment policy manuals, reports, and other internal information
- Distribute information quickly without printing costs
- Help employees work collaboratively, and decrease the amount of time employees spend in meetings
- Decrease computer training time by providing a standard interface—a Web browser—for all information retrieval

A number of major corporations have taken the intranet plunge. Xerox's WebBoard intranet allows employees to access the corporate telephone directory and employee newsletter. Visa intends to connect member banks by intranet. MCI employees share sections of program code and internal company information. And CBS News' intranet connects CBS with its network affiliates.

> **NOTE**
>
> Just as networks need network administrators, intranets need intranet administrators, often called **Webmasters**. See Session 13 to find out how a large hospital system is using an intranet to help provide quality patient care.

Intranets require the software required to build and maintain a World Wide Web site. Many database companies are providing Internet and intranet versions of their database development products. Microsoft, Borland, Oracle, Lotus, and PowerSoft all offer intranet-ready database development tools.

When you browse the Internet, most of the "work"—locating and transmitting data—happens not on your PC, but on the Internet server you're connected to. Intranets place increased stress on a company's hardware by greatly increasing demands on network servers. Often, companies purchase separate servers and intranet server software to handle intranet traffic. One server may provide access to the World Wide Web, while another handles security by checking each user's account and password before allowing access. The addition of a security system called a **firewall** on an Internet server prevents unauthorized users from entering the corporate intranet from the Internet.

> **NOTE**
>
> The strength of an intranet—easy access to internal information—is also its largest potential drawback. In any company, the largest security risks come from employees. With the focus on the invader from outside the system, most companies build intranets with inadequate internal protection for sensitive documents. Once you have been allowed intranet access without appropriate safeguards, you're free to browse the entire system.

The intranet server software field is dominated by Internet giant Netscape, but Microsoft and Lotus are also major players, with Microsoft Internet Information Server and Exchange, and Lotus Domino. The line between groupware and intranet software is getting fuzzier with every new product release, as Internet software incorporates groupware features, and groupware provides Intranet tools. Moreover, the growth in intranet spending has led to a number of alliances between hardware, software, and communications companies to provide integrated services. Netscape and AT&T are collaborating to provide seamless solutions, and Digital Equipment Corporation, Microsoft, and MCI have partnered for intranet work.

SPECIAL TOPIC: COMMUNICATING WITH CUSTOMERS

Customers are the individuals using your product or service now, or who may use it in the future. Your customers may be end users, people who purchase a product or service for their own use at home or in business. Your customers may also include one or more distributors who purchase your product for resale to end users. In the service and governmental sectors, customers are often referred to by other names—clients, patients, students, recipients, or constituents.

You can use communications technology to support customer communications in a number of ways:

- Provide sales staff and customer-support personnel with mobile computing and communication technologies, and enable more direct visits to customers and less time in the sales office (where customers generally aren't).

- Work from a customer's factory or business and connect back to your business network through dial-up services.

- Add computerized voice mail to telephone systems to allow customers to leave detailed messages for specific individuals.

- Create computerized customer databases and contact managers, so employees can track information on individual customers, the products or services they use, and prior contacts with your organization.

- Use fax back services to help customers troubleshoot problems in off hours. The customer who calls your support department can select help documents from a menu and have the documents faxed to their home or office.

- Establish a Web site to allow potential customers to find out about your products and services or print answers to FAQs. Include site-based e-mail, so site visitors can easily request more information. Allow customers to purchase directly from the Web page.

- Send customer bulletins electronically to online customers via e-mail.

- Extend intranet access to customers.

- Purchase or lease dedicated lines for information exchange with critical clients and distributors. This is commonly done in manufacturing and distribution.

Customer communication revolves around two issues: response and support. You need to respond to customer requests on a timely basis with accurate information, and provide support for customers as they use your product or service. When a customer has a question or problem, they judge your business by the quality and timeliness of the response received. Today's technology provides some new ways to maintain and extend your customer base.

What You Have Learned

Business communication systems have grown from their roots in the telephone system. Telephone companies provide public systems for connectivity. Businesses can also create private telephone systems for internal use. When telephone systems are used to transmit computerized data, transmitted data must be verified for accuracy.

The actual links between computers can be created with cable or wireless transmitters and receivers. When computers are linked, a network is created. There are two types of networks: client-server networks, and peer-to-peer networks. Networks allow employees to send and receive e-mail and participate in scheduling. Special client-server, groupware, and intranet applications take advantage of the power of connectivity, creating new opportunities for employee interaction and group work.

Focus Questions

1. What is a dial-up connection?

2. What is a leased line? Why would a business invest in a leased line?

3. Name and describe the three communications modes.

4. List and describe two communications media.

5. How does a client-server network differ from a peer-to-peer network?

6. What is a packet?

7. What is the purpose of a network login?

8. Describe two types of client-server applications used on distributed systems.

Knowledge Reinforcement

A. There are two struggles for market dominance being conducted in the connectivity arena: NetWare vs. Windows NT, and intranets vs. groupware. How do these struggles differ? How are they the same? Is it possible for any company to gain a permanent advantage in the computer industry? Is it possible for any technology to gain a permanent advantage?

B. Review the list of ways to improve customer communications listed in this session's Special Topic. Select three methods and explain how the methods could be implemented successfully but actually result in decreased customer satisfaction.

C. What qualities would make an individual a good network administrator?

D. What factors would you consider if you were deciding whether to install a network in a small business?

Further Exploration

Borland Corporation:
http://www.borland.com

Institute of Electrical and Electronic Engineers (network media and cabling standards):
http://www.IEEE.org

Lotus Corporation:
http://www.lotus.com

Microsoft Corporation:
http://www.microsoft.com

Netscape Communications Corp.:
http://www.netscape.com

Vocabulary

- computer-aided manufacturing (CAM)
- computer-integrated manufacturing (CIM)
- critical path
- electronic data interchange (EDI)
- Just in Time (JIT)
- middleware
- prototype
- slack
- virtual manufacturing

SESSION TWELVE

Computers in Production

Sessions 12 through 14 focus on how computer technology has transformed the world of business. In each session, you'll get an inside look at the impact of computers in one company. This session examines the use of computer technology in businesses that create products from raw materials. At the end of this session, you will be able to

- Identify what production and computer systems have in common
- Describe how computers can be used to shorten production time
- Compare and contrast CAD, CAM, and CIM
- Discuss how computers are used to control quality
- Describe the uses of project management software

SECTION 12.1: CREATING A PRODUCT

In today's demand-driven economy, getting a well-designed product "on the shelves" as efficiently as possible is a major factor in business success. Computers play a crucial role in improving the quality of products and the efficiency with which they are produced. Every product goes through a production cycle—a series of steps that results in an output, beginning with product specifications and moving through design to implementation and evaluation. Today, computers are being put to work in every step of the production process.

Take the publishing industry as an example. It wasn't long ago when authors submitted their typewritten manuscripts to their publisher through the mail. Any research required for the book was done by visiting research facilities and interviewing knowledgeable sources over the telephone or in person. All editing was completed manually. The manuscript was retyped for final submission and then was typeset by a printer before being sent to the printing press. It was then bound, boxed, and shipped to distributors for sale.

The production of this book took a much different course. First of all, much of the research work for the book was done using the Internet, which made obtaining information much easier and opened up whole new topics that might otherwise have been ignored. Although the telephone still played a role, many of the book's sources were contacted through e-mail. People who might not have otherwise agreed to a personal interview were more than willing to answer a question or two through electronic mail.

The authors and editors used Windows-based PCs running Microsoft Word to write and edit the manuscript. The manuscript and accompanying art work (screen captures and diagrams) were originally submitted on floppy disks. This allowed the editors to make their comments directly in the manuscript and provided the art department with high-quality graphics that could be easily reproduced. Figure 12.1 shows an example of text from Session 1 of this book after our editor, Bonnie Bills, made her comments. On-screen, each reviewer's comments appear in a different color.

Editors then used e-mail to return the manuscript to the authors for review. In this way, the authors and editors could exchange the manuscript several times in a day to incorporate all the necessary changes. Electronic publishing specialists and graphic designers then went to work, using PCs and Macintosh computers to turn the manuscript and art work into publishable pages.

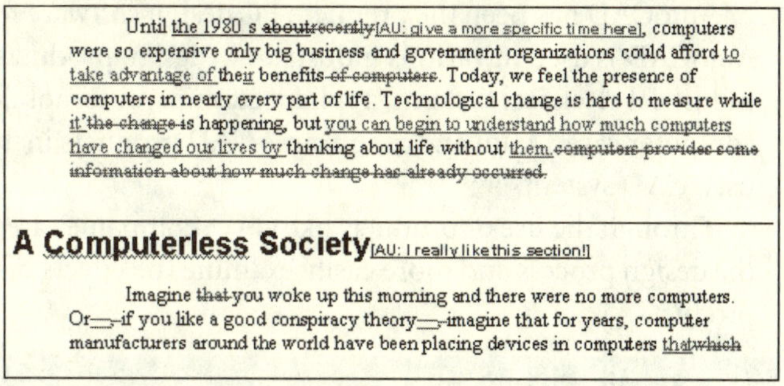

Until the 1980 s ~~aboutrecently~~[AU: give a more specific time here], computers were so expensive only big business and government organizations could afford to take advantage of their benefits ~~of computers~~. Today, we feel the presence of computers in nearly every part of life. Technological change is hard to measure while it'~~the change~~ is happening, but you can begin to understand how much computers have changed our lives by thinking about life without them. ~~computers provides some information about how much change has already occurred.~~

A Computerless Society[AU: I really like this section!]

Imagine ~~that~~ you woke up this morning and there were no more computers. Or—~~,~~ if you like a good conspiracy theory—~~,~~ imagine that for years, computer manufacturers around the world have been placing devices in computers that~~which~~

Figure 12.1 Early version of a manuscript edited in Microsoft Word

Through computerization, production efficiency is greatly improved and the time that passes between order and delivery (lead time) is significantly decreased. These two factors alone are enough to convince most production-oriented businesses that computerization is essential to their survival in today's fast-paced marketplace. In broad terms, the series of steps to produce a product—the production cycle—can be separated into three phases: product specifications and design, manufacturing or implementation, and quality management or evaluation. Although many businesses have essentially the same general information system needs, production-oriented businesses have needs that are specific to each of the three phases of the production cycle. In addition, they must manage the entire production cycle in order to meet timelines and control costs. Computers have become essential tools in helping companies effectively manage the production cycle.

SECTION 12.2: DESIGNING A PRODUCT

Traditional product design is a highly manual process. Product engineers hand-draw each component of a proposed product and create physical models of individual components and groups. The models are in turn adjusted to reflect improvements or problems introduced in the modeling stage. A **prototype** of the finished product is created and tested, and the information learned from the test is used to refine the prototype. Finally, manufacturing specifications are developed based on the prototype.

Computer-aided design, or CAD, uses computer systems to design new products. CAD is a powerful tool in the hands of a skilled draftsperson, allowing him or her to create detailed views and schematics, then store the drawings for future revision. CAD software streamlines the design drafting process, and allows a manufacturer to quickly adapt existing products for use in specialized markets.

AutoCAD has been the premiere PC design software for over a decade. AutoCAD is used in various industries to design products as diverse as homes, industrial electrical systems, appliances, ships, automobiles, printers, and computer cases. Mini and mainframe CAD products include CATIA, a widely used CAD system.

Through the use of products like CAD, companies are able to streamline the design process and more easily examine the effects of design changes on a product.

CAREER CAPSULE: CAD DRAFTER

Use CAD software to prepare assembly drawings. Ability to read and understand engineering change orders. Experience in specific product setting a plus.

Wage Levels: $15K | $35K | $55K | $75K+

Education Levels: High School | Associates Degree | Bachelors Degree | Postgraduate Degree

NOTE

Computer technology costs money, not just for hardware, but for implementation, training, software, and reduced output while employees are learning to use new systems efficiently. While a new $50 million mainframe computer looks impressive, in most businesses productivity gains are coming from installing smaller PC networks in every area of the business. This allows individual departments to develop systems that meet their special needs, resulting in more departmental ownership of their piece of the production cycle.

Using Computers to Design Advertising Inserts

Valassis Communications, Inc., one the of 500 largest manufacturing companies in the United States and the leading sales promotion company in the industry, offers a broad array of consumer promotion techniques. These include Valassis Inserts, free-standing advertising inserts distributed to over 56 million households each week through Sunday newspapers (see Figure 12.2). Over 100 different customized inserts are published each week for over 300 newspapers. Valassis uses a variety of software and hardware solutions to shorten the design-to-manufacture cycle, trim lead time, and meet customer needs.

12.2 ■ DESIGNING A PRODUCT

Figure 12.2
Free-standing inserts

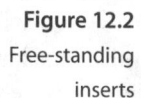

Courtesy of Valassis Communications, Inc.

In the 1970s, Valassis used a traditional product design cycle. Pieces of colored paper were cut to represent the anticipated size of each customer's insert content and attached to layout pages to create a prototype. As customer orders were confirmed, the prototype was adjusted by moving the scraps of paper until a new acceptable design was created. Because each piece's position influenced the position of the others, last-minute adjustments were impossible.

> *We could not be a low-cost, high-speed producer in this market without computers. Our computerized solutions allow us to accept business that our competitors can't.*
> —Amy Courter, Vice-President, MIS,
> Valassis Communications

The CAD programs designed to create durable goods like appliances weren't designed to provide the optimal page layout solutions required in insert publishing. So Valassis's Management Information Systems (MIS) department designed and coded a graphic Insert Publication (IP) system to run on their cluster of Digital Equipment VAX super minicomputers. Today, sales managers and assistants enter anticipated or actual content blocks for all inserts in the IP system database. The IP system then uses the blocks to design the page layout for all the inserts.

As the sales department confirms the actual content, forms specialists in the IP department use the IP system to create new layouts until a final layout can be produced. (The layout still requires human intervention to make sure, for example, that coupons for canned dog food and canned chili aren't placed on facing pages.) The IP system (see Figure 12.3) ensures that Valassis has the shortest lead time in their industry and allows the company to reflect last minute customer requests in product design. Valassis continues to improve the IP software in an effort to trim the time it takes to get products out the door, while creating more complex products.

Figure 12.3
Using the Insert Publication system

Courtesy of Valassis Communications, Inc.

Designing Hardware and Software

Ideally, a business would be able to design products and processes at leisure and ensure perfection before implementing a design in manufacturing, but the speed of the production design cycle has decreased, not increased, in recent years. In 1980, in the computer hardware industry the hardware cycle, measurement of the time between major changes in technology was estimated at five years. Currently, the hardware cycle is eighteen months. This means hardware manufacturers must continually design or redesign products to remain competitive. Computer industry insiders credit microprocessor manufacturer Intel's success to the shortness of their design-to-manufacture cycle. Intel processors are in the hands of computer manufacturers six months to a year before competing processors. Solid information technology keeps Intel in the front of the processor market.

> **NOTE**
>
> The shortness of the hardware and software cycles has a definite impact on PC consumers. It's depressing to see your new, state-of-the-art computer on sale a year later for half what you paid. Many users feel "left in the dust" by wave after wave of new and improved hardware and software. On the other hand, these are exciting times for users as companies continue to crank out faster, cheaper, more capable products.

The software cycle is even shorter than the hardware cycle—only nine to twelve months between major shifts in software technology. New releases or add-in updates of state-of-the-art software products such as Microsoft Internet Explorer and Netscape Navigator are released every few months with new features and functionality. How do companies create new software so quickly? By using rapid application development methods and tools. With RAD, the goal is to create a great (not perfect) word processor, game, or programming language interface that can be modified and improved in later versions. Corporate information services departments, like the MIS department at Valassis, use RAD to quickly create programs and applications for internal use.

> *Prototyping has improved our software development responsiveness. We have to accept new business and know that we have the expertise to find a solution. We can't just sit and analyze—to stay competitive, we have to jump in and try new technologies.*
>
> —*Amy Courter, Valassis Communications*

The Valassis Impact Promotions division (VIP) was launched less than a decade ago as a print provider for special promotional materials like single-page inserts and die-cut promotions. Today, VIP is transforming itself into an *information provider*, offering market selection statistics and data to customers, particularly in the fast food industry. VIP can't put their customers on hold while new software systems are tested; neither can they risk investment in large systems that may not perform as anticipated.

To assist VIP in developing and testing new systems and processes, Valassis has recently undertaken a PC initiative, annually placing over 100 microcomputers on employee desktops. MIS and VIP employees are using Visual Basic, Access, and Delphi software as prototyping tools to create software systems that support rapid information retrieval and will allow VIP personnel to easily develop new advertising products. The new systems are tested with limited use in VIP, then fine-tuned before being fully implemented in VIP and other divisions. PC prototyping allows Valassis to test new ideas on a limited basis before creating enterprise-wide applications and gives departments increased flexibility to build new, auxiliary product lines.

> *By using prototypes, users will be able to evaluate and request changes to their systems as the systems are being developed. And once the systems are in production, users will be able to respond more quickly to customers.*
> —Mark Schultz, VIP Redevelopment Project Leader, Valassis Communications

Computerized Prototype Testing

Even prototypes that aren't related to computers or computer software can be tested using computers. Computerized testing is designed to replace prototype testing by simulating test conditions. For example, a model created in a CAD program can be tested in a simulated wind tunnel. Like real wind tunnels, simulated wind tunnels are used to test the effect of wind and other types of currents on aircraft, automobiles, submarines, and buildings designed for high-wind areas. Computerized testing saves time that would have been spent building, transporting, and testing a physical prototype. An engineer can make changes to the model, then run the simulation again to see the effects of the modifications.

Simulations can be simple text-based models, or complex models that include multiple variables. For example, a real wind tunnel includes winds at various speeds coming from different directions. These two numerical variables (speed and direction) can be easily simulated on a PC. A more complex model for aircraft testing would include variations in wind speed, temperature, precipitation, and runway conditions. Simple simulation and testing is done with PCs, but more complex computerized testing with numerous variables is conducted on mainframe or supercomputers.

Simulations provide distinct advantages over "real-life" testing. Simulations provide a level of safety that can't be guaranteed when testing prototypes. For example, pharmaceutical researchers are using computer models of the human body to test potential new drugs for adverse reactions. Computerized testing is particularly valuable when the test must include changes over extensive periods of time, because time is just another variable in a simulation. The model can be sped up to simulate the passage of years within a few hours.

Virtual Manufacturing

Although computer simulations provide a way to test a product after it has been produced, up until recently there was no way to develop a computerized model of what it would take to manufacture a product. Using **virtual manufacturing** or VM, companies can now create models of the product that will be created in production as well as the production processes that will be needed to create it. Software that supports virtual manufacturing allows a manufacturer to design a product, then analyze the product to see how (and if) it can be produced.

Virtual manufacturing allows engineers and production employees to walk through difficult parts of the process before implementation. It is a relatively new concept, and is expected to radically change production in the next decade. The payoffs can be great—by modeling the manufacturing process, virtual manufacturing can help identify and solve production problems that can be corrected in product design, long before the product ever reaches the production stage.

SECTION 12.3: USING TECHNOLOGY IN MANUFACTURING

Just as there are a variety of computer tools to speed the design-to-manufacture cycle, there are a number of software and hardware combinations that assist in the implementation or manufacturing stage.

CAM and CIM

Computer-aided manufacturing, or **CAM**, is a group of technologies that support the manufacturing process. CAM adds intelligent technology (processors and memory) to machine tools so that a machine can be programmed to perform new tasks. The result is **flexible manufacturing**, the ability to manufacture new products without completely retooling a machine or plant. CAM's roots are in tool and die manufacturing, where one machine could be programmed to create different dies. Today, many processes use CAM technologies, from programmable printers such as the one shown in Figure 12.4, to robotic assembly units as shown in Figure 12.5.

Figure 12.4
Harrison 9000 press, Valassis Communications

Courtesy of Valassis Communications, Inc.

Middleware (software that bridges a gap between two existing applications) converts drawings from CAD systems into machine instructions for CAM applications. A numerical control programmer uses middleware and numerical control (NC) software to create the programs that instruct a flexible manufacturing machine how to create the part. For example, UG/Genius 4000, part of the Electronic Data Systems Unigraphics system, takes Unigraphics CAD and CAM specifications to a database that can be accessed by a flexible manufacturing system. **Computer Integrated Manufacturing** (**CIM**) takes CAM to another level by allowing one machine to pass data and program code directly to another without returning the data to a centralized database.

Computers and Just in Time

Just in Time (JIT) is an inventory management strategy with a profound impact on lead time and the entire manufacturing process. With JIT, materials are delivered to a customer just as they are needed, eliminating the need to warehouse materials. For a company to serve as a JIT supplier, they must be

Figure 12.5
Palette robot arm assembly, Valassis Communications

Courtesy of Valassis Communications, Inc.

able to guarantee products on demand, since delays from a supplier result in downtime for the customer. Some Just in Time systems rely on fax machines to provide a communications link between customers and suppliers. Customers fax their orders to suppliers, who verify the order by telephone or return fax. This is a cumbersome system, however, as it requires an employee to monitor the fax and either enter information into an order entry system or actually carry the fax to the next step in the process.

Increasingly, JIT manufacturers are using **electronic data interchange (EDI)** to communicate directly with customers and suppliers. Customers are connected directly to the manufacturer, and can place orders on a computer at their site. Then, the EDI software transmits the customer's order to a computer at the supplier's location. The manufacturer's computer confirms the order, then forwards it to the shop floor.

EDI configurations usually use leased lines and asynchronous modems to ensure consistent, continuous communication. Some manufacturers are implementing EDI by including their suppliers and customers in their communications systems through an intranet. Computerized Just in Time systems are customized for each implementation. Increasingly, EDI applications are PC rather than mainframe based, which means that even small companies can afford to implement JIT and compete with larger firms for lucrative accounts.

SECTION 12.4: MANAGING PRODUCT QUALITY

In the early 1980s, quality became the focus of American business. Automotive manufacturers speak of "world-class quality," and commercials on television and ads on the Internet advertise "high-quality" goods and services. There are two ways to think about quality: as a standard that products (or services) can be quantitatively compared to and as a continual improvement process. Computers and improved software make it possible to manage product quality in a production setting. Without technology, measuring and comparing quality and improvement are expensive, labor-intensive processes.

Quality Methods

There are several different quality management methodologies used in today's businesses: TQM (Total Quality Management), TQC (Total Quality Control), the Crosby method, the Deming method, to name a few. Most businesses begin with a particular methodology, then modify it to suit their needs. Software is available for almost every methodology to help employees and managers learn about and implement quality methods.

Measuring Quality

Regardless of method, there are techniques used at the process and product level to determine whether individual manufacturing components are meeting quality standards. Measuring quality is not a new concept. Statistical control charts were used to monitor production at Bell Labs in the 1920s. In the late 1940s, the U.S. government began requiring the use of quality control measures by suppliers. W. Edwards Deming introduced statistical quality control measures in Japan in the 1950s. The quality test used is related to the product being tested: How many errors are there in every thousand lines of software code? How many TGWs (things gone wrong) in a vehicle? How many bottles of your favorite soft drink didn't seal properly?

In a manufacturing setting, there are three points where quality can be checked: preproduction, during production, and postproduction. In preproduction quality assurance, some raw materials and prefabricated components are sampled (checked) before they are introduced into production. After production, finished products are sampled to ensure they meet quality standards.

For many products, sample testing is done with computerized machines that check quantifiable qualities: dimensions, hardness, temperature, and color. Other products must be submitted to human testing for overall appearance, smell, or flavor. A spreadsheet can be used to calculate the number of items that should be sampled and generate a randomized list of actual items for sampling. For example, a company with 1,000 products to test won't sample them all, particularly if they have to destroy the sample in the testing process, if testing is costly, or if time is limited. Instead, they can use the statistical functions of a spreadsheet program like Excel or formal sampling software to determine how many products should be tested to produce a representative sample. The spreadsheet's random function could then generate 10 random numbers between 1 and 1,000 to select the specific products to be sampled.

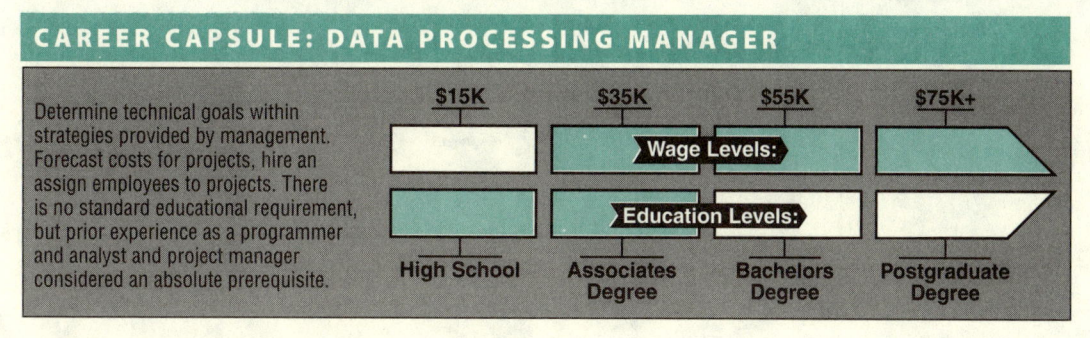

CAREER CAPSULE: DATA PROCESSING MANAGER

Determine technical goals within strategies provided by management. Forecast costs for projects, hire an assign employees to projects. There is no standard educational requirement, but prior experience as a programmer and analyst and project manager considered an absolute prerequisite.

	$15K	$35K	$55K	$75K+
Wage Levels:				
Education Levels:				
	High School	Associates Degree	Bachelors Degree	Postgraduate Degree

To monitor performance and then compare actual performance to an acceptable range, companies use statistical process control (SPC) techniques during the production process. They first take samples and then compare the results of those samples to an established range of acceptable performance. Control charts, like the Excel control chart shown in Figure 12.6, show the performance benchmarks for each part of the process and the established range of acceptability. If all variations are within the range, the process is in control. If variation in any process falls outside the range, like #7 in Figure 12.6, the process isn't in control, and the source of the variation must be identified and corrected.

Figure 12.6
Control chart created in Excel

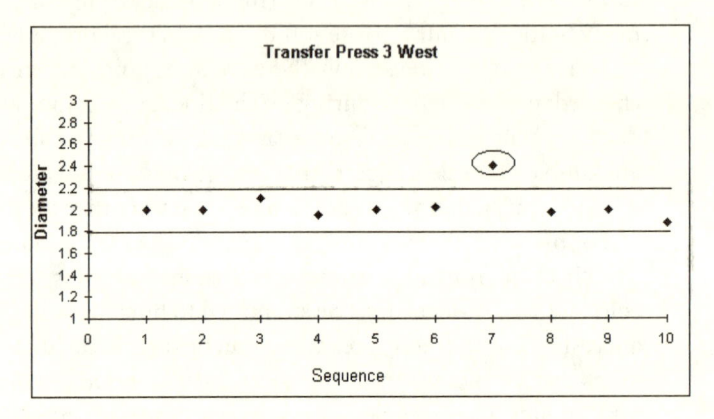

Another type of chart called radar chart (also called a spider chart) is also used to present variations from a standard. Companies use radar charts for SPC or to show variations between work groups, as shown in Figure 12.7.

Figure 12.7
Radar chart

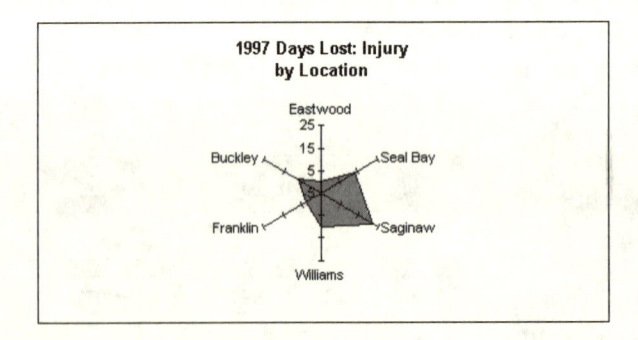

There are many other ways that computers are being used to measure and monitor quality. As more parts of the production cycle itself are computerized, quality management is becoming more integrated into the production process, resulting in higher quality products at lower costs. This is not only good news for businesses but should also translate into better products for consumers.

SECTION 12.5: MANAGING PRODUCTION WITH COMPUTERS

Before any product reaches the store shelves, a company has to invest resources—including personnel, money, facilities, and equipment—into the production process. In order to assure that the project is completed in a particular time frame with the specified resources, companies typically assign a project manager to oversee the process. A project manager coordinates the efforts of project team members and ensures that resources are utilized in the most efficient manner. A project manager will generally use one of three common methods to manage projects, and there is software available to support each methodology:

- Critical Path Method (CPM)
- Program Evaluation Review Technique (PERT)
- Gantt Charts

CPM, PERT, and Gantt all begin by breaking the total project into individual projects (also called work packages or tasks). Then, the project manager identifies the relationships between the tasks. For example, the painter can't paint the walls until the drywaller has hung drywall and finished the walls with "mud" and the sanding crew has sanded the walls. If the drywall hanger is behind schedule, the sanders and painters will also fall behind.

When the relationships between tasks are clearly defined, they are placed in a chronological order. Then, software tools are used to determine the **critical path**—the tasks that must be done before others—and **slack**—the tasks that have some "elbow room" because a longer, critical path task is occurring at the same time.

A diagram helps the manager and project team members see the workflow in a way that's intuitively easy to understand. Figure 12.8 shows a critical path chart created in Visio diagramming software for the design and prototype of a computerized database project.

Figure 12.8
A critical path chart shows how the timelines of various tasks relate to each other.

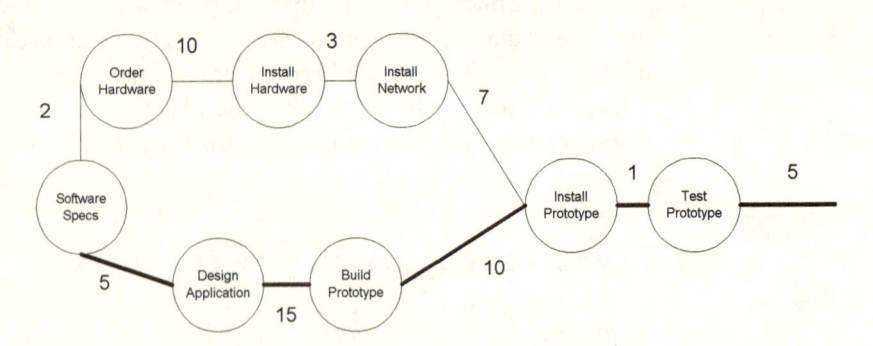

PERT weighs project tasks by looking at three different lengths of time the tasks might take: the most likely time, the optimistic time, and the pessimistic time. A probability is assigned to each likelihood. Then, the project manager uses a statistical package or a spreadsheet to determine the most probable timeline. A modified version of PERT, such as the one shown in Figure 12.9, is widely used in production planning.

Figure 12.9
A modified PERT chart shows the length of time each part of the project will probably take.

August 8	2	August 10	August 10	10	August 20
Order Hardware			Install Hardware		
August 8	3	August 11	August 11	12	August 23
August 8	6	August 14			
Software Specs				
August 8	7	August 15			

Gantt charts are frequently used to represent timelines in an easy-to-read form. Gantt charts show overlapping timelines, and are often used to manage completion times. A Gantt chart created in Excel is shown in Figure 12.10.

Managers can use general application programs like Excel and Visio to diagram relationships and create charts, but to actually manage project components, they often use software specifically designed for project management. Microsoft Project, a popular Windows-based application for project

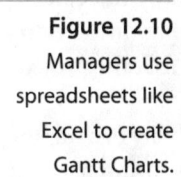

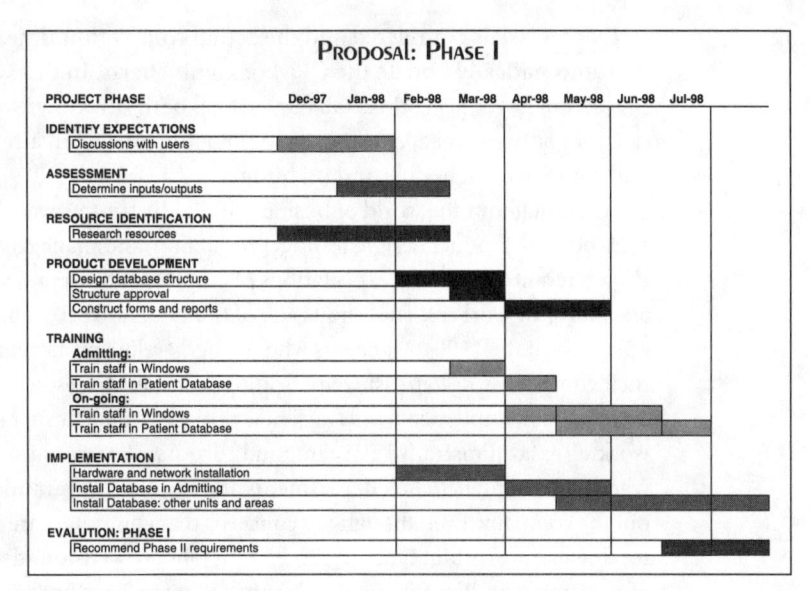

12.5 ■ MANAGING PRODUCTION WITH COMPUTERS   297

Figure 12.10
Managers use spreadsheets like Excel to create Gantt Charts.

management, supports both CPM and Gantt methods. Managers use project management software like Project to enter the people and other production resources needed for a project and then assign those resources to specific tasks. They can also plan the estimated completion times of each task, as shown in Figure 12.11.

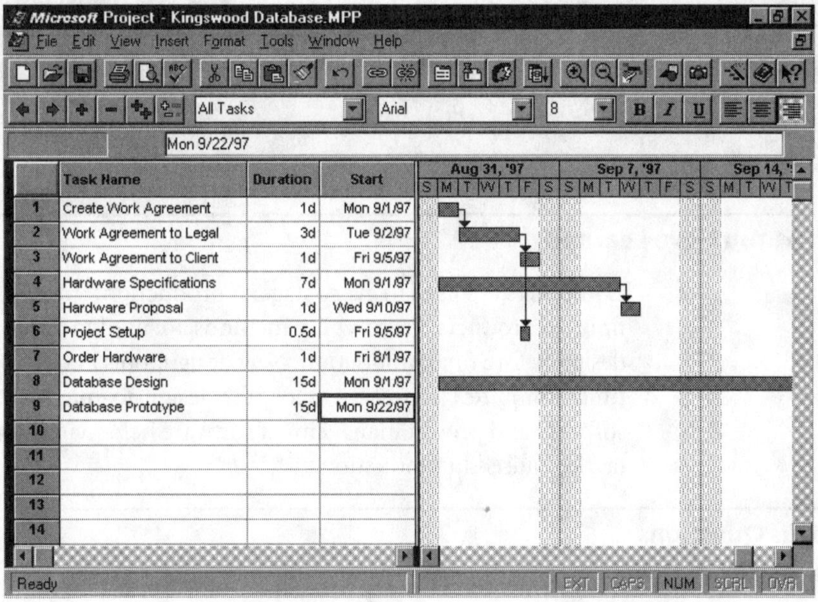

Figure 12.11
Microsoft Project allows managers to track complex projects.

Once a task is completed and the actual completion time is entered, Project will automatically update the CPM or Gantt charts. In this way, Project lets a project manager keep close tabs on critical path slowdowns that threaten to delay an entire project and makes them better able to ensure that the project will come in on schedule and on budget.

All throughout the world of business and industry, the availability of computerized tools for product design, testing, production, and management are changing the job requirements and expectations of employees from project managers to assembly line workers. The "shop rats" of the 1970s are becoming the skilled CIM operators of the 1990s. Managers who formerly relied on secretaries to handle all their computer work are using applications such as Microsoft Project, Excel, and Visio to plan, implement, and track new projects. Many former secretaries are now working as administrative assistants and corporate communications specialists who use computers to link departments and improve communications throughout the company. Even though the concerns that computers are partly responsible for downsizing certain types of production jobs are well-founded, there are plenty of new opportunities for people who are willing to learn how to apply computerized solutions to the production process.

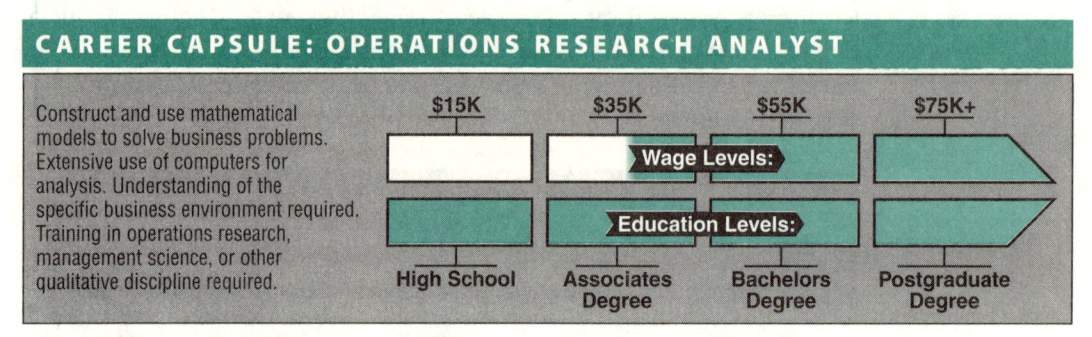

CAREER CAPSULE: OPERATIONS RESEARCH ANALYST

Construct and use mathematical models to solve business problems. Extensive use of computers for analysis. Understanding of the specific business environment required. Training in operations research, management science, or other qualitative discipline required.

Wage Levels: $15K — $35K — $55K — $75K+

Education Levels: High School — Associates Degree — Bachelors Degree — Postgraduate Degree

What You Have Learned

Computers are used in every stage of production, from design through testing finished products. Prototyping methods are used to check the viability of a design before final production. New design tools like CAD tools decrease lead time; computerized testing speeds the design-to-manufacture cycle. Design software and project management software help managers coordinate the tasks required in production.

Focus Questions

1. What do production systems and computer systems have in common?

2. How can computers be used to shorten the time it takes to produce a product?

3. What is prototyping? How does Valassis use computers in prototyping?

4. Compare and contrast CAD, CAM, and CIM.

5. What is Just in Time?

6. What software is used for project management?

Knowledge Reinforcement

A. Like many other large corporations, Valassis Communications is adding microcomputers to a mainframe or minicomputer environment. What advantages do users gain by having access to PCs? What possible disadvantages?

B. Can a company reach a point where they can achieve no further decreases in lead time? If yes, what are the implications for business technology strategies as a business approaches that point?

C. What are the advantages of information technology planning? What are the disadvantages? Considering the current speed of technological change, should IT planning be abandoned? Why or why not?

Further Exploration

CAD/CAM software:
http://mfginfo.com

IBM Manufacturing Solutions:
http://clearlake.ibm.com

Manufacturing Online:
http://www.chesapk.com/mfgworld.html

Project Management:
http://microsoft.com

Project Management Certification:
http://www.iol.ie

Unigraphics:
http://www.ug.eds.com

Vocabulary

- automated warehouse
- 2-D (matrix) bar code
- bar code (symbol)
- batch system
- inventory control system
- inventory tracking system
- point of sale (POS)
- real-time systems
- source data capture
- spamming
- symbology
- transaction capture
- transaction system
- virtual warehouse

SESSION THIRTEEN

Computers in Distribution

THIS SESSION FOCUSES ON THE COMPUTER systems used to track and value inventory and distribute goods to consumers. In this session, you'll see how Valassis Communications uses computers to help with distribution decisions, how Federal Express uses computers for real-time tracking, how retail outlets track sales, and how resellers are using the Internet. At the end of this session, you will be able to

- Name and identify the uses for bar code symbologies
- Discuss how firms use computers to distribute products
- Explain the differences between batch and real-time systems
- Discuss the challenges and opportunities of sales on the Internet

SECTION 13.1: DISTRIBUTING GOODS AND SERVICES

Decisions about how to distribute a company's services and goods impact every area of the business. Distribution affects manufacturing goals, pricing decisions, marketing requirements and, ultimately, product cost. In the simplest distribution system, a business creates a product or service and distributes it directly to its customers—like an artist selling pottery at an art fair, or a dentist giving you a root canal. More complex systems involve intermediaries: wholesalers and retailers between the producer and the customer. The steps that a product or service passes through on its way from a producer to a consumer is called a distribution channel. When a small producer sells directly to a consumer, it's easy to track product locations and sales. As the distribution channel involves more intermediaries, companies rely on computers to manage one or more of the four parts of distribution: warehousing, inventory, transportation, and scheduling.

SECTION 13.2: WAREHOUSING AND INVENTORY

Businesses need warehousing because there is a gap between production and purchasing. For example, a factory that produces blue jeans may make 5,000 pairs of size 36 button-front jeans in a single run. Unless there are 5,000 people with 36-inch waists queued up outside the factory with credit cards in hand, the jeans will have to be warehoused. Two computer systems, often integrated, help manage the company's stock of jeans. A computerized inventory control system helps company managers determine that the inventory contains an acceptable number of pairs of jeans of each style and size. Inventory tracking systems record the warehouse location of each type of jeans.

Item Identification

With thousands of items to control and track, computers play an important role in item identification. It's inefficient to have a clerk type full descriptions of each item at each stage of the distribution channel, so most items are coded for easier identification. The product's code is entered into the various product databases used by the producer, wholesalers, and retailers. However, even when the most proficient users enter information by keyboard, there is a chance of error, particularly when the information being entered consists of numeric or alphanumeric codes rather than words.

In Session 5, you were introduced to the use of bar code technologies as simple methods of inputting data into a computer. A **bar code**, also called a **symbol**, is a group of bars and spaces that represents a group of letters or numbers. Bar codes provide a consistent way to enter information and reduce errors. A user swipes a light pen or other input device across the bar code, and the code's characters are entered as if they were typed from a keyboard.

Just as ASCII and EBCDIC provided two different systems for encoding characters, there are various systems called **symbologies** that specify how characters will be represented in bar codes. There are two groups of bar code symbologies: linear and matrix. The more common linear symbologies and their normal uses include

- CODABAR, used in medical and library applications
- Code 128, an alphanumeric code used in shipping
- Code 39, used in manufacturing
- EAN, a European retail code
- UPC-A and UPC-E, North American retail codes

Each symbology has a set group of characters that the code represents. For example, UPC codes represent eleven digits (no letters); the first six digits are assigned to the manufacturer by the Uniform Code Council, and the manufacturer assigns the last five digits to individual products. (A twelfth check digit, used for error checking, is added to the code.) Code 128 is so named because it can be used to code all 128 ASCII characters.

A complete bar code system includes a printer for creating bar codes, a scanner to read the symbols, a computer, and software to receive the bar coded information. Bar code scanners like light wands and pens read all of the linear bar codes. The input device and software for a linear bar code system cost less than $1000, and can greatly reduce errors and increase warehouse productivity.

> **NOTE**
>
> Bar code scanning can be used anywhere repetitive data is entered. Grocery stores are a perfect place for scanning since most goods sold come pre-coded with a UPC symbol. But even small medical offices often scan patient visit information, using a small scanner and charts with codes for common diagnoses and treatments.

Matrix or **two-dimensional bar codes** are a new innovation. Matrix bar codes are compact, and can hold large amounts of information. Unlike a regular bar code, a matrix bar code can't be scanned by "swiping" across the surface, but must be scanned all at once with a camera-like charge coupled device, or CCD:

2-D bar codes have their drawbacks: reading them requires special, more expensive equipment, and the reading can't be as easily checked for errors. However, the denser 2-D codes have already found several niches in product identification and distribution. A 2-inch label can encode all the characters in this paragraph. Since more information can be represented in a smaller area, tiny 2-D symbols are used to label small parts like computer chips and electronics components. The ability to pack a lot of information into a small space means that a shipping company can encode the complete sender and destination names and addresses in the square inch label shown above.

Bar codes play an important role in distribution, by decreasing data entry errors and eliminating keyboard entry of routine, repetitive information. When packages and products can be rapidly scanned at each point in the distribution channel, the products you want to purchase are delivered more quickly and at a lower cost to your home or local retailer.

Distribution Centers

Warehouses that hold goods for a short period of time are called *distribution centers*. Warehouse employees use bar code technology to record shipments as they are received, temporarily stored, separated, and loaded on trucks to be shipped. Some large companies have taken the next step in computerization by completely automating their warehouses.

Automated Warehouses

Automated warehouses are state-of-the-art distribution centers. In **automated warehouses**, bar-coded products are stored in bar-coded bins. As products are received, their identity and storage location are scanned into a database. When products need to be removed and shipped, automated, scanner-equipped robots called *pickers* remove the items from the bins and place them in shipping containers. Much of the heavy work of a warehouse is done by the pickers, and automated warehouses need few human employees.

General Motors uses automated warehouses in many of their production facilities for tools and tool replacement parts like saw blades and drill bits. These automated warehouses replaced "tool cribs," which were staffed by employees. When a GM employee needs another drill bit, they go to the automated warehouse and enter their employee number (or have it scanned from a bar code on their employee ID card) and the part number into the warehouse order computer. The picker retrieves the item for the employee, and drops it in an output bin by the computer.

> **NOTE**
>
> Automated warehouses may solve a lot of problems, but they can also create others. According to employees interviewed in one General Motors plant, the technicians who created the database for the automated warehouse misnamed some of the parts: a torx driver was named a stardriver, a handle was given a name that still hasn't been identified. The warehouse contains parts that no one can retrieve, because no one knows what names the technicians used for the parts.

The automated warehouse uses inventory software to print lists of items that need to be reordered. The entire warehouse is enclosed with fence, so employees can't remove items unless they request them through the computer. If a part is listed in the database, management knows it must be in the warehouse, so warehouse inventory can easily be controlled. Automated warehouses reduce costs by cutting "shrinkage" and the number of items broken through mishandling, and by eliminating time spent taking physical inventories.

Inventory Control Systems

Computerized **inventory control systems** help managers make good business decisions about the type and number of items they hold in inventory. The value of the items in inventory is often the largest asset listed on a company's balance sheet. Products enter an inventory through purchase, or, in the case of a manufacturer, through production. Products leave an inventory when they are sold and shipped to a customer or distribution channel intermediary.

Before an inventory can be controlled, management must set goals for the inventory system. Because of the relationship between customer service and inventory levels, "managing inventory" means something different in every company. For some businesses, the best inventory is no inventory. For example, a mail order firm which uses electronic data interchange (EDI) software with its suppliers may try to have an empty warehouse at the close of business every day. All items received from suppliers are shipped to customers the same day, keeping warehousing and inventory carrying costs low. In these companies, the computerized inventory control system directly links order entry with purchasing and receiving with shipping, so each product ordered by a customer is immediately ordered from the proper supplier, and a product received from a supplier is immediately shipped to the customer. In this setting, inventory control is easy: purchasing simply doesn't order anything from a supplier that hasn't already been ordered by a customer.

Other companies have a reputation for always having the part or product you require. In these companies, every item they carry should be represented in the inventory every day so they can fill customer orders. Companies like Quill Corporation, a business office supply house, and MicroWarehouse, a computer software mail order company, advertise next day delivery on most items. For these companies, inventory control systems must take into account the largest reasonable number of each item that might be ordered in a single day and the amount of time it takes to receive new products from suppliers, to calculate when additional products should be ordered.

Instantly calculating the number of mouse pads on hand and determining whether to purchase more can easily be done using pencil and paper. However, when a business carries thousands of different items and sells vast quantities each day, the individual items can no longer be controlled manually. No matter what inventory goals a business sets, inventory control is easier with a computerized inventory control system, and control of a high-volume inventory control system is impossible without computers.

Inventory Tracking

Inventory tracking systems are used to trace and assign a value to inventory items. The heart of an inventory system is a database that includes a record for each inventory item, including an item number and item description. The additional fields in an item record depend on the type of inventory being tracked. Even small businesses that can control inventory manually often track inventory on computer, so there are dozens of off-the-shelf PC inventory tracking systems.

Businesses with specialized needs can use database software like Access or Paradox to create a tracking system. An Access inventory database is shown in Figure 13.1.

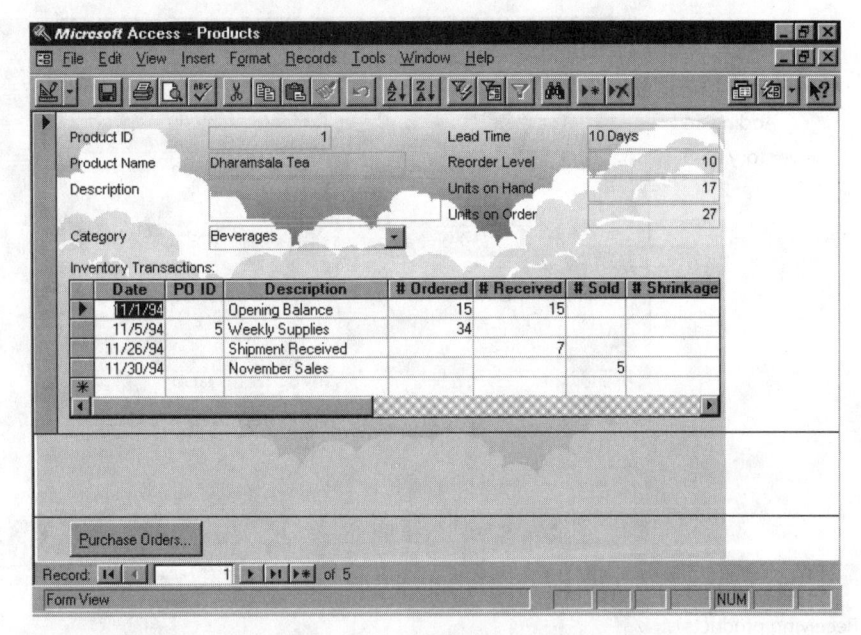

Figure 13.1
Inventory tracking database

[Screenshot of Microsoft Access - Products form showing Product ID 1, Product Name "Dharamsala Tea", Category "Beverages", Lead Time 10 Days, Reorder Level 10, Units on Hand 17, Units on Order 27, and Inventory Transactions table with entries for 11/1/94 Opening Balance, 11/5/94 Weekly Supplies, 11/26/94 Shipment Received, and 11/30/94 November Sales.]

In manufacturing, items that are in the manufacturing stage are a part of inventory called WIP: work in progress. The value of WIP and finished goods combined is the value of the manufacturer's inventory. While manufacturers used to guess at the value of WIP, computer-aided manufacturing (CAM) allows manufacturers to precisely determine the value of a product at every stage of manufacturing, so WIP can be exactly valued. Manufacturers that don't use CAM often use spreadsheets to model material and labor inputs at key points to get a better handle on WIP value.

Inventory tracking systems vary in complexity, but are often included in corporate accounting systems. Inventory is an asset, and inventory value, purchases, and sales are used to calculate a company's cost of goods sold for income statements. Quickbooks, a high-quality accounting package for small businesses, includes an inventory tracking module. New inventory items are entered in the database, as shown in Figure 13.2.

As products are purchased, they are entered in the Quickbooks inventory, which creates a bill for the amount due the supplier (see Figure 13.3). When products are sold, an invoice or cash receipt is created that automatically subtracts the products from the inventory. Bar-coded products can be scanned into and out of the inventory.

Figure 13.2
Adding an inventory item

Figure 13.3
Receiving products

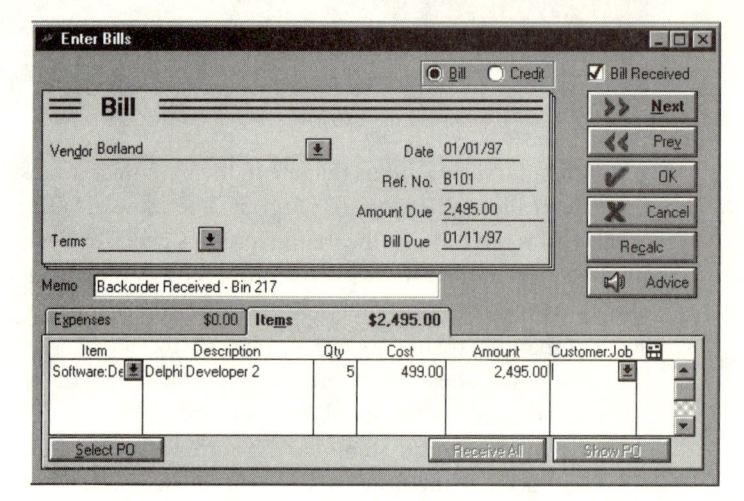

Inventory tracking systems allow users to adjust inventory quantities after a physical inventory or a catastrophic loss (like theft or fire). Reports from inventory tracking systems include the status of inventory items, status by vendor (to speed reordering), valuation summaries and details, and price lists.

SECTION 13.3: COMPUTERS IN TRANSPORTATION

The ultimate goal of most companies is to move their products out of the warehouse and on to the customer. Computerized systems to schedule and track transportation must take into account several key factors. These include:

- Time—when a product must be delivered
- Reliability of transport alternatives
- Price—the acceptable range of transportation costs
- Geography—the distance from the warehouse to each step in the distribution channel

The mode of transportation that a company chooses is largely dependent on these factors and on the type of products they are distributing. A well-designed computer system will help a company determine the most efficient and cost-effective method of transporting their products.

Transportation Scheduling Systems

Think about a shipping clerk who turns to a computer, retrieves information, and then applies the information to the physical objects stacked on the floor. That's distribution.
—Kevin McNally, Valassis Communications

At Valassis Communications, computerized scheduling systems help ensure that inserts are transported on time. Valassis Communications has no warehouses for the free-standing inserts (FSIs) they produce. Each insert is created for inclusion in a particular newspaper on a specific publication date, and must be scheduled and transported on time, or it has no value. Distribution scheduling for an FSI begins when the decision is made to print the product. Scheduling is broken into three functional parts: Traffic, Scheduling, and Shipping.

The Traffic department is responsible for transportation contracts. Because all their transportation requirements are one-way, Valassis uses commercial shippers rather than purchasing a fleet of trucks. Because of the distances involved, a percentage of the inserts need to be transported by air. Transportation costs are based on two factors: insert weight, and the number of miles an insert will be transported. Traffic negotiates short- and long-term contracts with commercial carriers for point-to-point delivery and enters the weighted mileage rates in a Page/Miles database.

Scheduling determines where a job will be printed. Valassis has insert printing plants in eight U.S. locations, and transportation costs can be decreased by scheduling printing in a plant closer to the final destination. Because scheduling has to happen before production, information about an insert is automatically moved to the computerized scheduling system as soon as it leaves the Insert Publishing system. The Scheduling department then assigns the insert to a plant. The Scheduling department uses Insert Publishing reports and the Page/Miles program to help make the decision about which plant to use. The Page/Miles program determines the optimal printing plant based on the information entered by Traffic employees and information from a Rand McNally Mile Maker database, which contains point-to-point mileage information for the United States and Canada. However, shipping costs are only one of forty-two factors (including paper and press time availability) that the schedulers must consider when selecting the printing plant for an insert, so final plant selection is determined by Scheduling department staff. Each plant can check the schedule database to view all scheduled jobs and pending unassigned jobs.

While the insert is being produced, transportation is arranged by the Shipping department. The Shipping department's database calculates the total weight of the shipment, assigns a carrier, and creates shipping documentation so it is ready when the carrier arrives to transport the inserts.

Transportation Tracking Systems

Federal Express is the world's largest express transportation company, transporting approximately 2,500,000 packages daily. Tracing 2½ million packages as they are transported to over 200 countries requires an enormous tracking system, so it isn't surprising that the FedEx database is one of the largest object databases in the world. Federal Express tracks every detail about each package. Most carriers can provide customers with the time and location where a package was picked up or delivered. With Federal Express, you can find out where a package is at any point during transportation.

> *Federal Express is committed to our PEOPLE-SERVICE-PROFIT philosophy. We will produce outstanding financial returns by providing totally reliable, competitively superior global air-ground transportation of high-priority goods and documents that require rapid, time-certain delivery. Equally important, positive control of each package will be maintained using real-time electronic tracking and tracing systems.*
> —*from the Federal Express Mission Statement*

FedEx opened operations in 1973 with service to 25 U.S. cities for overnight small package delivery based on a hub and spoke transportation system designed by founder Frederick W. Smith. All packages were taken to the FedEx hub in Memphis, Tennessee, where they were sorted and put on planes to their destination city. Industry critics scoffed at the idea of transporting a package from Dallas to Memphis, then back to Fort Worth, less than an hour from Dallas. But the success of FedEx has more than quieted the critics. Today, FedEx uses two national hubs, eight international gateways, and six regional sorting facilities to sort and route shipments ranging from standard letter packs to individual packages weighing 150 pounds.

NOTE

Smith proposed the hub and spoke system in a university term paper in 1965. He got a C on the paper.

FedEx's Customer Operations Service Master On-Line System (COSMOS) is a transportation transaction capture and reporting system. When a customer calls for package pickup, the customer service agent who receives the call enters customer information in COSMOS, which notifies the dispatcher closest to the customer. The dispatcher relays the customer pickup request to a Digitally Assisted Dispatch System (DADS) computer in a FedEx courier's van.

Each FedEx shipping slip, called an airbill, is bar-coded with a unique tracking number. The tracking number is the individual package's record number in the COSMOS database. Couriers use handheld computers called SuperTrackers to scan the tracking number and enter package information, such as transportation requirements and the destination address. When the courier returns to the van, the SuperTracker, shown in Figure 13.4, is plugged into a socket that relays the package information to the dispatch computer, which forwards the information to COSMOS.

At the end of the day, the courier takes all the pickups to the city station, where each package's arrival is recorded in COSMOS. Packages are consolidated into bar-coded containers and delivered to waiting FedEx aircraft. Containers are delivered to the nearest sorting facility, where domestic and international documents are sorted into outbound containers. The sorting facilities, like the Memphis SuperHub, are highly mechanized with elevators, beltways, and automated diverters with bar code readers that send packages down the proper beltways. The Memphis SuperHub sorts and tracks 800,000 packages daily in just two hours, and each transportation transaction is captured in COSMOS.

Figure 13.4
SuperTracker

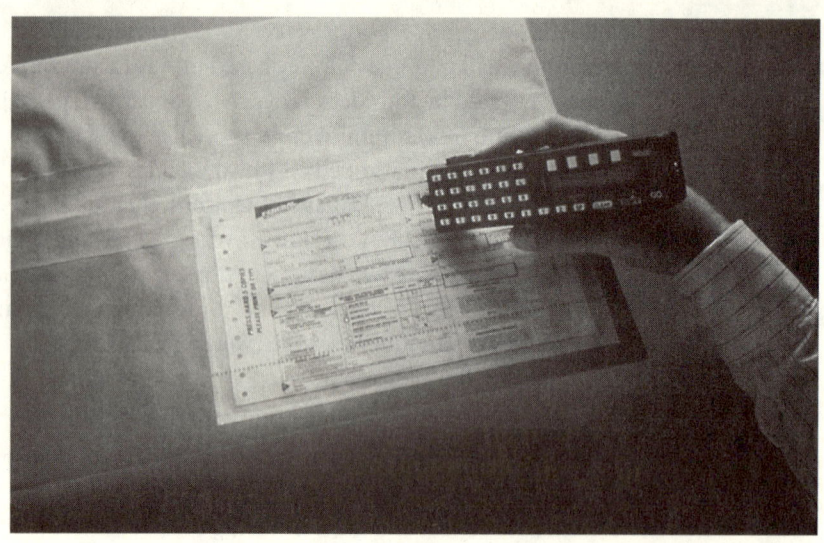

Courtesy of Federal Express Corporation

By 3:30 in the morning, all packages have been sorted, and most of the FedEx aircraft have departed for their destination cities. There, employees again sort the packages from containers into courier vans, ready for delivery. Each package has been tracked at all handling points, from the time the customer called for pickup until the package was delivered.

NOTE

Recently, FedEx has expanded into warehousing by establishing a Federal Express Partsbank near the Memphis airport. Companies store essential parts in the Partsbank, which are then retrieved and shipped to customers by FedEx.

Tracking information in COSMOS isn't just used by FedEx employees—it's accessed by Federal Express customers by telephone and the Internet. As a FedEx customer, you can phone a FedEx call center 24 hours a day, 7 days a week to receive real-time tracking information about a shipment. You can also connect to the FedEx home page and see the status of a shipment, including when it was delivered and who received the shipment.

As part of their commitment to customers, FedEx created FedEx Ship, PC software that helps customers manage package distribution (see Figure 13.5). You simply enter shipment information, and FedEx Ship dials a FedEx call center and connects to COSMOS. COSMOS generates and downloads a tracking number for the shipment and notifies the closest dispatch office to route a courier to your home or business.

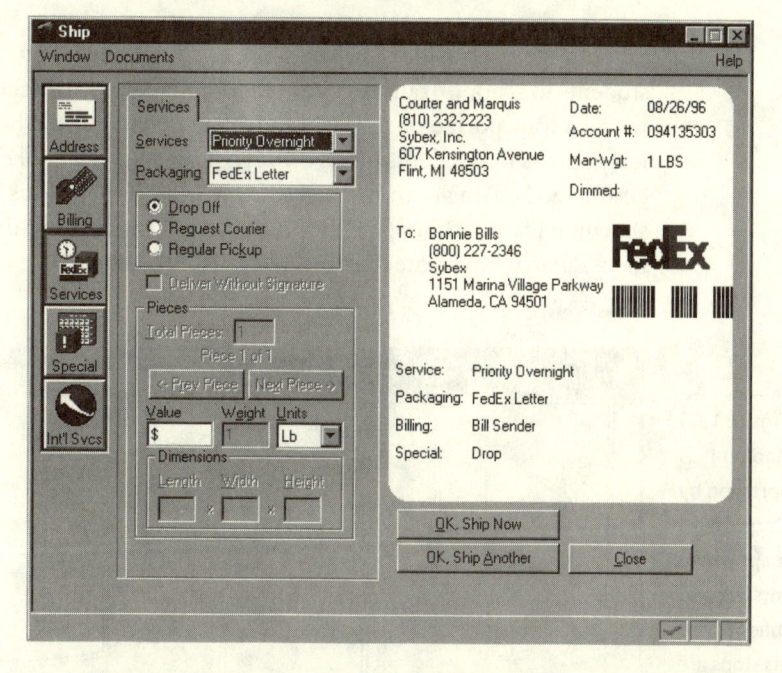

Figure 13.5
FedEx Ship software

You can print an airbill on your own printer, and FedEx Ship logs information about the shipment in a database on your computer for later reporting. FedEx Ship also includes a tracking component, so you can double-click on a shipment in your database and connect to COSMOS for tracking information.

Transportation for the Service Sector

Transportation isn't reserved for the delivery of products. Other types of service industries also have transportation requirements:

- A maintenance and cleaning service needs to transport employees to customer's homes or businesses
- An auto dealership's service department provides drop-off services for customers if a vehicle needs to be kept for repair
- A library creates a "Books on Wheels" program to deliver library lending services to neighborhoods

Transportation in the service sector has special considerations. For one, people generally resist the idea of being warehoused and insist on relatively clean and comfortable transportation modes. And don't even think about tattooing bar codes on people, even if it would make life easier.

A good example of transportation in a service industry is the U.S. public school system. Outside of urban areas, K-12 school districts usually transport students to school. Transportation requirements are stringent: every student must be transported on a timely and efficient basis, and school begins at different times for students based on age. Increasingly, school districts are using customized busing optimization software like MapNet Plus Transportation, shown in Figure 13.6, that manipulates a district map and the student enrollment database to create the optimal transportation plan.

Figure 13.6
MapNet Plus Transportation by Ecotran Corporation maps where students live and identifies where their bus stops are located.

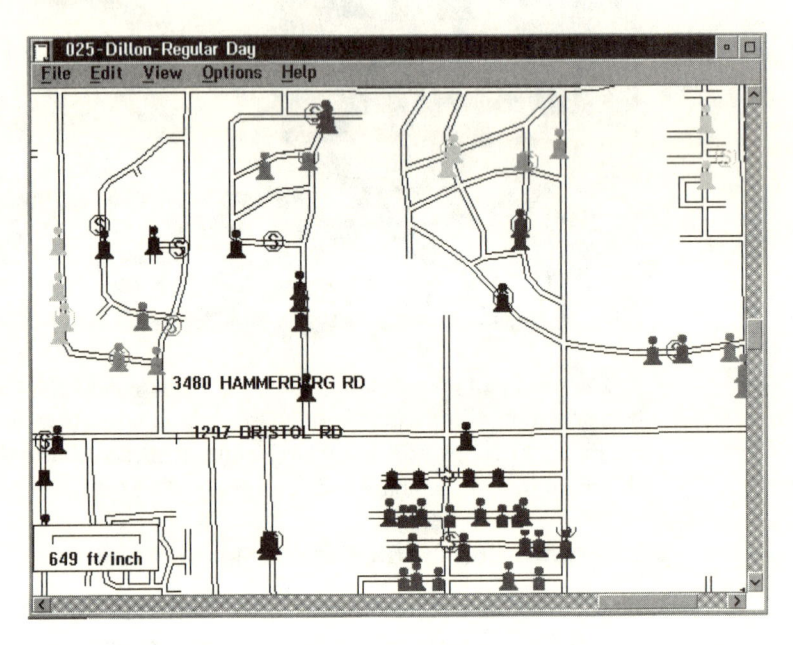

SECTION 13.4: COMPUTERS IN MARKETING AND SALES

In many respects, marketing and selling are two sides of the same coin. Marketing focuses on customer requirements, including product design and post-purchase service, and selling focuses on delivering existing product.

■ **Marketing**

With a new business or venture, market analysis includes thorough research about existing products and producers, and the size and definition of potential markets. Today, much of this research is done on the Internet. For example, a computer training company can research other training firms or check the Department of Labor's databases to find the demand levels for trainers. Searching for "computer training" returns tens of thousands of international resources.

When potential markets have been identified, more research is done to precisely define the markets and separate them into separate segments. A different product might be required for each market segment. Several firms create customized software to help with market research, analysis, and segmentation. For example, Palo Alto Software's Marketing Plan Pro includes an analysis program that helps users select and explore target markets, including segmentation strategies. Maps and Data is used in conjunction with Microsoft Office 95 for market analysis. Maps and Data includes data from the latest U.S. Census correlated with census tract maps to help identify potential customers for specific products.

Sales

Computers serve a number of purposes in the world of sales, including product marketing or demonstration, transaction capture, and as a tool to access online shopping.

Product Demonstration

In the 1980s, General Motors provided Test Drive demos on floppy disks to dealerships and customers who were interested in purchasing GM vehicles. The Test Drive demos announced new product features and allowed consumers to add features to a standard vehicle and find the estimated retail cost of the new car or truck. Today, General Motors dealerships use PROSPEC software (from Clear with Computers, Inc.) to demonstrate vehicle features, customize, and order a GM car, truck, or van for individual customers. PROSPEC includes information on the features available on each vehicle make and model, and financing options. To promote their RAV-4 utility vehicle, Toyota created a special MTV-style CD-ROM with music and full-motion graphics. The CD-ROM includes a "tour" of art galleries and compares the RAV-4's features to famous works of art.

Computers are also used to help users visualize customizable products and services ranging from room additions to cosmetic surgery. High-end hair salons use computer-enhanced imaging to show customers how their hair will look when cut in different styles. You can also see how your kitchen or bathroom will look after renovations before signing a contract, or how your body will look after plastic surgery.

The computer industry uses product demonstrations in the form of software demos, which they distribute to potential buyers. These demos are either less functional than full-fledged versions of the software or are time-bounded so that they can't be used after a certain date or number of days. Demos were introduced as a method for selling shareware, but mass distribution of demos has been taken to new heights by the online services. CompuServe, America Online, and Prodigy produce disks and CDs that contain the software to access their services and provide users with 5 to 50 hours of free online time. These online service disks are bundled in magazines, mailed directly to homes and businesses, included with book club membership materials, and even snuggled next to the dessert in American Airlines' in-flight lunch bags. These disks are so pervasive that environmentally conscious computer users no longer purchase blank disks—they erase and reuse the never-ending stream of online service disks.

Transaction Systems

Sales transactions occur when an item is purchased by a customer. The product can be tangible, like groceries, or an intangible like a class registration or a hospital admission. **Transaction systems** are manual or electronic systems that track transactions. Specific transaction systems go by other names: student registration, hospital admission, order entry, or sales transaction systems.

Manual Systems

Manual transaction systems were the mainstay of American business until the 1980s, and many small businesses still use manual systems to track sales. For example, you make a purchase at the local Ma & Pa Hardware. A sales clerk hand-writes your receipt, noting the quantity, cost, and description for each item purchased, along with your name or "Cash." The store's copy of the receipt is their record of the transaction. Every week, a bookkeeper takes the receipts and enters the totals for orders into a sales ledger, posts amounts due to the commercial customers' accounts for invoicing, and reorders products based on the prior week's sales.

There are obvious drawbacks to the manual transaction system. If clerks are in a hurry, they may write incomplete descriptions or customer names. Each time information has to be copied, the possibility of error increases—transcription errors can easily be made when copying prices from products or totals from receipts. And every transaction piece is entered many times: on the order form when the hardware orders a product, on the receipt at the time of purchase, and as summary data in the ledger and customer accounts.

Batch Systems

Electronic transaction processing systems provide an improvement over manual systems. In a simple order entry system, for example, orders are manually logged during the day, then recorded on punched cards. At the end of the work day, the entire batch of cards are processed against an order entry database, and managerial reports generated to show the day's transactions. Such **batch systems** have one significant drawback: the system's information is retrospective, not current. The batch report shows you what was, not what is, and as each day's batch piles up, the information in the order entry database becomes increasingly outdated.

Some colleges and universities still use batch processing for student registration. In a typical batch registration system, students are given an envelope and a punched card that contains their name, student number, and other identifying information. Then, for each class they want to take, students select a punched card, which identifies the class section and meeting time. A class is full when there are no cards left for the class. At the end of the registration day, the student's card and class cards are placed in the envelope and processed. After processing, administrators know which classes are filled and how many seats are left in each class.

There are other uses for batch systems. Most automated teller machine (ATM) transactions are supported by batch systems. Deposits and withdrawals are collected throughout the day, then verified and posted to customer accounts at a specified time. This means that you are not allowed to withdraw more money than an account had as of the last posting. This is only a minor inconvenience, since customers are used to waiting for deposits to clear through the banking system.

Real-Time Systems

Today, many transaction processing systems are **real-time systems**, where information is entered directly into a comprehensive system. When a user accesses the system, the report presented is up-to-the-minute, including all transactions that have occurred. A real-time system assumes, however, that there's some method to enter transactions immediately. Real-time systems only provide access to the information in the system—they can't report on the pile of class registration forms that are stacked on a clerk's desk, waiting to be entered.

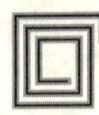

> **NOTE**
>
> The clerk is holding batches of registration forms, effectively making the real-time system a batch system. Would this still be a real-time system? The programmers who developed it would say "Yes"; the users (including the clerk) would say "No." To avoid this type of data backup, many real-time system developers include processes like requiring students to wait for a computer-printed proof of registration to ensure that the system lives up to its real-time capabilities.

Why aren't all computerized systems real-time systems? Real-time systems cost more than batch systems, are more difficult to design, and require reliable communications between all the input and output points of the system. An organization needs to determine how important real-time information is before rewriting batch systems to provide real-time reports and information.

Transaction Capture

Well-designed transaction processing systems place a premium on capturing transactions as they occur. This practice is called **source data capture** or **transaction capture**. Transaction capture increases efficiency and decreases errors by capturing all sale information directly to a database when the sale is completed. Transaction capture is used in many types of transaction processing systems, but was designed for retail sales.

Sales transaction capture systems are called **point of sale** (POS) systems. Retail POS systems use wand or gun readers to capture bar code information. Gas stations use POS pole displays, which combine a card authorization system, printer, and LCD terminal. Customers with credit or debit cards pump their own gas, and pay at the pole display.

Sales and Marketing on the Internet

For rural North Americans in the early part of the twentieth century, the Sears catalog represented a kind of shopping freedom that had formerly been reserved for urbanites. The catalog let farmers and residents of small towns shop for a wide variety of goods without traveling to the nearest large city. Eventually, thousands of businesses offered catalog shopping. The Sears catalog is gone, but catalog shopping has become a convenience that millions of Americans take for granted. Online shopping is simply the newest extension of shopping convenience.

Many of the products you purchase in person or by catalog can be purchased online. Grocery stores in several major metropolitan areas provide online grocery order services. Store personnel fill and deliver the order for a small service charge, or you can pick up the order at a designated time.

Not surprisingly, many computer stores have online catalogs, which reference databases that contains product information. If you search the Internet for Microsoft Office 97, you'll see listings from a variety of computer stores; a few clicks of the mouse, and you have comparative prices from a half dozen resellers. Such product pricing and availability information are two of the major bonuses consumers gain from online shopping. Instead of looking through a stack of catalogs to find one source for a particular software title, you can find four sources in minutes on the Internet.

Are you interested in entertainment? Browse the online catalog and fill your virtual shopping cart at Amazon Books (the "Earth's Largest Bookstore"), VideoFlicks video store, or the Columbia CD Club. If you'd rather experience entertainment in person, order event tickets through Ticketmaster OnLine. If the event is in another city, make your airline reservations through an online travel agent or directly on an airline's World Wide Web page. Don't worry about buying T-shirts at the theatre; when you return home after *Phantom of the Opera*, order your souvenirs online from the Really Useful Company Store.

Not all businesses will thrive on the Internet, and online shopping won't meet all customers' needs. But the convenience of online shopping has earned it a permanent niche in the economy.

Online Marketing

The growth of telemarketing in the 1980s resulted in an angry backlash of consumers tired of running to answer the telephone only to find a salesperson at the other end of the line. The backlash against online marketing is no less angry.

> *There are no mass markets on the Internet—only microcommunities with distinct histories, rules, and concerns. These communities are gathered into thousands of discussion forums ranging from hundreds to thousands of participants, but there are no groups of "millions." The challenge of the Internet-facilitated business is to find a way to reach these virtual communities on their terms, respecting their local customs.*
> —Michael Strangelove, "How to Advertise on the Internet:
>   An Introduction to Internet-Facilitated Marketing"

Until recently, most Internet users had grown up with the Internet, and were aware of the generally accepted protocols and netiquette that govern the online community. Now, however, the exponential increase in Internet users means that there is a large number of users who haven't spent enough time online to appreciate the culture. Some of those new users are business people who see the power of the Internet as a cheap direct marketing tool.

Small companies that sell Internet e-mail address lists or send multiple copies of advertising e-mail have sprung up seemingly overnight. Much of the direct marketing e-mail is sent to Usenet newsgroups that the advertisers believe have some interest—however tangential—in the advertised product. Some users pay connect time to receive 20 or 30 unwanted e-mail messages advertising products and services every day. Widely broadcasting inappropriate e-mail messages to a group is called **spamming**, a term coined by Internet MUD (Multiple User Dungeons) users from Monty Python's 1987 "Spam" skit. Spamming isn't tolerated on the Internet, and commercial spamming is considered to be incredibly bad manners. Many Usenet groups hold organized boycotts of companies that spam.

Does this mean businesses can't advertise on the Internet? No, but it means they have to promote their goods and services in ways that are consistent with the rules and practices of the online community. The companies that do this successfully construct Web sites that have useful information, and wait for users to come to them. E-mail mailing lists are built by asking site visitors to provide an e-mail address if they would like additional product or informational updates.

What You Have Learned

Computers play a significant role in decisions about the distribution of goods and services. Bar codes are used in warehousing and inventory control because they provide a consistent way to enter information and reduce errors. Automated warehouses provide industries with a secure and easy way to access warehoused items and control inventory. Computerized inventory tracking systems combined with computer-aided manufacturing allow manufacturers to precisely determine the value of a product at every stage of the process. Transportation scheduling and tracking systems help to make sure that products get to their destinations in the most expedient ways. Computers see wide use in sales and marketing, including marketing on the Internet.

Focus Questions

1. Name two reasons that modern business systems rely on computers for physical distribution of products.
2. Name three bar code symbologies and identify their normal uses.
3. What are automated warehouses and why are they useful?
4. How does Valassis use computers in scheduling distribution?
5. How does Federal Express use SuperTrackers to aid in their business?
6. How do batch and real-time transaction systems differ?
7. What is the major challenge businesses face when selling on the Internet?

Knowledge Reinforcement

A. What advantages do consumers receive when a retail store uses bar codes and POS? What disadvantages?

B. Collect samples of bar code symbols from products or deliveries you receive and identify (1) where each symbol was used; (2) how the symbols are similar; and (3) how the symbols differ.

C. Visit the registration office of a college or university to see what type of transaction processing is used in their registration system. Ask a staff member and a student for their opinions of the system's strengths and weaknesses.

D. Visit an automobile dealership and view a computer-based product demonstration. Would the demonstration help convince you to buy a particular vehicle? Why or why not?

E. Locate and visit the Web page for one of the sellers listed in the session. Would you purchase products online? Why or why not?

Further Exploration

Amazon Books:
http://amazon.com

Bar Code Standards:
http://mfgx.com/info

Columbia House CD Club:
http://www.columbiahouse.com

Federal Express:
http://www.fedex.com

PythOnline (Monty Python Site):
http://www.pythonline.com

The Really Useful Company Store:
http://www.reallyuseful.com

Ticketmaster Online!:
http://www.ticketmaster.com

VideoFlicks:
http://www.videoflicks.com

Vocabulary

- cellular digital packet data
- clinical workstation
- computerized medical record
- debit card
- digital library
- electronic medical record
- electronic signature
- mobile data terminal (MDT)
- mobile imaging unit
- National Information Infrastructure (NII)
- proprietary software
- rendering

SESSION FOURTEEN

Computers in Service Industries

SERVICE INDUSTRIES, WHICH PROVIDE SERVICES instead of producing material goods, make up 70 percent of the gross national product. This session focuses on how different service industries are using computers to improve the efficiency and effectiveness of the services they provide. At the end of this session, you will be able to

- Identify the ways computers are used in several major service industries
- Discuss the ways law enforcement organizations are using computers to fight crime
- Identify issues facing the banking industry as they encourage customers to use online banking
- Describe the ways in which computers are contributing to the art of animation
- Identify ways the health care industry is using computers to improve patient care

SECTION 14.1: DEFINING SERVICE INDUSTRIES

Service industries range from auto repair shops and car washes to human service organizations and the postal service. Lawyers, architects, doctors, hospitals, hotels, police/fire departments, banks, real estate agencies, stock brokers, schools, travel agencies, and airlines are all part of the service industry. Some service industries have a profit motive and some are set up not to make a profit. The primary characteristic they have in common is that their products are intangible.

Regardless of the profit objectives of the organization, the use of computer technology in service industries is sky-rocketing. Some service industries such as life insurance and banking were pioneers in the use of computers in business. In fact, one of Charles Babbage's goals for the Difference Engine was to be able to calculate and print actuarial tables for the prestigious insurance company Lloyd's of London, a task Babbage had formerly done manually. Governmental organizations played a pioneering role in the use of computers in the service industries when the U.S. government contracted with Herman Hollerith to automate the 1890 census (see Session 2 for a review of the Difference Engine and Hollerith's Tabulating Machine).

Today, the use of computers and computer technology is becoming an integrated element in most service industries. Whether keeping client or patient records, improving the flow of mail through the postal system, or monitoring environment cleanup operations, computers improve efficiency, provide comprehensive analyses of large amounts of data, and make information much more available to the people at the front lines. It would be well beyond the scope of this book to discuss in detail how computers are used in each of the service industries. Instead, we will provide snapshots of different types of service organizations and an in-depth look at one major health care provider to show how computers are influencing the business of providing services.

We'll Leave the Computer On for You

It won't be long before the only light left on at your favorite hotel or motel will be the light of a computerized kiosk where you insert a credit card, enter your address and phone number, and take out a room key. Automated check-in kiosks work like automated teller machines and are expected to become as popular within a few years. Hotel clerks won't be replaced completely, but their job responsibilities will focus on answering questions and resolving guest problems or complaints. The most significant advantages of automated check-in are that it is faster and more convenient for hotel guests and reduces the amount of staff the hotel has to have on duty.

It won't be long before "smart cards" replace your credit cards, and you won't even have to enter your address and phone number to secure a room. A smart card is a computerized wallet-sized card that can hold personal information like a calendar and address book, *and* serve as a credit or debit card. Although smart cards are still in the development phase, once they become available, they are expected to replace just about everything you now carry in your wallet and personal planner.

Virtual Real Estate Shopping

Whether you are interested in buying a new house or renting commercial property for a business, the real estate industry is making it easier with computer technology. In a non-technological world, real estate shopping usually means perusing page after page of black-and-white photographs and abbreviated descriptions of properties and then selecting some properties to visit. Today, shoppers can search for desirable properties next door or on the other side of the world in digital catalogs on the World Wide Web. Real estate Web sites, such as the site shown in Figure 14.1, allow users to search for property, applying a number of criteria such as location, price, and square footage. Properties meeting the search criteria are then displayed with color photographs, descriptions, and in some cases, floor plans.

For those interested in leasing, buying, or managing commercial properties, a number of software products exist that simplify this often complex process. Deciding where to locate a business is often the first decision prospective clients face when they approach a brokerage firm. Demographic mapping software allows brokerage firms to provide their clients with information about social and economic conditions, road conditions, and traffic information, and conduct analyses of the impact their business would have on the community.

Specially designed financial analysis software provides property managers with the tools they need to analyze properties and produce projected cash flow estimates to help prospective owners know what revenue a particular building might generate. Other software is designed to assist the owners and property managers of commercial buildings with space planning and facility management. Facility management software links data about a client's needs with computer-aided design (CAD) drawings of facilities. Property managers can show prospective tenants 3-D conceptual drawings that show remodeling changes the tenant has requested. These drawings can also be used to improve lighting and HVAC (heating, ventilation, and air conditioning) systems. Once the tenant moves in or new owner takes over, property management software generates maintenance schedules to help manage the building maintenance.

Figure 14.1
TIRI Better Homes and Gardens commercial real estate Web site

Managing Your Money Electronically

Online banking and bill-paying services are nothing new for banks. Many banks have had **proprietary software**, software designed especially for and owned by a company, since the mid-1980s. Banking software allows customers to dial in using a modem, access their bank accounts, and authorize payments to creditors. The most significant improvement in home banking is occurring because banks are moving their home banking services to the Internet. Internet banking means that you'll have access to services from more banks, and will be able to use a familiar and friendly interface, a Web browser, to use the services. As more and more of us choose to have our paychecks direct deposited, home banking is definitely the wave of the future. And once your check is in the bank, electronic bill paying is a natural next step.

Electronic bill paying frees customers from having to write checks and address, stamp, and mail envelopes. Over 60,000 vendors now accept payment online, and the number is growing everyday. Many banks prefer online payments because they reduce bank costs associated with handling, processing, and storing physical checks. Vendors who have offered to receive online payments like it because they receive payments more promptly and don't have to open envelopes to process payments or worry about having checks returned for insufficient funds.

Banks are also offering other online services including account balances and histories, transfers between accounts, and customer service. Because of the popularity of software products such as Quicken and Managing Your Money, successful online banking services are integrating their services with personal financial management software so that users can exchange information between them rather than having to reenter account activity (see Session 8 for more about personal financial management software). Other banking services, like loan application and approval and certificates of deposit sales, are being added to the list of available online services.

The only reason left for actually visiting a bank is to make a cash withdrawal. But even cash may soon become a thing of the past, as debit cards become more popular. **Debit cards** are cards similar to credit cards, but they charge cash purchases directly to your bank account.

The biggest hurdle for online banking to overcome is the threat of illegitimate and unauthorized access to account information. The fear that personal financial information can be intercepted and manipulated by online computer criminals is a real fear. However, banks have implemented sophisticated scrambling software that encrypts credit card and account numbers so that online hackers only reap unusable, scrambled data. Banks remain vigilant to stay a step ahead of the digital bank robbers of the twenty-first century.

CAREER CAPSULE: SECURITIES & FINANCIAL SERVICES SALES REPRESENTATIVES

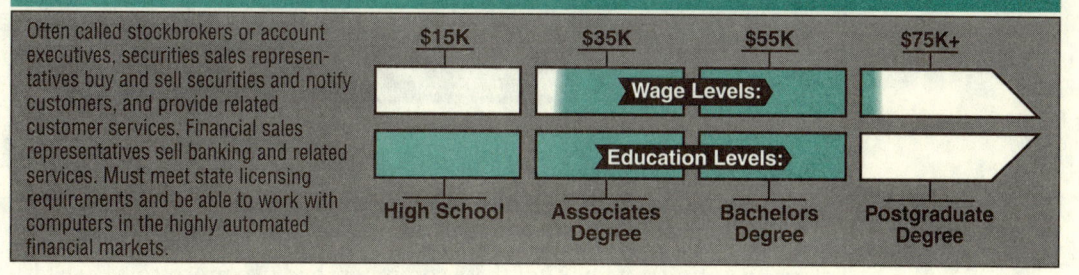

Often called stockbrokers or account executives, securities sales representatives buy and sell securities and notify customers, and provide related customer services. Financial sales representatives sell banking and related services. Must meet state licensing requirements and be able to work with computers in the highly automated financial markets.

Wage Levels: $15K — $35K — $55K — $75K+

Education Levels: High School — Associates Degree — Bachelors Degree — Postgraduate Degree

■ Digital Entertainment

The entertainment industry has developed innumerable applications for computers, from computer animated movies to programs that can predict the success of video sales. While digital effects are becoming quite commonplace—appearing in everything from movies like Jurassic Park to Reese's Peanut Butter Cup commercials and network sports broadcasts—the technology to produce digital effects is far from common and incredibly expensive.

Movie Animation

Sophisticated animation and special effects work for movies is done by a handful of special effects shops like Industrial Light and Magic and Pixar Animation Studios. Pixar, founded by Steve Jobs, founder of Apple Computer, changed the field of computer animation in 1986 with the release of the 3-D animated movie *Luxo, Jr.*, (see Figure 14.2), about a couple of animated desk lamps. As simple as this may sound, *Luxo, Jr.* went on to win 30 filmmaking awards and an Academy award nomination: the first computer-animated movie to be nominated for an Oscar.

Figure 14.2
Luxo, Jr. from Pixar Animation Studios

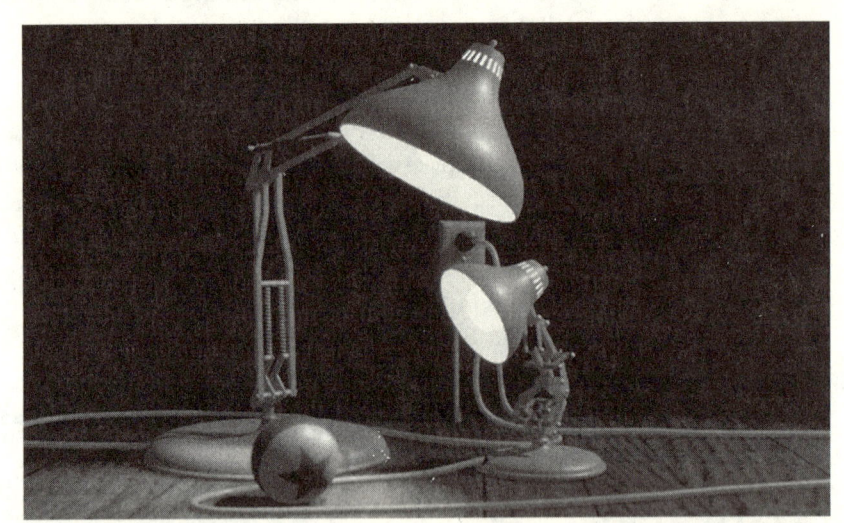

Luxo Jr. ©1986 Pixar

Pixar was a pioneer again with its production of the movie *Toy Story*, the first full-length, entirely computer animated movie. To create *Toy Story*, Pixar clustered 117 Sun SPARCstation20 workstations running on Sun's Solaris operating system. 87 of these computers had two processors, 30 had four processors and the server had eight processors. Together they processed 16 billion instructions per second. This computer bank, dubbed the Rendering Farm, was responsible for **rendering** each of the 114,000 frames in the movie. Rendering is the process in which 3-D computerized images are produced through the application of lighting, textures, and shading to computer drawn models.

Pixar's Rendering Farm with all 117 workstations is only 19-inches deep, 14-feet long, and 8-feet high. It can be upgraded—the process of adding more or faster processors, memory, and storage—to increase performance four-fold without taking up additional space. Even with all that computer power, though, it took from 2 to 13 hours per frame for final processing of Toy Story. One single-processor computer, however, would have to run continuously for 43 years to produce the same movie.

And rendering isn't the only aspect of animation the computer can help with. Pixar has also developed a program called Menv (Modeling Environment), which is an animation tool used to create 3-D computer models of characters that have controls built in to aid in the animation process. With these controls, animators can isolate specific frames of a desired motion—for example, the movement of a character's lips—and let the computer complete the animation. This eliminates the need to create precise frame-by-frame animation and achieves a much greater fluidity of motion.

Releasing Movies for Video

Once a movie is produced and has made its run in the theaters, movie studios are interested in capitalizing on the lucrative home video market. Deciding which movies will succeed in the home market and how many copies of a video will sell is no easy task. Market research software that can analyze the success of previously released products and apply those results to new products helps the film industry with the dilemma. Movies are especially suited to this type of analysis, since each movie has similar characteristics: number of stars, number of weeks in theaters, types and quantities of reviews. Each of these factors for past video successes and failures is plugged in to create a model that can be applied to new releases. The model not only makes predictions about future sales, but also analyzes what factors influence whether a movie will be successful. Armed with this information, movie producers are more likely to release videos that will be financially successful and also satisfy customer demand for videos they want to see.

SECTION 14.2: IMPROVING YOUR HEALTH

The health care industry is one of the largest industries in the Unites States. Most physicians and health care executives today are convinced that managing the volume of patients and the complexity of their care can only be accomplished using sophisticated computerized systems. As with any industry, computer information systems have become an essential ingredient in the management of health care institutions. Health care is unique in the magnitude and critical nature of information that has to be maintained about customers. In some industries, a technical problem with computer equipment or a customer database may result in a financial loss to the business or a disgruntled customer. In the health care business, technical problems or data loss can literally mean the difference between life and death.

Henry Ford Health System (HFHS), located in Detroit, Michigan, has invested significant resources to develop and implement a long-range information technology strategic plan. Developing an information systems network that meets the diverse needs of the patients, clinicians, researchers, students, and leaders in a large hospital system requires extensive planning, coordination, and willingness to evaluate new technological developments.

The Evolution of Health Care Information Systems

Dr. Richard Ward, Director of the Center for Clinical Effectiveness at HFHS, says the evolution of computer information systems in health care started 15 or 20 years ago, when the large mainframe computers in hospitals were used only for administrative purposes, billing, and patient registration systems. Individual clinical departments had needs that were not being addressed by the mainframe system, and these departments began to develop departmental information systems, such as a pathology department database to track laboratory tests. Eventually, these departmental systems developed into broader clinical information systems, made available throughout the organization, that contained data related to individual patients' illnesses and treatment. These clinical information systems, the first step toward an electronic medical record, allowed health care professionals to look up clinical information about their patients online. However, because the information was limited to a few reports and physician's orders, all of the electronic information had to be replicated in a paper record.

An **electronic medical record**, according to the Medical Records Institute, is a complete replacement of the paper record and is distinguished from the **computerized medical record**. A computerized medical record is structured the same as the paper record and in effect, duplicates the paper record. Most documents are created on paper and then scanned into a document imaging system. Documents are indexed for easy retrieval, and because they cannot be modified in their electronic form, are protected as legal documents.

Documents in an electronic medical record, on the other hand, are created using a computer. When a hospital moves to electronic medical records, there are no paper document equivalents. Even documents that originate outside the hospital system are scanned into the electronic record. The hospital must have a security system that controls who has access to the record, how data integrity is maintain, how and where the record is available, and how **electronic signatures** are handled. An electronic signature is a code or image that is assigned through a system of passwords to individual users to replace the physical signature on a document. The signature may be a scanned image of the person's actual signature or an established personal code.

The first definitive step toward an electronic medical record at HFHS came with the introduction of the Medical Information Management System (MIMS) in the late 1980s. Currently available throughout HFHS's 55-site health care network, MIMS is a compilation of data sources, including laboratory reports, physician's notes, discharge summaries, cardiology information, prescriptions, radiology reports, encounter histories, patient demographics, appointments, surgical histories, and other clinical data. Although it does not yet replace the paper medical record, MIMS provides care givers with immediate access to patient information, information that was previously unavailable in urgent or emergency situations. For patients, this means a higher quality of emergency and trauma care.

> *Our goal is to develop a team of staff who, through the use of computer information systems, can provide a system of seamless care across the various levels of care from the hospital to rehabilitation to home care and outpatient services.*
> —Dr. Richard Ward, Director, Center for Clinical Effectiveness, Henry Ford Health System

The next stage of computer development in health care involves the use of computers to manage work flow and help physicians manage each patient's disease appropriately. When a patient is seen in a medical clinic, there are many steps involved in providing even the simplest treatment: taking a patient's history, assessing the patient's condition, ordering necessary tests, reviewing the test results, diagnosing the patient's illness, developing a treatment plan, prescribing medications, and following up with the patient. A computerized workflow information system follows the patient's care every step of the way. Combining access to information with expert systems, the ideal work flow system helps the physician assess the patient's condition, order appropriate tests, diagnose the patient's illness, prescribe medications, and send reminders to the patient for regular tests such as mammograms and Pap tests.

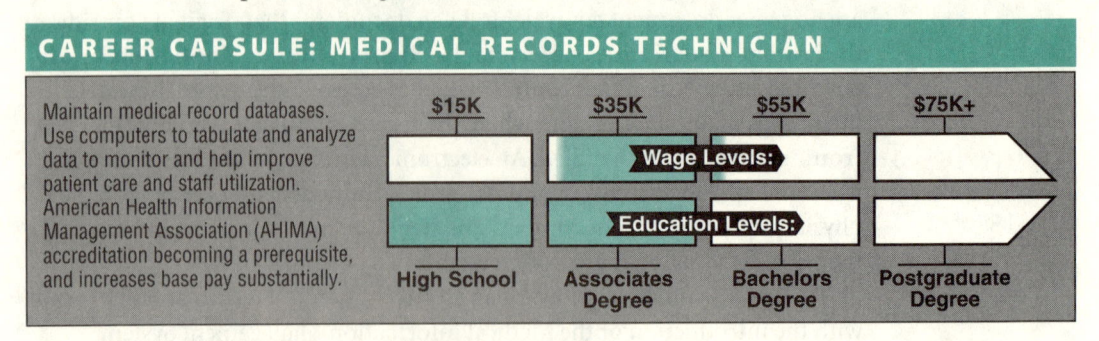

CAREER CAPSULE: MEDICAL RECORDS TECHNICIAN

Maintain medical record databases. Use computers to tabulate and analyze data to monitor and help improve patient care and staff utilization. American Health Information Management Association (AHIMA) accreditation becoming a prerequisite, and increases base pay substantially.

Wage Levels: $15K — $35K — $55K — $75K+

Education Levels: High School — Associates Degree — Bachelors Degree — Postgraduate Degree

Expert Systems and Practice Guidelines

Advances in medical science have made the amount of information a physician must consider when making decisions about clinical care unfathomable. It's impossible for physicians to keep up-to-date on all the latest medications, their side effects, and their interactions with other medications. The same is true for new treatment approaches, medical procedures, and the results of medical research. Experts systems help physicians pinpoint the information they need to determine the best treatment for their patients. According to *Healthcare Informatics*, expert systems have been particularly helpful in avoiding adverse drug reactions from improperly prescribed medications. Expert drug information systems can compare the data known about a patient with the research available on a particular medication and alert the physician to possible allergies, side effects, and other reactions the patient may experience.

Creating and maintaining your own expert system requires time and commitment, but ensures that the system matches policies and procedures within your organization. Expert systems like the practice guidelines in the HFHS Clinical Policy Library, shown in Figure 14.3, help physicians make clinical decisions based on the current research into a particular illness. HFHS posts the Clinical Policy Library on an intranet, so its medical staff can easily access the information when determining patient treatment. (See Session 11 for a review of intranets.) Physicians who are members of the Medical Group are given special access to the site.

The Clinical Policy Library contains the practice guidelines established by Henry Ford Medical Group (HFMG), physicians for a variety of medical illnesses. Figure 14.4 shows the first page of the practice guidelines for breast

Figure 14.3
The Henry Ford Health System Clinical Policy Library

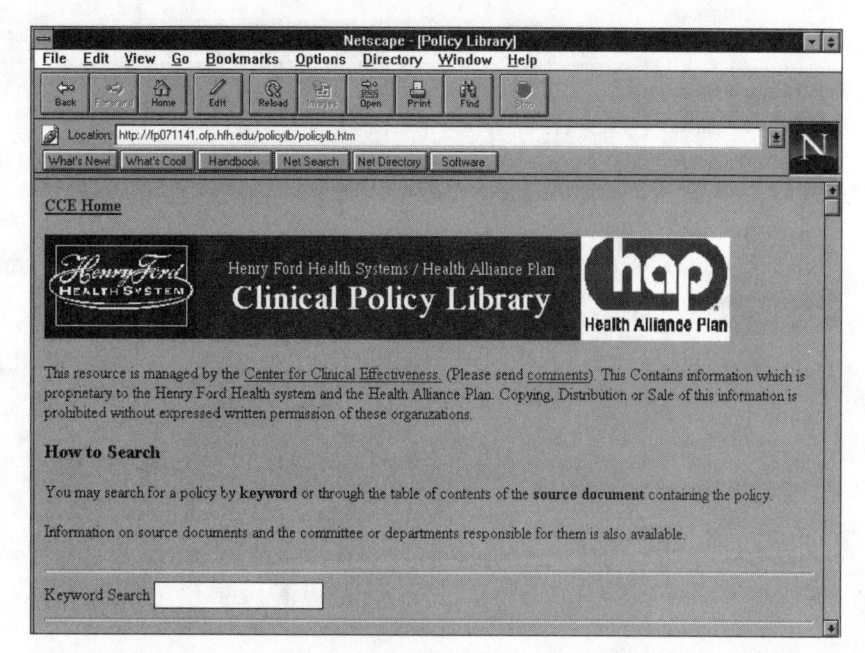

cancer screening with mammography in average risk women in the 40–49 age group. The Clinical Practice Committee of the HFMG develops and continually updates the guidelines after extensive computer and manual research and analysis of current medical literature. Physicians receive training in the practice guidelines through monthly in-service sessions. After training, whenever they need to review practice guidelines for a particular case, all they have to do is log on to the Internet and open the HFHS intranet site. And because they are already on the Internet, they are just a hot link away from medical journals and other medical resources, if they need to look up information outside of the scope of the practice guidelines.

In addition to HFMG's own practice guidelines, HFHS also participates with 31 group practices across the country that are connected to a Lotus Notes server. This server includes a practice guidelines database developed and managed by the Group Practice Improvement Network and the Institute for Healthcare Improvement. Notes also includes electronic mail capabilities, allowing physicians to access people involved in developing practice guidelines. Joint efforts like this groupware network help improve the overall quality of patient care throughout the country.

Figure 14.4
Henry Ford Health System's clinical policy analysis and recommendations regarding breast cancer screening

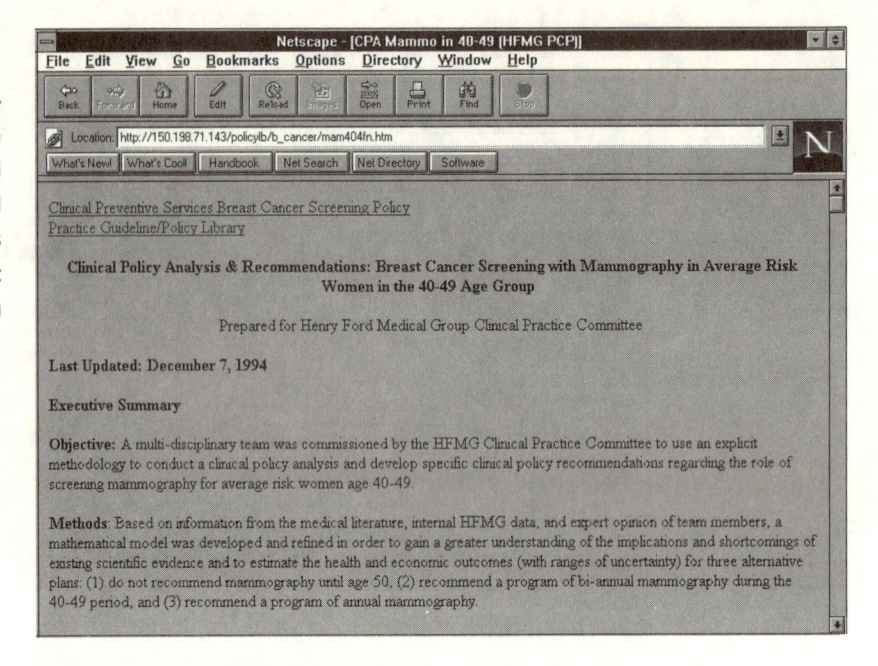

> *We look at information as one of the most important diagnostic tools we have. Improved availability of information means improved health care.*
>
> —Gail Warden, President and CEO,
> Henry Ford Health System

Clinical Workstations

By the year 2000, HFHS plans to completely replace the paper medical record with **clinical workstations**. Clinical workstations are handheld computers about the size and weight of a 1-inch medical record file folder. The workstations are wireless and can be used in the clinic or carried by the physicians while visiting patients in the hospital. The primary input device is a special pen-like device; however, voice input will also be an option. In addition to storing medical records, the clinical workstations will communicate physician orders for consults, tests, and procedures, produce patient instructions, report on test results, and correspond with patients. They will also be able to access library and reference resources, and run standardized reports.

Whether or not all physicians will one day use clinical workstations, it is evident that hospitals and medical personnel have a growing need for computers that extend far beyond that of their billing departments. Computers are an integral component of patient treatment and promise to help the health care industry find ways to reduce costs while providing high-quality care.

SECTION 14.3: COMPUTERS IN THE WAR ON CRIME

Law enforcement personnel have long been hampered by the difficulty of obtaining information about possible suspects in criminal investigations. In the past, police investigating a crime in one city had a very difficult time finding information about similar crimes in other cities (or in some cases even in other precincts in the same city). Police released suspects, only to find that they were wanted for a crime by another law enforcement agency. Computers are beginning to make it harder for criminals to pass through the system, unnoticed by law enforcement personnel.

For police officers riding in patrols cars, having information available at their fingertips makes routine traffic stops far from routine. Rather than having to radio in license plates and driver's license numbers to a dispatcher, police cars are equipped with notebook computers and cellular modems that are connected to the **cellular digital packet data** system (CDPD). CDPD is a digital wireless transmission method, using Internet Protocol (IP), which enables users to transmit packets of data over the same cellular voice frequencies used for cellular voice transmissions. CDPD transmissions are encrypted, and because transmissions hop between channels to find open frequencies, CDPD is highly secure. CDPD allows police officers to use the computer to access databases with information about the driver and the vehicle they are driving—including whether the vehicle has been reported as stolen, outstanding warrants of the driver, prior criminal history, and other pertinent information. And by avoiding radio calls that can be easily intercepted, the police avoid inadvertently notifying possible accomplices who are waiting for the driver.

Michigan State Police use their cruiser-mounted notebook computers, shown in Figure 14.5, to generate reports and record and print traffic tickets. Soon the cruisers will be online with the court systems so tickets will be automatically forwarded to the local traffic court at the time they are written.

Figure 14.5 Michigan State Police trooper writes a ticket using a notebook computer

Some cruisers are being equipped with **mobile data terminals** (**MDTs**), which allow private messaging between vehicles so that police can discreetly communicate with other officers on patrol. An MDT can also provide access to the National Law Enforcement Telecommunications System, a private messaging system with users including the U.S. Department of State, Interlope, U.S. Customs, and Naval Investigative Services.

One data source police officers access is the National Crime Information Center (NCIC), started in 1967 by the FBI. This active collection of databases holds 24 million records and is accessible by 57,000 law enforcement and criminal justice agencies in the United States, Canada, the Virgin Islands, and Puerto Rico. The NCIC databases include missing and unidentified persons, license plates, foreign fugitives, violent felons, U.S. Secret Service protective files, stolen vehicles and vehicle parts, stolen boats, terrorists and members of violent gangs, stolen and recovered guns, stolen and recovered goods, deported felons, and stolen, embezzled, or counterfeited securities.

NCIC will soon be replaced with a new system called NCIC 2000, which will include a large fingerprint database, mug shots, and other images (like signatures). Squad cars will be equipped with **mobile imaging units**, which include a miniaturized fingerprint scanner and camera. This will allow police to transmit fingerprints, signatures and other images for matching with existing data. In addition, NCIC 2000 will provide access to protection orders and the names of people on probation or parole. NCIC is expected to be fully operational in the fall of 1999.

SECTION 14.4: LIBRARIES

If you haven't visited your public library recently, you may be surprised to know that libraries are on the cutting edge of the technological revolution. Libraries are storehouses of knowledge and their goal is to help people access that knowledge. There is not a more appropriate role for librarians to assume than that of electronic information specialist.

The move to electronic information didn't happen overnight. Libraries started by converting the boxes of index cards in the card catalogs to electronic databases where users could search by book or media title, author, or subject. In some libraries, the electronic card catalog also shows whether the book is on the shelf or has been checked out. Because many libraries belong to a consortium, users may search other libraries for a book and have the book sent to their local library. Card catalogs are often available online, some directly through the Internet and others through a special library phone number.

Circulating books is only a very small part of what a library is all about. The University of Michigan School of Information and Library Studies (SILS), which provides professional degree programs that train librarians to become information specialists, recently changed its name to the School of Information. No longer limited to the printed tomes on library shelves, information specialists are now trained to sift information from a variety of resources, including the world wide library available on the Internet. The School of Information's mission statement says its field of study is information: how it's created, identified, collected, structured, managed, preserved, accessed, processed, and presented; and how it is used in different environments, with different technologies, and over time.

The ability to connect to a broad set of resources without concern for their physical location or hampered by time constraints will stimulate the development of new communities based on individuals with common interests who will be able to interact with one another without limits imposed by geography or social convention.
—University Of Michigan School of Information

Anyone who has surfed the World Wide Web knows that it can be a daunting ordeal to find a specific piece of information. It often feels like playing the slot machines—you just keep putting in your quarters, hoping that one of them will hit it big. A skilled information specialist has been trained to search the Internet and hit the jackpot with minimal effort.

Students at SILS maintain a World Wide Web site called the Internet Public Library, shown in Figure 14.6, where you, or anyone, can ask them a question. These information specialists in training research the question using both traditional and electronic sources and return with an answer. If they can't find what you're looking for, they will at least point you in the right direction. With the unprecedented growth in the number of available information sources, knowing where to find a reliable answer, whether it's on the Internet or in some dusty old book on the shelves, is one of the most valuable skills anyone can develop (unless, of course, you know all the answers already). As a result, information specialists are becoming some of the most highly prized professionals in this information age.

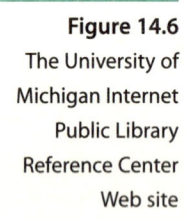

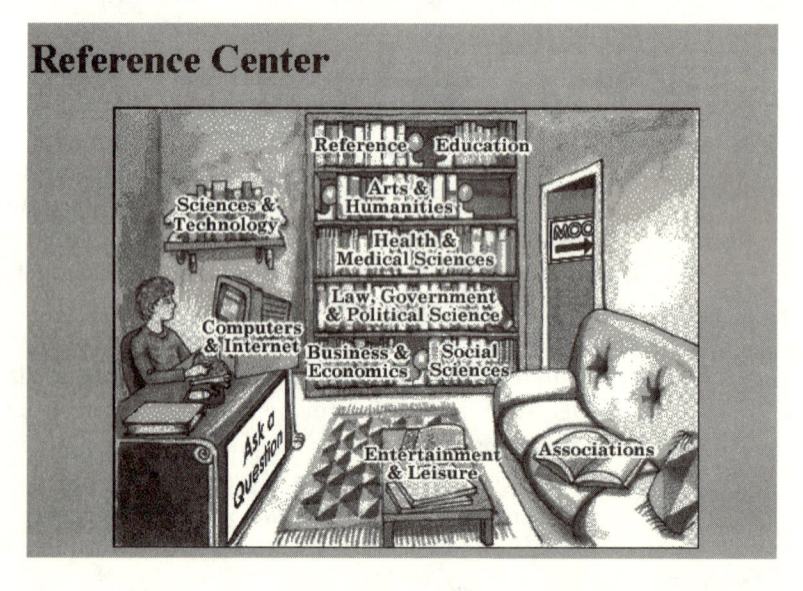

Figure 14.6
The University of Michigan Internet Public Library Reference Center Web site

Digital Libraries

The **National Information Infrastructure** (**NII**), the United States government's initiative to build the "information superhighway," has identified digital libraries as a key ingredient to make information available to every American. **Digital libraries** are electronic storehouses of materials, collections of books, and other print resources that have been converted to electronic format for easy search and retrieval. Digital libraries allow people to access their collections without geographic limitations. Six universities were funded by the Digital Library Initiative and sponsored by the National Science Foundation, Advanced Research Projects Agency (the originators of the Internet, as you learned in Session 10) and the National Aeronautics and Space Administration to research and develop digital libraries.

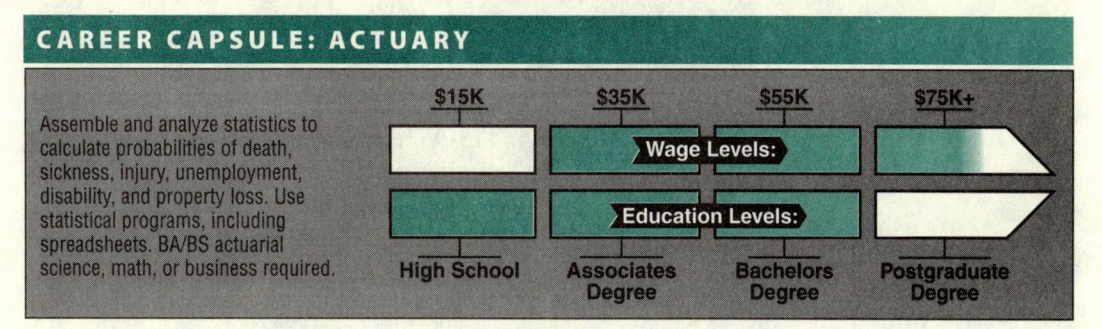

CAREER CAPSULE: ACTUARY

Assemble and analyze statistics to calculate probabilities of death, sickness, injury, unemployment, disability, and property loss. Use statistical programs, including spreadsheets. BA/BS actuarial science, math, or business required.

	$15K	$35K	$55K	$75K+
Wage Levels:		●	●	
Education Levels:	●	●		
	High School	Associates Degree	Bachelors Degree	Postgraduate Degree

---

The key challenges to creating digital libraries concern making large amounts of electronic information accessible in a usable form. This doesn't just involve posting it on the Internet, but involves developing technologies that can translate each specialty's jargon into common language so that someone unfamiliar with a particular field can still access information on it. It also means developing ways that information can be searched across collections on the World Wide Web. "Today on the Web you will find things by browsing documents. Tomorrow on the Web you will find things by searching repositories. In the new millennium beyond the Web, analysis of environment technology will let you correlate things across repositories to solve problems," say Bruce Shatz, principal investigator of the Digital Library Initiative at the University of Illinois, and Hsinchun Chen, associate professor of Management Information Systems at the University of Arizona, in their article "Building Large-Scale Digital Libraries" (*Computer*, 1996). The ultimate goal of the researchers is to develop search tools that can access information across many different electronic databases and apply artificial intelligence to combine the world's knowledge to help users answer questions and solve problems.

Digital libraries have a long way to go before they will totally replace books (and some people say they never will). However, digital access to books and print resources provides avenues previously unavailable to many people. For example, it no longer requires a trip to Washington, D.C. to visit the incredible resources of the Library of Congress. As the Library of Congress works to digitize its collections, the Library of Congress Web site, shown in Figure 14.7, brings its extraordinary riches directly to your home or business.

Figure 14.7
The Library of Congress Web site

In every service industry, computers are playing an increasingly significant role. As more people become computer literate and technology develops to make databases and other information sources even more accessible, records of every type will be primarily maintained on computer. Major advances in computer hardware like those experienced from 1930 to 1990 are not expected in the immediate future. Now the emphasis is on how the power of computers can be harnessed to move us from the Computer Age into the Information Age.

What You Have Learned

Service industries have developed many different uses for computers. In all cases, one of the primary uses is to make information more available to customers or employees. In some cases, as in the hotel and banking industries, computers provide convenience to customers, while at the same time, they make record keeping and processing easier. The entertainment industry has put computers to work in redesigning animation. The health care industry employs computerized record keeping and is introducing expert systems to help physicians make decisions about patient care. Computers in squad cars have given law enforcement a significant edge in identifying vehicles and suspects by providing access to international databases of criminal information and other records. The National Information Infrastructure has identified digital libraries as one of its primary objectives to make information available to every American. The service industries are playing a key role in the transition from the Computer Age to the Information Age.

Focus Questions

1. How did the service industry play a role in the development of computer technology?

2. List three reasons why vendors may prefer electronic bill paying by their customers?

3. What is the biggest hurdle for online banking to overcome before it becomes an accepted practice for many account holders?

4. Describe two different ways computers are being used in the entertainment business.

5. What is the difference between computerized medical records and electronic medical records?

6. How can expert systems aid physicians in prescribing medications?

7. Why is CDPD valuable to law enforcement?

Knowledge Reinforcement

A. If you went to see your physician, and they sat down at a computer and entered all of your information, how would you feel? Do you think computers make health care more personal or less personal? Support your position.

B. Recently, a computer consultant in Oregon purchased the Department of Motor Vehicles records for the entire state and posted them on the

Internet so anyone could look up a license number and find out to whom it belonged. The consultant reasoned that since the records were public information, everyone should have access to them and that it would help residents identify suspicious cars in their neighborhoods. Residents of the state were outraged and the publisher shut down the site. Do you think public records such as Department of Motor Vehicles records, criminal records, and court records should be available to everyone on the Internet? What would be the possible benefits? What are the possible abuses?

C. Do you think digital libraries will ever replace books? Why or why not?

D. Identify one service industry not discussed in this session and find out at least one way in which computers are used in that industry. Discuss how computers have helped that industry and what the possible dangers are, if any.

Further Exploration

"Consult an Expert: Your Computer" by Polly Schneider. *Healthcare Informatics,* May 1996.

Digital Library Initiative; Building Large-Scale Digital Libraries:
http://www/computer.org:80/pubs/computer/dli
http://www.dlib.org

Federal Bureau of Investigations Home Page:
http://www.fbi.gov

FedWorld: Technological Resources of the United States government:
http://www.fedworld.gov/

The Internet Public Library Reference Section:
http://www.ipl.org/ref/

The Library of Congress:
http://lcweb.loc.gov

Medical Records Institute:
http://www.medrecinst.com

University of Michigan School of Information:
http://www.si.umich.edu

SESSION FIFTEEN

Vocabulary

- agent
- DVD-ROM
- eye-tracking hardware
- fault tolerant
- natural speech input
- PC/TV
- personal area network
- plug-and-play hardware
- sensate liner
- social user interface
- ubiquitous computing
- universal service
- wearable computer
- Web TV

New Technologies, New Challenges

IN THE FIRST SESSION, WE LOOKED AT WHAT today's world would be like without computers. As we move into the twenty-first century, computers will be increasingly integrated into society and our lives. In this session, we will look at the future direction of computers and what implications this future has for each of us. At the end of this session, you will be able to

- Describe the major trends in computer development
- Discuss how computers could impact the lives of mainstream society
- Identify critical issues that will affect the future of computers
- Know how to stay informed about future technological developments

347

SECTION 15.1: PUTTING THE PERSONAL INTO PERSONAL COMPUTERS

Although personal computers have been around over two decades, the fact of the matter is that personal computers aren't really very personal. Compared to the giants of yesteryear, the PC sitting on your desktop today is an incredibly powerful machine. However, a computer system that can respond to your personal needs, learn how you like to have things done, and adjust to your particular work habits is still on the drawing board.

In the last 10 years, PCs have been sold with a lot of promises. We have been told that computers will organize our lives, streamline our work loads, provide us with endless hours of entertainment, connect us with people around the globe, balance our checkbooks, and assure ourselves and our kids of the best possible education. However, PCs do not always make life easier for the people who own them. Buying a computer is not like buying a television. A television plugs into a wall plug and a cable or antenna wire, and is operated with easily understandable push buttons. Except for programming the dreaded VCR, most of us feel very comfortable installing and using a television system. Computer systems, on the other hand, require a higher, less intuitive level of technical expertise. Even after the peripherals have been correctly plugged in, many users aren't able to successfully run programs or access previously stored files. New software packages generally include more built-in help than they did 10 years ago, but novice users still require extensive training to use them effectively.

Reliability continues to be a number one concern among competent computer users. Compatibility between myriad software applications designed for countless hardware configurations can present nightmares for users. Even **plug-and-play hardware**, hardware designed to install without complications on computers that support this feature, doesn't always live up to its name. And if hardware and software don't present enough problems, most computer users will eventually be victimized by a new generation of vandals who spread damaging computer viruses via computer disks and online services.

To be a competent computer user today, you need to be **fault tolerant:** able to adjust to the possibility that everything may not always go smoothly. You need to be willing to take precautions, such as backing up your hard drive in case of catastrophic data losses. You need to perform routine maintenance on your hardware, study how to use software applications, and stay informed about new releases and upgrades that may help you accomplish your objectives.

You may be asking yourself, "Is it worth it? Maybe I'll just wait until they get all the kinks worked out." That's certainly one approach. Just as it was not advisable for everyone to own an automobile 20 (or even 100!) years after they were invented, today's computers are not for everyone. At this point in its evolution, the computer has not proven itself to be valuable enough for everyone to be willing to put up with the accompanying frustrations. However, if the hardware and software manufacturers have their way, computers will soon become the most common household appliance. Bill Gates, President of Microsoft Corporation, has a vision of a personal computer in every household. He's committed to making the computers of tomorrow as appealing to people as today's televisions and telephones. To make this vision a reality, personal computers have to become more flexible, more personal. They will have to adjust themselves to users, rather than making users adapt to them. Very few of us know the inner workings of a telephone, but when we need it, it works. Computers have not reached yet that level of reliability, and until they do, Gates's vision will not be realized.

Making Friends with Your Software

It is not easy for users to decide which applications are best suited to their business or personal needs and be assured that they will be able to learn how to use the features they need most. Users want software that completes complex tasks, but is simple to use. Software publishers are striving to make software easy to use, more understandable, and, at the same time, more powerful. The greatest challenge facing software developers is how to incorporate the features people want and make them easily available.

The next generation of PC software will take into account the interests and work habits of the user, and actually learn how the user likes to do things. In his book *The Road Ahead*, Gates promotes the idea of building personal **agents** into software products. The primary job of the agent will be to make itself available when you need assistance. As long as you're comfortable with the tasks you are trying to accomplish, the agent will stay in the background. If you get lost or ask for help, the agent will reappear to assist you. Because the agent watches and remembers what you do, it will try to anticipate problems and help you avoid mistakes you've made before. Eventually, an agent might even be able to take over certain tasks for you, such as scanning and prioritizing electronic mail based on criteria you set up (or based on what the agent remembers from prior experience).

We're working to perfect softer software. No one should be stuck with an assistant, in this case software, that doesn't learn from experience.

—Bill Gates, The Road Ahead, *1995*

These agents may include a **social user interface**—a software interface that takes on a personality such as a cartoon character or celebrity—to interact with the user. The latest version of Microsoft Office (Microsoft Office 97) is the first attempt to introduce agents into an application designed for business use. The Office Assistant, shown in Figure 15.1, is an animated character that assists the user by anticipating needs and providing advice. It adapts and learns from the user and stops giving advice when the user has mastered a particular task. Microsoft provides nine different images and personalities that users can choose from.

Figure 15.1

Clippit, one of the Microsoft Office 97 Office Assistants

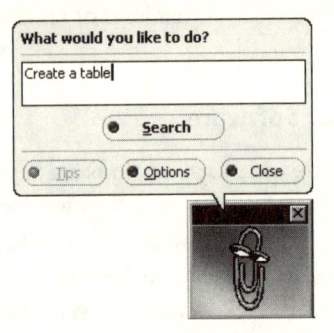

Although some people may shy away from a computer with a personality, it's expected that many people will like the Office Assistant and find it comforting when stress is high. (Misery loves company!)

Whether or not you choose to buy a personal computer for home, you'll be hard-pressed to stay away from PCs all together. It will be increasingly harder to find a job that does not require knowledge of personal computing. Only low-paying, unskilled jobs will be exempt. While you may only be required to learn one or two custom applications used by your employer, the broader your knowledge, the more marketable your skills become. Applications occasionally crash, and a knowledgeable computer user can intervene and prevent a relatively minor problem from becoming a crisis. It never hurts to be seen as a hero when things go awry.

SECTION 15.2: CONNECTING THE WORLD

In the nineteenth century, the telegraph and telephone made their respective debuts, opening up entire new frontiers in the world of personal communication. It quickly became possible to communicate with other people across town or across the world. One hundred years later, the Internet explosion is writing another new chapter in the book of human communication.

People who live in isolated villages in remote areas of the globe can access the same information as a corporate executive who occupies the corner office in a Manhattan high rise. People in war torn Bosnia-Herzegovina, for example, used the Internet to appeal for worldwide support for peace in their country. In April 1995, when the siege of Sarajevo was in its fourth year, an electronic forum was organized on the Internet to promote direct dialogue between the inhabitants of Sarajevo and the worldwide Internet community. While other media outlets were constrained or blocked, the Internet allowed people from all over the world to hear firsthand what was happening in the war zone, as shown in Figure 15.2. As the Internet continues to expand, it is becoming impossible for governments to block access to information as they were able to do in the days of the Cold War.

Figure 15.2
Sarajevo Pipeline lets Internet users around the world dialog directly with residents of Sarajevo through the ZTN.

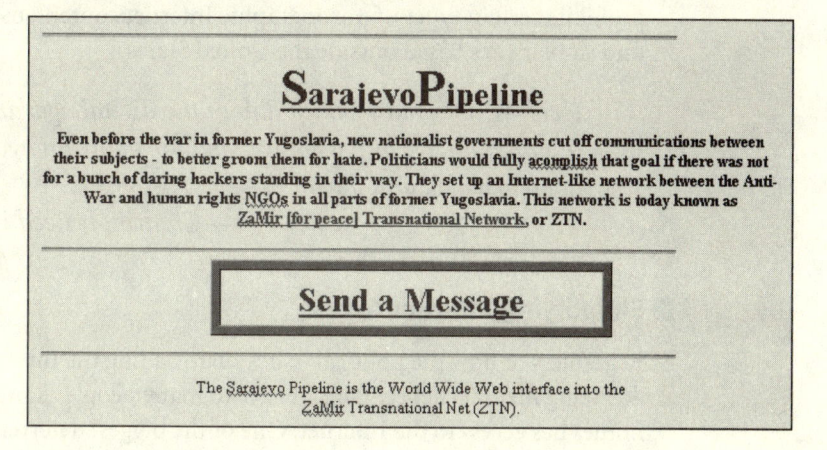

Making the Internet Safe and Available

Although the Internet offers incredible promise, it also presents new dilemmas and policy issues. In the Telecommunications Act of 1996, the U.S.

Congress gave the Federal Communications Commission a mandate to develop ways to make the Internet accessible to all people regardless of economic standing. The FCC responded with a policy called **universal service**, which calls for deep discounts for Internet access to schools, libraries, and rural health facilities. The FCC is also exploring tax breaks and other subsidies to those who cannot afford access.

> *If we allow the information superhighway to bypass the less fortunate sectors of our society, we will find that the information rich will get richer while the information poor get poorer.*
> —U.S. Vice President Al Gore

Access to information raises a host of issues related to censorship and security. Many people are convinced that children must be shielded from the obscenity and the pornography available on the Internet, and that the government should pass laws that regulate its content. Many others fear that government involvement in Internet access will result in government control of the Internet's content. Both sides of this issue must be viewed in a global context, since Internet content cannot be controlled by any single government. Information moves freely from one country to another without pausing for customs inspections. Therefore, if the United States government prohibits certain types of pornographic Internet content, users can simply find similar sites based outside the United States.

> *Here we are at last smack dab in the digital age; an age of promise; an age of possibility; and for many an age of anxiety, apprehension, and alarm.*
> —Chairman Reed Hundt, FCC

■ Simplifying Internet Access

Regardless of how the political issues surrounding the Internet are resolved, accessing the Internet remains illusive to many people. A minority of U.S. homes has access to the Internet. One of the biggest deterrents is the fear that it is too complicated to connect. A number of computer and television manufacturers are responding to these concerns with **Web TVs**, boxes that can be easily connected to televisions and telephone lines that allow non-computer users to surf the Net through the familiar television. Televisions and computers will soon be intimately interconnected with the introduction of **PC/TVs.** These new devices will have full computer capability, handle MPEG-2 video (full-screen video), and use new gas plasma active LCD technologies that result in higher resolution than is currently available on computer monitors. Through the use of high-speed cable modems, television programming will become totally controlled by the viewer. You'll be able to watch any show you want to see, at any time of day.

Some predict that, in a not too distant future, Internet access will be as available as telephones. Already, some future-oriented entrepreneurs are installing Internet access sites in restaurants, shopping malls, and airports. It won't be long before you'll be seeing connections in gas stations, waiting rooms, and your favorite sports bar.

SECTION 15.3: NEW WAYS TO INTERACT WITH COMPUTERS

In order to make use of a computer, you have to have a way to input data. The keyboard and the mouse are by far the most common ways available today to provide input to a computer. However, to use either one you are required to learn skills that have nothing to do with the purpose of a computer—not a very efficient use of time and resources. It is for this reason that computer researchers are actively working to develop more user-friendly input technologies. One of the fastest growing areas of research involves developing technology that will recognize natural forms of input such as human voices and eye movement.

"Open the Pod Bay Doors, HAL"

In the movie *2001: A Space Odyssey*, human crew members issued commands, conducted research, and asked the artificial intelligence computer questions by verbally addressing their requests to HAL, the on-board computer. One of the most sought after and illusive new technologies is a software system that allows users to use their own voices—the natural human output device—to tell a computer what they want it to do. Users could enter text in a word processor, numbers in a spreadsheet, or application commands by voice rather than mouse or keyboard.

Although forms of voice recognition technology have been around for more than 50 years, their hardware requirements have made them undesirable for general use. With advancements in processing speeds and digital storage, voice recognition is quickly becoming an obtainable goal. It is expected that dictation-quality voice recognition systems will be available by the end of 1997. However, because they will have limited vocabularies and will be expensive, these systems will be specialized for use in fields such as medicine and law. It will only be another few years, though, before high-quality voice recognition systems will be available for general use.

Natural speech input is by far the hardest technology to develop, because it requires programming software to recognize and interpret the complex language patterns of human speech and automatically adapt to the differences between users. Today's voice recognition technologies—for example, IBM's VoiceType Simply Speaking software—must be configured by each user. You need to read nearly 300 different sentences as they are displayed on screen so that the software can "learn" how you pronounce the words, as shown in Figure 15.3. However, while you are teaching the software how you speak, the software also is training you to speak in ways it understands by making you reread sentences that contain pronunciations it doesn't recognize. Some experts estimate comprehensive natural speech input that won't require hours of user programming will be available on a limited basis by 2002 (*2001* was just a little premature).

Figure 15.3
IBM's VoiceType software allows you to dictate rather than key text in a word processor.

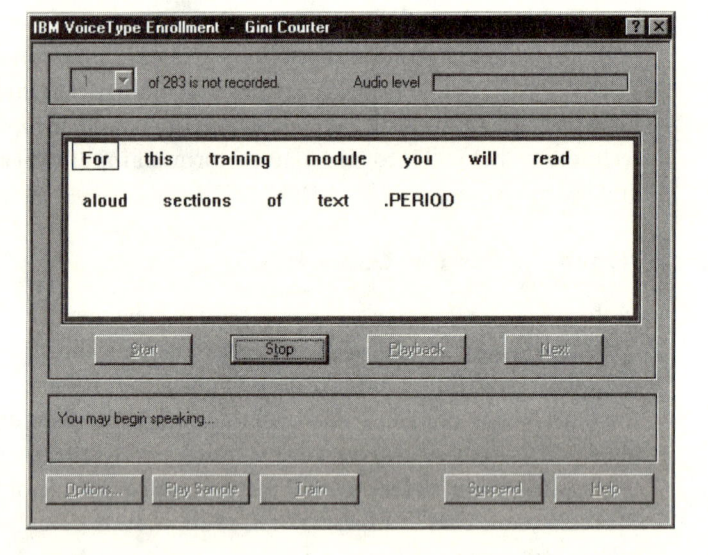

■ Look, Ma, No Hands!

Another type of input technology being developed could replace the mouse as a primary method of selecting objects on the screen. When users of **eye-tracking hardware** look at the screen and rest their eye on an object (typically, an icon or menu choice) for 250 milliseconds, the command behind the object is activated. Because users don't have to take their hands off the keyboard, their speed increases, and they no longer have to be concerned about eye-hand coordination.

Eye tracking is especially valuable to people who don't have the use of their hands or arms due to physical disabilities. Although other input devices exist for the physically disabled, none of these work for the severely disabled who may be only able to move their eyes. Eye-tracking hardware combined with voice technology offers hope that the disabled will soon be able to use graphical interfaces such as Windows.

One of the biggest constraints to implementing voice recognition, eye-tracking hardware, and other innovative input technologies is their requirement for high-capacity storage and increased amounts of memory. In the next section, you'll learn about some of the developments in the area of digital storage and memory.

SECTION 15.4: PHENOMENAL STORAGE AND MEMORY ADVANCES

There is an old adage that our need for space increases to the size of the room or home we occupy. The same appears to be true for digital storage. 5¼-inch floppies were quickly replaced by 3½-inch floppies because of their increased storage capacity and their convenience. It soon became impractical to install programs using 20 or 30 diskettes, so most applications today are sold in CD-ROM format. Many reference applications are written to fill the capacity of today's CD-ROMs, and software publishers are running out of room again. The first **DVD-ROM** players (digital video display–read only memory) are being demonstrated as this book goes to press. DVD-ROM disks hold 4.7 gigabytes of data, about seven times the capacity of CD-ROMs.

The first DVD-ROM software title, the Encyclopedia Electronica from Xiphias Publishing, contains over 80 minutes of MPEG-2 video footage, 25,000 hypertext articles, and 15,000 chronological stories. DVD-ROM disks are predicted to stimulate the development of 3-D games and provide the capability of watching full-length movies on a computer monitor. Given the rate of development for new storage devices, we can expect to see another big advance soon after the turn of the century.

Faster than a Speeding Bullet

Today's powerhouse personal computers have 64MB or maybe even 128MB of RAM. By 2002, we can expect to begin seeing 1GB dynamic random access memory chips. In late 1996, Samsung Electronics announced the development of 1GB chips capable of manipulating the equivalent of 8,000 newspaper pages. Samsung is planning to invest $272 million to develop these incredibly fast circuits. The chips will be used in PCs, video conference systems, medical systems, personal digital assistants, satellite telecommunications, 3-D graphics, high-definition television, and other multimedia products, allowing users to run applications 20–50 times larger (and, therefore, more sophisticated) than today's applications. Clearly, these chips will change the face of computers as we know them.

SECTION 15.5: MOVING COMPUTERS BEYOND THE DESKTOP

For computers to become more personal, they have to spend more time with us—not on our desktops or packed in a traveling case and stored in the trunk. As we move into the future, computers will be integrated into our world in ways that are hard to even imagine today. Researchers at IBM's Almaden Research Center are working on new technologies that could lead to **personal area networks**, networks that use the natural salinity and the low levels of electrical charges in our bodies to transmit digital information from one part of the body to another or from one person to another. IBM has already developed a prototype that allows two people to exchange business card information by shaking hands.

Even before personal area networks become practical, wearable computers will help move computers out of the office. **Wearable computers** include a wide range of products—from headsets that include tiny computer screens to intelligent long johns that can evaluate the medical condition of a wounded soldier. The Massachusetts Institute of Technology's Media Lab is one of the labs conducting extensive research on wearable computers. Wearable computers, often include a small video monitor that is worn like an eyepiece so the computer is readily available. Although still in the prototype stage, these small computers could include cameras and other types of input devices that could record sights and sounds that the user perceives, storing the information for later retrieval. It is envisioned that devices like these will augment memory, just like glasses and hearing aids augment vision and sight.

The U.S. military is interested in another type of wearable technology called **sensate liners**. Sensate liners are constructed of conductive polymers woven into the clothing worn by combat soldiers. The liners would include biological sensors that could tell medical personnel the condition of the soldier, including their blood pressure, pulse, respiratory rate, temperature, and a host of other medical indicators. They would also include physical sensors that could detect penetration of a bullet or other projectile, the amount of bleeding and blood loss, and how much the person is moving. This information could help determine who should be treated first and provide information to medics before they actually arrive on the scene.

The Army can already detect whether a soldier might be going into hypothermia through the use of a computer the size of pill that is swallowed to track core body temperatures. Because a lot of the research conducted for the military serves as a catalyst to the development of products for civilians, we can anticipate that these advances will result in making the computer more personal for all of us—or *in* all of us.

■ Receding into the Shadows

The history of computers has been characterized by several advances that significantly changed our relationship with computers. In the first "wave" of computing, many people shared the use of one mainframe computer. Then with the introduction of the personal computer, a one-to-one relationship was born. No longer dependent on other people's machines, in the second wave of computing we assumed the freedom and the headaches that come with managing our own personal piece of high technology. Mark Weiser of Xerox PARC has begun work on what he calls the third wave—**ubiquitous computing**. Ubiquitous computing, or ubicomp, is unobtrusive computing, where technology fades into the background so that the focus moves to function rather than hardware or the user interface.

> *Our computers should be like our childhood: an invisible foundation that is quickly forgotten but always with us, and effortlessly used throughout our lives.*
> —Mark Weiser of Xerox PARC

At this point in our history, when we work with a personal computer, it becomes the center of attention; to accomplish our task, we must adapt ourselves and our work to the computer's way of doing things. In Mark Weiser's world, we will be able to stay focused on our work, using the computer tool much like we use a pen and a pad of paper. Weiser objects to the development of computerized assistants and other forms of social interfaces, because they increase the emphasis on the computer, drawing our attention away from the task we're using the computer to accomplish. Weiser believes computers should be transparent aids by being reliable, predictable, ever-present, and hidden in the background. As they take the place of message pads, notebooks, dry-erase board, books, and innumerable other objects in our normal work and personal environments, computers should become smaller, cheaper, and significantly more plentiful. Proponents of ubiquitous computing foresee homes and offices filled with hundred of wireless computing devices—all doing different things—so easy to use we will not even think about them.

To imagine the workplace of ubiquitous computing, envision every slip of paper, every notepad, every desktop enhanced with computing devices. Circling an interesting item in the morning paper, for example, will automatically transfer the item to your office where you can store it in an electronic file for later reference. Rather than parking a computer on your desk, the desk itself will be a computer—giving you plenty of space to work, places to keep messages, and the ability to have a number of documents open in plain sight. When you need to communicate with someone, you will merely mention the person's name and the computer will browse the person's various communication tools, locate them, and connect you. A report you want to discuss will appear on your colleague's desktop so you can work on it together. When you finish, you'll send the report and a video file of your meeting along to your boss, who'll review the document while watching the video on the video-capable front wall of their office. When you turn out your office lights and lock the door, your desk will signal your car that it's time to go home. The car will leave the automated parking lot and pick you up at the door.

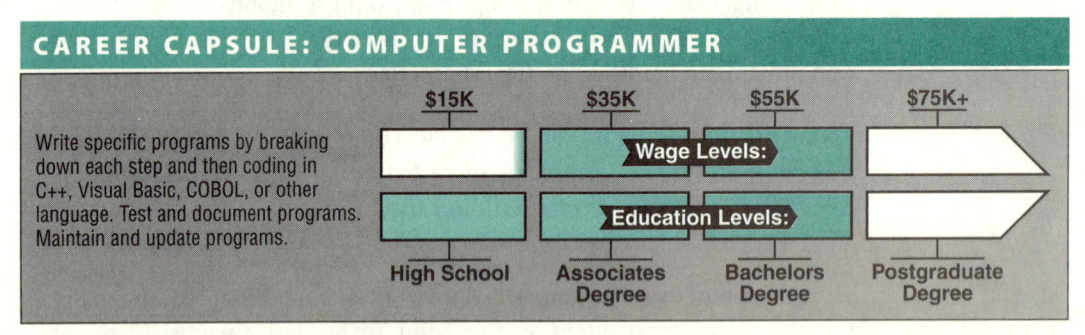

CAREER CAPSULE: COMPUTER PROGRAMMER

Write specific programs by breaking down each step and then coding in C++, Visual Basic, COBOL, or other language. Test and document programs. Maintain and update programs.

Wage Levels: $15K | $35K | $55K | $75K+

Education Levels: High School | Associates Degree | Bachelors Degree | Postgraduate Degree

Of course, ubiquitous computing is not confined to work environments. A world of ubiquitous computing will be a world where technology is threaded through our lives until we are unable to distinguish it from the most mundane parts of our existence. Coffee cups that keep our coffee warm, clothing that communicates its care instructions directly to the washer and dryer, and televisions and sound systems that automatically mute when you answer the phone are examples of ubicomp.

One Thing's For Sure

We began this session with a vision of the future where computers will become more powerful, and at the same time, more personable. In this vision, we will have intelligent, computerized assistants who will help us to complete our work. At the end of this session, we presented a somewhat different view of the future where computers fade into the woodwork and become powerful by their invisibility, permeating our lives so completely that we will take little notice of their presence. During our lifetimes, reality will fall somewhere in the middle while computer theorists and manufacturers struggle between "Bigger is Better" and "Small (and ubiquitous) is Beautiful." Whether computers remain a focal point or fade into a more passive usefulness, learning about computers and how to make the most of new technologies will remain an important task for those who hope to prosper in the next millennium.

What You Have Learned

The next phase of hardware and software development, currently underway, is to simplify computers and make software easier to learn and understand. New development in input devices such as voice input will play a significant role in making computers accessible to more people. Increased memory and increased storage capabilities will bring high-resolution, full-screen video to the computer and bring the computer, the Internet, and the television closer together. Computers will also begin to become more integrated into our lives, working behind the screens rather than taking center stage as they do now.

Focus Questions

1. Why is it important to be fault tolerant when working with today's computers?
2. How will a personal agent help the average computer user?
3. Name two hardware advances that will allow for the integration of the television and the personal computer.
4. What is the significance of DVD-ROM to the software industry?
5. Describe the three waves of computing to date.

Knowledge Reinforcement

A. Do you think computers should have social user interfaces? Why or why not?

B. How do you feel about the idea of personal area networks? Do you think there are valid applications for computers that use our body processes to operate?

C. Read Chapter 10 of Bill Gates's book, *The Road Ahead*, called "Plugged In at Home." Do you think Bill Gates's and Mark Weiser's views of the future are radically different? What features of the new Gates house would you like to have? Which ones don't you like? Explain your reasons.

D. Some people compare ubiquitous computing to Big Brother—computers everywhere, watching and recording everything that happens. Do you think computers should be behind the scenes or would you rather they stay in the forefront? If possible, read Mark Weiser's essay "Open House" (see reference below) before answering the question.

E. List at least three things you intend to do to stay abreast of new technological developments in the field of computers.

Further Exploration

21st Century Eloquence (information about voice technology):
http://www.voicerecognition.com/

Federal Communications Commission (information on universal access to the Internet):
http://www.fcc.gov

IDRG Eye Tracking Project:
http://www.cms.dmu.ac.uk/Research/IDRG/ET/

Mark Weiser and Ubiquitous Computing:
http://www.ubiq.com/weiser/

Open House by Mark Weiser (a fascinating essay about ubiquitous computing):
http://www.itp.tsoa.nyu.edu/~review/current/focus2/open00.html

The Road Ahead. Bill Gates. Penguin Books, 1995, 0-670-77289-5.

Sarajevo Pipeline (direct access to news and information about the war in Bosnia):
http://MediaFilter.org/mff/spipe.html

Sarajevo Online (promotes direct dialogue between inhabitants of Sarajevo and the Internet community):
http://www.worldmedia.fr/sarajevo/index.html

Things That Think Research (information about research underway at the MIT Media Laboratory):
http://ttt.www.media.mit.edu/tttpic/researchpic.html

"What Pupils Teach Computers" by Allan Joch. *Byte*, July 1996, pp 99–100. A look at eye-tracking hardware.

Xerox Palo Alto Research Center (PARC) Projects (a look at research underway at PARC):
http://www.parc.xerox.com/Projects.html

APPENDIX

Manufacturers and Products

APPENDIX ■ MANUFACTURERS AND PRODUCTS

Company	Product
21st Century Entertainment, Inc.	Pinball Arcade
Adobe Systems Incorporated	PageMaker™ for Macintosh
Alexei Pazhitnov (original design); copyright Microsoft Corp.	Tetris
America Online, Inc.	America Online™
Apple Computer Corporation	Macintosh Finder Operating System Apple IIE Message Pad 130 with Newton® 2.0
Art Data Interactive	Chess Wars—a medieval fantasy
Atomic Games and Microsoft Corporation	Close Combat
Autodesk	AutoCAD™
Banner Blue Software	Family Tree Maker
Borland Corporation	Paradox
Broderbund® Software, Inc.	Myst® New Print Shop Planix Home Architect 3D
Bullfrog Software	Theme Hospital
Cognos® Corporation	Impromptu
Compuserve Corporation	Compuserve™
Corel®	Print House™ WordPerfect® Office Suite
Cray Research, Inc.	Cray Supercomputer
Cybermedia, Inc.	First Aid 95
Cyrix Corporation	Cyrix 686 PC
Delrina Corporation	Echo Lake™
Digital Directory Assistance, Inc.	Phone Disc Select Phone
Digital Equipment Corporation	Alta Vista™
Disney Interactive	Toy Story Animated Storybook

Company	Product	(*continued*)
Epic MegaGames	Tyrian	
GoldMine Software Corporation	GoldMine	
Gyration®	GyroPoint®	
Hasbro. Inc.	Scrabble® Monopoly®	
Hewlett® Packard Company	HP 5000 LaserJet 5 DeskJet 660C	
IBM®	IBM Mainframe and Minicomputer PC-DOS Voice Type™ Simply Speaking	
Intel® Corporation	Pentium® Microprocessor	
Interplay Productions	Descent II	
Intuit® Corporation	Quickbooks® Quicken® Turbo Tax®	
Iomega® Corporation	Zip™ Drive	
Janna Systems Inc.	Janna Contact™	
Knopf New Media	National Audobon Society Interactive CD-ROM Guide to North American Birds	
Linguistic Technology Corporation	English Wizard™	
Logitech	Trackman™	
Lotus Development Corporation	Lotus Smart Suite™ Lotus Notes™	
LucasArts Entertainment Company	Afterlife™ Pipe Dream™	
Maxis	Sim City 2000 and other Sim products	
McAfee Associates, Inc	McAfee Virus Scan	

■ MANUFACTURERS AND PRODUCTS   365

Company	Product (continued)
MECC	The Oregon Trail and The Amazon Trail
Micrografx®	Hallmark's Card Studio
MicroProse	Civilization II
Microsoft® Corporation	Fury3 Microsoft® Clip Art Galley Microsoft® Internet Explorer Microsoft® Money Microsoft® Office Microsoft® PowerPoint™ Microsoft® Publisher Microsoft® Works Microsoft Encarta® 96 Encyclopedia Microsoft Flight Simulator Microsoft Office for Windows® 95 Minesweeper MS-DOS SideWinder™ 3D Pro Windows® 3.1 and Windows® 95
Multicom Publishing, Inc.	Better Homes and Gardens® Healthy Cooking CD Cookbook
Netscape Communications Corporation	Netscape Navigator
Nico Mak Computing, Inc.	Win Zip®
Nolo Publications	Living Trust Maker WillMaker
PC-cillin	TouchStone Software Corporation
PKWare, Inc.	PKZIP
Prodigy Services Corporation	Prodigy™
Quark, Inc.	Quark Xpress
Quarterdeck Coporation, Inc.	CleanSweep®
Rand McNally & Company	Rand McNally Quick Reference Atlas

■ MANUFACTURERS AND PRODUCTS   367

Company	Product *(continued)*
	Rand McNally StreetFinder™ 1996 Edition Rand McNally TripMaker™ 1996
SAP Aktiengesellschaft Systeme	SAP R/3®
Softkey® Multimedia, Inc.	American Heritage® Talking Dictionary for Windows 95
Solomon™ Software	Solomon™
Symantec™	Norton Anti-Virus Norton Commander ACT!™
TalonSoft™	Battleground: Shiloh, Battleground: Waterloo, Battleground: Gettysburg
Texas Microsystems, Inc.	Texas Micro Hardbody Handheld PC
The Software Toolworks, Inc.	Mavis Beacon Teaches Typing® New Grolier Multimedia Encyclopedia Release 6
ThunderBYTE Inc.	ThunderBYTE Anti-Virus
Timex®	Data Link™ Watch
Vertisoft Systems, Inc.	Remove-It®
Virgin Games, Ltd.	Dune™
Visio Corporation	Visio®

We wish to extend a special thanks to the following companies:

- Federal Express—Memphis, Tennessee
- Henry Ford Health System—Detroit, Michigan
- IntegrationWare—Chicago, Illinois
- Karman Ainsworth School District—Flint, Michigan
- Twilight Technologies—Grand Blanc, Michigan
- Valassis Communications, Inc—Livonia, Michigan

Glossary

2-D (matrix) bar code Denser bar code that can hold large amounts of information.

4GL A fourth-generation language that allows users to enter natural-language commands to work with a database.

abacus The first computing device, computations were made on it by sliding stones on a board or beads on a series of wire racks.

access time The average length of time that passes between the moment a computer requests information from a storage device and the moment the computer finds and starts to read the information.

add-ons Additional software designed to enhance a primary software product. Also called *add-ins*.

agents Program help features that make themselves available when you need assistance.

Howard Aiken Inventor of the electronic Mark I (1944), a computer used to calculate gunnery tables.

Analytical Engine Babbage's general-purpose computing machine designed to multiply and divide large numbers with great accuracy (it was never built). Numbers would be read from punched cards, and results placed on another set of cards for reuse in later calculations (nineteenth century).

application Software that enables users to complete specific tasks.

architecture The design of a computer's system board, including the connections for other components.

arithmetic logic unit (ALU) Part of the CPU that processes mathematical and logical operations.

ARPANET Advanced Research Projects Agency–funded project to connect university computer scientists and engineers together via their computers and telephone lines. Predecessor of the Internet.

ASCII American Standard Code for Information Interchange. ASCII uses 7 or 8 bits to represent a character; in 7-bit ASCII, the other bit is used for error checking.

assembly language Second-generation language that is converted to machine language with an assembler.

asynchronous A communications method that uses start bits and stop bits to signal the beginning and end of transmitted packets. Dial-up connections are asynchronous.

Atanasoff-Berry Computer (ABC) The first electronic computer, invented by John Atanasoff and Clifford Berry (1942).

John Atanasoff Coinventor of the ABC computer in 1942.

Charles Babbage Eighteenth-century inventor of the first steam-driven computational devices, the Difference Engine and the Analytical Engine.

backups Archival copies of data that can be restored if original data is lost.

bar code (symbol) A group of bars and spaces that represents a group of letters and/or numbers.

batch systems Systems where transactions are temporarily stored, then processed in batches.

baud A measurement of signal speed related to bits per second. Baud is a measurement of data transmission speed.

Tim Berners-Lee Swiss software engineer who invented the World Wide Web (1992).

binary digit (bit) The smallest unit of data that can be manipulated by a computer. A bit can have a value of 0 or 1.

BIOS Basic Input Output System. The interface between computer hardware and the operating system.

George Boole Nineteenth-century inventor of Boolean algebra, an algebraic system using only 0s and 1s.

browser A program designed to display and move between Web pages—for example, Netscape Navigator and Microsoft Internet Explorer.

bus Wiring pathways in the system board to carry data and instructions, which travel as low-voltage electricity, between the CPU and components.

Vannevar Bush Inventor of the Differential Analyzer, the first machine that could solve differential equations (1930).

bus LAN A network topology where computers are connected to a common communications line that originates at the file server.

business software Programs designed for business use—for example, business systems software and productivity software.

business systems software Software designed to support the basic functions of a business, including financial functions, manufacturing functions, and client tracking functions.

byte An 8-bit unit used to represent one character.

cache A designated area of memory that holds frequently used instructions and data so they can be quickly recalled by the processor.

capacity The amount of data, measured in bytes, that can be held in memory or on a storage device.

cathode ray tube (CRT) Monitor technology that uses a vacuum tube that forms the screen display at one end and has a socket at the other end. The monitor image is produced by electron beams that are generated in the neck of the CRT and shot against colored phosphors on the face of the CRT.

cell The basic unit of a worksheet or table. A cell is the intersection of a row and a column.

cell address In a spreadsheet, the column letter and row number that describe a cell's location.

cellular digital packet data (CDPD) A digital wireless transmission method, using Internet Protocol (IP), which enables users to transmit packets of data over the same cellular voice frequencies used for cellular voice transmissions. CDPD transmissions are encrypted, and because they hop between channels to find open frequencies, CDPD is highly secure.

central processing unit (CPU) A processor that includes two major parts: the arithmetic logic unit (ALU) with its connected registers, and a control unit that contains a clock, a program counter, an address decoder, and an instruction decoder.

client A computer other than the server in a client-server network.

client-server database An application that utilizes the processing power of local workstations and one or more central servers.

clinical workstations Wireless handheld computers

about the size and weight of a 1-inch medical record file folder carried by physicians.

clip art Graphics and other objects that can be imported into applications and then positioned, resized, and edited.

coax (thinwire) A copper wire, covered with a plastic insulator and wrapped with a metal mesh shield, used for cable television and computer networks.

COBOL The Common Business-Oriented Language, COBOL was the first high-level computer language that wasn't specific to a particular machine.

code A computer program or a section of a program.

Colossus The first large electronic valve programmable logic calculator, Colossus was designed specifically for cryptoanalysis in the Second World War.

command-line interface A text-based interface where users enter one-line commands to give instructions to the computer.

commercial online information services CompuServe, America Online, and other fee-based services that provide access to various databases, e-mail, and the Internet.

communication systems Business systems that connect computers, allowing employees to work collaboratively and access shared information easily.

communications software Software that allows computers to connect using telephone lines.

compiler A program that generates an object code version of a program that is then run through yet another program, called a *linker,* to create a final machine language version.

compression Removing repetitive and unnecessary bytes before files are stored or transmitted, resulting in smaller, more compact files.

computer A simple electronic device that takes data, processes the data according to a series of instructions called a program, and produces information.

computer literate Somewhat knowledgeable about computers, including their capabilities, functions, and components.

computer system A combination of computer hardware and software designed to work together.

computer-aided design (CAD) Using specialized design or drafting software to create new product wireframes and specifications.

computer-aided instruction (CAI) Tutorial software that helps users learn a skill or group of skills.

computer-aided manufacturing (CAM) Adding intelligent technology (processors and memory) to machine tools so that a machine can be programmed to perform new tasks.

computer-integrated manufacturing (CIM) Integrated manufacturing that allows one machine to pass data and program code directly to another without returning the data to a centralized database.

computerized medical record A computerized version of a paper medical record, used for reference.

conceptual computer A construct that allows generic discussion of computers and their functions. The five parts of the modern conceptual computer are input, processor, output, memory, and storage.

connect time The length of time a user's computer is connected to a host or online service.

connectivity All the methods used to build connections between computers, thereby connecting users.

control unit Part of the CPU that manages the flow of data to the registers and ALU.

conversion utility A program that allows users to open a document created by another application and have it automatically converted to the format used by the active application.

coprocessor A dedicated processor like a DMA processor or math coprocessor that takes over specific tasks from the CPU, increasing overall system performance.

cuneiform The earliest writing, dating from 3500 B.C.E.

data mining Software that examines data using an engine to find relationships.

GLOSSARY

data source A database, spreadsheet, or table that contains data that can be used by another application.

data warehouse A subject-oriented, central storehouse of electronic data that can be accessed by managers and other decision-makers within a company for data analysis and extraction.

database A collection of information organized into categories for fast and easy retrieval.

debit cards Cards similar to credit cards that charge cash purchases directly to your bank account.

decision support One of the primary functions of a management information system.

dedicated lines (leased lines) Permanently connected phone lines between two locations.

delimited text A file type created in any application that uses commas or other characters to separate fields and records.

desktop computer A microcomputer that fits on a desktop.

desktop publishing Using page-layout software to produce printed materials.

detail report Database output that includes record level data.

development tools Programming languages and add-in software products used by programmers to write software.

device driver Programs that provide specific information to the operating system computer about a particular piece of hardware.

dial-up connection A connection that uses telephone lines and a modem.

Difference Engine The first steam-driven calculating machine, Babbage's Difference Engine was designed to provide printed output (nineteenth century). Work on the Difference Engine was never completed.

Differential Analyzer The first machine that could solve complex, multivariable differential equations (1930).

digital libraries Electronic storehouses of materials, collections of books, and other print resources that have been converted to electronic format for easy search and retrieval.

digital photographs Digitized versions of photographs that can be used in computer documents.

direct (random) access An access method where data can be stored in and retrieved from any specific location on a device such as a CD-ROM or floppy disk.

distributed system A system where two or more computers are connected so that processing for system tasks can happen in multiple locations.

DMA channel A system board channel that transmits data from the disk drives to memory without passing through the CPU, speeding up both the CPU and data retrieval to memory.

domain A two- or three-letter designation that identifies the type of institution in a URL—for example, *gov* for government and *com* for commercial.

domain address The URL address of a host computer.

DOS Microsoft's microcomputer operating system with a

command line user interface. Also called PC-DOS or MS-DOS.

dot-matrix printers Printers that form an image by using columns of small pins in 9-, 18-, or 24-pin configurations that strike a ribbon to form a pattern of small dots on a page.

download The process of electronically transferring a file to your computer.

DRAM Dynamic RAM, the type of RAM used in most computers. Information is stored electrically on DRAM chips, which need a steady flow of electricity to remain active.

drilling-down A program feature that allows a user to select part of a summary display (like a state on a map) and get more detailed information.

duplex (full duplex) A simultaneous two-way communication channel—for example, a telephone connection.

DVD-ROM Digital video display–read only memory disks hold 4.7 gigabytes of data, about seven times the capacity of CD-ROMs.

dynamic data exchange (DDE) A communication protocol that allows applications to exchange data and commands supported by many operating systems.

EBCDIC Extended Binary-Coded Decimal Interchange Code invented by IBM in which 8-bit combinations of numbers each represent a specific digit, letter, or symbol.

John Presper Eckert Coinventor of the ENIAC computer (1946) and UNIVAC, the first commercial computer.

editing Inserting, deleting, copying, or moving text or objects

EDSAC Electronic Delay Storage Automatic Calculator, the first electronic computer that used stored programs (1949).

EDVAC Electronic Discrete Variable Computer, the first computer designed to use von Neumann's stored program techniques.

electronic bulletin boards An electronic information or message posting site equipped with a PC and modem.

electronic data interchange (EDI) Connectivity solutions that allow organizations to communicate directly with customers and suppliers.

electronic medical record A complete replacement of a paper medical record, EMRs are created using computers and contain all required patient information.

electronic presentation software Software used to create overheads, 35 mm slides, and on-screen presentations—for example, Microsoft PowerPoint or Lotus Freelance Graphics.

electronic signatures A password-protected code or image assigned to an individual user that can legally replace the physical signature on a document.

e-mail A service that allows users to send electronic messages to other users.

ENIAC The first general-purpose computer, ENIAC included over 18,000 vacuum tubes and weighed 30 tons (1946).

enterprise network A WAN that connects all the users in an organization.

entertainment software Games and game-like programs.

environment A user interface run in addition to an operating system—for example, Windows 3.1.

exception report Database output that identifies records that do not follow the expected process.

executable program file Machine language code that can be run by the computer.

expansion slots Sockets used to directly connect other kinds of cards and modules to the system board.

expert systems Software programs that help determine a correct solution to a problem (or make a reasonable prediction) based on the user's answers to a series of questions.

external A peripheral device that is installed outside the computer case.

extremely low frequency (ELF) radiation Low levels of radiation produced by televisions and CRT monitors.

eye-tracking hardware Input device that tracks the human eye and activates the command behind any object the user's eyes rest on for 250 milliseconds.

facsimile (fax) The transmission of images over telephone lines by converting text, characters, and graphics into a digitized pattern of small dots.

FAQ An introduction to a group or Web site listing answers to frequently asked questions.

fault tolerant Able to adjust to the possibility that something may go wrong.

fax back services Sending a fax on request, often used for technical assistance hotlines.

fiber-optic cable Bundles of optical fibers surrounded with a protective plastic shell; used for network communications.

field A category of data in a database.

field code In a word processing document, a variable code that is replaced with information from the system, an application, or a data source.

file extension Three letters following a filename that identify a file's type—for example, EXE for executable program code or BMP for a Windows Bitmap Graphic.

File Transfer Protocol (FTP) System that lets users move files from one computer to another.

filters Criteria used in a database to display specific records.

firewall Security software that prevents unauthorized users from gaining access to intranets through an organization's public Web pages.

floppy diskette A magnetically coated plastic disk used as a removable storage media. Data is stored on and retrieved from the diskette by the drive's magnetic read/write heads.

formatting Changing the appearance of part or all of a document.

formula An equation used in a spreadsheet or table.

gas plasma Single-color laptop display consisting of sheets of glass separated by a gas called plasma that fluoresces when electrically charged.

Bill Gates President and founder of Microsoft Corporation, the world's largest software company, and author of *The Road Ahead*.

generations of computers The four distinct stages of commercial computer development, beginning with UNIVAC.

gigabyte (GB) 2^{30} or 1,073,741,824 bytes.

Gopher A search tool that allows users to search through computers on the Internet through the use of a menu.

graphical user interface (GUI) Display format that allows users to use a mouse or other pointing device to point and click on objects to launch programs, open files, and issue commands.

groupware (workgroup software) A document-based client-server database application that operates like a combination of a database and e-mail and is designed to allow many users to interact with the same group of documents—for example, Lotus Notes.

half duplex A two-way, non-simultaneous communication channel—for example, walkie-talkies.

handheld computer Portable computer with functionality limited to specific tasks.

hard disk Large, internal, nonremovable read/write storage device.

hardware The physical parts of a computer.

high-level language A third-generation programming language like FORTRAN or COBOL.

Hollerith card A punched card used to enter and store computer data (nineteenth century). Modified Hollerith cards are still used with some computers.

Herman Hollerith Inventor of the first electromechanical computer, which was used to tabulate the U.S. Census of 1890.

home page The first or primary page of a Web site.

Grace Hopper U.S. Navy Admiral, the inventor of the first compiler and a coinventor of COBOL (1950s).

host The central computer in a network.

hypertext A method of presenting information on-screen that allows the user to move from topic to topic in a non-linear way, by clicking on links that connect documents. Hypertext is widely used on the World Wide Web.

Hypertext Markup Language (HTML) Language that supports hypertext links. HTML is used to create Web pages.

Hypertext Transfer Protocol (HTTP) The protocol used by servers set up to handle Web documents.

icon In a GUI, a small picture that represents a program or instruction.

impact printers Printers that make an image by striking or pressing a key or stylus against a ribbon or paper—for example, dot matrix printers and plotters.

Information Engineering A four-step software design methodology that begins with strategic planning.

information systems The combinations of software, hardware, and skills that support the mission and objectives of the business.

Information Technology (IT) planning A process to help businesses decide how computer systems can help them achieve their company's objectives.

ink-jet printers Printers that create an image by spraying ink on paper.

input Data that is entered into a computer (noun). To enter data into a computer (verb).

install Adding software to a computer system, including copying software files to the computer's hard drive. Also, adding hardware to a computer, including installing drivers.

integrated Products that share a common interface and are designed to work together.

integrated circuit A semiconductor module that contains many transistors or components.

Integrated Services Digital Network (ISDN) A standard designed for high-speed transmission of digital data that allows one line to carry up to three separate signals.

Intel Currently the world's foremost chip manufacturer, Intel invented the microprocessor.

internal A peripheral device that is placed inside the computer case.

Internet The world's largest computer network.

Internet service provider (ISP) A fee-based company that provides users with dial-up access to the Internet.

interpreter A program that translates programming language into machine language line by line as the program is entered, and each time it is executed.

intranet A World Wide Web site that is only accessible to an organization's employees.

inventory control systems Systems that help managers make decisions about the type and number of items in inventory.

inventory tracking systems Database systems used to trace and assign a value to inventory items.

IRC A worldwide chat system, Internet Relay Chat allows users to type messages and receive immediate live responses from other users.

Jacquard's loom Nineteenth-century pattern weaving machine. Jacquard's loom was the first machine to use a stored program or pattern.

kernel The heart of the operating system, the kernel handles memory and file operations.

keyboard An input device that allows users to enter text by pressing alphabetic and numeric keys.

kilobyte (KB) Roughly a thousand bytes: 2^{10}, or 1,024 bytes.

Augusta Ada King, Countess of Lovelace The first computer programmer, King translated a series of lecture notes on Babbage's work, and developed programs for the Analytical Engine (nineteenth century).

knowledge applications A range of applications, from tutorials on computer use to dictionaries and encyclopedias on CD-ROM or disk.

laptop computer Portable computer weighing 8–15 pounds that has all the components of a desktop computer.

laser printers Printers that produce an image by directing a laser beam onto a round drum, charging a pattern of particles on the drum. As the drum rotates, it picks up an electrically charged powder called toner which adheres to the paper and creates an image.

links In a hypertext system, the connections between areas of text within or between documents.

liquid crystal display (LCD) The active matrix or dual-scan matrix display commonly used in laptop computers.

listservs Internet mailing lists. Sending e-mail to the listserv sends it to all of the listservs subscribers.

local area network (LAN) A small to midsized computer network, generally limited to a small geographic area.

login The two pieces of information required for network access: a user ID and a password.

machine language A computer language that uses only 0s and 1s.

magnetic storage Storage methods, like floppy disks and hard drives, that use media coated with an oxide-based material that can hold a magnetic charge.

mail merge A word processing feature that combines a document with field variables and database records to create a separate document for each database record.

mailing lists Lists of users who express interest in receiving e-mail about a particular topic area.

mainframe A large, multiple-user computer.

management information system System that provides reports based largely on data from a company's transaction processing system.

John Mauchley Coinventor of the ENIAC computer (1946) and UNIVAC, the first commercial computer.

media Disks, tapes, CDs, and other magnetic or optical units used in storage devices.

megabyte (MB) 1,048,576 (2^{20}) bytes. Modern microcomputers have between 4 and 64 megabytes of memory.

megahertz (MHz) Millions of cycles per second. Megahertz is the measurement used for CPU clock speed.

memory The working surface of the computer, directly accessible to the computer's processor. RAM chips are used for microcomputer memory.

menu A list of mutually exclusive choices presented for user selection.

microcomputer Small, personal computers with one or more microprocessors.

microminiaturized circuit Integrated circuits with hundreds of components (LSI) to millions of components (ULSI) on a single chip.

microprocessor A single, small CPU chip that contains all the critical functions required in a microcomputer processor.

Microsoft Windows Graphical user interface designed for IBM-compatible personal computers.

middleware Software that bridges a gap between existing applications.

MIDI Musical Instrument Design Interface, a standardized interface that allows computers and MIDI-compatible musical instruments to communicate.

millisecond One thousandth of a second.

minicomputer A midsize, multiuser computer used in business applications.

mobile data terminal (MDT) software Allows private messaging between vehicles so that police can discreetly communicate with other officers on patrol or access the National Law Enforcement Telecommunications System.

mobile imaging units Units that include a miniaturized fingerprint scanner and camera to allow police to transmit fingerprints, signatures, and other images for matching with existing data.

modem A combination modulator/demodulator that allows computers to communicate across telephone lines.

monochrome Monitors that display a single color on a lighter or darker color background.

mouse A small input device used to move an on-screen pointer in graphical user interfaces.

multimedia A computer with full-color video and audio capabilities. Also, a document that uses video and audio.

multiuser A computer or system able to support simultaneous access by multiple users.

nanosecond One millionth of a millisecond or one billionth of a second.

Napier's bones Invented by John Napier (seventeenth century), the "bones" were strips of wood, bone, or ivory with numbers painted or etched on them that could be arranged to multiply two large numbers.

National Information Infrastructure (NII) The United States government's initiative to build the "information superhighway."

natural language English, Dutch, Greek, or other spoken and written human language.

natural speech input Programming software to recognize and interpret the complex language patterns of human speech and automatically adapt to the differences between users.

network Computers and peripheral devices that are connected by cable or wireless communications media and able to communicate with each other.

network account Network access rights for an individual established by the network administrator.

network administrator A designated individual who is responsible for maintaining a network, including establishing new accounts and granting user rights.

network communication protocol Specifications that describe the contents of transmitted packets—for example, TCP/IP.

network standard Standard that specifies how a transmitted signal travels on the network—for example, Ethernet.

node Any computer (client or server) in a network.

notebook computer Portable computer weighing 4–8 pounds that includes all the components of a desktop computer.

object code Program code that has been compiled but has not been converted to executable code.

object linking and embedding (OLE) A protocol that allows one application to exchange data with other Windows applications.

office automation systems Systems that use a variety of technologies to streamline routine tasks involved in the processing and managing of work in an office.

office suite A collection of applications that includes a word processor, a spreadsheet, and other applications.

online bill paying A banking service that allows you to connect via modem to a banking institution and pay bills with electronic transfers.

online help Help files included with a program that can be accessed on-screen.

open database connectivity (ODBC) A protocol that supports drivers used to connect to databases created with a variety of database management systems.

operating systems Programs that control the basic functions of a computer, including moving instructions and data in and out of memory, printing, and reading information from a disk.

optical character recognition (OCR) Software technology that allows scanned text to be stored or manipulated as text rather than as a digitized graphic.

optical storage Storage devices, like CD-ROMs, that use a laser to read or write data.

output Information from a computer.

packet Part of a communication that contains your computer's network address, the address of the computer or device you're sending the file to, and one section of the file being transmitted.

parity checking A simple method for transmission error-checking, parity can be odd, even, or none.

Blaise Pascal Seventeenth-century inventor of the Pascaline.

Pascaline Machine that could add and subtract, patented by Blaise Pascal in 1649.

password A code that a user must enter to gain access to network resources.

PC/TV Devices with full computer capability, handling MPEG-2 video (full-screen video).

PCMCIA card A plug-in card for laptop computers based on standards developed by the PC Memory Card International Association.

peer-to-peer network A local area network that does not include a server.

pen computer A small portable PC designed to accept input from a special pen device.

peripherals All computer hardware except processors: input, output, memory, and storage devices.

personal area networks Networks that use the natural salinity and the low levels of electrical charges in our bodies to transmit digital information from one part of the body to another or from one person to another.

personal computers Microcomputers designed to be used by one person at a time.

personal digital assistant (PDA) Handheld computer with software designed to replace schedulers and address books.

personal financial management software Home software products used to track income and expenses, pay bills, and assist with other common financial tasks.

personal information manager (PIM) Software designed to replace traditional personal information tools like planners and address books.

pixels Individual spots on a display screen that can display a particular color.

platform The combination of a computer's processor and operating system—for example, a Pentium PC running Windows 97.

plug-and-play hardware Components designed to meet the plug-and-play standard and which can be configured by plug-and-play-capable operating systems.

point of sale (POS) terminal A workstation that includes an optical input device for capturing sales transactions.

ports Connections for internal or external devices on the motherboard or expansion cards.

private branch exchange (PBX) An internal telephone system, including hardware and cabling.

productivity software Software that allows you to be more productive and work more efficiently.

program A series of computer instructions written in a programming language.

programming language Software used to write computer programs, which are then translated into machine language the computer can implement.

prompt A text string that lets the user know the operating system is ready to receive commands.

proprietary software Software designed especially for and owned by an organization.

prototype "First draft" of a finished product, suitable for user testing.

query A construct used to retrieve specific information from a database.

random-access memory (RAM) Memory chips that can be installed on the system board and directly accessed by a computer's processor.

rapid application development (RAD) A software design practice that creates and continually improves on prototypes to create a final software system.

read-only memory (ROM) ROM, PROM, EPROM, or EEPROM memory chips cannot be erased with normal processor operations. ROM chips come with data or programs that can only be read, and typically are used to hold instructions for what a computer should do each time it is turned on.

real-time systems Systems where transaction information is entered directly into a database.

record All the data about one individual or item in a database table or spreadsheet.

registers Part of the CPU. Registers are small memory areas that temporarily hold the data the ALU is working with and will require for the next operation.

relational database A database that separates fields into two or more related tables.

render Add light sources and color to convert an outline or wireframe object to a 3-D object.

resolution For monitors, the number of pixels displayed horizontally and vertically on a monitor; for printers, the number of dots printed per inch.

rights The ability to read, write, delete, or use particular files on a network. Rights are granted to individuals and groups.

ring LAN Network topology where communications are

carried in a ring that connects all the computers and the file server.

scanner An optical input device that produces a digitized image of text or graphics.

Wilhelm Schickard Seventeenth-century inventor who built the first mechanical adding machine.

scrolling Moving vertically or horizontally within a document on-screen.

search To access data in a document or database based on one or more keywords entered by the user.

search engine A Web application that allows you to search for particular Web sites based on keywords or concepts—for example, Alta Vista and Yahoo!

search results Information or topics returned as a result of a user request.

semiconductor Materials like germanium and silicon that conduct better than glass or rubber, but not as well as copper or steel.

sensate liners Liners woven into combat fatigues that include biological and physical sensors.

sequential access Data access methods that store and retrieve information sequentially—for example, all magnetic tape access is sequential.

server In a client-server network, a large computer that holds special network software, applications, and shared data.

shell Program that takes commands from the user and passes them to the operating system kernel.

simplex A one-way communication channel—for example, a TV broadcast.

sims Modeling simulators like SimCity.

site A series of related Web pages.

social user interface A software interface that takes on a personality such as a cartoon character or celebrity.

software piracy Making illegal copies of commercial software or shareware.

software Programs. Software is divided into two broad categories: applications, and systems software.

source data capture A type of transaction process where data is embedded in and recorded during a transaction—for example, scanning products at a retail store.

spamming Widely and inappropriately broadcasting electronic mail messages.

spider A search engine utility, also called a robot, that retrieves a document and all documents referenced by the first document.

spreadsheets A program used to manipulate and analyze numerical information.

star LAN A LAN topology where each workstation is connected to the server.

Steve Jobs Homebrew Computer Club member and cofounder of Apple Computer.

storage Nonvolatile device that houses programs and data for later retrieval.

stored program Instructions that are maintained separately from a process or processor. The first stored program was stored on cards for use in Jacquard's loom. John von Neumann is the father of the modern stored program concept.

streaming technology Audio and video Web

applications that begin playing the media file as reception begins, rather than waiting until the entire file has been downloaded.

subdomain Part of a URL, usually the name of a server, network, or company.

subnotebook computer Extremely lightweight portable PC with smaller input and output devices.

summary report A report that provides totals for a particular time period.

supercomputer The largest size of computers, custom-constructed for a specific purchaser with extremely large data processing needs.

swap file A hard drive file created by an operating system to temporarily hold part of the data normally held in the computer's memory.

symbology A system that specifies how characters will be represented in a bar code—for example, UPC.

synchronous A communications mode where data is transmitted at a set rate, timed by a common clock. Almost all the communication inside a computer happens synchronously, timed by the CPU clock.

system board (motherboard) The main circuit board in a computer that contains the CPU, bus, and expansion slots.

system call An instruction issued by the operating system.

system development life cycle A specific series of steps used to guide a systems analysis and design process.

system resource allocation Assigning hardware to different programs and functions so that the computer is operating efficiently.

system software Software that allows the computer to carry out basic operational functions, including input and output.

systems analysis and design A methodology used to research and design business software systems.

TCP/IP A communication protocol (Transmission Control Protocol) and addressing protocol (Internet Protocol) developed for the Internet and now the dominant standard for networks of all types.

Telnet A system that allows users to access other computers, then run applications or access files that are housed there.

terminal Combination keyboard/monitor workstations for mainframes and minicomputers.

terminal Mainframe or minicomputer access device that includes a screen, keyboard, and connection to the mainframe, but no processor.

text insertion Adding text to a document without overtyping existing text.

thinwire (coax) A copper wire, covered with a plastic insulator and wrapped with a metal mesh shield, used for cable television and computer networks.

thread In a bulletin board or newsgroup, an original message, responses to the message, responses to the responses, and so on.

topology The cabling design for a network: bus, ring, or star.

tower computer A desktop-sized microcomputer with a case designed to stand alone rather than underneath the monitor.

transaction An event that happens in a business: a student registration, a sale, the receipt of an invoice.

transaction processing systems Business systems that capture information about the events that occur in a business.

transistor An electrical rectifier or amplifier made from semiconductive materials. Transistors replaced vacuum tubes.

Alan Turing British mathematician who described a model of a computer called a Universal Turing Machine that would process data and programs, allowing the machine to perform a variety of functions (1936). One of the developers of Colossus.

tutorial software Software that helps users learn a particular skill or group of skills.

twisted-pair Cable used for short-distance data transmission and for lower density voice transmission, even over long distances.

ubiquitous computing Unobtrusive computing, where technology fades into the background so the focus moves to function rather than hardware or the user interface.

UNIVAC The first commercial computer, introduced in 1951 by Remington Rand.

universal resource locator (URL) A string of characters that identifies the name and address of each document available to the Web.

universal service An FCC policy that calls for deep discounts for Internet access to schools, libraries, and rural health facilities.

upgrade To add more or faster processors, memory, storage, or peripheral devices to an existing computer.

Usenet newsgroups Text-based Internet topical discussion groups.

user ID A unique name that identifies a user to the network.

user interface The text or graphic part of a program that the user interacts with to issue commands.

utilities Programs that are used in conjunction with the operating system to control and use a computer's hardware, or manage data and program files.

virtual manufacturing Simulations that model a product that will be created and the production processes that will be needed.

virtual memory An operating system feature that allows the computer to use part of storage as memory by creating a swap file.

Virtual Reality Modeling Language (VRML) A programming language used to create 3-D, "walk through" Web sites.

volatile memory Memory like RAM that must be constantly refreshed electrically.

John von Neumann Author of "First Draft of a Report on the EDVAC" in which he developed the design for the first digital computer, capable of using stored programs (1944). Von Neumann's conceptual computer included an input unit, memory area, arithmetic unit, control unit, and output device.

WAIS Wide Area Information Servers provide a full-text indexing system for documents searched in specific databases.

wearable computers A wide range of computer products designed to be worn by the user, from headsets that include tiny computer screens to intelligent long johns.

Web page A document on the World Wide Web.

Web TV A box that can be easily connected to televisions and telephone lines to allow non-computer users to surf the Internet through the familiar television.

Webmaster The administrator of an intranet or Web site.

wide area network (WAN) A network that connects users across long distances—for example, the Internet.

Winchester disk The original IBM hard disk drive. *Winchester disk* is commonly used to refer to any hard disk drive.

Windows 95 A 32-bit operating system for PCs. Windows 95 is the first version of Windows that is an actual operating system.

word processor A program designed to create text-based documents like letters.

workstation (client) A computer other than the server in a client-server network.

workstation A microcomputer and its peripherals, including a keyboard, monitor, and printer.

World Wide Web A graphical, hypertext navigation tool for the Internet

zoom control A program feature that allows a user to expand or contract a view displayed on a monitor.

Index

Note to the Reader: Throughout this index, **boldface** page numbers indicate primary discussions of a topic. *Italic* page numbers indicate illustrations.

Numbers

16-bit microprocessor, 90
28.8KB modem, 121
2-D (matrix) bar code, 304, 369
32-bit microprocessor, 90
64-bit microprocessor, 90

A

Aaron's World Famous Virtual Computer Museum, Web site, 96
abacus, 27, *28*, 369
ABC (Atanasoff-Berry Computer), *39*, 39, 370
access time, of storage device, **70**, 369
ACT! (Symantec), 248
active matrix LCD panel, 113
actuary, 341
Ada 95, 139
Ada programming language, 33
adapters
 audio card, 118
 video cards, 110, **112–113**
add-ons, 162, 369
adding machine, mechanical, 29
address book, 247
address channel, 92
administrator of network, 268
Advanced Research Projects Agency (ARPA), 202, 341
adventure games, **169–170**
advertising
 computers for design, **284–286**
 on online services, 205
Afterlife, 165
agents, 349, 369
Aiken, Howard, 41, 51, 369
air travel
 computer use, 7–8
 computerized reservations, 9, *10*
 traffic control, 9
airbill, 311
AIX (IBM UNIX), 129
ALGOL, 137
ALL-IN-1, 240

Allen, Paul, 81–82
Almaden Research Center, 356
alphabet, 27
Alt key, 101
Alta Vista, 217–218, *218*
Altair, 79, *80*
ALU (arithmetic logic unit), 66, 370
Amazon Books, Web site, 322
Amazon Trail, *161*, 161
America Online (AOL), 204, 206, *207*
 online service disks, 316
American Heritage Talking Dictionary, 157, *158*
American Standard Code for Information Interchange (ASCII), *65*, 65, 370
analog signals, 120
Analytical Engine, 31–34, 369–370
Analytical Society, 31
animated objects, on Web pages, 222
announcements, 190
Apple Computer Corp., 18, 84–85
 disk drives, 83
 Lisa computer, 85–86, 129
 Macintosh computer, 86
 Macintosh operating system, 129, *130*
 Message Pad 130, 88, *89*
 public stock offering, 85
 Web site, 195
Apple DOS, 129
Apple I computer, 80–81, *81*
Apple II computer, 84
Apple IIE computer, *59*
Apple IIGS, 190
AppleWorks, 176
application generators, 138
applications software, 126, **140–143**, *141*, 370
 data sharing between, 242
arcade-style games, **167**
architectural drawing, 189
architecture, 370
archival copies of files, 94
archivists, 69
arithmetic logic unit (ALU), 66, 370
arithmetic problems, 66
Army, 357

ARPANET, 202, 370
artificial intelligence, 60
ASCII (American Standard Code for Information Interchange), *65*, 65, 370
assembler, 136
assembly language, 136, 370
assembly lines, 38
Association for Computing Machinery, 173
asynchronous communications, 260, 370
AT&T Bell Labs, 119, 129
Atanasoff, John, 39, 370
Atanasoff-Berry Computer (ABC), *39*, 39, 370
Atari, 82
 video games, 59
atlas software, 158
attributes (properties), 139
audience, for home computer market, **152–153**
audio
 from home software, 153
 as input, 107–108
 on World Wide Web, 220
audio card, 118
audit flags, in tax preparation software, 183
auditory learners, 153
AutoCAD, 284
automated teller machine (ATM) transactions, 317
automated warehouses, **304–305**
automatic teller machines, 6, *7*
autonomous route guidance systems, 187
A/UX (UNIX for Mac), 129
auxiliary memory, 67

B

Babbage, Charles, 31–35, *32*, 326, 370
BACKUP command (DOS), 133
backups, 94, 370
 utilities to create, 134
Bank of America, 54
banks
 automated teller machine (ATM) transactions, 317
 computer use, 6

online bill paying services, 181–182, 328–329, 380
   proprietary software, 328–329
banners, 190
Banyan Vines, 268
bar code scanners, 303
bar codes, 109, 303, 370
   for mail, *12*
   Web site, 322
Bardeen, John, 52
BASIC computer language, 81, 135, 137
Basic Input Output System (BIOS), 127–128, 370
batch transaction systems, **317**, 370
batteries, 30
Battle Chess, 168
Battleground (TalonSoft), 170–171
baud, 121, 370
behaviors (methods), 139
Bell, Alexander Graham, 35
Bell Labs, 119, 129, 293
benchmarks, 294
Berners-Lee, Tim, 207, 214, 216, 370
   Web site, 224
Berry, Clifford, 39
Better Homes and Gardens Healthy Cooking CD Cookbook, 157
bill paying, online, 181–182, 328–329, 380
binary digit (bit), 63, 370
binary numbering system, *64*
BIOS (Basic Input Output System), 127–128, 370
bit, 63, 370
"black box," 9
Blue Mountain Home Page, Web site, 148
BMP file extension, 193
Boeing, 18
Bombe code-breaking machine, 40
Boole, George, 35, 370
Boolean algebra, 35, 39
Borland Corporation, Web site, 148, 279
Bosnia-Herzegovina, 351
Brattian, Walter, 52
Bricklin, Daniel, 84
browsers, **216–217**, 370
BSD UNIX, 129
bubble forms, 109
budgeting, 182
bulletin boards, electronic, **203**, 374
bus LAN, 266, *267*, 370
buses, **92**, 370
Bush, Vannevar, 38, 370
business analysis, 145

business software, **140–142**, 370–371
Business Software Alliance, 146
   Web site, 148
business systems software, 371
bytes, **63–65**, 371

C

C++ programming language, 139
C shell, 129
cable, **260–261**
cable systems, 258
cache, 62, 371
CAD (computer-aided design), 106, 189, 283–284, 327, 372
CAD/CAM software, Web sites, 299
CAI (computer-aided instruction), 158, 372
calculus, 29
calendar interchange protocol, 251
calipers, 106
CAM (computer-aided manufacturing), **289–290**, 372
camcorders, 118
capacity, 371
   of memory, 63, 65
   of storage, **69–70**
Caps Lock key, 101
careers in computers, **14**, 350
   actuary, 341
   archivists, 69
   CAD drafter, 284
   computer and office machine repairer, 109
   computer programmer, 358
   data processing manager, 293
   digital imaging technician, 188
   electronic pagination system operator, 241
   equipment operator, 115
   library technician, 209
   medical records technician, 334
   operations research analyst, 298
   paralegal, 214
   PC salesperson, 93
   private detective or investigator, 220
   product cost estimator, 237
   securities and financial services sales representatives, 329
   technical writer, 167
   word processor, 244
Carolson, Chester A., 55
cassette tape recorder, for data storage, 83
catalog shopping, 318

category list, in encyclopedia, 155, *156*
cathode ray tube (CRT), 57, 111, 371
CATIA, 284
CBS News, 275
CBS television network, 50
CCD (charge coupled device), 334
CD Magazine Online, Web site, 172
CD-ROM drives, *22*, 69, 93–94
   purchasing decisions, 197
CD-ROMs, 355
   educational software on, 154
cell address, 177, 371
cell in spreadsheet, 177, 371
cell phones, 262
cellular digital packet data system (CDPD), 337, 371
census of 1890, 35–37, 326
central processing units (CPUs), 66, 371
centralized systems, 272
Cerf, Vinton, 202
channels, 92
charge coupled device (CCD), 334
Chen, Hsinchun, 341
Chess Challenger, 168
chess games, 173
Chess Master, 168
Chess Wars: A Medieval Fantasy, *168*, 168
children, and Internet access, 352
Chrysler, 18
CIM (Computer Integrated Manufacturing), 290, 372
city planning simulation, 163
Civilization I and II, 170
client-server applications, 273
client-server database, 371
client-server networks, 264, **265–266**
clients, 264, 371
clinical workstations, **336–337**, 371
clip art, 110, **192**, 371
clock channel, 92
clock speed, 66
Close Combat, 171
coaxial cable, 260–261, 371
COBOL (Common Business-Oriented Language), 54, 137, 371
code, 134, 371
   errors in, 138
coders, 40
color monitors, 111, 112
color phosphor, 111
color printers, 113
   laser, 116
Colossus computer, 40–41, 371
Colossus Rebuild Project, Web site, 46

Columbia House CD Club, Web site, 322
COM domain name, 215
command keys, 101
command line interface, 85, 129, 371
commercial online services, 120,
    204–206, 371
  pricing, 213
commercial properties, 327
commercial software, 145–146
communications, 351
  with customers, 277
  protocols, 202
  software for, 176, 372
  verification in, 258–260
communications media, 260–262
communications modes, 258
communications systems, 228,
    257–262, 372
comparative data in management information systems, 233–234
compatibility of computer systems, 348
compiler, 51, 137–138, 372
compression of files, 119, 372
  software for, 134
CompuServe, 204–205, 208
  online service disks, 316
CompuServe Information Manager, *205*
computer architecture, 60, 91
computer chips, 55
computer generations, 50–60, 376
  first—vacuum tubes, 50–51, *52*
  second—transistors, 52–55, *53*
  third—integrated circuits, 55–57
  fourth—microminiaturized circuits, 57–59, *58*
  future, 60
Computer Integrated Manufacturing (CIM), 290, 372
computer literate, 17, 372
computer models, 9
computer programmers, 54
Computer Shopper, 198
computer stores, 198
computer system, 4, 372
computer system parts, 61–71
  input devices, 61
  memory, 61–65
  output, 71
  processors, 66
  storage, 67–71
computer types, 17–22
  mainframe computers, 19

microcomputers, 19–22
minicomputers, 19
supercomputers, 18, *18*
computer-aided design (CAD), 106, 189, 283–284, 327, 372
computer-aided instruction (CAI), 158, 372
computer-aided manufacturing (CAM), 289–290, 372
computerized medical record, 332–333, 372
computerized voice mail, 277
computerless society, 4–8
computers, 372
  in 19 c., 30–35
  in 20 c., 38–39
  benefits of, 10–11
  history, Web site, 46
  increasing dependence on, 8–10
  personal rewards from, 16–17
  purchasing, 195–199
  wearable, 356
  what they are, 4–8
  in World War II, 39–44
computing, ubiquitous, 357–358
Computing-Tabulating-Recording Company (CTR), 37
conceptual computer, 61, 372
connect time, 204, 372
connectivity, 255–276, *256*, 372
  basics, 256
  communications systems, 257–262
  computer networks, 262–264
  distributed systems, 272–276
  local area networks, 264–268
  network applications, 270–272
  network use, 268–270
contact managers, 248
contracts, 184
Control (Ctrl) key, 101
Control Program for Microcomputers (CP/M), 128
control unit, 66, 372
control unit clock, 66
conversion utilities, 242, 372
cookbooks, 157
copper telephone wire, 261
coprocessors, 66, 372
COPY command (DOS), 133
copyright, 146
Corel Corporation, Web site, 253
Corel Print House, 190–191

Corel WordPerfect, HTML from, 221
Corel WordPerfect Suite, 180, 241
costs, of computerization, 11–13
counting, history, 26–27
CP/M (Control Program for Microcomputers), 128
CPUs (central processing units), 66, 371
Cray T-90 supercomputer, *18*, 18
credit cards, 327
Critical Path Method (CPM), 295–296, *296*
Crosby method, 292
cross-platform performance of Internet, 274–275
crossword puzzles, 168
CRT (cathode ray tube), 57, 111, 371
cryptoanalysis, 40
CTR (Computing-Tabulating-Recording Company), 37
Ctrl (Control) key, 101
cuneiform, 27, 372
custom software, 142
customers
  access to FedEx tracking information, 312
  communication with, 277
cyclical redundancy check (CRC), 260
Cyrix, 90, *91*

D

D Day, 41
daisy wheel printers, 115
Dark Ages, 28
data, sharing between applications, 242
data channel, 92
data frame, 260
data management, changing role, 236–238
data mining, 236, 372
data processing manager, 293
data source, 373
  for mail merge, 243
data warehousing, 235, 373
database development tools, 244–245
databases, 138, 178–179, *179*
  data sharing by, 242
DataMind Corporation, 236
  Web site, 253
DDE (dynamic data exchange), 243–244, 374
debit cards, 329, 373

decimal numbering system, 63, *64*
decision making, expert systems for, 238
decision support, 372
  analysis tools for, 233
dedicated lines, 257, 372
Deep Thought program, 173
DEL command (DOS), 133
delimited text file, 243, 373
Delphi, 139, 145
Deming, W. Edwards, 293
Deming method, 292
demographic mapping software, 327
dependence on computers, **8–10**
Descent II, 162
design tools, **189**
Desk Set, 54
desktop computers, 21, 373
  value of, 78
desktop publishing, **190–191**, 373
detail reports, 233, 373
development teams, 143
development tools, 139, 373
device drivers, **132–133**, 373
Devol, George Jr., 55
dial-up connection, 257, 373
Difference Engine, 31, *33*, 326, 373
Differential Analyzers, 38, 41, 373
differential equations, machine
  to solve, 38
digital camera, 108, 187–188
digital communication lines,
  network of, 122
digital entertainment, **329–331**
Digital Equipment Corporation, 19
  PDP-1 minicomputer, 54, *55*
digital imaging technician, 188
digital libraries, **341–342**, 373
Digital Library Initiative, Web site, 344
digital photographs, 187, 373
Digital Research Laboratories, 128, 217
digital signals, 120
Digital VAX family of computers, 19, *20*
Digitally Assisted Dispatch System
  (DADS) computer, 311
digitizers, 106
direct access storage, **68–69**, 94, 373
direct memory access channels (DMA
  channels), 92, 373
Direct Memory Access (DMA)
  processor, 66
disk cleaning, utilities for, 134
disk drives, 54
distributed systems, **272–276**, 373
distribution centers, **304–305**
distribution channel, 302

distribution of goods, **302–320**
  transportation, **308–314**
  warehousing and inventory, **302–308**
DMA (Direct Memory Access) channels,
  92, 373
DMA (Direct Memory Access)
  processor, 66
domain names, 215, 373
doping, 52
DOS command line, 129
DOS operating system, 128–129, 373–374
  utilities, 133
DOS shell, 129
dot-matrix printers, 114–115, 374
downloading files, 374
  from Internet, 220
dragging, 103
DRAM (dynamic RAM), 61, 92, 374
drilling-down, 158, 374
drum plotters, 115
dual-scan matrix LCD panel, 113
dumb terminal, 240
Dungeons & Dragons, 169
duplex communication, 258, 374
DVD-ROM players, 355, 374
dye-sublimation printing, 117
dynamic data exchange (DDE),
  243–244, 374

E

e-mail, 202, **209–210**, 374
  for business communication, 270–271
EBCDIC (Extended Binary-Coded
  Decimal Interchange Code), 64–65,
  65, 259, 374
Echo Lake, 187, *188*
Eckert, John Presper, 41–42, 43–44, 374
Edison, Thomas, 35
editing, 374
EDSAC (Electronic Delay Storage
  Automatic Calculator), 43, 374
EDU domain name, 215
educational simulations, **162–165**
educational software, **153–165**
EDVAC (Electronic Discrete Variable
  Computer), 43, 374
EEPROM (electrically erasable PROM),
  62–63
Egypt, 27
EISA (Enhanced ISA), 93
election returns, 50
electric battery, 30
electric generator, 35

electrically erasable PROM (EEPROM),
  62–63
electromechanical computer, 37, 37
electronic bulletin boards, **203**, 374
Electronic Control Company, 43
electronic data interchange, 292, 374
Electronic Delay Storage Automatic
  Calculator (EDSAC), 43, 374
Electronic Discrete Variable Computer
  (EDVAC), 43, 374
electronic mail, 202, **209–210**, 374
  for business communication, 270–271
electronic medical record, 332, 374
electronic music keyboards, 119
Electronic Numerical Integrator and
  Computer (ENIAC), *41*, 41–42, 374
electronic phone books, 178–179
electronic presentation software,
  245–246, 374
Electronic Recording Method of
  Accounting (ERMA), 54
electronic rectifier vacuum tube, 38
electronic signatures, 333, 374
electrostatic plotters, 115
ELF (extremely low frequency) radiation,
  112, 375
employment, workplace computer
  skills, **15**
Encyclopedia Electronica (Xiphias
  Publishing), 355
encyclopedias, **154–156**, *155*
Engelbart, Douglas, *57*, 57, 77–78, 119
  mouse invention, *102*, 102
  Web site about, 96
Engelberger, Joseph, 55
English Wizard, *138*, 138
ENIAC (Electronic Numerical Integrator
  and Computer), *41*, 41–42, 374
Enigma, *40*, 40
enterprise network, 268, 374
enterprise technology planning, 228
entertainment, digital, **329–331**
entertainment software, **143**,
  165–171, 375
  adventure games, **169–170**
  arcade-style games, **167**
  military and strategy games, **170–171**
  puzzle games, **168–169**, *169*
  sports games, **171**
  traditional games, **167–168**
  Web sites, 172
Entertainment Software Rating Board
  (ESRB), 166–167
  Web site, 172
environment, 130, 375

EPROM (erasable PROM), 62–63
eraser-heads, 105
ERMA (Electronic Recording Method of
    Accounting), 54
errors, in program code, 138
Esc (Escape) key, 101
Ethernet cards, 78
even parity, 259
Everton Genealogical Helper,
    Web site, 195
exception reports, 233, 375
executable program file, 137, 375
expansion slots, **93**, 375
expert systems, 60, **238–239**, 375
    for health care, **334–335**, *335*
Extended Binary-Coded Decimal
    Interchange Code (EBCDIC), 64–65,
    65, 259, 374
external devices, 375
    disk drives, 83
    modems, 121
    ports, 93
extremely low frequency (ELF) radiation,
    112, 375
eye-tracking hardware, 354–355, 375
    Web site, 360
eyestrain, resolution and, 111

F

facility management software, 327
facsimile (fax machines), **119–120**, 375
Fairchild Semiconductor, 55
family computers, *See* home computers
family history, **187–188**
Family Tree Maker, 187
fan-folded paper, *114*
FAQ (Frequently Asked Questions), 375
    for newsgroups, 211
    Web site, 224
Faraday, Michael, 35
fast food restaurants, computer use, 5–6
fault tolerance, 348, 375
fax back services, 277, 375
fax machines, **119–120**, 375
fax/modem card, purchasing
    decisions, 197
Federal Bureau of Investigation,
    Web site, 344
Federal Communications
    Commission, 352
    Web site, 360
Federal Express, 310–313

FedEx Ship, 312–313, *313*
    Web site, 322
FedWorld, Web site, 344
fiber-optic cable, 261, 375
field codes, 375
    for mail merge, 243
field in database, 178, 375
file extensions, 192, 375
file formats, 242
    for graphics, 192, 193
File Transfer Protocol (FTP), 212, 375
files
    archival copies, 94
    compression of, 119
    downloading from Internet, 220
    software for compressing, 134
filters, 192, 375
financial management software, **180–182**
Finder, 129
firewall, 276, 375
First Aid 95, *135*
"First Draft of a Report on the EDVAC"
    (von Neuman), 42–44
fixed imaged video, 108
flash memory, 63, 67
flatbed plotters, 115
flatbed scanners, 108, 109
Fleming, John Ambrose, 38
flexible manufacturing, 289
flicker, 112
Flint, Charles, 37
floppy disk drives, *22*, 67, 83, 94
floppy diskettes, 82, *83*, 375
Flow-Matic programming language, 54
Flury, Jim, 249
flyers, 190
fonts, for Web pages, 221
Ford, Henry, 38
FORMAT command (DOS), 133
formatting, 375
formula, 177, 375
FORTRAN (Formula Translator), 54,
    136–137
4GLs, 138–139, 369
Frankston, Bob, 84
Freeware, 146
    for hobbies, 184
FTP (File Transfer Protocol), 212, 375
full duplex communication, 258
full-motion video, 108, 118
function keys, 101
Fury3, 162, *163*
fuzzy logic, 60

G

games, 143
Gantt Charts, 295, 296
gas plasma display, 113, 375
Gates, Bill, *76*, 76–77, 81–82, 349, 375
GB (gigabyte), 65, 376
GBH button, 104–105
genealogy, **187–188**
General Motors dealers, PROSPEC soft-
    ware, 315
generations of computers, **50–60**, 376
geostationary orbit, 262
germanium crystal, 52
gigabyte (GB), 65, 376
Gina Smith's On Computers (radio talk
    show), 220, *221*
global positioning system (GPS), 187
GMAT, study software for, 160
Goldstine, Adele, 41
Gopher, *212*, 212, 376
GOV domain name, 215
graphic tablets, 106
graphical user interfaces, 85–86,
    129–132, 376
    for Internet, 207
graphics, 190
    file formats for, 192, 193
    for home software, 152
graphics input, 107–108
gray-scale monitors, 111
Group Practice Improvement
    Network, 335
group scheduling software, 272
groupware, 274, 376
Guidestar Navigation Information
    System, 186
Gutenberg, Johannes, 29
GyroPoint (Gyration), *103*, 103, *104*

H

half-duplex communication, 258, 376
Hallmark Card Studio, 191
handheld computers, 88, 376
    Windows CE for, 247
handheld scanners, 108, 109
hard disk drives, 67, 82, 94, 376
    purchasing decisions, 197
    video requirements, 118
    virtual memory space on, 128
hard-wired programming, 42

Hardbody Handheld PC (Texas Microsystems), *88*, 88
hardware, 4, 376
  design cycle, 286–287
  device drivers for, 133
  eye-tracking, 354–355
  input devices, 21, **61**, **100–110**
  input/output devices, **118–121**
  for networks, **263**
  operating system and, 128
  output devices, 4, 21, **71**, **110–118**
  plug-and-play, 348
Harvard-IBM Automatic Sequence Controlled Calculator, 41
health care
  clinical workstations, **336–337**
  expert systems and practice guidelines, **334–335**, *335*
health care industry, **331–337**
Healthcare Informatics, 334
help
  for home software, 153
  online, 153, 380
Henry Ford Health System (HFHS), 332
Henry Ford Medical Group, Clinical Policy Library, 334
Hewett Packard, 82
  HP 5000 printer family, *114*
  HP Color LaserJet 5 printer, *116*
  HP DeskJet 660C printer, *117*
high-level language, 136–137, 376
high-volume printer, *114*
history
  of computers, 46, 96
  of counting, 26–27
  fax machines, 120
  first music on computer, 119
  of mouse, *102*
  online communication, **202–209**
hobby software, **184–189**
  design tools, **189**
  genealogy and family history, **187–188**
Hoerni, Jack, 55
Hollerith, Herman, 36, 326, 376
Hollerith card, *36*, 36, 376
Hollerith Tabulating Machine, *37*
home banking, 328
home computers, **151–173**
  audience for software, 152–153
home page, 216, 376
home productivity software, **175–198**
home software, features of
  best-selling, 152

home use of computers, 16
Homebrew Computer Club, 80
Honeywell, 53
Honeywell v. Sperry Rand, 44
Hopper, Grace, *51*, 51, 376
  Web site, 72
hospitals, 8
host, 202, 376
hot links, 155
hotels, automated checkin kiosks, 326
HotWired Online Magazine, Web site, 123
hub and spoke transportation system, 311
hypertext link, 77–78, 376
  in reference tools, 155, 215, *216*
Hypertext Markup Language (HTML), 139, 215, 221, 376
Hypertext Transfer Protocol (HTTP), 214, 376

I

I/O processors, 66
IBM 5100 microcomputer, 82
IBM Corporation, 19, 38, 53
  agreement with Microsoft, 85
  Almaden Research Center, 356
  cooperation with Microsoft, 130
  first personal computer, 85
  first portable computer, 82
IBM PC-DOS, 128
icons, 129, 376
IEEE Computer Society, Web site, 73
IF-THEN scenarios, 238
Imagewriter II printer, 190
impact printers, **114–115**, 376
Impromptu, 138
in-vehicle guidance ssytems, 186
In-Vehicle Map Systems, Web site, 172
India, 27
industrial robots, 8, 55
Industry Standard Architecture (ISA), 93
information
  access to, 352
  database storage of, 178
information engineering, **145**, 376
information provider, 287
information specialists, 339, 340
information systems, 228, 376
  expert systems, **238–239**
  management information systems, **232–238**

office automation systems, **240–248**
  transaction processing systems, **228–232**, *230*
information technology planning, 228, 376
  development, 249–251
information transmission, 7
infrared technology, for wireless mouse, 102
ink-jet printers, 117, 377
input, 4, 377
input devices, 21, **61**, **100–110**
  digitizers, 106
  graphic tablets, 106
  joysticks, **105**, *106*
  light pens, 106
  microphone, 107
  multimedia, **107–108**
  pointing devices, **102–105**
  source data automation, **108–110**
  for text entry, **101**
  touch screens, **105**
  trends, **353–355**
input/output (I/O) devices, 100, **118–121**
input/output (I/O) process, operating system and, 128
insert publishing, 284–286, *285*, *286*
installing, 377
  software for PCs, 126, 152
Institute of Electrical and Electronic Engineers, Web site, 279
Institute for Healthcare Improvement, 335
integrated, 377
integrated circuits, **55–57**, 377
integrated office suites, **240–248**
integrated products, 179–180
Integrated Services Digital Network (ISDN), 257–258, 377
IntegrationWare, 249
  Web site, 253
Intel, 58, 61, 377
  microprocessor development, 78
  microprocessors, 90
IntelliQuest, 207
interactive learning, **158–161**
interlacing, 112
internal devices, 377
  disk drives, 83
  modems, 121
Internal Revenue Service, 183
International Business Machines (IBM) Corporation, 38

Internet, 16, 120, **208–216**, 376
  accessing, **213–214**
  beginnings, 202
  e-mail, **209–210**
  funding, 214
  growth, **206–207**
  and intranets, **274–276**
  mailing lists, **210–211**
  programming languages, **139**
  research using, 282
  sales and marketing on, **318–320**
  simplifying access, **352–353**
  Usenet newsgroups, **211**
  World Wide Web, **208–209**
Internet addresses, **214–216**
Internet banking, 328
Internet Explorer (Microsoft), 217, *218*
Internet Protocol (IP), 202
Internet Public Library, **340**, 340
  Reference Section Web site, 344
Internet service provider (ISP), 213, 376
The Internet Sleuth, 219
Internet Society, Web site, 224
interpreter, **137–138**, 377
intranets, 120, **274–276**, 377
  and security, 276
inventory, **302–308**
inventory control systems, **305–306**, 377
inventory management, with Just in Time
  (JIT), **290–292**
inventory tracking, **306–308**, *307*, 377
Iomega Zip drives, 94
IRC (Internet Relay Chat), 212, 377
ISA (Industry Standard Architecture), 93
item identification, in warehousing and
  inventory, 302–304

J

Jacquard's loom, 30–31, 377
Janna Systems, Janna Contact '95, 248
Java, 139, 222
Jazz drives, 94
jigsaw puzzles, 168
job skills, 350
Jobs, Steve, 80, *84*, 330, 382
joysticks, **105**, *106*
JPG file extension, 193
Just in Time (JIT), **290–292**

K

Kasparov, Garry, 173

KB (kilobyte), 65, 377
Kennedy, John, 55
Kepler, Johannes, 29
kernel, of operating system, 128, 377
keyboards, *22*, 61, *101*, 101, 377
  electronic music, 119
Al-Khwarizmi, Muhammed ibn, 28
Kilby, Jack, 55
kilobyte (KB), 65, 377
kinesthetic learners, 153
King, Augusta Ada (Countess of
  Lovelace), 32–33, *34*, 377
knowledge software, 142, 377

L

LANtastic, 268
laptop computers, *87*, 87, 377
  PCMCIA card for, 121
  pointing devices for, **103–105**, *104*
  for travel, 185
large-scale integration (LSI), 57–58
laser, 261
laser devices, 60
laser printers, **115–116**, 377
law enforcement, **337–339**
Laws of Gravity, 29
LCD (liquid crystal display), 113, 378
leased lines, 257, 292, 372
LED (light emitting diode), 261
legal help, **184**
leisure time software, 184
letter-quality printers, 115
libraries, **339–342**
  digital, **341–342**
Library of Congress, Web site, *342*,
  342, 344
license
  for clip art, 192
  for software, 146
Liebniz, Gottfried Wilhelm, 29–30
life cycle, for software development,
  144, 383
light pens, 106, 303
linker, 137
links, 77, 378
liquid crystal display (LCD), 113, 378
Lisa computer, 129
LISP, 138
listservs (mailing lists), 202, **210–211**, 378
Living Trust Maker, 184
loan tracking, 182
local area networks (LAN), **264–268**, 378

logarithms, 28
logical errors, 138
logical problems, 66
login, 269, 378
LOGO, 138
lossy transmission, 259
Lotus 123, 244
Lotus Corporation
  Domino, 276
  Notes, 274
  Smart Suite, 180, 241
  Web site, 253, 279
LSI (large-scale integration), 57–58
Luxo, Jr., 330

M

machine language, 134, 136, 378
  converting programming
    language to, 51
  for first-generation computers, 50
Macintosh computer, 86
Macintosh operating system (Mac OS),
  129, *130*
Magnetic Ink Character Recognition
  (MICR), 109
magnetic storage, **68**, 69, 378
mail merge, in word processor, *243*,
  243, 378
mail order, 198, 306
mail sorting, 11–12
mailing lists, 202, **210–211**, 378
main memory, 67
mainframe, **19**, 50, 77, 272, 378
management information systems,
  232–238, 378
  data mining, **236**
  data warehousing, **235**
Managing Your Money, 329
manual transaction systems, **316**
manufacturing, 364–367
  computers for managing, **295–298**
  plants production scheduling, 310
  technology and, **289–292**
  virtual, **289**, 384
Manufacturing Online, Web site, 299
MapNet Plus Transportation, *314*, 314
maps, 184–186
Marconi, Guglielmo, 38
Mark I, 41
market research, on video releases, 331
marketing, **314–315**
  on the Internet, **318–320**

Markkula, Arnas (Mark), 84
mass production, 38
mass-storage cube, 60
Massachusetts Institute of Technology, Media Lab, 356
math coprocessors, 66
matrix bar code, 304, 369
Mauchly, John, 41–42, 43–44, 378
Mauchly, Kay McNulty, 42
Mavis Beacon Teaches Typing, 158–159, *159*
MB (megabyte), 65, 378
MCI, 275
mechanical adding machine, 29
media, 67, 378
Medical Information Management System (MIMS), 333
medical records, electronic, 332
Medical Records Institute, Web site, 344
medical records technician, 334
medical simulations, 165
megabyte (MB), 65, 378
megahertz (MHz), 66, 378
memory, 42, **61–65**, **92**, 378. *See also* RAM (random access memory); ROM (read-only memory)
    flash, 63, 67
    measuring, **65**
    trends, **355–356**
    virtual, **70–71**, 90, 128, 384
    volatile, 61
memory modules, 92
menus, 129, 378
Menv (Modeling Environment), 331
Mesopotamia, early writing, 27
methods (behaviors), 139
MHz (megahertz), 66, 378
microcomputers, **19–22**, 378. *See also* personal computers
    Web site for history, 96
microminiaturized circuits, **57–59**, *58*, 378
MicroPro, 176
microprocessors, *58*, 58–59, 66, **90**, **91**, 378
    computers by type used, 91
    development, 78
    purchasing decisions, 197
microsecond, 70
Microsoft, 76, 82
    Access, 231, *232*, 244, *245*
    Clip Art Gallery, 192, *193*
    cooperation with IBM, 130

DOS, 128
Encarta '96 Encyclopedia, *155*, *156*
Excel, *234*, 234, 244
Flight Simulator, 162
Internet Explorer, 217, *218*
Internet Information Server and Exchange, 276
Money, 182
PowerPoint, Slide Sorter view, *246*, 246
Project, 296–297, *297*
Publisher, *191*
QuickBASIC, 137
Web site, 148
Windows, 86–87, 129–130, 378
Windows 3.1, 130, *131*
Windows 95, 131, *132*, 385
    expert system in Troubleshooting system, *239*, 239
Word, HTML designer, 221
Works, 180
    word processor, *177*
Microsoft Office, 180, 241
    agents in, *350*, 350
MicroWarehouse, 306
microwave transmission, 262
Middle East, 27
middleware, 290, 378
MIDI (Musical Instrument Design Interface), 119, 378
MIL domain name, 215
military games, **170–171**
millisecond, 70, 378
MILNET, 202
mind games, **173**
Minesweeper, 168
mini floppy diskettes, 83
minicomputers, **19**, 54, 378
minutes per page (mpp), 117
mobile data terminals (MDTs), 338, 379
mobile imaging units, 339, 379
modems, **119–120**, *121*, 292, 379
money management, **328–329**
monitors, *22*, 71, **110–113**
monochrome monitors, 111, 379
Morse, Samuel, 35
motherboard, **91–92**
mouse, *22*, 57, 86, **102–103**, 379
    first, *102*
    and Windows, 130
moveable type print, 29
movie animation, **330–331**
movies, releasing on video, **331**
MS-DOS (Microsoft Disk Operating System), 85

multimedia, 19, 379
multimedia kit, 118
multiplayer adventure games, 169
multiple-part forms, printing, 115
multitasking, and RAM requirements, 197
multiuser systems, 19, 379
    Windows NT for, 131
Musical Instrument Design Interface (MIDI), 119, 378
Myst, *170*, 170

N

nanosecond, 70, 379
Napier, John, 28
Napier's bones, 28, 379
National Aeronautics and Space Administration, 341
    Ames Virtual Windtunnel, 18
National Audobon Society Interactive CD-ROM Guide to North American Birds, 157
National Center for Atmospheric Research, 18
National Crime Information Center (NCIC), 338–339
National Information Infrastructure (NII), 341, 379
National Law Enforcement Telecommunications System, 338
National Science Foundation, 341
natural language, 379
    programming language and, 135
natural speech input, 354, 379
NET domain name, 215
netiquette, 320
Netscape Communications Corporation, 276
    Web site, 279
Netscape Mail, 209, *210*
Netscape Navigator, *217*, 217
network account, 379
network administrator, 268, 379
network applications, **270–272**
network communication protocols, 264, 379
network computers, as corporate security risk, 237
network standard, 263, 379
networks, **262–264**, 379
    client-server, 264, **265–266**
    hardware for, **263**
    peer-to-peer, 264, **265**

schedule software for, 272
security for, **270**
software for, **263–264**, 266, *268*
use of, **268–270**
New Jersey, driver's licence, 17
New Print Shop, 190
newsgroups, 211
Newton, Sir Isaac, 29
1984 (Orwell), 17
Nintendo, 143
nodes, 264, 379
noise, from printers, 115
Nolo Press, Web site, 195
non-interlaced monitors, 112
nonimpact printers, **115–117**
nonremovable storage, **67**
notebook computers, *87*, 87, 379
police use, 337, *338*
Novell GroupWise, 274
Novell NetWare, 266
numbering system, positional, 28
numerical control programmer, 290

O

object code, 137, 379
object linking and embedding (OLE), 242, 379
object-oriented programming (OOP), 139, 222
obscenity, 352
ODBC (Open Database Connectivity), 242, 380
odd parity, 259
off-the-shelf software, 140, 229
office automation systems, **240–248**, 379
office suites, **240–248**, 380
 applications in major, 241
 contact managers, **248**
 database development tools, **244–245**
 at home, **179–180**
 presentations, **245–246**
 spreadsheets, **244**
 tracking and scheduling, **247–248**
 word processing, **242–244**
OLE (object linking and embedding), 242, 379
online bill paying, 181–182, 328–329, 380
online commercial services, advertising on, 205
online communication, history, **202–209**
online help, 153, 380
online marketing, **319–320**

online shopping, **318–320**
OO-COBOL, 139
OOP (object-oriented programming), 139, 222
open database connectivity (ODBC), 380
operating systems, 56, **127–132**, 380
 and application software, 140
 graphical user interfaces, **129–132**
 and purchasing decisions, 196
 text-based, **128–129**
operations research analyst, 298
optical character recognition (OCR), 108, 380
optical disks, 94
optical fibers, 261
Optical Mark Recognition (OMR), 109
optical storage devices, 60, **68**, 380
Oregon Trail, *161*, 161
ORG domain name, 215
Orwell, George, *1984*, 17
OS/2 operating system, 130
Osborne Computer Corporation, 85, *86*
"out of memory" error, 70
output, 380
output devices, 4, 21, **71**, **110–118**
 monitors, 71, **110–113**
 printers, 21, 71, **113–117**
 sound, **118**
overhead projector, LCD panel for, 113

P

packets, 263, 380
PageMaker, 190
pagers, 262
palmtop computer, 89
Palo Alto Research Center (PARC), 78
Palo Alto Software Marketing Plan Pro, 315
paper backups of computer records, 8
Paradox, 244
paralegal, 214
parallel processing, 60, 66
parity checking, 259–260, 380
Pascal, Blaise, 29, 380
Pascaline, 29, *30*, 380
passive matrix LCD panel, 113
password, 269, 270, 380
PC Memory Card International Association, 121
PC salesperson, 93
PC/TVs, 352–353, 380
PCI (Peripheral Component Interconnect bus), 93
PCMCIA card, 121, 380
PCT file extension, 193
PDAs (personal digital assistants), 88, *89*, 380
peer-to-peer networks, 264, **265**, 380
pen computers, 88, 380
Pentium microprocessor, 90
Perfect Works, 180
performance optimization, utilities for, 134
Peripheral Component Interconnect bus (PCI), 93
peripheral memory, 67
peripherals, 100, 380
personal area networks, 356, 380
personal computer components, **90–94**
 buses, **92**
 hard drives, 67, 82, 94
 memory, **92**
 microprocessors, **90**, *91*
 ports, **93**
 slots, **93**
 storage devices, **93–94**
 system board, **91–93**
personal computer skills, **16**
personal computers, **19–22**, **75–96**, 380. *See also* Apple Computer Corp.; IBM Corporation
 beginnings, **76–82**
 competition, 85–87
 sales in 1980s, 85
 trends, **348–350**
personal digital assistants (PDAs), 88, *89*, 380
personal financial management software, **180–182**, 380
personal freedom, 17
personal information managers (PIMs), 247, 380
 printing for, 248
PERT (Program Evaluation Review Technique), 295, *296*, 296
pharmaceutical research, 289
Phoenicians, 27
Phone Disc, 179
phonograph, 35
photocopying, 55
photographs
 collections, **192**
 digital, 187, 373
 processing on disk, 187
 scanning, 109

physically disabled, 355
pickers, in warehouse, 304
pinball manufacturers, 59
Pipe Dream, 168
Pixar, 330–331
   Menv (Modeling Environment), 331
pixels, 111, 381
Planix Home Architect 3D, *189*, 189
platforms, 381
   and Internet, 274
platters, 68
plotters, 115
plug-and-play hardware, 348, 381
point-and-shoot cameras, 188
point-of-sale (POS) system, 110, 318, 381
pointing devices, **102–105**
   disadvantages, 106–107
   for laptop computers, **103–105**, *104*
police, notebook computer use, 337, *338*
Popular Electronics, 79
pornography, 352
portable computers
   memory cards for, 63
   purchasing decisions, 197
ports, 93, 381
positional numbering system, 28
postal service delivery, 120
power companies, computer use, 5
power-on self test, 127
PowerBuilder, 139
presentations, **245–246**
price
   of commercial online services vs. ISPs, 213
   of computers, 11, 198
printers, 21, 71, **113–117**
   dot-matrix, 114–115
   impact, **114–115**
   ink-jet, 117
   letter-quality, 115
   nonimpact, **115–117**
   purchasing decisions, 198
   thermal, 117
printing press, 29
privacy, right to, 17
private branch exchange (PBX), 258, 381
processors, **66**
Prodigy, 204, 205, *206*, 208
   online service disks, 316
ProDos, 129
product cost estimator, 237
production, *See* manufacturing
production cycle, 283

design phase, **286–287**
productivity software, 142, 381
   databases, **178–179**, *179*
   financial management, **180–182**
   home office suite, **179–180**
   legal help, **184**
   printing and publishing, **190–192**
   spreadsheets, **177–178**, *178*
   tax preparation software, **183**
   word processors, **176–177**, *177*
products, 364–367
   creating, **282–283**
   demonstrations, **315–316**
   design, **283–289**
   quality, **292–295**
program, 4, 381
   vs. software, 143
Program Evaluation Review Technique (PERT), 295, *296*, 296
programmable read-only memory (PROM), 62–63
programmer analysts, 144
programmers, 134
   numerical control, 290
programming
   for games, 166
   hard-wired, 42
programming languages, **134–140**, 381
   Ada, 33
   assembly language, 136
   BASIC computer language, 81
   conversion to machine language, 51
   Flow-Matic, 54
   FORTRAN, 54
   Java, 222
   in personal computers, 135
project management
   software for, 296–297, *297*
   Web site, 299
project manager, 295
Project Mercury, 82
PROM (programmable read-only memory), 62–63
prompt in DOS, 128–129, 381
properties (attributes), 139
proprietary software, 328–329, 381
protocols, 202
   for calendar interchange, 251
   network communication, 264
prototypes, 8–9, 283, 287, 381
   computerized testing, **288–289**
public domain software, 146
public telephone lines, speed, 257

publishing industry, 282–283
punched cards, 36, 317
purchasing, computers and software, **195–199**
puzzle games, **168–169**, *169*
PythOnline, Web site, 322

Q

quality, measuring, **293–295**
quality management, **292–295**
quality of output, from ink-jet printers, 117
Quark Xpress, 190
quartz integrated circuit, 55
Quattro Pro, 244
query of database, 179, 381
query generators, 138
Quickbooks, *229*, 229–230, *230*
   inventory tracking module, 307, *308*
Quicken, 88, *181*, 181, *182*, 182, 329
Quill Corporation, 306

R

Rabdologia, 28
radar chart, 294
radiation, from monitors, 112
radio, 38, 258
radio stations, computer use, 5
RAM (random access memory), 61, 79, **92**, 381
   minimum requirements, 196–197
   trends, **355–356**
Rand McNally
   Mile Maker database, 310
   Quick Reference Atlas, 158, *159*
   StreetFinder, 186
   TripMaker, *185*, 185
random access storage, 68–69
Rapid Application Development (RAD), 145, 287, 381
read-only memory (ROM), 62, 381
   self test instructions in, 127
read/write CD drives, 69
read/write heads, 68
read/write memory (RWM), 62
read/write optical disk drives, 94
real estate, virtual shopping, **327–328**
real-time transaction systems, **317–318**, 381
Really Useful Company Store, Web site, 322

record in database, 178, 381
recreation, software for, **184–189**
reference tools, **154–158**
refresh rate, 112
registers, 66, 381
relational database, 244–245, 381
reliability, of computer systems, 348
Remington Rand, 44
   UNIVAC introduction, 50
removable media PC storage devices, *94*, 94
removable storage, **67**
Renaissance, 28
RENAME command (DOS), 133
rendering, 189, 330–331, 381
report generators, 138
Report Program Generator (RPG) language, 137
research, using Internet, 282
resolution, 381
   of monitor display, 111
   of printer, 116
RESTORE command (DOS), 133
restore process, utilities for, 134
retail stores, computers in, 6
right to privacy, 17
rights, 269, 381
ring LAN, 381
Roberts, Ed, 79
robots, 218
   in warehouse, 304
ROM (read-only memory), 62, 92, 381
   self test instructions in, 127
Roman Empire, 28
Roman numerals, 28
royalties, for clip art, 192
Rubenstein, Seymour, 176
RWM (read/write memory), 62

S

SABRE, 9, *10*
safety standards, for monitors, 112
sales, **315–317**
   on the Internet, **318–320**
   transaction systems, **316–318**
sample testing, for quality measuremetn, 293
Samsung Electronics, 356
Sarajevo, 351
   Web site, 361
SAT, study software for, 160

satellites, for microwave transmission, 262
scanners, 108, 382
scheduling, 247, **248**, 251
   on networks, 272
   for transportation of goods, **309–310**
Schickard, Wilhelm, 29, 382
school system, busing schedules, *314*, 314
scientific research,
   supercomputers for, 18
scrolling, 382
search, 382
   method for encyclopedias, 154
search engines, **217–219**, 382
   Web sites, 224
search results, 382
secondary memory, 67
security
   for banks, 329
   intranet and, 276
   network login and, 269
   for networks, **270**
   notebook computers as risk, 237
   voice recognition for, 107
Sega, 143
Select Phone, 179
semiconductor, 52, 382
sensate liners, 356–357, 382
sequential access storage devices, **68–69**, 94, 382
serial port, 121
servers, 264, 382
service industries, **325–342**
   defining, **326–331**
   transportation for, **313–314**, *314*
SF-Lovers, 202
shareware, 146
   for hobbies, 184
Sharp Wizard, 247
Shatz, Bruce, 341
shell, 128, 382
Shockley, William, 52
Sholes, Christopher, 35
shrinkage, 305
signatures, electronic, 333
silicon, 52
Sim City 2000, 162, 163
SIMMs (single inline memory modules), 61, *62*, 92
simplex communications, 258, 382
sims, 164, 382
simulation, 288
   educational, **162–165**

single inline memory modules (SIMMs), 61, *62*, 92
site, 382. *See also* Web sites
skilled employees, 11–13
slack, 295
slide rule, 28
slides, in electronic presentations, 246
slots, **93**
smart cards, 327
Smith, Frederick W., 311
"snail mail," 120, 210
social user interface, 350, 382
society, without computers, **4–8**
software, 4, **125–147**, 382
   applications software, 126, **140–143**, *141*
   browsers, **216–217**
   design cycle, 287
   development, **143–145**
   development life cycle, 144, 383
   educational, **153–165**
   entertainment, **143**, **165–171**
   ethics, 145–146
   installing, 126
   for networks, **263–264**, 266, *268*
   for project management, 296–297, *297*
   public availability, 145–146
   purchasing, **195–199**
   requirements for, 196
   and user needs, 349
   version numbers, 131
   voice recognition, 353–354
software developers, 134
software piracy, 146, 382
solid-state appliances, 53
Solitaire, 167
Soloman, Les, 79
Solomon Software, 142
   Solomon IV, 230, *231*
sound output devices, **118**
Source, 204–205
source data automation input devices, **108–110**
source data capture, 318, 382
Soviet Union, 56
spamming, 320, 382
speakers, *22*, 110, 118
specialized software, 142
speech technology, 107–108
speed, interpreted vs. compiled programs, 137
Sperry-Rand, 53
spider, 218, 382

spider chart, 294
sports games, **171**
spreadsheets, **177–178**, *178*, 382
  in office suites, **244**
  in quality testing, 293–294, *294*
  for trends analysis, *234*, 234
Sputnik, 56
SQL (structured query language), 138
SRAM (static RAM), 62
Stanford Research Institute, 57
star LAN, 265, *266*, 382
start bit, 260
static RAM (SRAM), 62
statistical process control (SPC), 294
steam engine, 31
stop bit, 260
storage, **67–71**, **82–83**, 382
  access time of, **70**
  device comparison, **69–70**
  direct access vs. sequential, **68–69**
  machine-generated data, *36*
  magnetic vs. optical, **68**
  removable vs. nonremovable, **67**
  trends, **355–356**
  use as memory, 70
storage devices, 21, **93–94**
  optical, 60
stored program, 31, 382
strategic planning, 145
strategic technology planning, 228
strategy games, **170–171**
streaming technology, 220, 382–383
street-level maps, 186
stress, 13
structured programming, 138
subdomain, 383
subnotebooks, 88, 383
summary report, 232–233, 383
supercomputers, **18**, *18*, 383
  solid-state technology in, 53
superconductors, 60
SuperSort, 176
SuperTrackers, *311*, 311
SVGA (super video graphics array), 112–113
swap file, 70, 383
Symantec, ACT!, 248
symbolic logic, 35
symbologies, 303, 383
synchronous communications, 260, 383
System 7 (Mac OS), 129
system analysts, 144
system board, **91–93**, 383
system call, 383

system case, *22*
system design, 145
system development life cycle, 144, 383
system protection, software for, 134
system resource allocation, 128, 383
system software, **126–140**, 383
  device drivers, **132–133**
  operating systems, **127–132**
  programming languages, **134–140**
  utilities, **133–134**, *135*
systems analysis and design, **143–144**, 383
systems analysts, 54

T

T1 dedicated line, 214, 257
T3 dedicated line, 257
tags in HTML, 221
TalonSoft, Battleground, 170–171
tape drives, 67, 94
tax preparation software, **183**
  personal financial software and, 182
TCP/IP, 202, 383
Telecommunications Act of 1996, 351–352
telegraph line, 35
telemarketing, 319
telephone, 35
  for business communications, 257
  cellular, 262
telephone companies, computer use, 5
telephone directories, electronic, 157, 178–179
television stations, 258
  computer use, 5
televisions, vs. computer use, 152
  vs. monitors, 111, 112
Telnet, 212, 383
terminals, 78, 240, 383
Tetris, 168, *169*
Texas Microsystems, Hardbody Handheld PC, *88*, 88
text insertion, 383
text-based operating systems, **128–129**
text-entry devices, **101**
Theme Hospital, 165
thermal printers, 117
thermal wax transfer, 117
thimble printers, 115
Things That Think Research, Web site, 361
thinwire, 261, 371, 383

thread, 203, 383
Ticketmaster Online, 319
  Web site, 322
TIF file extension, 193
time-sharing, 56, 77
Timeline feature, in encyclopedia, *156*, 156
Timex DataLink Watch, 89
toggle key, 101
token-ring LAN, 266, *267*
toner, 115, 198
topology, of network, 265, 383
Total Quality Control (TQC), 292
Total Quality Management (TQM), 292
touch pad, 105
touch screens, **105**
tower computer, 21, *22*, 383
Toy Story, 118, 330–331
Toy Story Animated Storybook, *160*, 160–161
TQC (Total Quality Control), 292
TQM (Total Quality Management), 292
trackballs, 103, *104*
tracking systems, for transportation of goods, **310–313**
trackpoint, 104–105
Tracy, Spencer, 54
Traf-O-Data, 82
transaction, 384
transaction processing systems, **228–232**, *230*, **316–318**, 384
  batch, **317**
  custom, 231
  real-time systems, **317–318**
  transaction capture, **318**
transatlantic telegraph cable, 35
transistors, 38, **52–55**, *53*, 384
Transmission Control Protocol (TCP), 202
transmission speed
  of fax modems, 121
  for network standards, 263
transportation, **308–314**
  computer use, 5
  scheduling systems, **309–310**
  for service sector, **313–314**, *314*
  tracking systems, **310–313**
travel, in-vehicle guidance sytems, 186
trends
  input devices, **353–355**
  personal computers, **348–350**
  RAM (random access memory), **355–356**
  storage and memory, **355–356**

trends analysis, spreadsheets for, *234*, 234
Turbo Pascal, 139
TurboTax, *183*, 183
Turing, Alan, 38, 173, 384
tutorial software, 158, 384
twisted-pair cable, 260, 384
2001: A Space Odyssey, 119, 353
two-dimensional bar codes, 304, 369
typewriter, 35

U

ubiquitous computing, 357–358, 384
  Web site, 360
ULSI (ultra-large-scale integration), 58
UNDELETE command (DOS), 133
underlining, for hypertext links, 215, *216*
Unigraphics, Web site, 299
UNIMATE industrial robot, 55
uninstall, utilities for, 134
Unisys, 19, 53
United States Postal Service, mail sorting, 11–12
UNIVAC computer, 50, 384
UNIVAC Corporation, 44
universal product code (UPC), 109–110
universal resource locator (URL), 214–215, 384. *See also* Web sites
universal service, 352, 384
Universal Turing Machine, 38–39
University of Michigan School of Information, 339–340
  Web site, 344
UNIX, 129
UNIX to UNIX Copy Protocol, 211
UPC (universal product code), 109–110
upgradable memory, 92
upgrade, 384
URL (universal resource locator), 214–215, 384
U.S. Bureau of Labor Statistics, 14
U.S. Census Bureau, **35–38**, 44, 326
U.S. Department of Defense, 33
Usenet newsgroups, **211**, 384
  Internet site, 224
user ID, 268–269, 384
user interface, 57, 152
  for Alto computer, 78
  command line, 85
  graphical, 85–86, **129–132**
  for operating system, 128
  social, 350

user rights, 269, 381
utilities, **133–134**, *135*, 384
  conversion, 242, 372

V

vacation planning, **184–185**
vacuum tubes, **50–51**, *52*
Valassis Communications, Inc., 284
  distribution scheduling, 309
  Impact Promotions division, 287–288
verification of communication, **258–260**
version numbers, of software, 131
very large-scale integration (VLSI), 58
VGA (video graphics array), 112–113
video
  releasing movies on, **331**
  on World Wide Web, 220
video cameras, 118
video capture boards, 108
video cards, 110, **112–113**
Video Electronics Standards Association, 112
video input, 107–108
video monitor, *See* monitors
video RAM (VRAM), 62
VideoFlicks, Web site, 322
virtual manufacturing, **289**, 384
virtual memory, **70–71**, 90, 128, 384
virtual reality, 162
Virtual Reality Modeling Language (VRML), 222, 384
virus detection and removal, utilities for, 134
Visa, 275
VisiCalc, 84, 176
Visio, 196, 295
Visual Basic, 139
visual learners, 153
VLB (Video Local Bus), 93
VLSI (very large-scale integration), 58
voice input, 107
voice mail, computerized, 277
voice recognition, 353–354
  Web site, 360
VoiceType Simply Speaking software, *354*, 354
volatile memory, 61, 384
Volta, Alssandro Guiseppe, 30
von Neumann, John, *42*, 42–44, 384
Von Neumann's computer system, 67
VRAM (video RAM), 62

W

WAIS (Wide Area Information Servers), 212, 384
wands, 110
Warcraft, 170
warehousing, **302–308**
  automated, **304–305**
  distribution centers, **304–305**
warranty, 198
Watson, Thomas, 38
Watt, James, 31
wearable computers, 356, 385
Web browsers, **216–217**
Web pages, 385
  creating, **221–222**
Web sites
  Amazon Books, 322
  Apple Computer Corp., 195
  bar codes, 322
  Tim Berners-Lee, 224
  Blue Mountain Home Page, 148
  Borland Corporation, 148, 279
  Business Software Alliance, 148
  CAD/CAM software, 299
  CD Magazine Online, 172
  Colossus Rebuild Project, 46
  Columbia House CD Club, 322
  on computer history, 46, 96
  Computer Museum, 96
  Corel Corporation, 253
  for customers, 277
  DataMind Corporation, 253
  Digital Library Initiative, 344
  on Douglas Engelbart, 96
  entertainment software, 172
  Entertainment Software Rating Board, 172
  Everton Genealogical Helper, 195
  eye-tracking hardware, 360
  FAQ (Frequently Asked Questions), 224
  Federal Bureau of Investigation, 344
  Federal Communications Commission, 360
  Federal Express, 322
  FedWorld, 344
  on Grace Hopper, 72
  HotWired Online Magazine, 123
  IEEE Computer Society, 73
  In-Vehicle Map Systems, 172
  Institute of Electrical and Electronic Engineers, 279

IntegrationWare, 253
Internet Public Library Reference section, 344
Library of Congress, *342*, 344
Lotus Corporation, 253, 279
Manufacturing Online, 299
Medical Records Institute, 344
Microsoft, 148, 195, 279
Netscape Communications Corporation, 279
Nolo Press, 195
project management, 299
PythOnline, 322
Really Useful Company Store, 322
Sarajevo, 361
search engines, 224
Things That Think Research, 361
Ticketmaster Online, 322
ubiquitous computing, 360
Unigraphics, 299
VideoFlicks, 322
voice recognition, 360
Mark Weiser, 360
women of computing, 46
Xerox Palo Alto Research Center, 361
Xerox PARC, 96
Web TVs, 352, 385
Webmasters, 276, 385

Weiser, Mark, 357–358
  Web site, 360
wide area networks (WANs), 78, 268, 385
Wilkes, Maurice, 43
WillMaker, 184
wills, 184
Winchester disks, 82, 385. *See also* hard drives
wind tunnel, simulation, 288
windows, 78
Windows 95 (Microsoft), 131, *132*, 385
  expert system in Troubleshooting system, *239*, 239
Windows CE, 247
Windows (Microsoft), 86–87, 129–130, 378
  version 3.1, 130, *131*
Windows NT, 131, 132
  networking software, 266, 268
WinZip, 146
WIP (work in progress), 307
wireless mouse, 102
wireless transmission methods, 261–262
wiring paths, *See* buses
WMF file extension, 193
women of computing, Web site, 46
word processor as career, 244
word processors, **176–177**, *177*, 385
  vs. desktop publishing, 192
  in office suites, **242–244**
WordStar, 176
work flow, managing in health care, 333–334

work in progress (WIP), 307
workgroup software, 274
workstations, 21, 264, 385
World War II, computers and, **39–44**
World Wide Web, 35, **208–209**, 385
  contributing to, **220–222**
  growth, **206–207**
  for meeting scheduling, 251
  real estate sites, 327, *328*
Wozniak, Stephen, 80, *84*
WPG file extension, 193

X

XENIX, 129
Xerox, 55, 77, 78
  Alto Workstation Computer, 78
  Palo Alto Research Center, Web site, 361
  WebBoard, 275
Xiphias Publishing, Encyclopedia Electronica, 355

Y

Yahoo, *219*, 219

Z

Zip drives (Iomega), 94
zoom control, 158, 385